D1036021

CINCINNATI'S GERMAN HERITAGE

Don Heinrich Tolzmann

Heritage Books, Inc.

Cover illustration is from *Cincinnati in Wort und Bild* by Max Burgheim, published in 1888.

Other Heritage Books from
Don Heinrich Tolzmann:
The First Germans in America
Ohio Valley German Biographical Index
German Chronicle in the History of the Ohio Valley
German Pioneer Life: A Social History
History of the German Element of Virginia:
Hermann Schuricht's History

Published 1994 by

HERITAGE BOOKS, INC.
1540-E Pointer Ridge Place
Bowie, Maryland 20716
(301) 390-7709

ISBN 1-55613-986-1

A Complete Catalog Listing Hundreds of Titles on
Genealogy, History, and Americana
Available Free on Request

Contents

Preface

The purpose of this work is to provide a general overview of Cincinnati's German heritage by means of a selection of the author's work on the topic.

DHT

Introduction

In Part One of this volume, an historical description of the German-American community of Cincinnati, from its beginnings up to the time before World War One, will be found. This is followed, in Part Two, by an examination of the community's experience of World War One. In Part Three, the postwar period is described.

This is then followed, in Part Four, by a survey, which reviews the German-American experience since the early 1900s, and brings history up to the recent past. Basically, this covers a period which I have described as the ethnic surival/revival period, as it covers the German-American experience since the world wars down to the recent past, when there has been a ethnic heritage and roots revival amongst German-Americans.

For those interested in further sources, three parts had been included. In Part Five, references to materials in the German-Americana Collection at the University of Cincinnati Blegen Library will be found. A list of the German-American newspapers, published in Cincinnati, can be found in Part Six, and information pertaining to Cincinnati German imprints will be found in Part Seven.

Part One

The German-American Community

CINCINNATI'S GERMAN-AMERICAN COMMUNITY:

AN HISTORICAL DESCRIPTION

Cincinnati, the Queen of the West, the El Dorado
of the German emigrant! Ask a German, who is
traveling into the interior from one of the
seaports, Where are you going? and the answer
will invariable be - to Cincinnati.   [1]

--Friedrich Gerstäcker

Immigration

Since the recording of immigration statistics in 1820, Germans

have constituted the largest single group of European immigrants. The

peak year of German immigration was 1882 while the peak year for the

Austrian Empire was 1907.[2] The German immigration to Cincinnati was

part of the great European immigration to American shores. The

nineteenth century German immigration can be divided into three

periods: before 1830, from 1831 to 1871, and after 1871. In the

---

[1]

Cited in Mack Walker, Germany and the Emigration 1816-1885.
Cambridge: Harvard University Press, 1964, p. 43.

[2]

See "Germans Constituted the Largest Single Group of Immigrants
to the U.S. During the Last 160 Years," Newsletter of the Society for
German American Studies 3:2, 1982, 2. Also see Günter Moltmann, Von
Deutschland nach Amerika. Zur Sozialgeschichte der Auswanderung im
19. und 20. Jahrhundert. Wiesbaden: Steiner, 1979, and also Willi P.
Adams, ed., Die deutschsprachige Auswanderung in die Vereinigten
Staaten. Berlin: John F. Kennedy Institut für Nordamerikastudien,
1980.

first period German immigration to Cincinnati was light, but it
increased substantially in the second period. "The inrush of Germans
in the middle half of the nineteenth century made Cincinnati into a
German city. For many years Cincinnati did not even try to assimilate
its German immigrants; instead they assimilated Cincinnati."[3] The
high point of German immigration to Cincinnati was reached in the
1880s. The German-speaking population rose from a mere five percent
of the population in 1820 to 34.9% by 1917.[4]

The majority of the first immigrants to Cincinnati came from the
southwestern area of the German-speaking sections of Europe. The two
largest groups appear to have been the Swiss and the Württembergers,
after which immigrants from Baden, Alsace and northern Germany,
especially Oldenburg, are the predominant groups. In addition to the
European German immigration a sizable, but inestimable, number of
German-Americans from Pennsylvania, Maryland and Virginia came to
Cincinnati. The pre-1830 immigrants consisted mainly of workers,
tradesmen, and farmers, with a small number of educators, such as
teachers and clergymen.

By 1800 the German element in Cincinnati amounted to 53 persons,
or slightly more than six percent, of a total population of
approximately 700. By 1820 the German-born population alone had

---

[3] Works Projects Administration, Writers Program, Ohio, The Ohio
Guide. New York: Oxford University Press, 1940, p. 79.

[4] August B. Gorbach, Das Hilfswerk und Cincinnatis deutsche
Vereine. Zweite Auflage. Cincinnati: S. Rosenthal & Co., 1917, p.
9.

reached 400, or 4.6%, of a total population of 9,600. This German-
born population then tripled to 1,120, or five percent, of a total
population of 24,381 by 1830.[5] Because of the upheavals in Europe
caused by the French Revolution and the Napoleonic wars, German
immigration was nothing more than a "trickle" until 1815. However,
after that the immigration picked up noticeably, especially after
1817, the year which brought drought, famine and starvation in
Germany. Thereafter the trickle became "a wide regular stream."[6]

The second immigration to Cincinnati contained a number of
refugees, e.g., the Thirtyers, the immigrants who came after the 1832
protest demonstration known as the Hambacher Fest, and the Forty-
Eighters, refugees of the failed 1848 German revolution. Although
small in number, they exerted a strong influence on the social,
cultural, economic and political life of the German element. However,
not all of the immigrants were political refugees: many were
laborers, tradesmen, merchants and manufacturers. The second period
differed from the first in that more immigrants came for economic,

---

[5] The 1820 statistic has been computed by the author through the
compilation of a list of immigrants referred to in local German
language histories: Max Burgheim, Cincinnati in Wort und Bild.
(Cincinnati: M. & R. Burgheim, 1888), H. H. Fick, Cincinnati und sein
Deutschtum. (Cincinnati: Roessler, 1901). Emil Klauprecht, Deutsche
Chronik in der Geschichte des Ohio-Thales und seiner Haupstads ins
Besondere. (Cincinnati: G. Hof & M.A. Jacobi, 1864). Heinrich A.
Rattermann, Gesammelte ausgewählte Werke. 12 bde. (Cincinnati: Im
Selbstverlage, 1906-12). Armin Tenner, CincinnatiSonst und Jetzt.
(Cincinnati: M. & R. Burgheim, 1878). The numerous statistics cited
here and in the following pages on the Einwanderung are drawn from the
U.S. Bureau of the Census, Census Reports, 1820-1910.

[6] Heinrich A. Rattermann, Werke, Vol. 16, p. 221.

rather than political reasons, although they were not as vocal as their refugee compatriots. Immigration continued from the areas that had contributed to the first immigration, but increased substantially from northern Germany, especially from Hanover and Oldenburg (specifically from Damme and Diepholz). Because of the Thirtyers and the Forty-Eighters Cincinnati became a well-publicized destination for the German immigrations as well as a German-American cultural center in the years before the Civil War.

By 1840 the German-born population numbered 3,440 out of a total of 46,282, but by 1850 this had literally "soared" to 30,758 out of a total population of 115,436. The population of Cincinnati in the 1840s had tripled, but the German-born population increased almost tenfold. At the eve of the Civil War, in 1860, the population of German stock in Cincinnati amounted to 30% out of a total of 161,044 Cincinnatians. In 1870 the German-born numbered 49,446 out of a total population of 216,239 while the German stock had now inched up to 34%, or 75,000.

After the Franco-Prussian War German immigrants were mostly from the working classes, but with far better educations than those of earlier periods. A few immigrated for political reasons, e.g., the Catholics dissatisfied with Bismarck's Kulturkampf and the socialists alienated by Bismarck's Sozialistengesetze, but for most the motivation to immigrate was economic. The 1870 U.S. Census indicates the origins of the German-born in Cincinnati as follows: Prussia, 30.3%; Bavaria, 19.7%; Hannover, 17.5%; Baden, 10.4%; Württemberg,

6.3%; Oldenburg, 4.7%; Hessen, 4.7%; Saxony, 1.9%; Austria, 1.1%; and other and unidentified states, 3.0%.

A high point in the German immigration was reached in the 1880s so that by 1890 the German stock reached its zenith with 57.4% of a total population of 296,908. At the turn of the century Cincinnati's population of 325,902 included 39,624 German-born citizens and a German stock of 109,875. In the last pre-war Census of 1910 there were 30,759 German-born and a German stock of 121,719 out of a total Cincinnati population of 363,591. In the 1910 Census for the first time information was included regarding the mother tongue of Americans. At this time there were 125,446 in Cincinnati who claimed German as their mother tongue. That there were several thousand more German-speaking Cincinnatians than the total number for the German stock indicates that their language was retained into the third generation and beyond. In 1917 the German-speaking population was estimated at 127,000, or 34.9% of the population.[7]

Over-the-Rhine

A section known as the Over-the-Rhine district, an area of 213.3 acres, became in the nineteenth century the central geographical locale of the German community. Its borders were defined by the Miami Canal, completed in 1831, on the west and south, and on the north and east by McMicken Avenue and Main Street. The old barge canal, known as the Miami-Erie Canal, had been locally dubbed as the "Rhine" since when one crossed over it one entered the German district. In mid-

-----

[7] Gorbach, Das Hilfswerk, p. 9.

nineteenth century, according to Rattermann, it divided "the German quarter from the English."[8] In actuality, the district never was completely German, nor were all the Germans settled there. It consisted of the first and fifth wards, but by 1840 Germans were not only in these wards, but also in the seventh ward, as well as elsewhere in the city. In the Over-the-Rhine wards Germans constituted in 1840 only 46.3% of the population. Nevertheless, they were the predominant element in the district. Settlement patterns indicate, however, that Germans preferred the western, northern and eastern edges of the city. As the German population grew it spread beyond the confines of Over-the-Rhine. In 1870 the German population was moving north along Vine Street until it came to McMillan. By 1890 it was concentrating in the area one mile north from McMillan to Howell "while along McMillan it had moved an additional half-mile east to its intersection with Burnet."[9] After 1900 Over-the-Rhine began to lose its character as the center of the German population, but as it dropped in number there, other areas of the city gained in German population. On the other side of the Mill Creek Valley, in Fairmount, Germans began to concentrate, for example. The German element in

---

8
    Rattermann, Werke, Vol. 12, p. 526. Rattermann here cites a poem by local poet, Dr. Adolph Bauer, entitled, "Over the Rhine. (19 Dezember 1852)" which was written in response to the nativism of an article in the Cincinnati Daily Times (17 December 1852) which had referred to the district as "where the hogs, dutch and souerkrout dwell in peace and harmony together . . ."
    9
    Dobbert, Disintegration, p. 38.

Covington, Kentucky also expanded.[10]

It is clear that because of the impact of the German immigrations, that the old Over-the-Rhine district could not contain the rapidly expanding German population. In 1890 already only a few of the city's wards showed a greater deviation than plus or minus ten percent from the city's average of 57.4% of German stock per ward. Wards 7 and 13 contained 80.1% and 71.3% respectively as the wards with the highest concentrations. Wards with lower percentages were 1, 18, and 20 with 37.9%, 36.8%, and 37.5% respectively. By 1910 German-Americans had, therefore, distributed themselves widely throughout all of Cincinnati's wards.[11]

As the population expanded and settled throughout the city, the Over-the-Rhine district lost some of its old German character as well as its economic and political significance, but it gained new importance as a social-cultural center with the numerous German houses, restaurants, churches, bakeries, open air markets, beer gardens and other shops and stores. A late nineteenth century German-American history called Over-the-Rhine the district in which "everything is German and even the American discards his formality and envelops himself in German Gemütlichkeit."[12] It still was the home

---

[10]
This study is not concerned with Covington and the Germans in Kentucky, but those interested in this topic should consult Ludwig Stierlin, Der Staat Kentucky und die Stadt Louisville, mit besonderer Berücksichtigung des Deutschen Elementes. Louisville: Louisville Anzeiger, 1873.

[11]
Guido A. Dobbert, "The Zinzinnati in Cincinnati," Cincinnati Historical Society Bulletin 22, 1964, 217.

[12]
Tenner, Cincinnati, p. 81.

of German music, theaters, newspapers, libraries, clubs, societies, and religious institutions. It was filled with "the little savings and loan societies where thrifty Germans could deposit their savings or borrow money from this early form of credit union."[13] In 1859 Turners had built the Turnhalle, a central point of nineteenth century social and cultural life, considered "a mighty fortress of German-American culture."[14] Among the popular beer gardens, theaters and opera houses of the district were the Arbeiter-Halle, the Männerchor-Halle, Heuck's, Schickling's, Wielert's Pavilion. According to a local history, "everywhere it is gemütlich in Over-the-Rhine."[15]

Life in the district has been well portrayed by Wittke:

> Cincinnati's German community, in its early years, was concentrated largely in an area north of where the canal entered the city, and was known as "over the Rhine." Here the Germans lived in neat little frame and brick houses built flush with the sidewalk, and with backyards fenced in with lattice work and planted with flower and vegetable gardens. Every Saturday, German housewives scrubbed the front steps of their homes until they were snow white. Here too the German Hausfrau nourished her family with German food and delicacies which quickly became part of the American culinary art. After working hours and on Sunday, the men sought recreation in the taverns, played euchre, skat and pinochle, or brought their families to the beer gardens to listen to old familiar German airs.[16]

Aside from being the original site of the German community and later a social cultural center, Over-the-Rhine reflected the impact of

---

[13] Wittke, The Germans, p. 11.

[14] Tenner, Cincinnati, p. 82.

[15] Ibid.

[16] Wittke, "The Germans of Cincinnati", p. 7.

the German immigrations since "their buildings -- where they worshipped, worked, played, lived and died -- still punctuate the face of the
city."[17]

The architectural impact of the German immigration extended beyond Over-the-Rhine to other sections of the city, and also found expression in the landscaping and park system, as exemplified by the
work of Adolf Strauch in Clifton and Spring Grove Cemetery.[18] In various parks monuments or statues could be found which related to the
German heritage, e.g., the Turnvater Jahn monument in Inwood Park.
Two architectural and engineering landmarks were associated with the
German heritage: the Suspension Bridge built by Johann A. Roebling,
and the Tyler Davidson Memorial Fountain, purchased in 1871 by Henry
Probasco, which was poured in Munich under the direction of Ferdinand
von Miller to depict the Genius des Wassers. In short, the imprint of
the German immigrations was to be seen in the material culture and architectural styles that originated in the Over-the-Rhine district and
spread to other areas of the city.[19]

―――――――――
[17]
     Carl M. Becker and William H. Daily, "Some Architectural
Aspects of German-American Life in Nineteenth Century Cincinnati," in
Don Heinrich Tolzmann, Festschrift for the German-American
Tricentennial Jubilee: Cincinnati 1983. (Cincinnati: Cincinnati
Historical Society, 1983), pp. 10-21.
[18]
     On Strauch see Heinrich A. Rattermann, "Deutsch-Amerikanische
Künstler: Der Pionier der Landschaftgärtnerei," Der Deutsche Pionier
10, 1878, 82-93. Also see his Adolph Strauch, der Begründer der
landschaftlichen Friedhöfe. Eine biographische Skizze. Cincinnati:
n.p., 1884.
[19]
     For a guide to the various sites, monuments, buildings, etc. in
Cincinnati see Max Burgheim, Der Führer von Cincinnati, ein
Vollständiger und zuverlässiger Wegweiser durch die Stadt und ihre
Umgebung. Zweite vermehrte und verbesserte Auflage. Cincinnati: M. &
R. Burgheim, 1876.

The Religious Camp

The first missionaries to the Germans in Ohio were from Pennsylvania, Maryland and Virginia, many of them the sons and grandsons of German-speaking immigrants. In 1792 the Moravian missionary to the Indians of Ohio, Johannes Heckewelder, visited the first settlement in southwest Ohio, Columbia, where he stayed with its founder, Major Benjamin Steitz, who had led 30 settlers, including several German Dunkards, to Ohio to establish the settlement (18 November 1788). From 1802-25 the Rev. Paul Henkel, a Lutheran clergyman from New Market, Virginia, ministered to Germans in southwest Ohio, but it was not until 4 September 1808 that the first German language religious service in Cincinnati was conducted by Heinrich Böhm, a Methodist itinerant preacher from Lancaster County, Pennsylvania. In 1814 the United Brethren in Christ sent a missionary, a Dr. Dreher, to Cincinnati where he is said to have preached before almost empty benches in the courthouse. These early beginnings may be regarded as the pioneer state of Cincinnati German Kirchengeschichte.[20]

Between 1814 and World War I, eleven independent German Protestant congregations were established. By 1870 their membership reached 30,400.[21] The independent congregations were exactly that:

20
A good survey of local religious life is found in Fick, Cincinnati, 113-32.

21
Joseph Michael White, "Religion and Community: Cincinnati Germans, 1814-1879," (Ph.D. Dissertation, Notre Dame University, 1980), p. 52.

independent, i.e., not affiliated with a particular denomination. The
pattern for this has been set by Cincinnati's first German church, the
Deutsche St. Johannes-Kirche, established in 1814, located at 12th and
Elm Streets. Its 1839 constitution indicated that services were to be
patterned on the Christian religion in accordance with the models
established by Luther and Zwingli, a broad statement indicating the
"union" outlook of transcending Lutheran and Reformed Church
differences. Although there was a tendency to transcend theological
differences, various problems arose because of regional and linguistic
differences among the independents. A debate, for example, in the St.
Johannes-Kirche regarding the relocation of the church pitted the
Swabians against the non-Swabians in such heated discussion that the
floor collapsed, dumping them all in the basement. The second German
Protestant church was formed by a secession of Palatines from St.
Johannes. The third independent Protestant church was caused in turn
by a secession of north Germans from St. Johannes also. Its
constitution (North German Lutheran Church) stated specifically that
church officers must speak Low German, Plattdeutsch.

In spite of their diversity, there was a gradual development of
cooperation among Cincinnati German independent Protestants. In 1840
members of the St. Johannes and the North German Church established a
Protestantischer Kirchhof-Verein, a cemetery association, which bought
land on Montgomery Road in Walnut Hills and made lots available to all
German Protestants.[22]   Second, the cholera epidemic of the summer of

---

[22]
See _Verfassung des Protestantischen Kirchhof-Vereins auf Walnut
Hills_. (Cincinnati, 1869).

1849 brought a high number of deaths and the need was felt for a
German Protestant orphanage; on 29 July a General Protestant Orphanage
Society was formed and administered by a committee of two
representatives from each of the then six independent congregations.
In Mt. Auburn an orphanage was built which by 1854 had 46 childrena nd
92 by 1875. Third, German Protestants were endowed with an
exceptional leader, the Rev. August Kröll, a liberal-minded graduate
of the rationalist University of Giessen. Born at Rohrback, Hessen in
1806, Kröll served at a German parish as an assistant after his
theological studies, but then decided in 1833 to immigrate to the
United States with the emigration society of Paul Follenius, the
Giessener Gesellschaft. After farming in Missouri and church work in
Louisville, Kröll came to Cincinnati where in 1841 he became pastor of
the first German congregation, St. Johannes-Kirche, a position he held
until his retirement in 1874. He brought stability not only to his
congregation, but a sense of unity to the other German Protestant
congregations. For three decades St. Johannes was the leading German
Protestant congregation and Kröll the leading Protestant spokesman in
Cincinnati.[23]

In 1849 he established a German Protestant newspaper, Die
Protestantischen Zeitblätter to encourage a united German Protestant
spirit in Cincinnati.[24] As editor he secured the services of the

---

[23] Heinrich A. Rattermann, "Pastor August Kroell," Der Deutsche
Pionier 6, 1874, 339-46.

[24] Karl J. R. Arndt and May E. Olson, The German Language Press of
the Americas. Vol. 1 History and Bibliography 1732-1968: United States
of America. München: Verlag Dokumentation, 1976, p. 450-51.

Rev. Friedrich Boettcher, a representative of liberal, rationalist
Christianity who was born in 1800 in Mackerock, Prussia and educated
at the University of Halle. The newspaper appeared for 30 years as a
weekly for the instruction and edification of "thinking Christians."
It presented a liberal, humanist Christian perspective. Many of its
articles encourage German Protestant unity by pointing to the example
of the various synods, the Catholics and the German Methodists. In
1856 Kroll wrote about the possibilities of a union of the local
independent churches.

In his articles he proposed a German Protestant mutual aid
society, a German Protestant educational program including Sunday
schools and musical lessons. Pulpit exchange between the churches
would be a possibility. A meeting was held in St. Paul's Church,
located at 15th and Race Streets, on 3 October 1856 to organize the
group, and by November a constitution of the Protestant Christian
Community appeared in the Zeitblätter. A board of 13 directors was
elected by local Protestants to administer the Community, whose
purpose was to fulfill and accomplish the Gospel, promote Christian
education and morality, and to aid the sick and needy. The
Zeitblätter was to be supported and youth instructed in the German
language, religion, cultural affairs and music. Hence, the union was
a very loosely knit one, but one that nevertheless brought about a
semblence of unity. In 1858 a German Protestant Sunday School Union
was established to provide a unified program of religious and cultural
instruction along liberal Christian lines.

In 1843 the Zion Evangelical Church, at Bremen between 15th and
Liberty Streets, was founded. It joined the Kirchenverein des
Westens, later known as the German Evangelical Synod, which had been
established in 1840 in St. Louis County, Missouri.[25] This church body
recognized the value of the symbolic confessions of the Lutheran and
Reformed churches as biblical interpretation, but declared the Bible
as the ultimate standard to be interpreted by the individual
conscience. In 1847 the Kirchenverein established its own catechism,
its Agende (worship-order) in 1857, and a hymnal in 1862. It also
published a journal for its membership, the Friedensbote, and
established a quality educational institution, the Eden Theological
Seminary. In 1867 Zion established its own normal school for children
of church members. As with other local Protestant churches, Zion
experienced a secession of members, and one that led to the founding
of Cincinnati's first Lutheran church. By World War I the German
Evangelical Synod had 12 churches locally.

In November 1849, 19 members of the Zion Evangelical Church
withdrew to form Holy Trinity Evangelical Lutheran Church. As a
result of a visit by the Rev. Friedrich Wyneken, later Synod
president, Trinity joined the Missouri Synod.[26] The church

25
   See Carl E. Schneider, The German Church on the American
Frontier. A Study of Religion among the Germans of the West based on a
History of the Evangelischer Kirchenverein des Westens, 1840-1866.
St. Louis: Eden Publishing House, 1939.
26
   See Trinity's congregational history: Kurzgefasste Geschichte
der Ev. Luth. Dreifältigkeits-Gemeinde zu Cincinnati, Ohio
(Cincinnati, Ohio, 1899).

established a day school for its children. The church came under attack from the secular press as well as that of the German Methodists because of its conservative orthodox theological views. Missouri Synod Lutherans shunned freethinkers, socialists, and radicals as they would the Teufel. Members received the Synod journal, Der Lutheraner, which was published 1844-1977. The cultural and intellectual center of the Synod, however, was the Concordia Seminary in St. Louis which acquired a reputation for its German scholarship. Second only to the preservation of an uncorrupted Lutheranism was the preservation of the German language. By World War I there were three German Lutheran churches in Cincinnati.

In 1833 several Lane Seminary students established a German Sunday School on Main Street to instruct German children in Christianity and the English language. A total of 250 attended this program. The Emigrant Friend Society, established in 1834, aimed to financially support the school. Also day and evening classes were initiated with the freethinkers Eduard Salomon and Julius Weyse, later members of the Turngemeinde, as teachers. By 1840 German-English bilingual schools were established in Cincinnati and this Emigrantenschule went out of existence. Germans in general were not pleased with the religious proseletyzing, the use of the English language, and Kirchendeutschen in particular disliked the use of freethinkers as teachers. In May 1856 the First German Presbyterian Church was organized with 37 members and in 1868 a Second German Presbyterian Church was formed, an indication that there was local support for the Presbyterians. By 1870 there were close to 500

members in both churches, and by World War I two more German
Presbyterian churches had been established.[27]

German Methodism originated in Cincinnati and is associated with
the work of Wilhelm Nast, born in Stuttgart in 1807. Nast studied at
the University of Tübingen, and immigrated in 1828. After teaching
classical languages and German at various educational institutions,
including the U.S. Military Academy, Nast was converted to the
Methodist faith in 1835. After his conversion the Ohio Conference
appointed him as the Methodist missionary to the Cincinnati Germans.
Upon arrival in the Queen City, Nast came under harsh attack from the
secular press which ridiculed the Methodists as Puritans. Slowly
Nast, however, built a following and conducted German services in the
two local Methodist chapels. In 1838 the Ohio Conference authorized
the publication of a German newspaper to be edited by him: Der
Christliche Apologete, the first issue of which appeared 4 January
1838. By 1869 it attained a readership of 15,000 subscribers.

The Apologete was an excellently edited newspaper intended not
only for German Methodists, but for the entire German-American
community. It contained Nast's many articles and essays on the
Catholics and other German Protestant denominations. In 1842 the

---

[27]
    See Calvin Stowe, Education of Immigrants. An Address delivered
before the Western College of Teachers during their Convention held in
Cincinnati, October, 1835, at the Request of the Emigrant Friend
Society (Cincinnati, 1835). James Weis, "The Presbyterian mission to
German Immigrants," Journal of Presbyterian History 43, 1965, 264-91,
and One Hundred Fifty Years of Presbyterianism in the Ohio Valley,
1790-1940 (Cincinnati, 1941).

mother church of German Methodism was constructed on Race Street between 13th and 14th Streets: the First German Methodist Church. By 1864 German Methodism had expanded to 18 districts across the U.S., with 26,145 members and 366 ministers. In 1879 there were 554 German methodists and 727 Sunday School children. At the eve of the first World War there were six German Methodist churches. Three educational institutions were maintained by the German Methodists: Baldwin-Wallace College, Central Weslayan College, and Iowa Weslayan University. Most Ohio students attended Baldwin-Wallace in Berea, Ohio. The literature published by the German Methodists is extensive: in addition to the 250 translations into German another 225 original works in German must be added. In 1900 German Methodists established Bethesda Hospital in Cincinnati under the direction of Pastor W. H. Trager.[28]

In 1852 a small group of German Baptists under the Rev. August von Puttkamer failed in their attempt to establish a Baptist congregation, but in 1855 the Ninth Street Baptist Church secured the services of Philip W. Bickel from the Baptist Seminary in Roch, New York, as a Baptist missionary to the Cincinnati Germans. After a three month trial period, a German Missionary Committee was formed to

---

[28] On German Methodism see Paul F. Douglass, The Story of German Methodism: Biography of an Immigrant Soul. (New York: The Methodist Book Concern, 1939); Carl Wittke, William Nast. Patriarch of German Methodism. (Detroit: Wayne State University Press, 1959); John Sinnema, "German Methodism's Ohio Roots," Journal of German-American Studies 8, 1974, 64-85; and C. Golder et al., eds., Geschichte der Zentral Deutscher Konferenz, einschliesslich der Anfangsgeschichte des Deutschen Methodismus. Cincinnati: Jennings & Graham (1901), pp. 140-98, 205-12, 323-30.

defray salary and other expenses. In 1857 the First German Baptist
Church was established and Bickel was ordained as its minister. In
1866 he became editor of the local German Baptist publication, Der
Sandbote, which by 1879 had a circulation of 3,000. However, by that
year the Cincinnati congregation had only 95 members and 175 Sunday
School children. The Baptists never made a great impact on the German
community; by World War I there was still only one German Baptist
congregation, the Deutsche Baptisten-Gemeinde, located at Corvine and
Walnut Streets.[29]

In 1846 the German Reformed Church's Board of Missions sent the
Pennsylvania German, Rev. Henry Kroh, as missionary to the Cincinnati
Germans. In the same year Kroh organized a congregation with seven
members, the First German Reformed Church. In 1851 Rev. Herman Rust,
from Bremen and a graduate of the Reformed Church seminary in
Lancaster, Pennsylvania, began his pastorate at this church. He was a
vigorous preacher against rationalism and was involved in several
local revivals. The secular press attacked him harshly, and during
the Forty-Eighter era Rust was said to have feared for his life. Due
to his work the Second Reformed Church was established in 1857.
Although he pushed for a German language Reformed Church periodical,
nothing came of his efforts. However, in the 1850s a Deutsches
Christliches Hospital was established in Over-the-Rhine on Brown

---

[29]
    See L.H. Donner, Twenty-Fifth Anniversary of the First German
Baptist Church of Cincinnati, Ohio. (Cincinnati, 1883); White,
"Religion and Community," pp. 130-35, and John Ramaker, The German
Baptists in North America: An Outline of Their History (Cleveland:
German Baptist Publication Society, 1924).

Street. By the Civil War, the two churches had 926 members and by

1870 1,695. These two congregations sustained their membership and

were the only two Reformed Churches in Cincinnati by the time of World
War I.[30]

In 1870 there were 49,960 German Catholics in Cincinnati,

undoubtedly the largest of all the church bodies established by

Kirchendeutschen.[31] In 1823 because of the need, Bishop Fenwick had

obtained the services of Friedrich Rese, a priest from Hannover, who

arrived in Cincinnati in September 1824. He first united 23 German

Catholic families (from local Protestant congregations) for Catholic

worship services. Then he traveled to Vienna. While he was there the

Leopoldine Foundation was established by Austrians to finance

missionary work in America, especially in Cincinnati.[32] Donations

began in 1830 with $25,000, which resulted in the Atheneum at Sycamore

and 7th Streets. It was considered the diocese's first seminary.

These donations continued until 1862. Also, donations were

forthcoming from the Society for the Propagation of Faith (Lyons,

France) from 1823-69 with which the St. Peter-in-Chains Cathedral,

[30]
See David Dunn, et al., A History of the Evangelical and
Reformed Church. (Philadelphia: Christian Education Press, 1961) and
John B. Rust, The Life and Labors of the Rev. Herman Rust, D.D.
(Cleveland, 1916).

[31]
White, "Religion and Community," p. 52.

[32]
Friedrich Rese, Abriss der Geschichte des Bisthums Cincinnati
in Nord-Amerika (Wien: Mechitaristen-Congregations-Buchhandlung,
1829).

8th and Plum Sts., was built. During Rese's Vienna visit Cincinnati German Catholics were served by Martin Kundig and Johann Martin Henni.[33] When Rese moved on to Detroit as archbishop there, the services of Father Henry D. Juncker from Lorraine were secured for the first ethnic parish in the West for German-Americans, Holy Trinity Church, which was dedicated 5 October 1834. In 1836 he was replaced by Henni who exerted a quite positive influence locally. He established a parish school that attracted 150 children from Catholic as well as Protestant homes. In 1837 the St. Aloysius Orphanage Society was formed to establish a German Catholic Orphanage. In April of that year Henni and the Society planned for the publication of a German Catholic newspaper to raise funds as well as to fulfill the need for such a publication. In July the Wahrheitsfreund, the first German Catholic newspaper in the U.S., was published with Henni as editor. It circulated in the tri-state region as well as across the U.S.[34]

The paper followed political affairs, especially as they related to the nativist movement, but did not endorse candidates. It did,

----

33
See Johann Martin Henni, Ein Blick in's Thal des Ohio (München, 1836), Martin Marty, Dr. Johann Martin Henni, Erster Bischof und Erzbischof von Milwaukee (New York, 1888), Heinrich A. Rattermann, "Dr. Johann Martin Henni, Erster Bischof und Erzbischof von Milwaukee," in Werke, Vol. 10, pp. 291-334; Peter L. Johnson, Stuffed Saddlebags: The Life of Martin Kundig, Priest, 1805-1879 (Milwaukee: Bruce, 1942) and also Johnson's Crosier on the Frontier: A Life of John Martin Henni (Madison: State Historical Society, 1959).
34
Arndt, The German Language Press, p. 457. By 1904 the paper had a circulation of 12,210.

however, engage in debates and disputes with Nast's Apologete and Kröll's Zeitblätter. Occasionally it contained abstruse theological articles, but was essentially maintained as a German Catholic family newspaper.

In 1842 a second German Catholic church, St. Mary's, at 13th and Clay Sts., was established to fulfill the needs of the rapidly expanding population.[35] In 1845 a third church was established on the initiative of Father Josef Ferneding: St. John the Baptist Church at Bremen and Green Streets. Father William Unterthiner, the first of many Austrian Franciscans, served as pastor. Other churches were established to meet the demands of the immigration.

In 1842 the German Catholic Cemetery Society, a lay group, was deeded land located in a Catholic cemetery (St. Joseph Cemetery in Price Hill) by Bishop Purcell. In 1858 Sisters of the Poor of St. Francis from Aachen, Prussia established St. Mary's Hospital at Linn and Betts Streets which cared for 800 annually by the 1860s.

German Catholics established numerous societies and organizations which by 1910 numbered 12,000 members in 80 Vereine, all of which affiliated with a German Catholic Zentral-Verband, which in turn was affiliated with the national organization of German Catholic societies, the Central-Verein, located in St. Louis.[36] By the

[35] See Diamond Jubilee of St. Mary Church, 1842-1917. (Cincinnati: n.p., 1917), and William J. Dammarell, Old Saint Mary's. A Challenging Church in a Changing City (Cincinnati: n.p., n.d.).

[36] Regarding the Central-Verein see Philip Gleason, "The Central Verein, 1900-17: A Cahpter in the History of German-American Catholics," (Ph.D. Dissertation, Notre Dame University, 1960) and also

outbreak of World War I, there were 44 German Catholic churches with 18,105 families, or 65% of the local Catholic population.[37] The importance of the local parish should be emphasized in the life of the German Catholic. Geographically one lived within a specific parish which provided worship, educational, social, and cultural programs for its parishioners. Splintering was prevented by the authority of the bishop and the clergy over doctrinal matters, practices and liturgy. The Cincinnati-born Rev. Anton Walburg was the major proponent of German Catholicism in the late nineteenth century. German Catholics could find their spiritual and cultural needs met in the framework of the church, especiaily in the local neighborhood parish, according to him. He described the Anglo-American culture as a "hotbed of fanaticism, intolerance, and radical ultra-views on matters of politics and religion. All the vagaries of spiritualism, mormonism, free-lovism, prohibition, infidelity, and materialism generally breed in the American nationality."[38] In 1904 Cincinnati obtained its first German archbishop, Henry Moeller, who, instaed of emphasizing isolationism or assimilation, focused on building a quality parochial education program.

---

his The Conservative Reformers: German-American Catholics and the Social Order. Notre Dame: Notre Dame University, 1968.

[37]
    August B. Gorbach, Deutscher Vereins-Wegweiser von Cincinnati, Ohio (Cincinnati: Deutscher Stadtverband von Cincinnati, 1915), p. 217.

[38]
    Zane L. Miller, Boss Cox's Cincinnati. Urban Politics in the Progressive Era.. (Chicago: University of Chicago Press, 1968), p. 135. Also see Anton Walburg, A Question of Nationality in its Relation to the Catholic Church in the United States. (Cincinnati, 1889).

By World War I there were 17 German Jewish congregations. In
1817 the first Jews (from England and Holland) had settled in
Cincinnati. They wrote to Jews in Germany describing the favorable
conditions in Cincinnati, thus starting the German Jewish immigration
to the city. The first German Jews joined the "English" cong .gation
as K.K. B'nai Israel was then known, but became dissatisfied for three
reasons. First, there was the problem of the use of a different
language. Second, there was felt to be a snobbery between the older
and the more recent immigrants. Third, the liturgy was not something
the German Jews were accustomed to. For these and other reasons
German Jews met in 1840 to organize a separate congregation, B'nai
Yeshrum, with S.E. Levy as president and Jakob Elsasser as temporary
minister. Their constitution declared they would worship according to
the rites, customs and usages of the German Jews. The new
congregation expanded steadily so that its quarters in the Workum
home, on Third Street, between Sycamore and Broadway, became too
small. On 14 October 1846 the cornerstone to the Lodge Street
Synagogue was laid, and the Gothic structure was completed in 1848.
In 1851 a school was established which offered instruction in Hebrew,
English and German; later the school confined itself to religious
subjects when it was felt that public schools had improved enough to
send children there. Membership grew over the years: 160 in 1848, 227
[39]
in 1871, 350 in 1898, and 400 in 1917.

---

[39]
James O. Heller, As Yesterday When it is Past. A History of
the Isaac M. Wise Temple - K. K. B'nai Yeshurun - of Cincinnati in
Commemoration of the Centenary of its Founding (Cincinnati: Isaac M.
Wise Temple, 1942), p. 229.

A great number of German Jews appear to have been from Bavaria.
Many of them were literate, educated individuals with a good Hebrew
education and a solid grounding in German literature. Most settled in
the central city and engaged in various commercial enterprises. By
1888 there were between 12,000 and 15,000 German Jews in
Cincinnati.[40]   Among the organizations they founded were the
Allemania, the Phoenix Club, and the Eureka. Among the women's groups
were the Old German Ladies' Benevolent Society and the German Ladies
Relief Society.

More congregations were established and the community grew. Like
others in the religious camp, German Jews established a whole variety
of local institutions. On Burnet Avenue the Jewish Old People's Home
was established in 1889; in 1891 Jewish Hospital was opened on Burnet
Avenue in close proximity to the Home for the Aged; and in 1896 a
United Jewish Charities of Cincinnati was established to which nine
organizations belonged. It conducted a broad range of social programs
and philanthropic activities. In 1875 Hebrew Union College was
established and acquired a reputation for its high scholastic
standards and achievements.

---

[40]
    Barnett, R. Brickner, "The Jewish Community in Cincinnati,
Historical and Descriptive, 1817-1933," (Ph.D. Dissertation,
University of Cincinnati, 1935), pp. 16, 346. Also see Ann Deborah
Michael, "The Origins of the Jewish Community in Cincinnati, 1817-
1860," (M.A. Thesis, University of Cincinnati, 1970). Also see Alan
I. Marcus, "The Allen Temple, formerly the Bene Israel Synagogue,
Cincinnati, Ohio, 1852-1974" typescript at the Cincinnati Historical
Society.

The outstanding leader of the Cincinnati German Jews was Isaac
Meyer Wise who became rabbi of the congregation Ben Yeshurun in 1854,
a position he held for 46 years. He founded the newspaper The
Israelite along with its German-language supplement Die Deborah which
bore the subtitle, "Jüdisch-amerikanische Familienzeitung."[41] This
paper appeared from 1855 to 1902. Wise, more so than any leader in
the religious camp, was an advocate of Americanization. In 1892 he
stated that, "American Judaism, i.e., Judaism, reformed and
reconstructed by the beneficient influence of political liberty and
progressive enlightenment, is the youngest offspring of the ancient
and venerable faith of Israel. The old soul is found in a new body;
that majestic palm tree is but transplanted into a more fertile soil
and invigorating clime . . . It is the American phase of Judaism."[42]
Wise and his colleagues led their congregations "toward the style of
American Protestant religious practices . . . in short, aimed at
making the German Jews as much like their Hilltop Gentile neighbors as
possible without entirely abandoning their religious
distinctiveness."[43] Cincinnati-style Reform Judaism, therefore,
introduced numerous reforms including the use of the English language.

---

[41]
Arndt, The German Language Press, pp. 438-39.
[42]
Heller, As Yesterday, p. 3. Regarding Wise see James Gutmann,
"Watchman on the American Rhine: New Light on Isaac M. Wise," American
Jewish Archives 10, 1958, 135-44 and Linda L. Glassman, "Wise and
Cincinnati: The Heart and Heartbeat of Reform Judaism," M.A. Thesis,
University of Cincinnati, 1965.
[43]
Miller, Boss, p. 131.

In 1889 Wise organized the Central Conference of American Rabbis
"which has continued to be a major force in modernizing and
intellectualizing American Jewry."[44]   Also to his credit was the
establishment of Hebrew Union College and the union of American Hebrew
Congregations in 1873. Beyond Cincinnati he was without question one
of the foremost figures in American Jewish religious life.

Among the German Jews there wa,s in spite of the Americanization
orientation of Wise and his colleagues, nevertheless at least a
substantial, but inestimable, number of German Jews who desired the
preservation and maintenance of their faith within the framework of
the German heritage, as was the case with others in the religious
camp. The foremost proponent of this perspective was Dr. Gotthard
Deutsch, a professor at Hebrew Union College. Born in 1859 in Kanitz,
Austria, Deutsch attended the rabbinical seminary at Breslau, Germany
where he studied under the notable historian Heinrich Graetz. He then
studied Jewish history and literature at the University of Vienna.
After teaching and serving as a rabbi in Austria for several years he
accepted a post at Hebrew Union College in 1891, where he served as
acting president in 1903.

In Cincinnati Deutsch wrote extensively for various publications,
such as the Israelite, Die Deborah, etc., as well as for the
Allgemeine Zeitung des Judenthums, the foremost Jewish newspaper in
Germany. Aside from his numerous journalistic contributions, Deutsch

---

[44]
Wittke, We Who Built America, p. 329.

authored many journal articles and several monographs. He maintained
an active role in the life of the German-American community during the
early decades of the century. Locally he was considered an articulate
representative of the German-American community.[45]

It can be seen that the religious camp is a discernable group and
that each religious group established its own particular institutions,
organizations, and often German language publications. Among them
were some exceptional leaders, e.g., Kröll, Nast, Henni, Wise and
Deutsch. German Catholics alone formed the largest single group among
the Kirchendeutschen. The importance of the maintenance of religious
values within the framework of the preservation of the German heritage
was the basic element shared in common, but even here exceptions to
the rule can be noted. However, many would agree with the phrase
coined by Henni, "Language saves faith."

The Secular Camp

In 1819 the first Verein in Cincinnati, a mutual aid society, was
established under the direction of the Rev. Lidwig Heinrich Meyer of
St. John's Church. On 31 July 1834 a German Society, a mutual aid
society patterned after the older German Societies of Pennsylvania,
Maryland and New York, was established by 200 Germans meeting in City
Hall. Heinrich Rödter, a refugee of the protest Hambacher Fest, was

---

[45]
Regarding Deutsch see "Gotthard Deutsch Memorial Number,"
Hebrew Union Monthly 8:5 (1922) and Guido A. Dobbert, "The Ordeal of
Gotthard Deutsch," American Jewish Archives 20, 1968, 129-50. On
Deutsch and Hebrew Union College generally see Samuel E. Korff, ed.,
Hebrew Union College - Jewish Institute of Religion at One Hundred
Years. (Cincinnati: Hebrew Union College, 1976).

elected president. In the course of the nineteenth century literally hundreds of Vereine were established. Within the framework of this chapter it would be impossible to trace the labyrinth of their history. Therefore, the status and structure of these organizations will be examined as they stood before World War I.[46]

In October, 1883 the Pastorius Celebration was held to honor the bicentennail of the founding of the first permanent German settlement in America by Franz Daniel Pastorius. The Fest, held in the Music Hall, was organized by a committee chaired by H.A. Rattermann with H.H. Fick as secretary. Addresses were given by Rattermann, Emil Rothe, Gustav Bruehl, Charles Reemelin, Isaac Meyer Wise, J.D. Cox and George H. Pendleton. Attempts to place this "German Day" celebration on an annual basis were unsuccessful until 1895.[47]

Under the direction of Cincinnati-born John Goetz Jr., the German Day Society was established to celebrate annual German Day on 2 September 1895, a celebration which also coincided with the 25th anniversary of the Battle of Sedan. The purposes of the Society were the preservation and protection of the German heritage and the celebration each September of a German Day. Affiliation was open to

---

[46]
   On the early organizations see William Anthony Rengering II, "Early Germans in Cincinnati and Biographical Studies of Four Representative Men," (M.A. Thesis, University of Cincinnati, 1951).
[47]
   "Two Centuries. Bi-Centennial of the First German Settlement in America. The Great Local Demonstration." Newspaper clipping in the Fick Collection of German-Americana, Special Collections Department, University Libraries, University of Cincinnati. This newspaper article contains the texts of the various addresses delivered at the 1883 Pastorius Celebration.

all local Vereine. With monthly meetings at the Central Turnhalle, the Society functioned as the first central organization of local secular societies. Its annual Fest attracted up to 25,000 with noteworthy speakers, such as Carl Schurz. It did not engage in political or religious questions, except when "Germandom directly or the German cause" stood in danger. [48] Philanthropic donations were made to charities, such as the Altenheim, to national events, such as the Turnfest and the North American Sängerfest, as well as to the creation of monuments, such as the Pastorius Monument, the Erkenbrecher Monument, and the Jahn Monument (in Inwood Park). After Goetz's death, the Society was led by Judge August H. Bode and by August B. Gorbach. In 1906 it was incorporated into a new local central organization, Der Deutsch-Amerikanische Stadtverband, or German-American City Alliance.

On 21 September 1906 Judge Bode, at the suggestion of Max Henning, president of the Ohio Alliance, called the first meeting of the Cincinnati Stadtverband, as a branch of the state Alliance, in the Turnhalle. Officials were elected and a constitutional committee appointed. In the April 1907 meeting a new president was elected, Judge John Schwab, with Heinrich Albertz as secretary. Both gave the new group "new life and drive" and gave "the liberal Germandom of Cincinnati . . . the boldest hopes." [49] Its first Volksfest (21 July

48
For a history of the Day Society see August B. Gorbach, Deutscher Vereins-Wegweiser von Cincinnati, Ohio. Erste Ausgabe. (Cincinnati: Stadtverband von Cincinnati, 1915) pp. 39-44.
49
Gorbach, Wegweiser, p. 24.

1907) attracted 10,000 people. The celebration was characterized by a festive atmosphere with German food, drink and music. Resolutions were adopted protesting all limitations on personal freedom (prohibition) and it was announced that only those candidates for public office would be supported who had "healthy views" on the matter. At the August state convention in Toledo, Cincinnati with its "efficient, energetic and fearless and conscientious leader" was chosen as state headquarters with Schwab as state president and Albertz as state secretary.[50] By 1915 the Cincinnati Stadtverband represented Vereine with 11,800 members, or as the local guide to Vereine called them, "over 10,000 voters."[51] According to the guide, the Stadtverband had become a political force that could not be ignored, especially when it came to school board elections. Here it endorsed German language instruction as well as physical education (Turnunterricht). Its platform stated that it did not engage in party politics, excluded religious questions, opposed immigration restrictions, laws hindering the attainment of citizenship, and all laws hindering personal liberty. In local elections it opposed prohibition, women's suffrage and supported home rule legislation. In 1910 a women's branch of the Stadtverband was formed by Mrs. Charlotte Neeb, the Frauenstadtverband, with membership open to all German-American women and organizations. It engaged in various humanitarian,

---

[50] Gorbach, _Wegweiser_, p. 28.

[51] Ibid.

philanthropic and charitable projects. For many recently arrived young women it succeeded in finding positions as teachers in the public schools.[52]

In June 1843 a Männerchor was established, followed soon by the Deutscher Gesangverein (1844) and the Liederfafel (1844), the latter of which held the first public German song concert. In 1849 singing societies from Louisville and Madison, Indiana met with those in Cincinnati to hold their first Sängerfest, at which time the North American Sängerbund was established. In 1896 local singing societies established a central committee, the United Singers, to prepare for the 1899 Sängerfest in Cincinnati, an organization which continued after the Fest. Affiliated with it were the 11 local singing societies. Its president, Charles G. Schmidt, was also president of the North American Sängerbund.[53]

By 1915 there were 12 trade union societies for the various trades, e.g., bakers, brewers, butchers, shoemakers, musicians, safemakers, printers, etc. Aside from being affiliated with the Stadtverband, the trade unions held strong ties with the Central Labor Council which drew its leadership from the German community. The Council reflected trade union views: it advocated the eight hour day, government ownership of the means of transportation and communication, free textbooks and free education from kindergarten to high school, union-owned and operated cooperatives as well as other socialist

[52] Gorbach, Wegweiser, p. 23.

[53] Ibid., pp. 51-75.

principles. The trade union movement in Cincinnati "became in many
ways an extension of ethnic community and class cohesiveness."[54]   Its
social life bore the imprint of old world Gemütlichkeit. The Labor
Council published its constitution in German and English, rally
speeches were given in both languages and its official paper, The
Unionist, printed occasional articles in German.

In 1915 there were 59 mutual aid societies out of a total of 110
societies. Mutual aid groups arose out of the need to provide mutual
financial support from a common fund intow hich members paid a small
amount at regular intervals. This provided funds for sickness, death,
unemployment, and educational scholarships to members and their
families. In short, they addressed economic problems of the ethnic
community. Many were regionally based, e.g., Austrian, Bavarian,
Swiss, Saxon, etc., while some were neighborhood oriented, e.g., the
Cincinnati Findlay Kasion, the Pleasant Liberty Klub, etc. Eight were
affiliated with the Pittsburgh-based German Beneficial Union. The
fact that the majority of organizations were regionally-oriented
mutual aid societies indicates the strong sense of fellow feeling in
providing aid and relief to fellow immigrants and their families.
Most of these groups also sponsored Feste, dances, picnics and various
social activities, but these were secondary to the basic goal of

------

[54]
    Barbara L. Musselman, "Working Class Unity and Ethnic Division:
Cincinnati Trade Unions and Cultural Pluralism," Cincinnati Historical
Society Bulletin 34, 1976, 125. Also see her "Trade Unionism in
Turbulent Times: The Central Labor Council of Cincinnati and Vicinity,
1889-1894," (M.A. Thesis, University of Cincinnati, 1971).

55
mutual aid.

There were three marksmen, or sharpshooter clubs, in 1915, all of which preserved the old custom of an annual Schützenfest. However, they also provided mutual aid in the case of a member's death to the surviving family members. Some of the marksmen clubs contributed to local charities, such as the Altenheim and orphanages.[56]

In 1915 there were three Turner societies, the oldest and most prestigious of which was the Cincinnati Turngemeinde with its large Central Turnhalle at 1409-1413 Walnut Street. It had been founded in 1848 by Friedrich Hecker and several other local Forty-Eighters, and was the first such organization in the U.S. The Turnhalle, considered "a mighty fortress of German-American culture," was a social, cultural and political center in the nineteenth century.[57] Over the years one found the following in the Turnhalle: art classes, physical education courses, a library, the German Theater, a band, and a chorus. Since 1859 it was affiliated with the North American Turnerbund, although a national Turnfest had been held in Cincinnati as early as 1852. Its well-trained militia, the Schutzen-Kompagnie, protected the community during the 1850s Know-Nothing nativist outbreaks of violence, and became the Ninth Ohio Regiment in the Civil War. Turners strongly supported the German-English bilingual program, and were responsible for the introduction of physical education into the public school

_____

55
   Gorbach, Wegweiser, pp. 98-172.
56
   Gorbach, Wegweiser, pp. 174-82.
57
   Tenner, Cincinnati, p. 82.

curriculum in 1892. From 1914-15 the Nord-Cincinnati Turnverein in Corryville published a monthly journal entitled Turner-Leben. In 1913 the Turngemeinde established the Deutschen Klub in its Turnhalle as a central meeting place for local Vereine (44 belonged). Here social activities could be held in private in spite of the "Puritanical" Sunday laws.[58]

There were 12 organizations that were cultural, educational, and musically oriented.[59] The United German Reading Club maintained a small library of 50 volumes and was dedicated to continuing education, the cultivation of knowledge of German literature and the preservation of the German heritage. The Aschenbrödel Klub was formed by local musicians whereas zither players established the Cincinnati Zither-Verein. The two most important groups in the cultural category were the Deutsche Literarische Klub and the Deutsche Pionier-Verein. The Klub, established in 1877, counted Cincinnati's foremost German men of letters as its honorary members: H.A. Rattermann, H.H. Fick, and Wilhelm Mueller. Meetings, lectures, discussions and social get-togethers were held. Many of its members were published authors; its song book contains several lieder written by Cincinnatians.[60] The

---

[58]
Regarding local Turner societies see Cincinnati Turnfest-Führer. Festschrift, hrsg . . . für das 25. Bundes-Turnfest des nordamerikanischen Turnerbundes abgehalten in Cincinnati vom 21.-26 Juni 1889. (Cincinnati: M. & R. Burgheim, 1889). On the establishment of the first Turngemeinde see Heinrich A. Rattermann, "Die Pionier-Turngemeinde Amerika's," Der Deutsche Pionier 7, 1876, 178-87.

[59]
Gorbach, Wegweiser, pp. 194-204.

[60]
See Deutscher Literarischer Klub von Cincinnati, Liederbuch, Cincinnati: G. Mühler, 1910.

Pionier-Verein was not regionally organized, but rather open to
Germans from all areas with the stipulation that one must be at least
40 and have resided in the U.S. for 25 years. Its purpose was to
renew and establish old friendships as well as to preserve the history
and memories of German pioneers for future generations by the
collection of relevant documentation. To reach this goal it published
an outstanding historical journal from 1869-1887, Der Deutsche
Pionier, which attained a national readership, especially under the
editorship of local historian H.A. Rattermann. Later the Verein
published an annual, the Vorstandsbericht which reported on the year's
activities and contained extensive biographical information on
members. In 1914 with 900 members it represented the largest local
Verein. Among its important members were: Gustav Bruehl, H.H. Fick,
Friedrich Hassaurek, Christian Moerlein, Karl L. Nippert, Charles G.
Schmidt, Jakob Seasongood, Friedrich S. Spiegel, Gustav Tafel, Isaac
Meyer Wise and E.G. Zinke. Its honorary member was Carl Schurz.[61] It
should be noted that this category of cultural organization was one
that attracted members of the elite, as did the following category.

There were seven German-American charitable organizations, most
prestigious of which was the Deutsche Altenheim-Verein, established in
1891. Its purpose was to provide a home for aged and needy men of
German descent. Its founders included: Frederick H. Alms, J.G.

---

[61] See Rainer Sell, "The German Language: Mirror of the German-
American Struggle for Identity as Reflected in Der Deutsche Pionier
(1869-1887) and the Activities of Der Deutsche Pionier-Verein von
Cincinnati," Journal of German-American Studies 11, 1976, 71-81.

Schmidlapp, Gustav Tafel, Christian Moerlein, Henry Wielert, Henry
Mühlhauser, Albert Erkenbrecher and others from the elite. Before the
war its president was Judge Schwaab. Reflecting its elite nature was
the fact that the Altenheim-Verein was not affiliated with the
Stadtverband.[62]

Local Vereine numbered 110 by 1915; central organizations, 3;
singing societies, 12; trade unions, 12; mutual aid societies, 59;
marksmen clubs, 3; Turnvereine, 3; cultural organizations, 13; and
charitable organizations, 7. To the external observer the superficial
conclusion regarding the Vereine could be that their central concerns
revolved around Feste, Gemütlichkeit, picnics and conviviality. All
of these aspects, to be sure, were part of the fabric of Vereinsleben,
but they were secondary to the actual purposes for which they had been
established and the needs they addressed, e.g., mutual aid, trade
union, cultural, etc.

The Elite

One was either born into the elite, or worked one's way up into
it the hard way. The two individuals who emerged from the elite as
ethnic leaders in the time period of this study represented both
possibilities: Judge John Schwaab and Judge A.K. Nippert.

Born 9 March 1855 in Bavaria, Schwaab had attended schools in
Zweibrücken and graduated from the Munich Military Academy. In
September 1880 he immigrated to Cincinnati where he became a teacher

---

[62]
    For information on the charitable organizations see Gorbach,
Wegweiser, pp. 205-212.

of German in the bilingual program of the city. Here he earned a
modest salary, but he married well: Caroline Wichard, descended from
Kaspar Molitor, a Forty-Eighter, and studied law in his spare time.
In 1893 he commenced the practice of law and became active in local
politics. In 1894 he was elected to the Board of Education, a
position he was re-elected to until 1913; he also served on the Union
board of High Schools for 25 years. As a member of the School Board
he represented the interests of the German community with regard to
the bilingual program, and was entrusted with the program's
supervision until 1903 when H.H. Fick was appointed Supervisor of the
German program.

Schwaab's entrance into the Republican Club of Hamilton County in
1895 led to his association with the Boss Cox machine. The prolonged
illness of machine member Judge William Lueders resulted in Schwaab's
appointment to fill in for him on the bench of the Police Court. the
early years of the century witnessed his rapid rise to social,
cultural and political leadership in the German community. In 1906 he
was elected president of the Stadtverband and in 1907 he was elected
president also of the Stadtverband and the Ohio German-American
Alliance. Before the war he also chaired the Theaterverein, the
organization which ran the local German theater. In 1915 he was
elected president of the prestigious Altenheim-Verein, an organization
predominantly reserved for members of the elite. Schwaab symbolized
not only the man who rose to the top, but was also a gifted and
talented ethnic leader with the ability to attract support from a

cross-section of the German community. By the time of the outbreak of
the war he was, furthermore, one of the vice-presidents of the
National German-American Alliance.[63]

Nippert was born in Frankfurt am Main on 12 June 1872, son of
Ludwig and Ida (von Uxküll-Gyllenband) Nippert. His father, a
Methodist minister, had been sent to Switzerland and Germany by the
Ohio Methodist Conference, and became the first dean of the Methodist
Theological Seminary in Frankfurt am Main. A.K. Nippert received his
preliminary education at the Musterschule in Frankfurt am Main and at
the public schools of Pittsburgh, Pennsylvania and Newport, Kentucky,
and graduated A.B. and L.L.B. in 1894 and 1897 from the University of
Cincinnati. He married Maude Gamble, the daughter of James M. Gamble,
an ingenious chemist who had become immensely wealthy by perfecting
the formula for Ivory Soap. Maude Gamble's mother was Fanny Nast, the
daughter of the father of the German Methodist church, Wilhelm Nast.
Nippert's familial background, therefore, made him one of the most
highly respected German-Americans in Cincinnati. His name signified a
synthesis of origins deriving from the Kirchendeutschen and the elite.

In 1897 he commenced the practice of law in Cincinnati. From
1913-1919 he served as judge of Hamilton County Common Pleas Court,
and was thereafter commonly referred to as "Richter Nippert." From

---

[63]
Dobbert, Disintegration, p. 308-10. An obituary of Schwaab
appeared in the Cincinnati Times-Star (30 March 1933). See also
William M. Morris and E.B. Krieger, The Bench and Bar of Cincinnati:
Commemorating the Building of the New Courthouse (Cincinnati: New
Court House Publishing Co., 1921). Schwaab was fond of relating the
story that he had arrived in Cincinnati in 1880 with a nickel in his
pocket, but in one month was earning fifty dollars per month.

1912 to 1913 he was on the board of directors for the University of Cincinnati. During the war Nippert became an active spokesman for German-American affairs.[64]

The most easily recognizable and best organized of those individuals who could be included in this category were the local teachers of German in the public schools. They were esteemed by and strongly supported by the German community, including Vereins- as well as Kirchendeutschen. By 1915 there were 175 teachers of German in Cincinnati. The tendency of German-American academicians and teachers to separate off from the Vereinsdeutschen began in the 1860s and 1870s across the U.S. This phenomenon occurred in Cincinnati also where teachers formed four of their own organizations.

In 1860 German secondary school teachers formed the Deutsche Oberlehrer-Verein which functioned as a board of directors for the bilingual program until the 1890s when Schwaab was elected to the school board and was entrusted with supervision of the program. The Verein met monthly to discuss educational affairs as they related to the public schools. Secondary school teachers all belonged to a larger group established in 1889, the Deutsche Lehrer-Verein, which embraced all local teachers of German. The purpose of the group was to maintain public interest and support in the bilingual program. Monthly gatherings consisted of business meetings, music, song,

---

[64] See the biography of Nippert in the National Cyclopedia of American Biography, Vol. 46, pp. 267-68; obituaries appeared in the Cincinnati Enquirer (7 August 1956), the Cincinnati Post (7 August 1956) and the New York Times (8 August 1956).

lectures and discussions. Aside from teachers the group accepted all
those interested in educational matters. In 1878 teachers had formed
their own mutual aid society, the Unterstützungsverein der deutschen
Lehrerschaft. In 1908 German women teachers were brought together in
a new society, Harmonie, founded by Charlotte Neeb, president of the
Frauenstadtverband. It was a social and cultural organization aiming
to provide the opportunity for teachers to discuss the most recent
ideas and developments in teaching languages and literature. Funds
from its Gartenfest were contributed to the German-American Teachers
Seminary in Milwaukee, Wisconsin.[65] The key person among local
teachers and academicians was the Supervisor of the German program in
the public schools, H.H. Fick.

Born 16 August 1849 in Lübeck, where he attended the
Grossheimsche Schule, Fick early developed an intense interest in
language, history and literature. In 1864, three years after the
death of his father, he immigrated to New York where he had been
offered a position in his uncle's business. He then moved to
Cincinnati to engage in a similar business venture as a salesman.
Dissatisfaction with the business world caused him to enter the
teaching profession after successfully passing his entrance exams. In
1870 he was appointed as a teacher of German in a public elementary
school in Cincinnati. Because of his artistic talents he also gave
art instruction. He gave great impetus to the art program: in 1872
an art exhibit was sent to the Vienna Exposition and the report of

---

65
   Gorbach, Wegweiser, p. 50.

Commissioner of Education claimed that Cincinnati "had gained an enviable reputation in this branch." From 1878-84 Fick was Superintendent of Drawing. In 1884 he moved to Chicago where he gave private lessons in German and art and married a teacher, Clementine Barna, with whom he founded a German-English school with another colleague. In 1890 he returned to Ohio to complete his Ph.D. at Ohio University (1892). Then he served until 1901 as principal of the Sixth District School and in 1901 was appointed Supervisor of German in the Public Schools, a position he held until 1918.

Fick was nationally known for his contributions to the field of education. He was elected seven times to the presidency of the National German-American Teachers Association which had its central office in Milwaukee at the German-American Teachers Seminary. He also served on the Seminary's board of directors for 40 years until 1918. He was co-editor and then editor-in-chief of the Association's educational journal, the Erziehungsblätter, for a total of 35 years. Locally Fick was, of course, greatly involved in the teachers' organizations. He also edited a local journal for children, entitled Jung-Amerika which contained prose and poetry by himself, his wife and other local authors. He also authored a series of textbooks for the bilingual program, an excellent local history, and a collection of poetry. He was highly respected among the Vereinsdeutschen with honorary memberships in the Pionier-Verein, the Turngemeinde and the Deutsche Literarische Klub. He was the main speaker at numerous

German-American programs and Feste in the tri-state region.[66]

Education

German language instruction was first offered in Cincinnati in 1824 by St. John's Church by the Rev. Ludwig Heinrich Meyer. It attained a peak enrollment of 427 pupils, but declined after 1835 after Meyer resigned. In 1824 German language instruction was also offered in the Catholic Trinity Church with classes held Wednesday, Saturday and Sunday evenings. As early as 1831 German was taught in a Catholic elementary school adjoining the Atheneum. In the 1830s other churches established schools also.[67]

Due to the pressure of the Cincinnati Germans the state legislature passed laws in 1839 allowing for the instruction of any school subject in a foreign language.[68] On 7 September 1840 the first German-English public school opened in Cincinnati, located in the North German Lutheran Church, with Joseph A. Heeman as teacher, the first public school teacher of German in Cincinnati. Also in

---

[66] For a biography of Fick see my German-American Literature. Metuchen, New Jersey: Scarecrow Press, 1977, pp. 273-84. Also see Fick's "Im Rahmen von sechs Jahrzehnten," Autobiographical manuscript, 1928. Fick Collection of German-Americana, University of Cincinnati Central Library.

[67] For a history of German instruction in Cincinnati see Edwin Zeydel, "The Teaching of German in Cincinnati: An Historical Survey," Cincinnati Historical Society Bulletin 20, 1962, 29-37; his "New Light on the Early Teaching of German in Cincinnati," Cincinnati Historical Society Bulletin 22, 1964, 257-58; as well as his general national survey, "The Teaching of German in the U.S. from Colonial Times to Present," German Quarterly 37, 1964, 315-92.

[68] See Ohio, Statutes of the State of Ohio of a General Nature. Vol. III. (Columbus: Samuel Medery, State Printer, 1854), pp. 2214-15.

appplication for this position has been the German travel author, Friedrich Gerstäcker. The school enrolled over 200 in one month so that a second school with 427 students was opened in November at St. John's Church. More schools and teachers were added in the course of the century.

To ensure the maintenance of the program Dr. Friedrich Roelker was elected to the school board in April 1842. Thereafter, local German-Americans demonstrated concern for continued representation on this board. By 1860 the Deutsche Oberlehrer-Verein was established by local German teachers, an organization which was entrusted with the administration of the German-English program. Later their authority was limited to that of an advisory board. By the turn of the century supervision had been entrusted to a member of the school board, Judge John Schwaab. In 1903 he turned this supervision over to the new Supervisor of the German program, Dr. H. H. Fick.

Fick enjoyed a national reputation as an educator as well as a poet. His pedagogical methods became known as the Cincinnati Plan, a German instructional program adopted in many localities. From five to nine hours per week were devoted to German instruction with particular emphasis on the learning of Lieder and poems. For the program he wrote a series of textbooks which were in national use. A 1911 textbook entitled Neu und Alt attempted to synthesize all that was good in the old and new worlds. It, therefore, contained readings on Schiller, Goethe, Franklin, Washington, Lincoln, and various German-American pioneers. Under Fick's leadership the bilingual program thrived. In 1915 there were 175 teachers with 17,000 students of

German.

Prior to the war the program had come under nativist attack at two different times. In the 1850s various Know-Nothings claimed that the program bred disloyalty and in the 1880s complaints were made that it interfered with "English studies." In response to the 1880s attacks a local German teacher, Hermann von Wahlde, authored several pamphlets that addressed these issues.[69] He concluded with regard to the opponent of German language instruction:

> He is not aware that also by means of German words the significance of our American banner, the grandeur of our Republic and the duty of every citizen to love it and to defend it in times of danger can be powerfully inculcated on the minds of children, and that it is done, frequently done, by German teachers of public schools and private schools, within the boundary of the United States.[70]

The Press

Since 1807, when a German almanac, Teutscher Calender auf 1808, by Robert Stubbs, translated into the Pennsylvania German dialect by Edward H. Stall, was published, over 200 German newspapers and periodicals have been published in Cincinnati.[71] At least six distinct categories for these publications can be identified: political/general interest newspapers; religious journals; labor

---

[69] See Hermann von Wahlde, Schriften pädagogischen Inhalts. Zweite vermehrte Auflage. Cincinnati: Albertz, 1899, pp. 59-72. These pamphlets are reprinted in English in this collection of pedagogical essays by Wahlde.

[70] Wahlde, Schriften, p. 62.

[71] Arndt, The German Language Press, pp. 433-59. For a study of the pre-Civil War press see Henry John Groen, "A History of the German-American Newspapers of Cincinnati before 1860," (Ph.D. Dissertation, Ohio State University, 1945).

newspapers; comic/satirical newspapers; Turner newspapers; and
literary/historical journals.

By 1910 the two major dailies, the Volksblatt and the Freie
Presse, had a combined aggregate circulation of 92,000 and by 1917,
112,000.[72] The Volksblatt commenced publication in 1836, the Freie
Presse in 1874. Both issued daily, weekly and Sunday editions. From
the beginning both publications were political antagonists, the Presse
usually taking the Republican position. An array of smaller special
interest publications addressed the needs of particular
subcommunities, organizations and institutions.

The purpose of the press was spelled out in an essay of Der
Deutsche Pionier: education, preservation and fructification.[73]
First, the press was to educate German-Americans about the social,
political, and economic conditions of the land, and to instruct them
on their duties, privileges and rights as American citizens. Second,
the press was to contribute to preservation of the heritage by the sue
and cultivation of an exemplary German and through the encouragement
of the retention of German customs and traditions, and through the
reporting of events in the old country. Third, by the preservation,
representation and spreading of German viewpoints the press should
attempt to imprint the formative nature of the growing nation. The
Cincinnati German press attempted to accomplish these goals in the

---

[72] Henry John Groen, "A Note on the German-American Newspapers of
Cincinnati Before 1860," Monatshefte 37, 1945, 67.
[73] "Die Pflicht der deutsch-amerikanischen Presse," Der Deutsche
Pionier 17, 1885, 127-28.

various types of publications it issued, e.g., political, religious, literary, etc. Its articles, editorials and essays debated current issues; short stories, articles and poems were published for edification and enlightenment; and news items from abroad appeared throughout the daily, weekly, monthly and quarterly publications.

Literature

In discussing local German literature this study is concerned with literature in its broadest sense as the aggregate of all writings of a people, and not limited to belles lettres. Although a definitive checklist of Cincinnati German publications has not been compiled a preliminary one has.[74] By World War I well over 200 books by Cincinnati German authors had been published, making these publications, next to Pennsylvania Germanica, one of the largest branches of German-American literature.

Regarding Cincinnati German literature several conclusions can be made. First, Cincinnati Germans had a predilection for poetry. Some 5,000 poems were published in their books. Also evident is the fact that many authors were concerned with German language instruction: the number of German grammars and readers is striking. Many books dealt with German-American history in general and Cincinnati German history in particular. Scholarly treatises covered a wide range of historical, philosophical and theological topics. Generally authors confined themselves to the humanities, although several scientific and

---

[74] See my "Musenklänge aus Cincinnati," Cincinnati Historical Society Bulletin 35, 1977, 115-29.

technical works were published.

In terms of organizations literary life centered on the activities of Der Deutsche Literarische Klub. This club aimed at furthering German-American literature and culture through lectures, writing and publication. Leading German-Americans of the day addressed its members: Udo Brachvogel, a New York German poet (1892); Dr. Julius Goebel, chairman of the German-American Historical Society (1907); and Dr. Kuno Francke, curator of the Germanic Museum at Harvard (1907). Dr. H.H. Fick presented numerous lectures and poems to the Klub; between the years 1878 and 1897 Fick gave 50 lectures on various topics such as German-American Newspaper Names (8 November 1891); German-American Original Poems (30 November 1892); A Stepchild of Our Time: German-American Poetry (25 October 1893); and Poems by Robert Reitzel (21 November 1894). On 26 March 1906 Fick gave the central address at a special service held to mourn the death of Carl Schurz. From 1877 to 1927 over 1700 meetings were held, and many of the lectures were published locally.[75]

Theater

According to Edwin Zeydel, the German stage performed an important educational function: "It has helped to keep alive in German immigrants a love of their native literature. It has helped,

---

[75] For a history of the Klub see Festschrift zum Goldenen Jubiläum des Deutschen Literarischen Klubs von Cincinnati 1877-1927. (Cincinnati: 1927) and its earlier history Geschichte des Deutschen Literarischen Klubs von Cincinnati. Erinnerungsschrift für das zehnte Stiftungsfest 26. November 1887. (Cincinnati: S. Rosenthal, 1877). A list of lectures presented in the Klub can be found in Vorträge gehalten im Deutschen Literarischen Klub von Cincinnati. Festgabe zum 20. Stiftungsfest. (Cincinnati: S. Rosenthal, 1897).

also, to furnish the second and third generations of German-Americans with a better understanding of the land of their fathers. Finally, it has done much to acquaint non-Germans with German drama and with the theater in general."[76]   Ethnic theater transcended all lines of division in the community since audiences included people from all walks of life. This was a strength, the fact that it had a wide appeal in the community, but also its weakness, since it could point to no single segment of the community as its institutional sponsor. Because of this the German theater was often referred to as the step-child and as a Schmerzenskind, or a child of sorrow.[77]

In 1843 the first German plays were presented, Die Lauten-Schlägerin by Christoph Schmidt and Genoveva by Ernst Raupach, under the direction of Stephen Meis, a teacher from the Catholic Trinity Parochial School. Before World War I several theaters were established: the Stadttheater of the Turngemeinde, the German Theater in Robinson's Opernhaus, and the Germania Theater. Dramatic performances were also held in various societal halls and places of entertainment. The only period in which there were no theatrical performances was in the 1881-82 season. In early 1881 a city ordinance against Sunday performances and presentations, the Stubbs Law, was passed. German-Americans petitioned in vain to the mayor for

---

[76]
    Edwin Zeydel, "The German Theater in New York City, 1878-1914," Deutsch-Amerikanische Geschichtsblätter 15, 1915, 308.

[77]
    For example see the article, "Das Schmerzenskind des amerikanischen Deutschtums, das Theater," Cincinnati Volksblatt (2 April 1875).

removal of the ban on Sunday performances which was viewed as "the
victory of the Puritans."[78] The law adversely affected theaters since
Sunday afternoon was the main performance time for the theaters.
Violations of the Stubbs Law caused fines and the arrest of German
actors. Because of this negative Zeitgeist there were no performances
1881-82. Thereafter the German theater survived due to two factors.
First, it shifted its schedule to the weekdays and, second, a new
Theaterverein was formed in 1890.

The Theaterverein aimed to place the theater on a sound financial
basis. Its directors in the pre-war period included those who were
prominent in the elite and the Vereine, including Leopold Markbreit,
Max Burgheim, Henry Hauck and Charles G. Schmidt. Its presidents
included Adolf Sander, Albert Mühlhäuser, and Judge John Schwaab. In
1913 a competing organization was formed, the German Theater Company,
with Dr. Karl L. Stoll as president.

The theater presented a kaleidoscope of the works from the world
literatures. For example, in 1861 plays by Shakespeare, Schiller,
Goethe, Raimund, Sheridan Knowles and others were presented; in 1870
there were plays by Lessing, Grillparzer, Schiller and Goethe, among
others. Among the noted actors on the Cincinnati stage was the poet
Konrad Nies, who in 1883 presented his monodrama Konradin von

---

[78] Ralph Charles Wood, "Geschichte des Deutschen Theaters von
Cincinnati," (Ph.D. Dissertation, Cornell University, 1932), pp. 55-
59. For a brief survey of the theater that is less comprehensive than
Wood see Max Heinrici, ed., Das Buch der Deutschen in Amerika.
(Philadelphia: National German-American Alliance, 1909), pp. 450-52.
See also Cincinnati, The General Ordinances and Resolutions of the
City of Cincinnati in Force April, 1887 (Cincinnati: Robert Clarke &
Co., 1887) pp. 772-76.

Hohenstaufen. A noteworthy guest in 1906 was the German author
Ludwig Fulda, in whose honor his play Jugendliebe was performed. A
memorable event was the April 1906 Schiller Celebration when Wilhelm
Tell was performed at Music Hall.

Art

The first German artist in Cincinnati, Friedrich Eckstein,
arrived in 1825-26 in the Queen City where he established the Academy
of Fine Arts.[79] Many more artists were to follow in the course of the
century, such as John Hauser who painted scenes of the Old West and
the American Indian. The one artist who best symbolized and
epitomized the pre-war symbiosis of German-American culture was Frank
Duveneck. Born in Covington, Kentucky in 1848, Duveneck worked as a
youth in Cincinnati with the decorator Wilhelm Lamprecht, and in 1870
traveled to Munich to study at the Art Academy. At that time the
Bavarian capital "was as much the Mecca of American art students as
was Paris . . ." In Munich he studied the work of Rubens and Van Dyck,
but "the marked feeling in his early pictures for accurate, detached
observation and a sure manipulation of pigment are characteristics
which recall the early work of Leibl."[80] In 1874 Duveneck held a
successful show in Cincinnati, but returned to Munich where he

---

[79]
    For a brief survey of local German-American art see Karl L.
Stoll, "Deutsche Werke im Kunstmuseum," Cincinnati Freie Presse:
Illustrierte Beilage (6 November 1927).
[80]
    Cincinnati Art Museum, Exhibition of the Work of Frank Duveneck
May 23 Through June 21, 1936 (Cincinnati: Cincinnati Art Museum), p.
8.

established his own school and following known as Frank Duveneck and
the Duveneck Boys. He also traveled widely throughout Europe
absorbing artistic influences there.

In 1890 he began his teaching career at the Cincinnati Art Museum
where he attracted a following, as in Munich. Until his death in 1919
he was Cincinnati's premier artist. He was depicted as "an artist
working with dignity in a great painterly tradition." Although a
realist, Duveneck was never superficial:

> His exact observation penetrated beneath the surface and
> revealed the character of personality of whatever he was
> painting. He was a consummate workman, a sure and vigorous
> draftsman, a good colorist, and an able designer. His interest
> was always in the normal aspects of man and nature. An ardent
> exponent in his own work and in his teaching of direct painting,
> he was a master of drawing with the brush.   81

Music

In 1867 Clara Baur, a German pianist and singer, founded the
Cincinnati Conservatory of Music based on the model of the Stuttgart
Hochschule für Musik. The College of Music, established in 1878, was
first directed by Theodor Thomas, born in Esens, Hannover. However,
German musical influences were perhaps most clearly apparent in the
May Festival and the Cincinnati Symphony Orchestra.

Local German singing societies with their colorful Sängerfeste
had already contributed by mid-nineteenth century to cincinnati's
reputation as "the city of festivals." [82]   In 1873 the first May

---

81
   Exhibition, pp. 12-13.
82
   Sylvia Kleve Sheblessy, 100 Years of the Cincinnati May
Festival (Cincinnati, 1973), p. 3.

Festival was planned by an executive committee chaired by Col. George
E. Nichols, who was ably assisted by his wife Maria Longworth Nichols.
The 12-man committee consisted of Anglo-Americans, such as John
Shillito, and Bellmany Storer, and four Germans, including H.A.
Rattermann. As some members belonged to the Harmonic Society (Anglo)
and others to the Orpheus Club (German), the first May Festival
represented Anglo-German musical cooperation. Although some Germans
complained that there was not enough festivity at the festival, they
were pleased that all of the composers on the program were German and
that the conductor was Theodor Thomas. The festival's locale, the
Exposition Hall, was replaced in time for the third Fest (1878) by the
Music Hall, due to the donations of Reuben Springer. Theodor Thomas
was succeeded by other German musical directors: Frank van der
Stucken (1906-12) and Ernst Kunwald (1914-16) in the pre-war period.
The Symphony Orchestra's forerunner was the Cincinnati Orchestra which
was begun in 1872 under George Brand to augment Thomas' May Festival
Orchestra. In 1895 the Cincinnati Orchestra Association was
established to form the Symphony Orchestra with stockholders and
guarantors. During the first season concerts were directed by van der
Stucken, Anton Seidl, and Henry Schradieck; van der Stucken was then
commissioned as conductor for the next season. Other pre-war
conductors included Stokowski (1909-12) and Ernst Kunwald (1912-17).

By 1910 President Taft and the German Ambassador, Count von
Bernstorff, attended the May Festival. At the Queen City Club toasts
were presented to the president, his wife, to the ambassador and to
Germany. Among the popular May Festival stars were Johanna Gadski,

Reinhold Werrenrath, Alma Gluck, and Marcella Sembrich, but most
popular was the great contralto, Ernestine Schumann-Heink. Between
1900 and 1914 she sang at eight festivals. Locally she was also known
for her wind-up Victrola recording of **Stille Nacht**.[83]

Politics

Already in the 1840s the Cincinnati Germans united for political·
purposes to form the Deutsche Demokratische Verein of Hamilton County,
an organization that came into being because of the nativist
tendencies of local Whigs. "It soon became evident that the
Cincinnati German-Americans, whenever they joined in concerted action,
held the balance of political power between the Whigs and Democrats . . ." The key phrase here is "concerted action" since the
German community, because of its very nature, did not usually engage in
concerted action, except in times of crisis or of pressing issues,
e.g., the 1850s nativist outbursts.[84]   Because of the community's
diversity it makes little sense to speak of a "German vote" in terms

---

[83]
    Sheblessy, **100 Years**, pp. 49-51. for further information on
musical history see Reba Robertson, "Musical History of Cincinnati,"
(M.A. Thesis, University of Cincinnati, 1941), Vernon Paul Schroeder,
"Cincinnati's Musical Growth, 1870-1875," (M.A. Thesis, University of
Cincinnati, 1971), and Louis Russell, "A History of the Cincinnati
Symphony Orchestra," (Ph.D. Dissertation, University of Cincinnati,
1972) and also his "The Cincinnati Symphony Orchestra Under the
Direction of Fritz Reiner, 1922-1931," (M.A. Thesis, University of
Cincinnati, 1963).

[84]
    Groen, "A Note on the German-American Newspapers," p. 70. For
coverage of the 1850s nativist phenomenon in Cincinnati see William
Baughin, "Nativism in Cincinnati before 1860," (M.A. Thesis,
University of Cincinnati, 1963) and his "Development of Nativism in
Cincinnati," **Cincinnati Historical Society Bulletin** 22, 1964, 240-55.

of a phalanx of voters at the polls. For example, the Vereine would staunchly oppose prohibition, but not so the German Methodists. However, in pre-war Cincinnati the Stadtverband, which claimed to represent 12,000 voters, did play a definite political role in endorsing and opposing candidates and issues. Because of this and the sizable German population, it is certain that the Germans were an element that had to be included in the strategy of any local politician.

Basically the Cincinnati Germans voted Republican. Of the eight mayors elected from 1897 to 1916, six were Republicans: Gustav Tafel (1897-1900); Julius Fleischmann (1900-05); Col. Leopold Markbreit (1908-09), Louis Schwab (1910-11), Frederick S. Spiegel (1914-15); and George Puchta (1916-17), all of whom were Germans.[85] Two non-German Democrats served in this period: Edward Dempsey (1906-07) and Henry Hunt (1910-11).

Before the interrelationships between the Republican machine of Boss Cox, the reformers and the Germans are examined, a few general points should be made. All too often reformers have painted a black and white picture of themselves as the crusading white knights and the machine as the smoking black dragon, a picture that does not always conform with reality. Although machine vices were manifold, they

---

[85]
      For biographical information see Fick, *Cincinnati*. Also see Melvin G. Holli and Peter d'A. Jones, eds., *Biographical Dictionary of American Mayors, 1820-1980: Big City Mayors*. (Westport, Conn.: Greenwood Press, 1981). For a discussion of the role of the Cincinnati Germans in nineteenth century politics see Heinrich A. Rattermann, *Die Stellung der Deutschen in den politischen Parteien*. (Cincinnati: S. Rosenthal, 1884).

should not obscure consideration of some of the positive services provided by the political machine. First, the machine recognized the pluralistic nature of American society: political bosses not only recognized the ethnic vote, they catered to, exploited and manipulated it. Second, the machine provided real services to large numbers of people. Precinct captains made it a point to address the particular needs of recently arrived immigrants, from finding them employment to finding them accomodations. In short, machines provided a whole variety of welfare services and privileges available from no other government agency. Third, machines afforded socio-political opportunities and elective office. Here was a legitimation of ethnic involvement in American political life. At a lower level the machine held contracts and franchises at its disposal which could be exploited in its own interests. The point here is that in spite of its well documented vices, the political machine of pre-World War I days performed a number of services for ethic communities.

Reformers, on the other hand, "were always an outlandish breed to the immigrants" with their repulsive platforms espousing temperance, sabbatarianism, and women's suffrage.[86] Their religious tolerance, or indifference, seemed to the immigrant to reflect a lack of interest in religion. Reformers found not only little support but stubborn opposition among the foreign-born populations. Often reformers attacked the recognized immigrant leaders as machine bosses.

---

[86] Oscar Handlin, The Uprooted. The Epic Story of the Grat Migrations that Made the American People. New York: Grosset & Dunlap, 1951, pp. 219-220.

Sometimes there was a tendency to ascribe poor government and the plight of the cities to the immigrant residents, a move "calculated to win the favor of the native born." Few reformers seriously addressed the needs and concerns of immigrants from their perspective. If the problems of immigrants were discussed the solution was seen in their Americanization. "The whole pack of innovations in the structure of government seemed to the foreign-born to be either mere tinkering or some subtle plot to steal control by undermining the familiar ways of political action."[87] The moralistic crusades of the progressives have been described by Richard Hofstadter as the movement of a displaced WASP elite to restore itself and its values to political power.[88]

The nature of American society had been profoundly altered by the millions of European immigrants. The German immigration to Cincinnati had swollen the German population from five percent in 1820 to over one-third by 1910. According to Hofstadter, progressivism has been traditionally viewed as a reforming liberal movement aimed at adjusting institutions to the new industrial age, but to Hofstadter progressivism related mainly to status anxiety of a displaced elite. By the end of the nineteenth century older Anglo-American families, clergymen, professors, lawyers and other professionals were feeling themselves displaced from their traditional seats of power by the new political machines supported by ethnic voters. They responded with the progressive movement to install their sort of people into office.

---

[87] Ibid.

[88] Richard Hofstadter, The Age of Reform: From Bryan to F.D.R. New York: Alfred A. Knopf, 1955.

George E. Mowry has depicted progressivism as a movement by a
particular class to reassert its declining position.[89] It should be
noted that, although Cincinnati had two early German-American mayors
in the nineteenth century (Ziegler and Baum), that almost the entire
century saw Anglo-American mayors until 1897 when the German period
began, lasting until 1917. Anglo-Americans had been definitely
displaced. A recent study of the Anglo Kulturkampf has found that the
leaders of the assimilationist crusade against the Germans in World
War I were "not from the conservative elements of the community, but
from its pre-war 'progressive' activists in civic, Social Gospel, and
political organizations."[90] According to this study, Social Gospel
ministers were some of the most forceful proponents of German-American
conformity to Anglo standards of behavior and culture.

Boss Cox, the son of a British immigrant, built an ethnically
oriented political machine. A large number of its members were
German: Simon Krug, Frank Krug, Frank Kirchner, Friedrich Bader,
Herman F. Cellarius, Lewis Kraft, Dan Bauer, Morris Bauer, Joseph
Schweninger. William H. Lueders, a lawyer and active member of
charitable organizations, provided contacts with the elite, as did
Judge August H. Doda, president of the German Day Society. Judge
Schwaab, president of the Stadtverband, owed his appointment to a

---

[89]
For example, see his "The California Progressive and His
Rationale: A Study in Middle Class Politics," Mississippi Valley
Historical Review, 36, 1949, 239-50.

[90]
Clifford H. Scott, "Assimilation in a German-American
Community: The Impact of World War I," Northwest Ohio Quarterly 52:1,
1980, 153.

judgeship to an associate of Boss Cox. However, the two leading
machine lieutenants were August Hermann and Rudolph K. "Rud" Hynicka.
The former was born in 1859 in Over-the-Rhine and he "never broke his
ties with that section of the city."[91] In 1891, when he joined the
machine, he was appointed to the board of administration. Hynicka was
captain of the ninth ward and in the 1890s was elected police clerk.
The machine held "court" on upper Vine Street at Schubert's or Pel's
saloon, or at their table in Wielert's beer-garden. Meetings also
were held at the Central Turnhalle.

What advantages did the German community get from the machine?
Aside from political recognition the community obtained jobs. With
control over five thousand city and county jobs "the German element
must have had its appropriate share."[92] Germans also appreciated the
low tax rates. Moreover, they were suspicious of reformers, fearing
the possible enactment and enforcement of blue laws. Under the Cox
machine it was possible to drink on Sunday. Nevertheless, the
machine's vices were apparent. For example, it was wondered how
Hermann could afford such fine and expensive furniture for his home.
In 1906-08 an anti-Cox reform mayor was elected, Edward J. Dempsey,
but his running mates included two German Protestants, a German Jew as
well as an Anglo-American Mason, born in England. To win, Deomcrats
recruited Germans to deliver German-language addresses, and Judge
Rufus B. Smith addressed local German-Americans on German Day,

---

[91] Miller, Boss, p. 85.

[92] Dobbert, Disintegration, p. 19.

extolling large amounts of praise on German influences on American
life.[93]

The only other progressive reform mayor in the 1897-1917 German
period was Henry T. Hunt (1912-13). He offered a foretaste of what
could happen should nativistically tinged Anglo progressives gain the
upper hand. The _Volksblatt_ derided him as a Judas since he declared
himself to be in favor of personal liberty, but voted for temperance
laws twice as a state legislator. The _Presse_ stated, "The Dutch
[would] get it in the neck" if Hunt was elected. Nevertheless, he was
elected and the judgments of the German language press became all too
true. Under the pretext to shut down "dives" Hunt closed 60 "dives"
and dance halls, and even "temporarily revoked the license of Central
Turner Hall after a detective discovered that girls in short dresses
were being served drinks at a public dance here."[94] It should be
remembered that the Turnhalle had been a central meeting place and the
Turnverein the major verein in the nineteenth century. By 1913 the
German press was strongly criticizing Mayor Hunt, his colleagues and
his policies. His welfare program was viewed as brutal and inhumane.
the press claimed that the German-Americans had helped to elect Hunt,
but that during his administration they had definitely taken a back
seat position. Also, he was supported by the _New York Times_ and
Collier's Weekly, the former of which, according to the German

-----

[93]
Rufus Smith, _The Influence of the Germans in the United States
on its Life and Institutions_. (Cincinnati, 1905).

[94]
Miller, _Boss_, p. 218.

press, constantly criticized Germany and the latter of which was no friend of the brewing industry. Moreover, Hunt's beliefs regarding personal liberty had been exposed by his harassment of Vereine to which he sent spies and snoopers who then sent reports to the local press on the "awful happenings." The next election for mayor pitted Hunt against Frederick S. Spiegel, a Prussian-born Jew. The Post attacked him as "one of the pitiful, surviving figures of an age in which the minds of many good men were, politically speaking, atrophied by the tyranny exercised by the gang." The Post saw the conflict as between good and evil, in which the opposing slate represented "all the horde that break the law and yearn for the protection of which they were deprived two years ago."[95] Hunt's defeat by Frederick S. Spiegel, however, brought a feeling of relief to many a Cincinnati German. Not only was Spiegel a member of the German community belonging to various Vereine, including the highly respected Pionier-Verein, but also a believer in personal liberty, and finally a welcome change to the last two years.

Thus stood political affairs on the eve of the First World War in Cincinnati. To the astute observer in the German community, especially among the Vereinsdeutschen and the editors of the German language press, the signs of nativist intolerance were already visible. The nativism of the following years, which H.L. Mencken described as "the Anglo-Saxon White Terror," represented the

---

[95]
Miller, Boss, pp. 210, 218, 236-37.

culmination of an ethnocultural conflict dating back to the nineteenth century.[96] The significance of the war was that it "was the occasion that converted latent tensions into manifest hostility."[97]

———

[96] H.L. Mencken, The American Scene. A Reader. New York: Knopf, 1965, p. 22.

[97] Luebke, Bonds, p. xiv.

Part Two

The World War One Experience

THE NATIVIST KULTURKAMPF

We shall not become Englishmen, and we shall continue to cherish
our memories but with steadfast devotion we shall stand by our
country which will need us now more than ever. We shall watch
over her internal peace, and we shall make every sacrifice which
is demanded of us.   1

Introduction

An examination of nativism against the German element in

Cincinnati reveals that traces of it were to be found even before

American entrance into the First World War. Although it reached its

hysterical zenith during the war period (1917-18), it continued until

1932 when the last piece of nativist-engendered legislation, the

federal prohibition legislation, was lifted. This nativist period

must be viewed as a whole and can be dated as having lasted from 1917

to 1932.

The Nativist Period, 1914-17

The German element was as "pro-German" as were many Anglo-

Americans "pro-British" in the 1914-17 neutrality period. The Freie

Presse felt that if it came to a European war it would be a
                                                    2
Kulturkampf between Germany and her foes.   So confident of German

---

1
Freie Presse, 2 April 1917.
2
Freie Presse, 27 July 1914.

victory was the Volksblatt that it advocated a discussion of the division of the spoils of war. Later, it proposed war with England, the raising of German-American and Austro-Hungarian volunteers and reservists, and the conquest of Canada.[3] However, most German-Americans in the first weeks of war were still enmeshed with local issues. On the day German declared war on Russia (1 August 1914) the Cincinnati Alliance opened its campaign against prohibition with a mass meeting at which President Schwaab declared that "Prohibition is a fight against the Germans."[4] At the same time the state Alliance, of which Schwaab was also president, presented the Ohio Secretary of State with a peitition against prohibition in Ohio that contained 280,000 signatures. On 8 August the first Stadtverband meting was held after the war's outbreak. Resolutions were passed against what was viewed as the negative stance of the local Anglo-American press against Germany and Austro-Hungary. A week later the Swabian Mutual Aid Society (15 August) condemned what it described as "the malicious Anglo-American press" that aimed to present Germany in a bad light.[5]

At its state convention in Toledo (21-23 August) the Ohio Alliance declared itself ready to answer the challenges of the Anti-Saloon League, and the "equally obnoxious advocates of female suffrage" through which "the fanatics of prohibition are planning to gain everything else that remains to be desired by them in the

[3]
Volksblatt, 29 July and 2 October, 1914.
[4]
Mitteilungsblatt des Deutschamerikanischen Nationalbundes (September 1914): 4.
[5]
Volksblatt, 16 August 1914.

state."[6] On the 23rd Japan declared war against Germany so the
Alliance drew up resolutions expressing concern over the Japanese
seizure of Tsingtau and indicted England for building up the Japanese
navy and military at the expense of the U.S. Copies were sent to the
President, Secretary of State, and Ohio members of Congress.

On 30 August a mass peace demonstration was held at the Music
Hall, a meeting widely advertised in local religious institutions a
week in advance. It was organized by Dr. Gotthard Deutsch with the
support of a committee consisting of Prof. J. L. Shearer, Rabbi H.
Englander, Rev. George G. Thayer, Miss Annie Laws, Dr. R. H. Reemelin
and others. This first mass demonstration for peace reflected the
widespread manner in which the war affected the local community.[7] On
4 September the Rev. A. Nemenz, St. Paul's Church, presented a well
attended lecture entitled "The Rise of Germany against a World of
Enemies," a presentation with special attraction since the minister
had just returned from Germany.[8]

In early September Dr. Oskar Mezger, German Consul in Cincinnati,
published a letter in the Freie Presse requesting that readers
subscribe to the recently established weekly journal The Fatherland,
published in New York and edited by George Sylvester Viereck. Mezger
recommended the journal as "an effective weapon" in the battle for

---

[6] Mittteilungen des Deutschamerikanischen Nationalbundes
(September 1914): 4.

[7] Freie Presse, 31 August 1914.

[8] Ibid., 5 September 1914.

fair play for Germany.[9]

At the September meeting of the German Literary Club complaints were raised regarding the objectivity of war reports in the _Times-Star_. August Gorbach wrote that it was clear that it was a question of "an organized anti-German press" which aimed to do everything to awaken antipathy against Germany. This issue had already been raised in August by the Bavarian Mutual Aid Society as well as at the Stadtverband meeting. Addressing this issue the German and Austro-Hungarian Aid Society sent a letter (25 September) to Charles P. Taft, publisher of the _Times-Star_, protesting the "one-sided pro-British war reporting." An unsatisfactory response from Joseph Garretson of the newspaper caused the Aid Society to reiterate its concerns in a second letter.[10]

A second mass demonstration was held in the Music Hall (11 October) with a twofold purpose: to protest "the distorted war reports and the renunciation of the Germans" and to show solidarity with the people of Austro-Hungary. Local press announcements from the Stadtverband invited all to attend. The hall was packed to the balconies with a chorus of 200 from the United Singers on the stage. A "hearty welcome" was accorded Mayor Spiegel as he entered the auditorium. Expressing their concerns for peace were the main speakers, Judge Schwaab, Nippert and Rev. Hugo G. Eisenlohr. The latter declared, "We do not beg for sympathy, we demand justice." The

[9] _Freie Presse_, 3 September 1914.
[10] _Volksblatt_, 26 September 1914.

mass meeting was organized by Rev. Hans Haupt, Gorbach, Nippert, Colon

Schott, Rev. Nemenz, Karl Pletz, H. H. Fick, Charles Schmidt, Prof.

Ludwig Wosececzek and others.   A Liederkonzert (15 November) was [11]

then sponsored in the Music Hall by the United Singers on behalf of

the relief work being done locally, with an address by Charles

Schmidt.   From mid-November to January 1915 a number of films on the [12]

war were shown at the Music Hall and elsewhere which, according to a

commentator, offered the chance to see conditions and events "as they

really were, not through the colored glasses of the enemies of

Germany."   In December 1914 Prof. Woseczek, who had helped organized [13]

the October mass demonstration, designed a postal card for the German

and Austro-Hungarian Aid Society that depicted the work of the relief

program: in one corner was Columbia and the suffering in the other (a

wounded German sailor and family and two Austro-Hungarian widows with

babies) gazing with "thank-filled" eyes to Columbia. These were

widely sold and used locally in support of the relief program. In

mid-January iron rings were also produced and widely sold locally on

behalf of the Aid Society. [14]

In February there arose the beginnings of a controversy between

the Stadtverband and the President of the University of Cincinnati,

William Dabney. Already at the January meeting of the German Literary

---

[11]
    Volksblatt, 12 October 1914.
[12]
    Freie Presse, 16 November 1914.
[13]
    August B. Gorbach, Das Hilfswerk und Cincinnati's deutsche
Vereine (Cincinnati: Deutscher Stadtverband, 1915), p. 73.
[14]
    Ibid., p. 83.

Club, Dr. Deutsch had spoken sharply against Dabney's 28 December 1914 speech in Columbus, Ohio in which he had denounced Germany as imperialistic and charged her with having started the war. [15] At the February meeting of the Stadtverband the issue was addressed and resolutions approved which protested this speech. Copies were sent to Dabney, members of the University's Board of Directors, as well as to Mayor Spiegel. It should be emphasized that the university was at that time a municipal institution rather than a state university. The Alliance also requested of Spiegel that in cases of vacancies on the Board of Directors, he should appoint only those who would not be inclined to grant Dabney the opportunity of disparaging the German-American community under the cloak of the university presidency. [16]

On 27 February a patriotic play entitled, "Fürs Vaterland" was written and produced by members of the Bavarian Männerchor. [17] In April Bernhard Ritter, editor of the New Yorker Staats-Zeitung, presented a lecture at Music Hall entitled "The Other Side of War." He also displayed pictures of the war which had been approved by the German General Staff. The speaker was introduced by Dr. Deutsch who bestowed "high praise" on the New Yorker. [18]

Summer festivals of 1915 related to the themes of war in Europe.

15
Volksblatt, 7 January 1915.
16
Gorbach, Hilfswerk, pp. 94-95. Also see Zane Miller, "Charles W. Dabney and the Urban University: An Institution in Search of a Mission," Cincinnati Historical Society Bulletin 38 (1980): 150-79.
17
Freie Presse, 28 February 1915.
18
Volksblatt, 21 April 1915.

The Stadtverband's Volksfest (12 June) was held in Reichrath's Park
with Joseph Keller, First Vice-President of the National Alliance, and
Mayor Spiegel as the main speakers.[19]   On 20 June the Sängerfest of
the Southern Ohio and Kentucky Sängerbund was held in Wiedemann Park
in Newport, Kentucky with six thousand people attending. Charles
Schmidt addressed the fest described as a demonstration of "German
social life."[20]

In July 1915 Schwaab declared that "the drink question is forced
upon us by the same hypocritical Puritans as over there are
endeavoring to exterminate the German nation." According to him, the
Germans in Europe were "a thorn in the flesh of an Englishman" because
of Germany's commercial growth, and in America the English aimed at
the suppression of German influence.[21]   At the same time a mass
demonstration (1 July) was held at the Music Hall to protest the
munitions trade. Addresses were held in English so that non-Germans
could attend. Resolutions were worked out by Judge Nippert. The
judge stated that American munitions makers were causing more tears,
sorrow, wounds, deaths, widows, and orphans than any nation currently
at war. The time had come, he urged, for American citizens to do
their duty in protesting against the export of munitions. He said,
"We protest first in the name of true neutrality and second in the

---

19
    Volksblatt, 13 June 1915.
20
    Freie Presse, 21 June 1915.
21
    Mitteilungen des Deutsch-amerikanischen Nationalbundes (August
1915):4.

name of Christian brotherly love and humanity . . ."[22]

At the end of July a folk festival for the Aid Society was held at the Zoo which attracted 10,000 people. Local Turners performed under the direction of Dr. Gustav Eckstein and members of the German Theater presented several sketches. The fest was organized by Schwaab, Schott, Schmidt, Weier, Gorbach, Mrs. Fick, Mrs. H.E. Wurlitzer and others. At the annual Ohio Alliance convention in Canton (21 August 1915) Schwaab stated that many of the proponents of prohibition were also opponents of Germany, but that one should soft-pedal the war question always. "Let us drive no friend out of our camp by making the European war into our war," Schwaab remarked.[23] However, the war intruded itself into German-American life. Responding to hysterical reports about German-American patriotism the Volksblatt queried "Did the hyphenates cause the tornado in Kansas?"[24]

Mass demonstrations continued: on 13 December 1915 Dr. Deutsch organized a mass meeting in the Grand Opera House to protest the treatment of Jews in Russia. The main speaker was Rabbi Jacob H. Kaplan, and Rev. L.B. Campbell represented Governor F.B. Willis.[25] In January 1916 J.W. Freiberg organized another mass meeting to call attention to the plight of the Jews in Russia and also those in Poland and Galacia. The main speakers at this event were Rev. Hugo C.

22
   Gorbach, Hilfswerk, p. 93.
23
   Freie Presse, 22 August 1915.
24
   Volksblatt, 11 November 1915.
25
   Freie Presse, 14 December 1915.

Eisenlohr and Judge Rufus Smith. The meeting was sponsored by the
American Jewish Relief Committee in Emery Auditorium.[26]

In 1915 President Wilson began his discussion of the dangers of
"hyphenism" and urged legislation against conspirators and those who
would plot against American neutrality. References to "hyphenated
Americans" were felt to be veiled slights against German-Americans.
The Volksblatt termed such references "an infamous insult, which we
shall not forget nor pardon."[27]

In March Congressman J. Campbell Cantrill published a letter from
the President of the University of Cincinnati, William Dabney, in an
interview with a newspaper. Dabney urged Cantrill to stand firm with
Wilson against Germany. The Cincinnati Stadtverband again registered
its protest in a letter to Dabney. It deplored his attempt to "foist
his dangerous notions, personal fallacies, and national antipathies
upon the community." It considered such actions "deserving of signal
and severest condemnation." Furthermore, it insisted that Dabney
"desist in the future from similar agitatory acts, or that, in case of
non-compliance, he be compelled to do so by the proper authorities."[28]

In early March the Aid Society sponsored the appearance of Dr.
Eugen Kühnemann from Breslau who spoke about the destruction and havoc
wrought by the war in East Prussia. He singled out the following as

---

[26]
   Volksblatt, 27 January 1916.
[27]
   Volksblatt, 9 December 1916.
[28]
   U.S. Congress, Senate Subcommittee on the Judiciary, Brewing
and Liquor Interests and German and Bolshevik Propaganda, Vol. 2.
(Washington, D.C.: Government Printing Office, 1919), pp. 2107-09.

having contributed the most to the alleviation of the distress in East Prussia: Prof. Shearer, Nippert, Schott, Deutsch, H.E. Wurlitzer, and others. Kühnemann's appearance led to the establishment of a local branch of the Society for East Prussian Aid. On 11 March, Nippert and Edward Brunhoff left for Cleveland and other Ohio cities to aid in establishing branches of the East Prussian Aid Society.[29]

Later in March news was received that Nippert had been appointed as the American delegate and representative of the East Prussian Aid Society to the convention in Berlin which would be attended by General von Hindenburg and Kaiser Wilhelm II; the New York Central Committee had recommended him for this position.[30] A farewell dinner was held in Nippert's honor (15 April) and before he left for Germany he received letters from Governor Willis and Secrtary of State Lansing. He also met with Theodore Roosevelt and Wilson before departing. Locally he was described as the Cincinnati Germans' "worthiest representative."[31] Upon his return a welcome fest was held in Emery Auditorium (20 July) which was organized by representatives of the Stadtverband, the German Day Society, the Pionier-Verein, the United Singers, the German Literary Club, and the Catholic Zentralverband. Jacob Hoffman of Westwood presented a poem dedicated to the judge, who then described his trip to Germany. Resolutions were ready by Dr.

---

[29] Volksblatt, 3 March 1916; Freie Presse, 13 and 17 March 1916.

[30] Freie Presse, 16 March 1916.

[31] Gorbach, Hilfswerk, p. 165.

Deutsch protesting against the tampering of federal mails sent from
neutral countries.[32]

In April President Wilson's note to Germany and his address to
Congress on the submarine controversy caused great concern in the
press. The Volksblatt claimed that "A war with Germany would be a
crime against civilization and be condemned by all fair-minded people
of the United States."[33] Judge Schwaab telegraphed Ohio's
representatives in Congress that "Your constituents are against
breaking off diplomatic relations with Germany and implore you most
earnestly to vote and work against any and all attempts that lead to
such a break." The Volksblatt telegraphed to representatives in
Washington, "Common sense is staggered and civilization shudders at
the thought that the people of the United States should become
involved in war for a mere technicality."[34]

A respite from war-related activities was offered on 19 May with
the celebration of the 75th anniversary of the introduction of German
language instruction into the puolic schools of Cincinnati.[35] Little
did the celebrators know that there would be no more such celebrating
with regard to anniversaries of the program.

The celebration was held in the Music Hall with the bilingual
program's chief architect, Dr. H.H. Fick, as main speaker. On stage

---

[32]
Volksblatt, 28 July 1916.
[33]
Ibid., 19 April 1916.
[34]
Ibid.
[35]
Volksblatt, 20 May 1916; Freie Presse, 20 May 1916.

was an 800-member children's choir singing such songs as: "Der Mai
ist gekommen," "Droben steht die Kapelle," and "Ade, du lieber
Tannenwald." The oldest German teacher, Marie Eichner, received a
bouquet of flowers as did Dr. Fick. Songs were presented by the
United Singers accompanied by Emilie Borger-Weissman at the organ.
Thereafter W. Wienecke, president of the Oberlehrer-Verein, stated
with respect to the bilingual program that he wanted "to make the
cultural values of the German people accessible to our children. That
is our holy duty . . ."[36] Dr. R.J. Condon, Superintendent of Schools,
gave a statistical overview of the bilingual program since 1840. Then
the last of the pre-war German-American mayors stated:

> The influence of the Germans in this city through their
> splendid congenial language ... their industry, thoroughness and
> ability for acquisition, their patriotism and love for home and
> friends, their inclination for music and art, their German
> culture have contributed so much to the present greatness of
> Cincinnati that so long as the Queen City exists the name of the
> noble character of its German citizens will stand forever.   37

Then the choir sang Fick's well known poem on the German mother
tongue, "Das Lied, das meine Mutter sang." After Fick's address,
which outlined the history of German language instruction, a display
of the photographs of 78 of Cincinnati's oldest German language
teachers was presented in the foyer of the Music Hall. On 21 May a
special dinner was held at the Gibson House to bring the celebration
to a close. Dr. Max Griebsch, Director of the German-American

---

36
  Gorbach, Hilfswerk, p. 14.
37
  Cited in Tolzmann, German-American Literature, pp. 278-79.

Teachers Seminary in Milwaukee, spoke, as did Dr. Gotthard Deutsch.[38]

In late May 1916 a German-American National Conference was held in Chicago with nearly 170 delegates from 26 states, most of them members of the National Alliance. A platform was adopted by the Resolutions Committee chaired by Judge Schwaab. This platform stated:

> We deplore and condemn all attempts to divide Americans and to insult or stigmatize any race, creed or color by invidious hyphenation. Men from every country of the world have found here a new home -- a land of liberty, of equal opportunity and equal justice -- and all have contributed their sweat and their blood to the upbuilding and defense of our great democracy. They may be hyphenated Americans, but their Americanism is unhyphenated. To attempt to arouse animosity and distrust toward any class or nationality as some have done through shrewd ambition or ungovernable temper, is a crime. A deaf ear should be turned to all demagogues that trade upon national antipathies and seek to extol their own loyalty by impugning that of others.   [39]

The Chicago Platform demanded "a neutrality that corresponds to the counsel which George Washington gave the American people in his farewell address;" urged "a foreign policy which defends with equal firmness and justice the existence of American interests" and condemned "every official procedure and every policy which shows inherent sympathy toward one belligerent nation and unmitigated antipathy toward another." It deplored "those speeches, made by public officials, or former public officials, which are intended to -- or which serve to -- produce a division among the American people on grounds of nationality." It hoped that no party would nominate a

---

[38]
   Freie Presse, 22 May 1916.

[39]
   Volksblatt, 1 June 1916. Also see *Verhandlungen der Deutschamerikanischen Konferenz in Chicago den 28. und 29. Mai 1916*. (n.p., n.p., 1916).

candidate whose views "could accentuate such a division."[40]   It also
hoped that both parties would nominate candidates in accordance with
the views in the platform. The Chicago meeting was significant since
it was one of the few national meetings of representatives of the
German element. From the Cincinnati perspective it was important
since the Resolutions had been written under the direction of Schwaab.

On 3 June a Family Fest was held in Philippi's Garden in Westwood
on behalf of the Aid Society and the same day a benefit fest at the
Zoo attracted 15,000 with Turner performances again directed by
Eckstein and an address by Mayor Puchta.[41]   Although a year earlier
Schwaab had advocated soft-pedaling the war issue because of the
desire not to alienate opponents of prohibition, he now stated at the
Ohio Alliance Convention (18 August 1916) that anyone who would betray
the land of his birth could also betray the U.S.[42]

In September the Aid Society sponsored several concerts of the
Third German Sea Battalion which had rcently occupied Tsangtau, China.
The main speaker was Judge Nippert who described the distress of war
prisoners in Siberia. The organizational committee again reflected
the involvement of the elite: Schwaab, Nippert, William Lueders,
Oskar Braun, Max Burgheim, Dr. Schwagmeyer, Colon Schott, August
Gorbach, Ernst Weier, H.H. Fick, Charles Schmidt, Prof. Louis Saar,
and William Guckenberger. Judge Nippert was especially active on

---

[40]
   Ibid.
[41]
   Volksblatt, 4 June 1916.
[42]
   Freie Presse, 20 August 1916.

behalf of the cause of war relief. On 4 September he spoke at the
Hungarian Aid Society's benefit fest in Price Hill.[43]

The fall brought with it the U.S. Presidential election. The
Ohio Alliance endorsed Hughes, as did most of the state alliances.
Charles Hexamer, national president of the Alliance, for the first
time endorsed a presidential candidate stating that after much thought
he had decided to vote for Hughes and Fairbanks. He stated that "No.
self-respecting American of German birth or extraction can vote for
President Wilson."[44] By the fall the nation's German-American press
overwhelmingly opposed Wilson. The Volksblatt claimed that the
Republicans recognized no such thing as "hyphenated citizens."[45] The
Freie Presse even claimed it preferred the bearded Hughes and
Fairbanks to the "smooth-shaven face, characteristic of typical
Englishmen."[46] Although Wilson campaigned under the slogan "He kept
us out of war," a report in the Freie Presse claimed it had been the
Kaiser who had accomplished this feat.[47] The Volksblatt especially
praised a statement by Hughes that "Unquestioning loyal and patriotic
support of the Government is one thing; approval of the fatuous course
which the Administration has followed is quite another."[48]

[43] Volksblatt, 5 September 1916.

[44] Child, German-Americans, pp. 134-35.

[45] Volksblatt, 9 June 1916.

[46] Freie Presse, 15 June 1916.

[47] Ibid., 10 October 1916.

[48] Volksblatt, 30 June 1916.

Early returns the morning after the election appeared to spell
defeat for the Democrats. The Freie Presse joyfully announced, "Oh
God! How it snowed! Hughes is elected. The answer of the hyphenates
to Wilson's insults!"[49]   These headlines surround a picture of the
American eagle with the victory banner of Hughes. The final returns
brought the disappointing news of Wilson's re-election for four more
years. The defeat of Hughes by Wilson meant troubled times ahead for
the German element.

By February 1917 the local German press saw the handwriting on
the wall as the Volksblatt declared "The war cloud is getting blacker.
A war seems inevitable. We must follow the example of the patriots in
the United States Senate who declare that the war cannot be justified,
but that everyone is obliged to support the Union."[50]   Prophetically a
local German paper stated in early February:

> Our condition will be very unpleasant. We will be watched
> with suspicious eyes and we will be charged with the most
> disgraceful plans. This attitude we can only combat with
> caution, and by avoiding everything which might give the least
> offense. Protest and indignation meets must absolutely cease.
> All outbursts of anger must be avoided. We must follow the motto
> of the suffering Kaiser, 'Learn to suffer without complaint.'
> Whether we will or no, we must do our duty as American citizens.
> We owe it to the oath of allegiance which we took to the union,
> we owe it to our families.   [51]

The Freie Presse felt that the U.S. was "being lured to
destruction by the Anglo-American press and financial magnates who

---

[49]
   Freie Presse, 8 November 1916.
[50]
   Volksblatt, 5 February 1917.
[51]
   Westliche Blätter, 4 February 1917.

were the creditors of England, a vampire nation which sought to escape
well-merited punishment at the hands of the unbeatable Germany by
getting the United States to send its young manhood into the
trenches."[52]   On 2 April 1917 Wilson read his war message to Congress
and by the 6th, war was declared against Germany. The Freie Presse
made a final confession of faith before the declaration of war:

> We shall not become Englishmen, and we shall continue to cherish
> our memories but with steadfast devotion we shall stand by our
> country which will need us now more than ever. We shall watch
> over her internal peace, and we shall make every sacrifice which
> is demanded of us. And when peace returns, we shall be the
> intermediaries between the two peoples whom a sad fate had
> divided, so that they may again join hands in the common tasks of
> peace for the service of mankind.   53

Before the war period is examined the war relief projects of the
Cincinnati German community should be examined. The war had united
the community, a unity that found expression in eight projects and
organizations. In all these programs and projects the various
elements of the community drew together as they had not ever before.

The German and Austro-Hungarian Aid Society was organized 14
August 1914 after the concept had been proposed at the August
Stadtverband meeting. Dr. August Schwagmeyer, a local physician, and
the Rev. Hans Haupt, St. Peter's Church, were elected president and
secretary of the new society.[54]   When the U.S. entered the war it had
raised $77,000 for the widows, orphans and those in need in Germany
and Austro-Hungary. The first annual report (1915) indicates the ways

52
  Freie Presse, 2 April 1917.
53
  Ibid.
54
  Volksblatt, 15 August 1914.

in which the community raised these funds. First, three churches (St. Peter's, St. John's, and St. Paul's) together with some lodges (the German Oddfellows), sponsored a bazaar in October 1914 which raised $3,906.33. Second, Ernst A. Weier, Speaker at the Nord Cincinnati Turnverein, presented a lecture on the Oberammergau Passion Plays, with slides at Emery Auditorium which collected $897.84. Third, the German Theater sponsored benefit performances netting $730.40. Fourth, a folk festival at the Zoo gathered in $1,350.60. Fifth, for three days in November 1915 an Alt Nürnberg fest was held at Music Hall raising $12,388.25. Sixth, many Vereine and private persons contributed to the Aid Society whatever they could. For example, Austro-Hungarian Vereine contributed $2,000; Mrs. Luise Schmid-Frei donated $304.30 from the Widows Home; the United Singers collected $477.65 at a concert; Mrs. Charlotte Neeb collected $220 at various meetings. Also, various Protestant churches gave $750 to the Aid Society.[55] Organizationally the Aid Society had nine sub-committees which had been set up to raise funds from various occupations and areas of the community: Businessmen; Doctors; Lawyers; Meat and Tannery Industries; Manufacturers; Manufacturers and Dealers Associations; Chamber of Commerce and Businessmen's Club; Brewers, Distillers and Liquor Trade.

Funds were raised by the holding of more benefit activities: a Hindenburg Fest (25 May 1916) gathered $400. A benefit at the Zoo

---

[55] Gorbach, Hilfswerk, pp. 56-148.

(3 June 1916) brought in $7,000; concerts by the band of the Third German Sea Battalion (6 September 1916) raised $1,427. In November 1916 the Aid Society was reorganized after the death of its president, Dr. Schwagmeyer. Colon Schott was elected to take his place with Haupt remaining as secretary. The board included Schwaab, Nippert, Heinrich Albertz, Dr. Ernst Kunwald, the Rev. A. Nemenz, Ernst Weier, William H. Lueders, and others from the community.[56]

The society for East Prussian Aid raised close to $70,000 in Cincinnnati. This was an international organization whose central U.S. office was located in New York. Funds raised in America were deposited in the German-American Bank of New York City for the purpose of rebuilding the villages in East Prussia that had been destroyed by the war between Germany and Russia. On 2 March 1916 a branch was formed in Cincinnati with Prof. John L. Shearer, President of Ohio Mechanics Institute, as president and Nippert as vice president. this organization, although more limited in scope than the Aid Society, succeeded in raising almost as much money. This was because it received greater support from the elite, whereas the Aid Society had been supported mainly by the Vereins and the Kirchendeutschen. Contributors to the Prussian Aid Society included: Charles Wiedemann ($5,000); William Cooper Procter ($5,000); Frederick H. Alms ($3,000); Louis J. Hauck ($2,500); Christian Moerlein's family ($2,500); William F. Doepke ($1,500); Adelheid Doepke ($1,500); Wilhelm H. Alms ($1,150); the Volksblatt ($1,200); the Freie Presse ($1,200); Mrs.

---

[56] Freie Presse, 18 November 1916.

Margaret Haffner and daughters ($1,200); Henrietta Billing ($1,200); Emilie L. Heine ($1,200); Mr. and Mrs. Ernst H. Hünefeld ($1,200); J.G. Schmidlapp ($1,200); Dr. and Mrs. Max Köhler ($1,200); the Lackman family ($1,200); James N. Gamble ($1,200); Katie Brill Nippert ($1,200); the Wurlitzer family ($1,200); Albert Nast ($1,100); the Mühlhäuser family ($1,100); the Windisch family ($1,100); the German and Austro-Hungarian Aid Society ($1,200); the German musicians of Cincinnati, through Dr. Kunwald, Director of the Cincinnati Symphony Orchestra ($1,300); Lawyers ($1,200); Teachers ($1,200); Physicians and Surgeons ($1,200).[57]

Germans from Hungary formed the Hungarian Aid Society on 10 August 1914 which raised a total of $4,382.88. The German Ladies Club established the "Quarter-Donation" fund drive which raised a total of $25,000. The group was led by Mrs. Max Burgheim, Mrs. Nippert, Mrs. Louis Victor Saar and others. On 25 January 1916 the American Jewish Relief Committee was formed at a mass meeting in Emery Auditorium to focus on the plight of the Jews in Poland, Galicia and Russia. J.W. Freiberg was elected president. The board included Ralph Mack, Joseph Lazarus, Dr. Julian Morgenstern and William Ornstein. At least $100,000 was raised.[58]

The amounts raised by these various groups was substantial; German and Austro-Hungarian Aid Society, $77,000; Society for East

---

[57]
    Freie Presse, 13 and 14 March 1916; *Volksblatt*, 3 March, 19 July and 31 October, 1916.
  [58]
    Gorbach, *Hilfswerk*, pp. 174, 178, 183.

Prussian Aid, $70,000; Hungarian Aid Society, $4,382.88; Quarter-

Donations, $25,000; American Jewish Relief Committee, $100,000. The

total amount of funds channeled through the individual religious

bodies and synods cannot be identified, but Gorbach estimated that

$50,000 was sent by private individuals to relatives in Europe so that

the total amount of funds raised for relief purposes in Cincinnati

(1914-17) totaled $426,382.88, or approximately $43.25 per person in

the German community.[59]

An indication of the unifying influence of the war on the

community was the formation of Der Deutsche Klub in 1915 by the

Turnverein. Prior to this date there had not been a central meeting

place for local Vereine. Indeed, several had their own clubhouses

while others met in restaurants and beer gardens, such as Grank Renn's

Mercer Halle (Vine and Mercer St.), Christ. Sachs' Deutsche

Gastwirtschaft (121 Elder St.), B. Flamm's Deutsches Gasthaus (Elder &

McMicken Ave.), and Henry Haefner's Deutsches Gasthaus (Liberty and

Elm St.). The purpose of the Klub was to provide a central meeting

place for local Vereine within the quarters of the Turnhalle on Walnut

St. The idea of such a central meeting place was first conceived in

1913 when Mayor Hunt closed numerous "dives." Such guest-houses, beer

halls and gardens had served as the meeting places of the Vereine. By

gathering in the Turnhalle the Vereine hoped to escape any future

invocation of Sunday "Blue" laws on local "dives." The unity caused

by the war no doubt led to the formation of the Klub, something which

---

[59] Ibid., pp. 146-47.

had not existed heretofore. Moreover, the Turnverein was considered a bulwark of personal liberty because of its historical opposition to limitations on individual freedoms. Each Verein paid a specific rent amount which entitled it to the use of space within the Turnhalle. By 1915 forty-four Vereine, including the Stadtverband and the Pionier-Verein, had made the Turnhalle their central meeting place.[60]

Another indication of the unifying influence of the war on the community was the establishment of the Germanistic Society of Cincinnati on 19 September 1916. Of special note about this organization was that it was one that attracted to its membership and to its leadership members of the elite who had previously stood aloof from involvement in German-American Vereine. Its specific purpose was the cultivation of German culture in America. It aimed to further the study of German literature, art, and scholarship in Cincinnati by holding monthly meetings with lectures, discussions, and social gatherings. Judge Nippert was chosen as its first president and Mrs. Gotthard Deutsch as secretary.[61]

The War, 1917-18

The declaration of war signaled the beginning of a hysterical, nativist crusade to eliminate all possible aspects and traces of the German heritage. "To a certain extent, the Germans' situation in

---

[60]
August B. Gorbach, Deutscher Vereins-Wegweiser von Cincinnati, Ohio. (Cincinnati: Deutscher Stadtverband von Cincinnati, 1915), pp. 45-46.
[61]
Volksblatt, 23 September 1916.

Cincinnati was similar to that of the Jews in Germany during the early
stages of Nazi persecution. It was not so much the acts of physical
violence . . . but the dread thereof and the knowledge that the public
at large would idly stand by, either approving or indifferent, in the
presence of misdeeds . . ."[62]

Nativism includes "every type and level of antipathy toward
aliens, their institutions, and their ideas," according to John
Higham. Nativists held that alien influences "originating abroad
threatened the very life of the nation from within." Nativism is
defined as "an intense opposition to an internal minority on the
ground of its foreign (i.e., un-American) connections." These
antipathies translate into a zeal to destroy those considered to be
enemies of the American way of life. Historically, nativism has risen
and fallen in relation to the intensity of nationalism.[63]

The "happy world" of the German-American community came to an
abrupt end in 1917 wwith the U.S. entry into World War I. The war
"cut deeply" into the heart of German-America, but as the editor of
the yearbook of the Deutscher Pionier-Verein commented, "The time of
argumentation was over, the majority of the people had spoken through
their representatives; the dice had fallen. They did not lay in our
hands to roll. The hour in which our feeling of duty and loyalty
would stand its most difficult test had struck."[64]

[62] Dobbert, Disintegration, p. 396.

[63] John Higham, Strangers in the Land. Patterns of American
Nativism, 1860-1925. New York: Atheneum, 1975, p. 4.

[64] Vorstandsbericht des Deutschen Pionier-Vereins (1917-18): 40.

Church leaders urged calm. At a mass meeting the Rev. Hugo Eisenlohr promised there would be united support for the war, but requested "a square deal" for German-Americans so that internal friction could be avoided. In a letter to local Catholics, Archbishop Moeller requested his flock to put their views aside and "assist in carrying out the design of our government" and that failure to do so would be "to rashly resist the ordinance of God Himself." Stadtverband president, Judge John Schwaab, immediately pledged his loyalty to the president. In spite of the numerous testimonies and protestations of loyalty, nativist sentiments and emotions gained the upper hand.[65]

The Christliche Apologete declared:

> The die is cast! ... War between Germany and America has become fact ... America was the light to all humanity ... How this beautiful dream has been shattered! Militarism shall be defeated by Militarism, War by War, Force by Force ...
>
> Henceforth all discussion of the war and its justification must stop. Every American owes his government loyalty and obedience.
>
> Americans of German extraction need no exhortation to be true to their adopted Fatherland, the Land of their choice, whose banner they honor and love and whose free institutions they highly treasure. They are loyal ...
>
> All disciples of the Prince of Peace, of whatever nationality, may properly deplore war, but at the same time they can and must be true subjects of the country to which they belong and whose protection they enjoy.
>
> Finally, a word to the citizens of the Reich: do nothing to raise suspicion and your rights here are fully guaranteed.[66]

---

[65] Freie Presse, 22 April 1917.

[66] Der Christliche Apologete, 17 April 1917.

The _Apologete_'s editorial, "Why All This Intolerance?" stated in part:

> The efforts which are now being made in our country to
> eliminate root and branch whatever has even the most distant
> connection with Germany is a hysteria, the likes of which we had
> thought impossible for the American people ... Americans have
> excelled in tolerance and open heartedness till now ...
> [67]

By the fall of 1917 public reason in Cincinnati was succumbing to

an anti-German hysteria. Rumors circulated that German-American

packing houses "were mixing ground glass in hamburger and other meat

products." [68] The first target super-patriots aimed at was the German

language bilingual instruction in the public schools.

It had not been enough that on September 19, 1917 the German

Textbook Censoring Committee removed from the public schools of

Cincinnati all books that were judged to be pro-German. The first

group to advocate the abolition of German in the public schools was

the Cincinnati American Women's Association, a spin-off organization

from a larger organization, the Cincinnati Women's Association. [69]

Public agitation against German instruction in the public schools

resulted in the drop of 13,856 students in 1916 to 7,546 by September,

1917. [70] As early as May 1917 the various opponents of Geman language

instruction organized to coordinate their efforts under the leadership

of Alexander Thomson, a paper manufacturer in Hamilton but resident of

---

[67]
    Ibid., 22 April 1917.

[68]
    Writers Program of Ohio, _Cincinnati: A Guide to the Queen
City._ Cincinnati: Wiesen-Hart, 1943, p. 94.

[69]
    Cincinnati Enquirer, 19 June 1917.

[70]
    Edwin Zeydel, "The Teaching of German," p. 37.

Cincinnati.[71] The anti-German language issue climaxed on Feb. 12,
1918 when the Committee of the Whole, and the Board of Education,
jointly announced that in response to public demand, and a vote by
council, German would be eliminated from the curriculum of the public
schools in the fall of 1918 when the schools opened. The Cincinnati
Enquirer reported that the "Board of Education approved cutting out
Teuton language lessons."[72] Another article declared, "Dropped! Hun
Language Barred."[73] In July "pink slip day" occurred as "Hun tongue"
teachers were stricken from the payroll of the public schools.[74] The
former supervisor of the German bilingual program in the public
schools, H.H. Fick, commented that the German language was crucified,
but "most of all they would have wanted to nail all of German-America
with it on the cross."[75]

In September 1918 the Academy of Medicine formed a committee to
confront the "Hun tongue" issue. the special committee, the Academy
of Medicine Against the Huns, voted unanimously in November 1918 to
banish all German literature from the academy archives and to
discourage all medical students from studying in Germany, or German
medicinal and surgical applications and techniques.[76]

---

[71]
Cincinnati Enquirer, 20 May 1917.

[72]
Cincinnati Enquirer, 12 February 1918.

[73]
Cincinnati Enquirer, 25 April 1918.

[74]
Cincinnati Enquirer, 9 July 1918.

[75]
Monatshefte, 19, 1918, 267.

[76]
Enquirer, 19 November 1918.

Other educational institutions were affected by the war-spirit.
A movement to expel Dr. Gotthard Deutsch of Hebrew Union College
because of his anti-war and pro-German views resulted in censure of
the learned professor. Nevertheless, members of the Board of
Governors of the college bore "the brunt of nativist taunts that the
college had not displayed the proper patriotic spirit in its handling
of the Deutsch case."[77]

The war hysteria spread to the campus of the University of
Cincinnati, where Prof. Martin Ludwich, who taught German in the
College of Engineering, was dismissed because he failed to become an
American citizen. Prof. Guy Allen Tawney of the Philosophy Department
was accused of being pro-German, becuase he had said in one of his
lectures that Germany had "outwitted all her commercial rivals, even
Great Britain." "Professor Tawney's patriotism is so well-known that
no investigation is necessary," said President Dabney.[78]

Physical evidence of the German-American presence in Cincinnati
was also targeted by super-patriots. Many cafes had their walls
redecorated to hide examples of the "Kaiser's art."[79] The statue of
Germania, located atop the Germania Building on Walnut Street, was
transformed, or "Americanized," into Columbia since Germania was

---

[77]
Dobbert, "The Ordeal," p. 153. Also, see Samuel K. Korff, ed.,
Hebrew Union College - Jewish Educational Institute of Religion at One
Hundred Years. (Cincinnati: Hebrew Union College, 1976).
[78]
Reginald McGrane, The University of Cincinnati. New York:
Harper & Row., 1965, p. 239.
[79]
Volksblatt, 28 March 1918.

deemed "un-American." [80]   The Father Jahn Monument in Inwood Park

became the object of vandalism and suspicion. Protests against the

monument with its German inscriptions were directed to the Parks

Commision claiming that to retain the monument was to "laud German

kultur and that it should be removed at once." The Commission decided

that "inasmuch as Jahn, who had been dead 70 years, and actually

suffered the same oppression against which America is fighting to free

the world, it would be improper, and inconsistent to remove" the

monument. [81]

The violence was more psychological than physical, but a few

cases of active violence did occur. An American pastor, the Rev.

Herbert S. Bigelow, who once served as president of the Constitutional

Convention of the state, but was now viewed as a pacifist and opponent

of conscription, was carried by auto to Kentucky, tied to a tree,

stripped, and whipped "in the name of the women and children of

Belgium." [82]   Tar and featherings occurred and in 1918 at least two

attempted lynchings of German-Americans in Cincinnati were reported.

Street fights broke out when people persisted in using German on the

street. [83]

---

[80]
Cincinnati Commercial Times, 3 May 1918.
[81]
Times-Star, 11 October 1918.
[82]
Freie Presse, 30 October 1917. Also see Daniel R. Beaver,
A Buckeye Crusader: A Sketch of the Political Career of Herbert Seeley
Bigelow (Cincinnati: n.p., 1957).
[83]
Volksblatt, 15 August 1918.

The German language press was objected to by super-patriots; on 11 October 1917 the offices of the Volksblatt were raided by local and federal officials, although no evidence of treason was found. A lawyer agitated in the city council that all German newspapeers be published bilingually. This did not pass, but federal law required all news relating to the war to be printed in English translation. On the Kentucky side of the river, the Volksblatt could be delivered only by mail since posters there warned against purchasing it at newsstands.[84]

German language books, journals and newspapers were removed from the shelves of the public library since they were condemned as being pro-German. At the 11 May 1918 meeting of the Public Library Board it was decided to remove the entire German collection into the sub-basement of the library:

> Resolved, that from this day until further notice the circulation and use within the library of all German books, periodicals and newspapers be entirely stopped with the exception that books and periodicals ... to be issued to students in the higher institutions of learning in Cincinnati when their applications for the same are endorsed by the proper authority.[85]

The Enquirer announced, "Kultur of the Kaiser's Kind not Promoted Through Library." James A. Green, board trustee, stated that the removal of 10,000 German books would prevent the use of the library "to further a reptillian and insidious propaganda." He noted that although the books had been fine a year ago, "since that time our

---

[84] Ibid., 29 July 1918.

[85] Public Library of Cincinnati and Hamilton County, Minutes of the Board of Trustees, 8 May 1918.

vision has been cleared and we are able to judge the real effect of the works." The library, according to Green, had been used by enemies of the U.S. and German literature published within the last 10 years "was tainted with the ideas and ideals which American boys are now giving their lives to combat." He stated, "we must do our part toward making it impossible for our country to be divided into hostile camps of Irish, German, Jewish, Roumainian or any other kind of hyphenated Americans. English is the language which must become universal in the United States and the library should be one of the instruments through which this is to be accomplished."[86] Under this authority Librarian N.D.C. Hodges ordered the removal of all German books from the main library and its branches. On 22 May the use of any scientific or technical material was prohibited if it contained the slightest degree of pro-German propaganda. However, in August the board resolved to allow state university students to use such material on the consideration that they present the written permission of their professor and university president.[87]

German family names were changed; e.g., Holtzinger to Holt, Schultz to Stratford, Sternberger to Stevenson.[88] Businesses changed names too; German Mutual Insurance Co. became the Hamilton County Insurance Co.; the German National Bank became the Lincoln National

----
86
   Enquirer, 9 May 1918.
87
   Public Library of Cincinnati and Hamilton County, Minutes of the Board of Trustees, 22 May, 7 August, 1918.
88
   Alvin F. Harlow, The Serene Cincinnatians. New York: Dutton, 1950, p. 203.

Bank; the West German National Bank became the West Bank & Trust Co.

Societies and institutions changed names; the North German

Schuetzengesellschaft became the Cincinnati Shooting Club and the

Altenheim became the Cincinnati Old Men's Home.[89]   The Nord Cincinnti

Turn-Verein announced it had decided to Americanize its name to North

Cincinnati Gymnasium, and the Vereinspraesident, Gustav Clements, said

"There is a peculiar atmosphere which pervades a Turnverein which is

not found in America ... In view of the fact that the organization is

composed entirely of Americans and strives for the physical betterment

of Americans, it should become 100 percent American."[90]   And on 9

April 1918 the Cincinnati City Council passed the following ordinance:

> Whereas, the United States of America is at war with Germany
> and Austria, and as a number of streets, avenues and places in
> the City of Cincinnati have names which commemorate political and
> military places and persons of those countries, amounting to
> propaganda in behalf of said foreign governments, and their
> ideals and institutions, intolerable to a free America; ... this
> council is of the opinion that there is good cause for the change
> of names ...   [91]

The following streets were among those changed: King Albert

became Dorchester St.; Bismarck to Montreal St.; Berlin to Woodrow

St.; Bremen to Republic St.; Brunswick to Edgecliff Point; Frankfort

to Connecticut Avenue; Hamburg to Stonewall St.; Hanover to Yukon

St.; Hapsburg to Merrimac St.; Schumann to Meredith St.; Vienna to

---

[89]
   Volksblatt, 10 January, 15 February, 4-5 April, 22 and 23 June,
1918.
[90]
   Enquirer, 5 April 1918.
[91]
   Council of Cincinnati, Eighteenth Supplement to Codification of
Ordinances with Other Information from January 1, 1918 to December
1918. Cincinnati, 1918.

Panema St.; Donnersberger to Melvin St.; Humboldt to Taft Rd.; Palais
Royal to South Crescent Ave. Significantly, German St. became English
St.

Dr. Ernst Kunwald, conductor of the Cincinnati Symphony
Orchestra, was interned (Ft. Oglethorpe) as an enemy alien, for
stating his heart was on the other side.[92] Professor Emil Heermann,
concertmaster of the orchestra, was also arrested, but released to the
custody of the faculty of the Conservatory of Music; he regained his
prestige by investing 75% of his income in Liberty Bonds. Three
members of the German Theater were arrested, causing the Theater to
close its doors.[93]

Prominent preachers in Cincinnati spoke against the Germans from
the pulpit. One declared in a sermon that "There are not enough
telegraph posts in Cincinnati to hang all the German Huns that should
be hanged." Another declared, "I would rather kiss a pig than shake
hands with a Hun." On one occasion the Secret Service called on the
superintendent's office of Bethesda Institutions (German Methodist) in
Cincinnati. They explained that it had been reported that a picture
of Bismarck was hanging in the superintendent's office. On the wall
were pictures of John Wesley, Wilhelm Nast, and Bishop Walden. John
Diekmann stated that he was not familiar with the "old German heros"
but that if Bismarck was one of them he would be pleased to take it

[92] Volksblatt, 2 December 1917.
[93] Volksblatt, 29 April 1918; Freie Presse, 29 April 1918.

down.   'Pointing to the bishop's portrait, one of the agents exclaimed
'That's the fellow!' and took it down."[94]

German-American societies canceled their meetings until the war's
end or else complied with the orders of the police chief that only
public meetings using the English language could be held. Such
meetings were usually held under police surveillance so that no German
language speeches or songs could be delivered. The editor of the
yearbook of the Deutscher Pionier-Verein noted that the 50th
anniversary of the Verein (15 June 1918) was conducted entirely in
English, but that after the fest all could go home "where they at
least between the four walls [of their homes] could still speak and
sing German." Pastor Andreas Nemenz, whose German language speech
was canceled for the anniversary of the Pionier-Verein in 1918, saw it
instead printed in the yearbook. It stated, "German-Americans would
have to endure 'accusations, persecutions, and slander' in silence."
In the meantime, the central organization of all local German-American
societies had been dissolved when, on 2 July 1918, the U.S. Senate
and the House with almost no discussion passed the bill to repeal the
charter of the National German-American Alliance. the Alliance and
all its local branches had, however, seen the handwriting on the wall,
and had voluntarily dissolved three months earlier. The Ohio
Alliance, headquartered in Cincinnati, gave the balance of its
treasury and a $300 Liberty Bond to the Red Cross.[95]

---

[94] Douglass, _Story_, p. 190.

[95] _Vorstandsbericht_ _des_ _Deutschen_ _Pionier-Vereins_ (1917-18), 29.

In spite of these nativist attacks, Cincinnati's German-Americans served well in the U.S. Army. The list of the war dead shows a high proportion of German surnames. To demonstrate German-American patriotism during the war, Charles W. Rattermann, son of the historian Heinrich Rattermann, edited a monthly, The Loyal American (1917).[96]

Cincinnati rejoiced at news of the Armistice. The Cincinnati Post called 11 November 1918 "The greatest day since the beginning of the world."[97] Citizens took to the streets with "sirens, whistles, rattles, tin cans, pots and pans, wash boilers, garbage containers, and metal waste baskets" and every kind of noise-making device. church bells rang all day long and all businesses closed. And "tons of confetti, tickertape, rice, corn, and wheat fell from the windows." On Fountain Square a coffin containing an effigy of the Kaiser (splattered with decayed fruit and vegetables) was soaked in oil and transformed into a flaming funeral pyre. The former German Emperor hung in effigy on dozens of lampposts throughout the city. On Sixth Street, a man brandishing a live rat shouted, "We've caught the Kaiser!" Arrayed in spiked helmet, flaring moustaches, and imperial uniform, a living embodiment of Kaiser Wilhelm was paraded down Vine Street in a cage mounted on a horse-drawn float. And "as the pandemonium continued into the night beneath the red sky with rockets and the glare of torches, an epoch in the history of Cincinnati

---

[96] See The Loyal American, 1917.

[97] Cincinnati Post, 12 November 1918.

came to a close."[98]

---

[98]
Writers Program of Ohio, *Cincinnati*, p. 95.

Part Three

Recovery and Reconstruction

Facsimile copy of: Don Heinrich Tolzmann,
**The Cincinnati Germans after the Great
War.** (New York: Peter Lang, 1987).

CONTENTS

PREFACE

This book focuses on the German-American community of Cincinnati in the years immediately following the Great War. It examines how German-American community institutions survived the hard times during and after the war. It also identifies and discusses what losses were incurred by the war, and what the impact of this was on the redefinition of German-American ethnicity.

I would like to acknowledge the assistance and advice I have received in the past from the following who are at the University of Cincinnati: Professors Roger Daniels, Zane L. Miller, Saul Benison, and Jerry Glenn. I would also like to gratefully acknowledge a grant from Inter Nationes in support of this work, and especially Dr. Goetz von Boehmer, Consul General of the Federal Republic of Germany, Detroit, who facilitated receiving this grant.

Don Heinrich Tolzmann
Cincinnati, Ohio
May, 1986

German Immigration to Cincinnati Before the Great War

According to the 1980 U.S. Census, the state of Ohio ranks third in the nation for the highest percentage of population with German ancestry; 40% of Ohioans claimed German descent. Few places surpass this statistic, but one which does is Cincinnati. It, along with Milwaukee and St. Louis, formed a corner in what became known in the nineteenth century as the German Triangle because of the high concentration of the German element in this area.

In the 1890 U.S. Census the German stock, the foreign-born and their children, numbered 57.4% of the population in Cincinnati. Ninety years later, in 1980, the German element, all those of German descent, in Greater Cincinnati is approximately 45%, the drop being due to the movement of new population to the area, as well as to out-migration, especially after World War II. The size of the German element in the 1920s was most likely some point between today's 45% and 1890's 57.4%. The best estimate would be somewhere midway between these two statistics, or 50%.(1)

Since the recording of immigration statistics in 1820, the Germans have constituted the largest single group of European immigrants. The peak year of German immigration was 1882 while the peak year for the Austrian Empire was 1907. The German immigration to Cincinnati was part of the great European immigration to American shores.(2)

Before the Great War German immigration to Cincinnati can be divided into three periods: Before 1830, from 1831 to 1871, and after 1871. In the first period German immigration was light, but it increased substantially in the second period. "The inrush of Germans in the middle half of the nineteenth century made Cincinnati into a German city. For many years Cincinnati did not even try to assimilate its German immigrants; instead they assimilated Cincinnati."(3) The high point of German immigration to Cincinnati in the nineteenth century was reached in the 1880s. The German element rose from a mere 5% of the population in 1820 to 57.4% by 1890.

The first Germans in southwest Ohio came in 1788 when Major Benjamin Steitz (Stites), a veteran of the American Revolution, led a group from New Jersey that included German Dunkards. They established Columbia in November 1788, the first settlement in the area. The Ohio and the beautiful surrounding river valley reminded Germans of the Rhineland with its vineyards. Germans also came to the area via service in the U.S. Army as soldiers stationed at Fort Washington which was established in 1789. Also, several German scouts were to be found in the area, such as Ludwig Wetzel. The most prominent local soldier was Major David Ziegler. Born in Heidelberg, he had served in the Prussian army before immigrating at the age of twenty-six to serve in the American Revolution. In 1802 Ziegler was elected the first president of the city council, a position now known as mayor.(4)

The majority of the first immigrants to Cincinnati came from the southwestern area of the German-speaking sections of Europe. The two largest groups appear to have been the Swiss and the Württembergers, after which immigrants from Baden, Alsace, and northern Germany, especially from Oldenburg, are the predominant groups. In addition to the European German immigration a sizable, but inestimable number of German-Americans from Pennsylvania, Maryland, Virginia, and New Jersey came to Cincinnati. This is demonstrated by the fact that Cincinnati's first German language publication, Teutscher Calender auf 1808, was printed in the Pennsylvania German dialect. The pre-1830 immigrants consisted mainly of workers, tradesmen,

and farmers, with a small number of educators, such as teachers
and clergymen.

Most prominent of the pre-1830 German element, next only
to Ziegler, was Martin Baum, a Maryland German who came to the
area in 1795. He is considered the founder of the Germandom of
the city of Cincinnati. Baum became one of the city's weal-
thiest citizens as a merchant, banker, and real estate agent.
He owned a foundry, the first sugar refinery, and held invest-
ments in steamboats. Through his agents stationed at New
Orleans, Baltimore, and Philadelphia, Baum attracted German
immigrants to Cincinnati to work in his various building enterprises, thus acquiring for the city the reputation as a destination for German immigrants. Today Baum's home is the Taft
Museum of Art, but in the early 1800s it was a center for
cultural activities amongst Cincinnati Germans. From 1807-12
Baum was mayor of Cincinnati. He helped organize a library,
several schools, the Western Museum, and a society for the
improvement of agriculture.

By 1800 the German element numbered slightly more than 6%,
or 53 persons out of a total population of 700. By 1820 the
German-born population alone had reached 400, or 4.6% of a
total population of 9,600. This German-born population then
tripled to 1,120, or 5% of a total population of 24,381 by
1830. Because of the upheavals in Europe caused by the French
Revolution and the Napoleonic wars, German immigration was,
however, nothing more than a trickle until 1815. Thereafter
the immigration picked up noticeably, especially after 1817,
the year which brought drought, famine and starvation in Germany. The trickle soon became a wide regular stream.

By 1830 Cincinnati had a well established reputation as a
destination point for German immigrants, a reputation that had
been established not only by Martin Baum, but also by a number
of German language publications which painted a favorable, and

sometimes glowing, picture of Cincinnati. In 1827 one of the most popular German authors of the century, Karl Postl, who wrote under the name Charles Sealsfield, published a work on the U.S. which contained a chapter devoted completely to Cincinnati and the state of Ohio. He wrote of the Queen City:

> There is no doubt that the commanding situation of this beautiful town, its majestic river; its mild climate, which may be compared to the south of France, and the liberal spirit of its inhabitants, contribute to render this place, both in physical and moral points of view, one of the most eligible residences in the Union. (5)

In 1829 Gottfried Duden published the most detailed and glowing account of Cincinnati which was considered the most widely read and influential single book for the history of the German immigration to the U.S. In this work Duden proclaimed:

> Cincinnati is called the most beautiful city of the entire West, and truly the European who involuntarily associates all kinds of ideas about savage life with the words American interior, would scarcely trust his eyes if he could suddenly be transported from his home to this city. (6)

The Rhine attained romantic adulation of German poets, but Duden seems to praise the Ohio River above and beyond the Rhine. ·He wrote that the "constant closeness of beautiful hills lends a certain charm to a trip on the Ohio such as perhaps can be found on no other river on earth." The surrounding region he described as "romantic and very fertile." Writing a little more than a decade after Duden was the well known travel author Friedrich Gerstäcker who wrote:

> Cincinnati, the Queen of the West, the El Dorado of the German emigrant! Ask a German, who is traveling into the interior from one of the seaports, Where are you going? and the answer will invariably be - to Cincinnati. (7)

All of the various German language publications which contained descriptions of Cincinnati contributed to its growing reputation on both sides of the Atlantic.

The second immigration to Cincinnati from 1831 to 1870 contained a number of refugees: the Thirtyers, the immigrants who came after the 1832 protest demonstration known as the Hambacher Fest, and the Forty-Eighters, refugees of the failed 1848 German revolution. Although small in number, they exerted a strong influence on the social, cultural, economic, and political life of the German element. However, not all of the immigrants were political refugees: many were laborers, tradesmen, merchants, and manufacturers.

In the second immigration most immigrants came for economic, rather than political reasons, and they were not as vocal as their political compatriots. Immigration continued from the areas that had contributed to the first immigration, but increased substantially from northern Germany, especially from Hanover and Oldenburg. Because of the Thirtyers and the Forty-Eighters Cincinnati became a well publicized destination point for immigration, as well as a major German-American center in the years before the Civil War.

By 1840 the German-born population numbered 3,440 out of a total of 46,282, but by 1850 this had literally soared to 30,758 out of a total population of 115,436. The population of Cincinnati in the 1840s had tripled, but the German-born population had increased almost tenfold. At the eve of the Civil War, in 1860, the population of German stock in Cincinnati amounted to 30% out of a total of 161,044. In 1870 the German-born numbered 49,446 out of a total of 216,239, while the German stock had now inched up to 34%, or 75,000.

During the third period of German immigration to Cincinnati in the nineteenth century, which began in 1871, immigrants

6

Die Fontaine, von der 5. und Walnut Strasse aus gesehen.

Fountain Square in Cincinnati as depicted by Max Burgheim,
Cincinnati in Wort und Bild (1891), a volume located in the
German-Americana Collection, Blegen Library, University of
Cincinnati.

came mostly from the working classes, but with far better education than those of earlier periods. A few came for political reasons: the Catholics dissatisfied with Bismarck's Kulturkämpf and the socialists alienated by Bismarck's Sozialistengesetze, but for most the motivation to immigrate was economic. The 1870 U.S. Census indicates the origins of the German-born in Cincinnati as follows: Prussia, 30.3%; Bavaria, 19.7%; Hannover, 17.5%; Baden, 10.4%; Württemberg, 6.3%; Oldenburg, 4.7%; Hessen, 4.7%; Saxony, 1.9%; Austria, 1.1%; and other and unidentified states, 3%.

A high point of German immigration was reached in the 1880s so that by 1890 the German stock reached its zenith with 57.4% of a total population of 296,908. At the turn of the century Cincinnati's population of 325,902 had a German stock of 109,875 (the foreign-born and their children). In 1910 the total population of Cincinnati was 363,591 and the German element numbered approximately 181,795, but only 125,446 claimed German as their mother tongue, according to the U.S. Census. Many of these could have been third, fourth, and fifth generation German-Americans. What this meant was that roughly one-half of the population was of German descent, and that every third person had German as his or her mother tongue.

Over-the-Rhine

A section of Cincinnati known as Over-the-Rhine, an area of 213.3 acres, became in the nineteenth century the central geographical locale of the German community. Its borders were defined by the Miami Canal, completed in 1831 (now Central Parkway), on the west and south, and on the north and east by McMicken Ave. and Main St. The old barge canal, known as the Miami-Erie Canal, had been locally dubbed as the "Rhine" since when one crossed over it one entered the German district in the nineteenth century. In mid-century, according to Rattermann, it divided "the German quarter from the English."(9) In actuality, the district never was completely German, nor were all the Germans settled there. It consisted of the first and fifth wards, but by 1840 Germans were not only in these wards, but also the seventh, as well as elsewhere in the city. In the Over-the-Rhine wards Germans constituted in 1840 only 46.3% of the population. Nevertheless, they were the predominant element in the district. Settlement paterns indicate, however, that Germans preferred the western, northern, and eastern edges of the city. As the German population grew it expanded beyond the confines of the Over-the-Rhine district. In 1870 the German population was moving northwards along Vine St. up to McMillan. By 1890 the German element was beginning to concentrate in the area one mile north from McMillan to Howell "while along McMillan it had moved an additional half-mile east of its intersection with Burnet."(10) After 1900 Over-the-Rhine began to lose its character as the center of the German element, but as it dropped in number there, other areas of the city gained in German population. On the other side of the Mill Creek Valley, in Fairmount, Germans began to concentrate, for example. The German element in Covington, Kentucky, on the other side of the Ohio River, also expanded.

It is clear that because of the impact of the German immigrations, that the old Over-the-Rhine district could not contain the rapidly expanding German population. In 1890 already only a few of the city's wards showed a greater deviation than plus or minus ten percent from the city's average of 57.4% of German stock per ward. Wards 7 and 13 contained 80.1% and 71.3% respectively, the highest concentrations. Wards with lower percentages were 1, 18, and 20 with 37.9%, 36.8% and 37.5% respectively. By 1910 German-Americans had, therefore, settled widely throughout all of Cincinnati's wards.

As the population expanded and settled throughout the city, the Over-the-Rhine district lost some of its old German character as well as its economic and political significance, but it gained new importance as a social-cultural center with the numerous German houses, restaurants, churches, bakeries, open air markets, beer gardens, and other shops and stores. A late nineteenth century German-American history called Over-the-Rhine the district in which "everything is German and even the American discards his formality and envelops himself in German Gemütlichkeit."(11) It still was the home of German music, theaters, newspapers, libraries, clubs, societies, and religious institutions. It was filled with "the little savings and loan societies (Bauvereine) where thrifty Germans could deposit their savings or borrow money from this early form of credit union."(12) In 1859 Turners had built the Turnhalle, a central point of nineteenth century social and cultural life, considered "a mighty fortress of German-American culture." (13) Among the popular beer gardens, theaters,and opera houses of the district were the Arbeiter-Halle, the Männerchor-Halle, Heuck's, Schickling's, and Wielert's Pavillion. According to a local history, "everywhere it is gemütlich in Over-the-Rhine." Life in the district has been quaintly portrayed by Carl Wittke:

> Cincinnati's German community, in its early years, was concentrated largely in an area north of where the canal entered the city, and was known as "Over-the-Rhine." Here the Germans lived in neat little frame and brick houses built flush with the sidewalk, and with backyards fenced in with lattice work and planted with flower and vegetable gardens. Every Saturday, German housewives scrubbed the front steps of their homes until they were snow white. Here too the German Hausfrau nourished her family with German food and delicacies which quickly became part of the American culinary art. After working hours and on Sunday, the men sought recreation in the taverns, played euchre, skat and pinochle, or brought their families to the beer gardens to listen to old famil-iar German airs.(14)

Die West Cincinnati Turnhalle.

One of the several Turnhallen in Cincinnati. From Max Burg-heim, _Cincinnati in Wort und Bild_ (1891), a volume located in the German-Americana Collection, Blegen Library, University of Cincinnati.

Aside from being the original site of the German community and later a socio-cultural center, Over-the-Rhine reflected the impact of the German immigrations since "their buildings - where they worshipped, worked, played, lived and died - still punctuate the face of the city." Indeed, the "most enduring architectural reflection of the German spirit" in Cincinnati may be found in the Over-the-Rhine district. (15)

The architectural impact of the German immigration extended beyond Over-the-Rhine to other sections of the city, and also found expression in the landscaping and park system, as exemplified by the work of Adolf Strauch in Clifton and Spring Grove Cemetery. In various parks monuments, or statues could be found which related to the German heritage, e.g., the Turnvater Jahn monument in Inwood Park. Two architectural and engineering landmarks were associated with the German heritage: The Suspension Bridge built by Johann A. Roebling, and the Tyler Davidson Memorial Foundation, which was completed in Munich under the direction of Ferdinand von Miller to depict the Cenius des Wassers. In short, the imprint of the German immigrations to Cincinnati was to be clearly seen in the material culture and architectural styles that originated in the Over-the-Rhine district and spread to other areas of the city. Taken together with its location on the banks of the Ohio River, Cincinnati acquired a distinctively German-American Stadtbild. (16)

The German-American Community

German-American community life at the turn of the century reflected to a great extent home town life in the Fatherland. Residents of German home towns were noted for their sense of community, strong local pride and their Geselligkeit, or sociability which found expression "in their pleasure in family and community feasts and frolics, in the celebration of anniversaries and namedays and in activities of the innumerable organizations to which they belonged - church, societies, choirs and instrumental groups, skat and skittle clubs, and the like."(17)

The German community was defined by the many organizations and institutions it established. Religious institutions represented the various faiths: Independent Protestant, German Evangelical Synod of North America, Lutheran Church - Missouri Synod, the Presbyterians, the Methodists, the Baptists, the German Reformed Church, the Catholics, and the Jews. Many of the religious bodies held their religious services in the German language and published their own books, newspapers, and periodicals in German. Cincinnati's first German congregation was the St. Johannes-Kirche whose old building is located at 12th and Elm. Cincinnati was the home of German Methodism, the creation of Wilhelm Nast whose Trinity Church stands across from the Music Hall. The Methodists published a high quality family newspaper, Der Christliche Apologete, from 1839 to 1941. This pioneer paper championed the cause of orthodoxy and took issue with nineteenth century rationalism. The Queen City was also the home of Reform Judaism. Isaac Meyer Wise became rabbi of the congregation Ben Yeshurun in 1854, a position he held for 46 years. He founded The Israelite along with its German language supplement Die Deborah, published from 1855 to 1902. In short, there was a wide variety of religious institutions available to meet the spiritual needs of the German community.

For those interested in societies and organizations there were over one hundred Vereine to choose from before the First World War: there were 12 singing societies, 12 trade unions, 59 mutual aid societies, 3 marksmen clubs, 3 Turnvereine, 13 cultural organizations, 7 charitable organizations, and 3 central organizations. Local Vereine affiliated with the Stadt-verband, commonly known as the German-American Alliance. It was a branch of the Ohio German-American Alliance which in turn belonged to the National German-American Alliance. Local Stadtverband President, Judge John Schwaab, was also president

of the Ohio Alliance and a vice president in the National
Alliance, a reflection not only of Cincinnati's importance in
German-America but also of Schwaab's ethnic leadership abili-
ties.

Best known of the local Vereine was the largest one, Der
Deutsche Pionier-Verein von Cincinnati. It had been established in 1869 to renew old friendships, establish new ones,
and to preserve the history of the German pioneers for future
generations. Before the war it had close to a thousand members.
The Pionier-Verein celebrated various Feste, such as Washington's birthday. its publications provide a lasting contribution. From 1869-87 it published the historical journal
entitled Der Deutsche Pionier which is a veritable mine of
historical information on nineteenth century Cincinnati German
history. It also published an annual in later years which contained extensive biographical information on members who had
died during the year. The Verein's honorary president was Carl
Schurz, and its members included prominent local citizens, such
as Christian Moerlein, Judge A.K. Nippert, Jakob Seasongood,
Friedrich S. Spiegel, Gustav Tafel, Isaac Meyer Wise and
others.

German-English bilingual instruction had been available in
Cincinnati's public schools since 1840. By 1915 there were 175
teachers of German with 17,000 students of German. Supervisor
of the program was Dr. H.H. Fick, who had authored a whole series of textbooks for use in the program that came to be known
nationally as the "Cincinnati Plan." A typical textbook of
Fick's was Neu und Alt which attempted to synthesize the best
from the Old and the New Worlds. Such school books contained
readings by and about Schiller, Goethe, Franklin, Washington,
Lincoln, and the German pioneers.

Many special interest German language publications were
available, such as the Brauer-Zeitung for brewery workers, but

the two major German-American newspapers were the Volksblatt and the Freie Presse. Both had a combined aggregate circlation of 92,000 by 1910. Both issued daily, weekly and Sunday editions. The press informed readers on the social, political, and economic conditions of the land and instructed them on their duties, privileges, and rights as citizens. It contributed to a preservation of the immigrant heritage by the use and cultivation of an exemplary German and through the encouragement of the retention of German customs and traditions, and by reporting on events from the old country. It also aimed to serve as the mouthpiece of the German community.

Well over 200 German language books had been published by Cincinnati German authors prior to the First World War, making these publications one of the largest branches of German-American literature. The local German Theater presented plays by Lessing, Grillparzer, Schiller, Goethe, Shakespeare, and others. For German imigrants it kept alive a familiarity with their native literature while for the American-born it transmitted an understanding of the land of their forebears. To non-Germans it provided a knowledge of the German drama. In 1906 the Schiller Celebration culminated in the performance of Wilhelm Tell in Music Hall, a high point in the history of the local German theater. (18)

World War I

The advent of war in Europe in 1914 struck many an American like a bolt of lightning from a clear blue sky. The German element was naturally pro-German, as Anglo-Americans were pro-British in the 1914-17 neutrality period. Cincinnati Germans concentrated and focused their sympathies on humanitarian war relief projects. Altogether a total of $426,382.88 was collected for the widows, orphans, and the suffering in Germany and Austro-Hungary. The U.S. declaration of war on Germany in

April 1917 resulted in a tragic display of hysteria directed against everything and anything German. Although carried on by nativist extremists, the majority silently approved, or at least did not speak out against the nativist hysteria.(19)

In July 1918 "pink slip" day occurred as "Hun tongue" teachers were stricken from the payroll of the public schools of Cincinnati, thus destroying a bilingual program dating back to 1840. In September the Academy of Medicine formed a committee to address the issues of the day, called The Academy of Medicine Against the Huns. A noted community leader, Dr. Gotthard Deutsch, a learned professor at Hebrew Union College, was censured for his outspoken views. At the University of Cincinnati Prof. Martin Ludwich, who taught German in the College of Engineering, was dismissed since he had filed to become a citizen. The Philosophy Department's Prof. Tawney was accused of being pro-German, but was not dismissed. The statue of Germania in the Germania Building on Walnut St. was Americanized into Columbia. The Father Jahn monument in Inwood Park became the target of vandalism. Tar and featherings occurred and two attempted lynchings of German-Americans were reported. The offices of the German press were raided by local officers and federal agents, although nothing incriminating was ever found. In 1918 the entire German collection of the Public Library was removed to the sub-basement. The _Cincinnati_ _Enquirer_ headlined "Kultur of the Kaiser's Kind Not Promoted Through Library."

Name-changing became the rage. The German Mutual Insurance Company became the Hamilton County Insurance Company and the German National Bank the Lincoln National Bank, for example. On 9 April 1918 the Cincinnati City Council passed an ordinance changing the street names "which commemorate political and military places and persons" in Germany and Austro-Hungary. Among those changed were: Bismarck to Montreal St.; Berlin to Woodrow St.; Bremen to Republic St.; Brunswick to Edgecliff Pt.; Frankfurt to Connecticut Ave.; Hamburg to Stone-

wall St.; Hanover to Yukon St., etc. Symbolically, German
Street was renamed English Street.

Dr. Ernest Kunwald, conductor of the Cincinnati Symphony
Orchestra, was imprisoned as an enemy alien for stating his
heart was on the other side. Prof. Emil Heermann, orchestra
concertmaster, was also arrested, but released to the custody
of the College Conservatory of Music. Three members of the
German Theater were arrested, thus causing the Theater to close
its doors. Under local police orders only English language
public meetings could be held. For the various singing societies this, of course, made the singing of German lieder an
impossibility. Many Vereine decided to postpone meetings until
the war was over.

In spite of these nativist attacks, Cincinnati's Germans
served well in the U.S. Army. The list of the war dead shows a
high proportion of German surnames. To demonstrate German-
American patriotism during the war, Charles W. Rattermann, son
of the well known local historian H.A. Rattermann, edited and
published a monthly entitled The Loyal American (1917).

World War I, without question, constituted the darkest
hour in German-American history. Because of the wrongs and
injustices committed against them, German-Americans especially
looked forward to the end of the war. Cincinnati rejoiced at
the news of the armistice. The Cincinnati Post called 11
November 1918 "The greatest day since the beginning of the
world." Citizens took to the streets with "sirens, whistles,
rattles, tin cans, pots and pans, wash boilers, garbage containers, and metal waste baskets" and every possible kind of
noise-making device. Church bells rang all day long and all
the businesses were closed. Also "tons of confetti, tickertape, rice, corn, and wheat fell from the windows." On Fountain Square a coffin containing an effigy of the Kaiser (splattered with decayed fruit and vegetables) was soaked in oil and

transformed into a flaming funeral pyre. The former German Emperor hung in effigy on dozens of lampposts throughout the city. On Sixth Street, a man brandishing a live rat shouted, "We've caught the Kaiser!" Arrayed in spiked helmet, flaring moustaches, and imperial uniform, a living embodiment of Kaiser Wilhelm was paraded down Vine Street in a cage mounted on a horse-drawn float. And "as the pandemonium continued into the night beneath the red sky with rockets and glare of torches, an epoch in the history of Cincinnati came to a close."(20)

Ethnic Survival After the War

The war may have marked the end of one period of German-American history, but it also marked the beginning of a new one, and that one has never been examined. This history of the Cincinnati Germans after the Great War demonstrates two basic conclusions that can be made. First, it demonstrates that the German-American community of Cincinnati survived the war-engendered anti-German hysteria, and that it did not vanish, disappear, disintegrate, or cease to exist. This is not to say that the Cincinnati German community did not survive the war unscathed, as will be seen. Indeed, it will be seen that the community was deeply affected by the war experience. As Moses Rischin has written, "Although German-Americans stoically endured their unpopularity, the price was high, the hurt deep." (21) Second, this history demonstrates that the Germanophobia engendered by the war did not subside with the mere signing of the November 1918 Armistice, but that it continued well after that date into the 1920s.

The conventional view of American historians has been that the war sounded the death knell on German-America, and that the war-engendered Germanophobia subsided almost immediately, or quickly after the signing of the Armistice. This view does not appear to correspond at all with the realities of German-

American community life.   It does not hold true in the case of
the Cincinnati Germans.(22)

Most historians, when writing about German-America between
the World Wars, have focused in actuality on the 1930s and the
response of German-America to the New Germany.   They have thus
focused on the pre-world War II period, and for the most part
overlooked the post-World War I period (1918-32), the period
which must be examined with regard to the study of the impact
of the Great War.

CHAPTER I

THE CINCINNATI GERMAN COMMUNITY AFTER THE GREAT WAR

... preserve and care for the community ...
hold together and in unity establish firmly
a proud German-America.(1)
--Der Deutsche Pionier-Verein, 1931

German Immigration in the Postwar Period

Since the 1880s, and especially in the decade before the
war the immigration from the German-speaking provinces of the
Austro-Hungarian Empire to the U.S. slowly increased. Immigrants sought economic opportunities and/or the chance to
escape military conscription into the Habsburg army. With the
dissolution of the Empire as a result of the First World War,
the immigration to Cincinnati increased. The Danube Swabian
immigration, as these immigrants were known, was reflected in
the formation of several new Vereine in Cincinnati in the
1920s. The immigration of this German Stamm was of special
importance for the German community for several reasons. In
Germany a distinction was made between those born in the German
Empire, Reichsdeutsche, and those born outside or abroad, Aus-
landsdeutsche. As a German-speaking minority group the Danube
Swabians were of the latter category. They had lived in small
communities throughout southeastern Europe. These settlements
were "enclosed communities" with German language churches,
schools, institutions, etc., where individuals "practiced their
customs and also spoke the mother-tongue with pride."(2) In
the literature on the Danube Swabians particular emphasis and
pride is placed on the fact that they lived outside of Germany,
but nonetheless preserved their heritage.(3) Such an immigration infusion after World War I could only exert a positive
influence on the German community. The two reasons cited by a

Danube Swabian historian as causing their postwar immigration, aside from economic factors, were the "envy and grudge" displayed towards them by their non-German compatriots in the former Austrian provinces.(4) Such disfavor together with the poor economic situation of the 1920s caused them to immigrate. In short, this group had, like the Cincinnati Germans, known disfavor, but was proud of its uniqueness as an ethnic group as well as its ability to preserve its ancestral customs and traditions. The Danube Swabians speak a dialect which has been called Honoratioren-Pfälzisch, a mixture of High German and dialect. Their ancestors came from Alsace, Lorraine, Luxemburg and southwestern Germany, and had settled in Austria-Hungary on the invitation of the Empress Maria Theresa.

The immigration from Germany was caused by the bleak socio-economic conditions of the 1920s. The Weimar Republic was heavily burdened with the Versailles Treaty, war debts, pensions to victims of the war, and with an expanding social welfare program. The Franco-Belgian occupation of the Ruhr in 1923 deprived Germany of essential raw materials, disrupted production, and increased the upward spiral of unemployment. Food riots occurred in August 1923. From 1920-23 government expenditure exceeded income annually at a rate varying from RM 6,136 million to 11,732 million. Debts were covered by the government's printing presses, i.e., by "floating debts." By 1923 close to two thousand printing presses ran night and day printing money. Dollar quotations for the Reichsmark increased from $8.90 (January 1919) to $4,200,000,000,000 (November 1923). As soon as one was paid one rushed to spend before the release of the next quotation, a situation literarily portrayed in Erich Maria Remarque's Drei Kameraden. Persons on fixed incomes and members of the middle class were left impoverished. In December 1923 only 29.3% of the German labor force was employed. The 1918-23 inflation period was followed by a period of boom and prosperity in 1923-29, but cut short then by the economic crisis of 1929-32. Unemployment rose sharply from

1,368,000 (1929) to 3,144,000 (1930). The basic economic crisis was complicated by international tensions externally and internally by nationalistic agitation which was setting the stage for a totalitarian system as the way out of the crisis. In the context of these conditions the German immigration is readily understandable.(5)

In 1920 the total population of Cincinnati was 401,247. The German element can be estimated as being approximately 200,623. The foreign stock from Germany, Austria, and Switzerland (the foreign-born and their children) numbered 98,762. For 1920 only 102,225 reported that German was their mother tongue, a drop of 25,000 from the 1917 estimate, and 23,000 less than the 1910 U.S. Census. The reason for this was the apparent reluctance of German-Americans to report information regarding their mother tongue. LaVern J. Rippley has noted that "Many families denied their origins and changed their names to hide their identities. Census records for counties with large German stock populations in 1910 showed radical drops in reports of nationality origin for Germans in 1920, indicating that many German people simply understated their German origins because of the ill-feeling about Germans at the time."(6) Glen G. Gilbert has also observed that with regard to the U.S. Census German-Americans have been hesitant in reporting information in politically sensitive years.(7) The actual number of those with German as a mother tongue was most likely, therefore, at least 127,000.

In 1930 the total population of Cincinnati was 451,247 and the German element could be estimated as being 225,623. The foreign stock from Germany, Austria, and Switzerland was 80,018. The mother tongue question was not included in the 1930 U.S. Census; only the mother tongue of the foreign-born was registered. Because of the passing of the immigrant generation, this could be estimated as being approximately 125,000.

From Over-the-Rhine to the Hilltops and to the West Side

In the 1920s Germans continued to move out of the old Over-the-Rhine district, a process already well underway before the war. George M. Henzel, who grew up in the district, attributed the move out of the area to the hilltop suburbs as the desire to demonstrate socio-economic mobility and status:

> Something in the German character, either brought over to America by the German immigrants, or burned into it by life in the tenements, was an overpowering desire for a brick house in the suburbs. A frame house, or a stucco or stone house, would not do.

He observed how Over-the-Rhine families saved money in local building and loan societies for the purpose of moving to the suburbs. After the war there was literally an exodus out of the area. "This same desire burned in the families of the businessmen in the area, and gradually they too, business and all, migrated to those hills." Even Henzel's parents "dreamed of a brick house up on the hill in the suburbs." This _Auswanderung_ meant that Over-the-Rhine was no longer "either a physical or ethnic community."(8)

Two false conclusions should not be deduced from the German-American exodus from Over-the-Rhine. First, it should not be concluded that German-Americans moved entirely helter-skelter, although they did, indeed settle in all wards of the city. As Henzel notes, Over-the-Rhiners "were buying a brick house in Price Hill, or Westwood or Cheviot."(9) German-Americans, hence, moved throughout the city, but concentrated especially on the west side of Cincinnati, resulting in somewhat of an east-west socio-cultural division of the city that is still evident. Second, it should not be concluded that because the population expanded and moved from the tiny Over-the-Rhine district that the community's cohesiveness was adversely

affected. Indeed, the complex organizational structure of the
secular and religious societies and organizations provided for
the institutionalization of ethnic interrelationships. Finally, it should be noted that the ethnic community should never
be completely equated with a specific geographical area. It
was more than the land it occupied:

> An ethnic community was more than a ghetto, a geogra-
> phic area in which a particular group was heavily
> concentrated. An ethnic community, like any other
> community, was a group of people who knew and cared
> about one another, enjoyed a common life, and shared
> common problems and concerns. The individuals in
> such a community related to one another in a variety
> of structured, or institutionalized, ways -- some
> informal, like the corner grocery or saloon, others
> formal, like the church, the school, or the fraternal
> lodge. Ethnic communities consisted of a network of
> such institutions, some as local as the nearby street
> corner, others as extensive as a national press.(10)

In conclusion, it can be observed that while it had been
appropriate to speak of the German community of Cincinnati in
the nineteenth century with respect to the Over-the-Rhine district, by the twentieth century, and especially by the 1920s,
it would be more appropriate to speak of ethnic neighborhoods
across the city, especially on the west side of Cincinnati.

German Community Leaders:

Judge John Schwaab, Judge A.K. Nippert and Dr. H.H. Fick

Three persons played an important role in the postwar
period in providing leadership and in setting an example for
the German-American community: Judge John Schwaab, Judge A.K.
Nippert and Dr. H.H. Fick. In thought, word and deed they
forged a German-Americanism that was appropriate for the time,
and one that was in accord with the Zeitgeist of the 1920s. An

understanding of their ethnic leadership is, therefore, essential to an understanding of the German community after the
Great War.(11)

Schwaab was born 9 March 1855 in Bavaria and had attended
schools in Zweibrücken and graduated from the Munich Military
Academy. In September 1880 he immigrated to Cincinnati where
he became a teacher of German in the bilingual program. Here
he earned a modest salary, but married well: Caroline Wichard,
descended from Kaspar Molitor, a Forty-Eighter. He also studied law in his spare time. In 1893 he commenced the practice
of law and became active in local politics. In 1894 he was
elected to the Board of Education, a position he was re-elected
to until 1913; he also served onthe Union Board of High Schools
for twenty-five years. As a member of the School Board he represented the interests of the German community with regard to
the bilingual program, and was entrusted with the program's
supervision until 1903, when Dr. H.H. Fick was appointed Supervisor of German.

Schwaab's entrance into the Republican Club of Hamilton
County in 1895 led to his association with the Boss Cox
Machine. The prolonged illness of machine member Judge William
Lueders resulted in Schwaab's appointment to fill in for him on
the bench of the Police Court. The early years of the twentieth century witnessed his rapid rise to social, cultural and
political leadership in the German community. In 1906 he was
elected president of the Stadtverband, or German-American Alliance, and in 1907 he was elected also president of the Ohio
German-American Alliance and vice-president of the National
German-American Alliance. Before the Great War he also chaired
the highly regarded Theaterverein, the organization which ran
the local German Theater. In 1915 he was elected president of
the prestigious Altenheim-Verein, an organization consisting of
members of the German-American elite which ran the German old
people's home. Schwaab symbolized not only the man who rose to

Richter John Schwaab,
Präsident des Stadtverbandes und des Staatsverbandes von Ohio.
Der erfolgreiche Führer des Deutschthums im Kampfe gegen
Beschränkung der persönlichen Freiheit.

Judge John Schwaab was described as "The successful leader of Germandom in the battle against limitation of personal liberty" in August B. Gorbach, _Deutscher Vereins-Wegweiser_ (1915), a volume located in the German-Americana Collection, Blegen Library, University of Cincinnati.

the top, but was also a gifted and talented ethnic leader with the ability to attract support from a cross-section of the German community.

Schwaab, as vice-president of the National Alliance, was involved through that position in a national leadership position. Also, in late May 1916 he participated as one of nearly 170 delegates for 26 states in the German-American National Conference held in Chicago. A platform was adopted by the Resolutions Committee which was chaired by Schwaab which is of value to look at as a reflection of his own views. The platform stated:

> We deplore and condemn all attempts to divide Americans and to insult and stigmatize any race, creed or color by invidious hyphenation. Men from every country of the world have found here a new home - a land of liberty, of equal opportunity and equal justice - and all have contributed their sweat and their blood to the upbuilding and defense of our great democracy. They may be hyphenated Americans, but their Americanism is unhyphenated. To attempt to arouse animosity and distrust toward any class or nationality as some have done through shrewd ambition or ungovernable temper, is a crime. A deaf ear should be turned to all demagogues that trade upon national antipathies and seek to extol their own loyalty by impugning that of others. (12)

Judge Schwaab led the Stadtverband, and indeed the German community, through the trying times of World War I, and skillfully engineered the survival of the Stadtverband as the new American Citizens League, which will be discussed later in this chapter. In 1931 he and his wife were honored at a gala festivity at the Hotel Alms on the occasion of their fiftieth wedding anniversary. Schwaab at that time had been named honorary president of the League, an indication of the high regard he was held in. Schwaab's strategy of ethnic survival in the 1920s consisted in making the German community as publicly subdued and reticent as possible. The purpose of this strategy was twofold. First, it aimed to maintain and preserve ethnic institutions. Second, by adopting a low profile Schwaab aimed to avoid any possible attacks or recurrences of the war-engendered anti-German hysteria. This strategy had the effect of submerging German ethnicity, and of making German-American institutions much less publicly visible. Several examples of how Schwaab went about this strategy can be mentioned here. The local German-American Alliance, which along with the state and national organizations, had its own charter revoked by Congress, did not cease to exist. Schwaab merely changed its name to the American Citizens League. Although it came to be known as the German-American Citizens League, its official name was the American Citizens League. The strategy here was to maintain the ethnic institution, and de-emphasize its ethnicity. In the 1920s a German-American Citizens League could have become a target for nativists, but not so an American Citizens League. Schwaab also set a personal example of de-emphasizing his ethnicity publicly. An example of this can be found in a biographical directory published in 1921 of Cincinnati judges and lawyers. Schwaab's biography contains many useful details regarding his life and work, but not one single reference in local, regional, and national German-American affairs. Although he was obviously widely recognized as an ethnic leader, the reader of his biography would know nothing of this. Schwaab's leadership style most likely was indicative of the subdued and submerged nature of German ethnicity that was being adopted elsewhere. His example was significant since he occupied the position as titular head of Cincinnati's Germandom. In retrospect his policy of ethnic survival could be criticized for tending to make German-Americans appear "invisible" but there can be no question that this was aimed at ethnic institutional survival, and also at the avoidance of any further nativist attacks. And it was also a strategy that proved to be successful. In the case, however, that a nativist attack should occur, Schwaab adopted the strategy that there should be a public and spirited defense, an example of which will be seen in Chapter IV when Schwaab himself came under nativist attack.

Alfred Kuno Nippert was born in Frankfurt am Main on 12 June 1872, son of Ludwig and Ida (von Uxküll-Gyllenband) Nippert. His father, a Methodist minister, had been sent to Switzerland and Germany by the Ohio Methodist Conference, and became the first dean of the Methodist Theological Seminary in Frankfurt am Main. A.K. Nippert received his preliminary education at the Musterschule in Frankfurt am Main and at the public schools of Pittsburgh, Pennsylvania and Newport, Kentucky, and graduated A.B. and L.L.B. in 1894 and 1897 respectively from the University of Cincinnati. He married Maude Gamble, the daughter of James M. Gamble, an ingenious chemist who had become immensely wealthy by perfecting the formula for Ivory Soap. Maude Gamble's mother was Fanny Nast, the daughter of the father of the German Methodist Church, Wilhelm Nast. Nippert's family background, therefore, made him one of the most highly respected German-Americans in Cincinnati. His name signified a synthesis of origins deriving from the religious community as well as from the elite.

In 1897 he commenced the practice of law in Cincinnati. From 1913-19 he served as judge of Hamilton County Common Pleas Court, and was thereafter commonly referred to as "Richter Nippert." From 1912 to 1913 he was on the board of directors for the University of Cincinnati. During World War I Nippert became one of the most active and articulate spokesmen of the German-American community. For example, when resolutions were passed in October 1914 to protest the anti-German Anglo-American press, it was Nippert who was called upon to work out the exact wording of the text. He was also a Vice President of the Society for Aid to East Prussia, and as such attended its general meeting in Berlin in 1916.

After the war Nippert continued to be active in German-American affairs, not as an elected member of community organizations and societies, but rather as a recognized spokesman who often addressed German-Americans at their functions and was widely respected for his political endorsements in the German-American press. Adding to his stature in the eyes of the German-American community was his successful bout with nativists in the postwar period, which will be examined in Chapter IV.

If Schwaab was a leader of ethnic community institutions, and Nippert a publicly vocal spokesman, then the cultural leader was to be found in the person of Dr. H.H. Fick. Born 16 August 1849 in Lübeck, where he attended the Grossheimsche Schule, Fick early developed an intense interest for language, history, and literature. In 1864, three years after the death of his father, he immigrated to New York where he had been offered a position in his uncle's business. He then moved to Cincinnati to engage in a similar business venture as a salesman. Dissatisfaction with the business world caused him to enter the teaching profession after successfully passing' his entrance exams. In 1870 he was appointed as a teacher of German in a public elementary school in Cincinnati. Because of his artistic talents he also gave art instruction, and provided great impetus to the art program. In 1872 an art exhibit was sent to the Vienna Exposition and the report of the Commissioner of Education claimed that Cincinnati "had gained an enviable reputation in this branch."(13) From 1878-84 Fick was Superintendent of Drawing. In 1884 he moved to Chicago where he gave private lessons in German and art and married a teacher, Clementine Barna, with whom he founded a German-English school with another colleague. In 1890 he returned to Ohio to complete a Ph.D. at Ohio University (1892). Then he served until 1901 as principal of the Sixth District School. From 1901 to 1903 he was Assistant Superintendent, and in 1903 was appointed Supervisor of German in the Public Schools, a position he held until 1918.

Fick was nationally known for his contributions to the field of education. He was elected seven times to the presidency of the National German-American Teachers Association which had its central office in Milwaukee at the German-American Teachers Seminary. He also served on the Seminary's board of directors for forty years until 1918. He was co-editor and then editor of the Association's educational journal, the Erziehungsblätter, for a total of thirty-five years. Locally, Fick was of course greatly involved in the teachers' organizations. He also edited a journal for children entitled Jung-Amerika, which contained prose and poetry by himself, his wife, and other local German-American authors. He also authored a whole series of textbooks for the bilingual program in Cincinnati, an excellent local history, and a collection of poetry. He was highly respected amongst Cincinnati Germans, and held honorary memberships in the Pionier-Verein, the Turngemeinde, and the German Literary Club. He was often invited to be the main speaker at programs and Feste in the tri-state region.

Fick had been under direct nativist attack since the outbreak of the war. As Supervisor of the German program he presented an obvious target. For example, one of his published lectures dealing with German instruction in the public schools was branded as an example of the threat of the German to the English language in America. His excellent series of school textbooks, which were used in Cincinnati and elsewhere, were condemned as glorifications of monarchy and German contributions to the U.S. On the average most of his textbooks were censored by 75%, but his textbook, Hier und Dort, a volume of 272 pages, was censored down to 30 pages. Any and all of the slightest references to Germany, its government, history, and its immigrants were cause for censorship. Even the word "Vaterland" was banned.

In May 1918 Dr. Fick found it necessary to tender his resignation to the school board since the program was to be eliminated in the forthcoming year. At his resignation it was emphasized that he had been patriotic in every manner. Nevertheless, he faced "verbal insults of the most shameless and vile manner." And of course it did not stop there. Fick wrote later "A systematic persecution of my entire family began, by which something unbelievable was accomplished in lies and the twisting of facts."(14) It was at this time of crisis that Fick demonstrated what kind of man he was and contributed to the ethnic leadership of the German-American community. It was perhaps his finest hour. Max Griebsch wrote of him:

> ... only now Fick showed his unending greatness. Another person would probably have despaired. However, he displayed a toned downness of spirit which let him preserve his equanimity where it required almost superhuman strength. He wrestled through to a philosophy of life which culminated therein that nothing that was humane was foreign to him, and which embraced all understanding and all forgiving.(15)

A colleague noted later how heavily Dr. Fick suffered from the defamations and accusations against his character and his family, especially as he had to witness "how everything that he had held high, held high in the service of true Americanism ... was pulled down." Nevertheless, he maintained his equanimity. He called him a man firmly rooted in the world of ideas of the German homeland, but a representative of an Americanism which transcended political boundaries to attain the "high ideals of freedom and humanity." He was noted for his humane qualities, his truthfulnes, and uprightness, his readiness to be of assistance to members of the communtiy, his friendly loyalty which brought him "respect and reverence" from all who knew him.(16)

Fick found strength and support in the postwar period from the German community. Dr. A.J. Bucher, editor of the *Christliche Apologete*, and F.W. Elven, editor of the *Freie Presse*, both employed him as a regular contributor to the press. He

also contributed on a regular basis to the Chicago Abendpost.
In serial form several book length manuscripts of his appeared.
He also was active in the 1920s as a member of the German Literary Club and the Pionier-Verein, whose annual publications
always contained one of his poems. In the late 1920s Fick
wrote:

> The war had been over for years: The uproarious
> defamation of the Germans may have abated in public
> and the evil word "Hun" may not be heard often any
> more. Brutal attacks and bodily harm belong to the
> past and yet often an unfriendliness makes itself
> felt in an unpleasant manner."(17)

According to Dr. Fick, the injustice committed against the
German element "could never be made good." Although he could
forgive, he understandably could not forget.

Amongst local German-American intellectuals Fick was without question the key person in Cincinnati. In the 1920s he set
a noble example for his compatriots in redefining how one could
be a German-American. Although he was not a systematic philosopher, he was an articulate individual who published extensively in the German press. It is, therefore, not difficult to
identify and enumerate the basic points in his Weltanschauung.
This consisted of, first of all, a stoic stance with respect to
the nativism of the time. A stoic is defined as one who
regards virtue as the highest good and teaches that men "should
strive to be free from passion, unmoved by joy or grief, and
able to submit without complaint to the unavoidable necessity
by which all things are governed."(18)

Certainly, there are stoic elements in the manner in which
he responded to nativism. Second, he obviously adopted the
cultural course of action that was being formulated and adopted
by German-American intellectuals elsewhere in the country.

Fick's whole orientation with regard to the role of the German community was non-political and cultural. His own ethnicity remained a simple and primary source of strength. In short, his example recommended a stoic indifference to the nativist Zeitgeist, an avoidance of ethnic group politics, and a steady cultural course of action within the framework of the German community. Although a man into his seventh decade, Fick ironically became a role model for the German community in the 1920s. He was called "the last representative" of prewar German-American cultural work. In a time of discontinuity he provided a thoughtful and introspective example of continuity. For the fiftieth anniversary of the German Literary Club in 1927 he wrote the introduction to the Club's history. Here he likened the history of the Club to the course of an old traveler. The course of the traveler in actuality reads much like an autobiographical statement of his philosophy. He writes that the traveler, having traversed a long, troublesome uphill course, could now stop to look around and orient himself [after the Great War]. At this point the traveler:

> ... then probably measures the accomplished distance, rests perhaps a bit, and strives, happy at the view to far and near, defying every phase of weather, towards the longed-for goal. A joyous call spurs him on; derogatory glances and words he leaves unnoticed; trouble and hindrances are easier forgotten in the knowledge of coming nearer to the destination.(19)

For Fick the goal was ethnic survival by means of the stoic, cultural course of action for the German community.

The importance of Fick is underscored by the loss felt in the German community at his passing in 1935. The Freie Presse described him as "Our true leader and friend." Another obituary recalled:

> ... his entire personality was so closely grown
> together with us, in him lived such a measure of
> life-affirmation, he lived so fully in our time from
> which he took everything which life offered to him,
> and to which he was willing to give what was within
> his power, that it hardly occurred to one that he
> belonged to a period lying much before us. (20)

At the funeral, representatives of the German Literary Club,
the Turngemeinde, the Pionier-Verein, the Citizens League, and
other Vereine were among those filling the crowded chapel at
Spring Grove Cemetery. Among the speakers were Dr. Bucher from
the _Apologete_, Pastor Hans Haupt, and Jerome Iffland. The
latter termed Fick's passing as a "great loss" for Germandom in
the entire U.S. Haupt spoke of the practical example Fick had
displayed in relation to the words of the German author Mathias
Claudius: "When you are truly depressed so that you can think
that no one can console you, then do something good to someone,
and immediately it will be better." According to Haupt, there
was no better illustration of this than Fick "in the days of
his deepest depression when he had to lay down his work. Never
was he friendlier or milder than in those days of his deepest
suffering." (21)

Societies and Organizations

The dissolution of the National German-American Alliance
in the spring of 1918 brought a nominal end to the German-
American Alliance of Cincinnati which merely re-surfaced as the
American Citizens League, a move cleverly orchestrated by Judge
Schwaab. Significantly the new organization was not entitled
"German-American" but rather "American." A 1936 edition of its
constitution indicates that for the period investigated by this
study the organization was known as the American Citizens
League, hereafter ACL, a name which gave no indication that it
was a German-American organization. This reluctance to refer

Dr. Heinrich H. Fick (1849-1935), director of German in Cincinnati schools, starting on his task of German textbook censorship.

From Don Heinrich Tolzmann, _Festschrift_ for the German-American Tricentennial Jubilee: Cincinnati 1983 (1982), a volume located in the German-Americana Collection, Blegen Library, University of Cincinnati.

to the organization as German-American reflects the xenophobia of the time. The ACL's constitution closely resembled that of the Stadtverband, although several points reflected the recent World War I experience. Its six basic purposes were enumerated as follows:

1. The preservation of the U.S. Constitution in every relation.

2. The protection of the rights granted to citizens under the U.S. Constitution.

3. Support foreign born in obtaining citizenship and instruction on duties and rights of American citizens.

4. The awakening and advancement of the feeling of unity in the population of German origin for the purpose of the preservation of the German language and lifestyle and for the common and energetic defense of just such wishes and interests which are in accord with the well being of the state and the duties of good American citizens.

5. The resistance of all unjust nativist attacks.

6. The resistance of all attempts to belittle the deeds of German-Americans for the adopted fatherland.

The constitution stated specifically that the League consisted of Vereine which were to be represented by delegates who must be U.S. citizens. Non-voting individual members were entitled to speak on the issues and to make motions during the business meetings. A special category was created for honorary members, the only one of whom during the period was Judge Schwaab. In one significant aspect the constitution differed from the Stadtverband, and that was in the area of politics. Whereas the old Stadtverband had actively endorsed and opposed political candidates, the new ACL excluded from it all organizations engaged in party politics. The president appointed six committees which indicate where the focus of interest in the ACL was: The Membership Committee, the Committee for Citizens' Rights, the Committee for German Affairs (the German School in the Turnhalle, German instruction, and the youth choir), Committee for the History of the State, the Publicity Committee, and the Social Affairs Committee (German Day). (22)

The ACL struggled to regain its old strength of pre-war days when 110 Vereine had been affiliated with it. In February 1919 only 30 Vereine were affiliated, but then the number of societies had decreased as a result of the war. In the 1920s there were 64 Vereine in Cincinnati, 45 of which were members of the ACL. There were approximately 5,000 members of local Vereine, or roughly half the amount that there were in 1915. The Vereinsdeutschen had, therefore, survived the war, but their numbers had diminished. According to Jacob Herz, a post World War II ACL president, "The First World War brought Germandom and the German Vereine great damage and everything went backwards." (23)

Not surprisingly the largest number of casualties amongst the Vereine was in the category of the small regionally-based mutual aid societies. In 1915 there had been 59, but by 1932 there were only eighteen left, a net loss of 41. All other categories of the Vereine proved to be relatively stable: This means that there was substantial ethnic institutional survival amongst the following organizations: the central organizations, the singing societies, the trade union societies, the marksmen clubs, the Turner societies, the cultural organizations, and the charitable societies. Indeed, if the loss of the 41 mutual aid societies is added to the 64 surviving Vereine that existed in 1932 the total is 105. This is not far from the 1915 total of 110.

There were several reasons for the decline of the small regional-based Vereine. During and after the war it became socially and economically advisable for German-Americans to cluster in larger organizations, rather than to maintain small societies. It should be remembered that during the war only English-language public meetings were permissible so that many Vereine simply postponed meeting until the war's end, and some of them never resumed meeting. The war, therefore, snuffed out some of these Vereine. While the ranks were being thinned out in the small Vereine, the larger community-wide organizations, such as the Pionier-Verein, expanded its membership in the 1920s. Without question German-Americans felt it was more advisable to belong to a larger, rather than a small German-American society, perhaps feeling that there was safety in numbers. Economic factors also contributed to the decline of the small Vereine. Prohibition deprived Vereine of one of their major sources of income--selling beer at their various meetings and Feste. Without this income flowing into the treasury it became difficult, and in some cases impossible for a Verein to financially survive. Another economic factor was the depression which exhausted funds of the small regional beneficial aid societies. Vereine here found it difficult to expend funds when members were sick or when there was a death in the family. Maintaining beneficial programs became too much for some of them. In short, if Darwin's law of the survival of the fittest was applied to the Vereine during and after the war, then it would have to be said that small societies and organizations found it socially and economically difficult, and in many cases impossible to continue their existence. The net result has meant that there are fewer societies, but that the surviving ones held larger memberships than before. This adverse set of circumstances may therefore be viewed as having reduced the number of Vereine, but in swelling the ranks of the larger ones.

The ACL met 6 December 1918 and decided not to assess the five cent per member dues from member Vereine in the hopes that no more societies would disaffiliate. The central task appeared to be that of survival and keeping together. And "if the immediate future was anything but rosy, courage should not be lost." It was felt "Better days are sure to come, so that the children, at least, will be harvesting the fruits of their having faithfully held together." The ACL placed emphasis on citizenship stating that it aimed to educate recently arrived German immigrants to become good American citizens so "that they don't get into trouble with the institutions of this country." Many, it noted, would ask:

> ... who has helped me? Such a questioner should think, however, that times and conditions have changed. While he came bearing his head proudly, the present German immigrant will be but tolerated and will land with his head bowed low by what has happened.(24)

Aside from its organizational work amongst the societies the ACL attained several modest accomplishments in the 1920s. The last annual German Day celebration was held 2 September 1916 with A.K. Nippert as the main speaker. In the spring of 1926 it was decided to again sponsor a German Day, and preparations were held so that after a decade German Day could again be held on 29 August 1926 at the Zoological Garden. The ACL sponsored German language Instruction in the Turnhalle in the 1920s and also sponsored a Kinderchor under the direction of William Kappelhoff, the father of actress Doris Day.

Judge Schwaab had been a gifted and skilled ethnic leader who had guided the Stadtverband through the war, and was responsible for its reorganization as the ACL. He was at ease with the various segments of the community and was known for his cultivated political contacts and associations with the Cox machine. He was named honorary president of the ACL shortly

after the war and was succeeded in office by John König,
Richard Greninger, Heinrich Albertz, and Henry Glöcker. All of
them were devoted Vereinsdeutsche and able leaders of the
Vereine, and although they did not surpass the stature, presence and abilities of Judge Schwaab, they led the Vereine well.
(28)

Although the ACL had survived the war it differed from its
pre-war days in terms of its political influence. As a result
of the war it was sheared of the overt political influence it
had exerted locally. First of all, it was deprived of two
basic issues it had rallied German-American votes around: personal liberty and the bilingual program in the Cincinnati
Public Schools. Prohibition was now a federal law, no longer
an issue on the local or state ballot, and repulsive as it may
be it was clearly beyond the scope of a local organization.
The destruction of the bilingual program in the public schools
was complete. No longer would this be an issue in local elections, nor would German-American representatives be sought to
run for the school board. Nevertheless the ACL voiced opposition to prohibition and supported in its constitution the
furthering of German language instructional programs, but in
view of the Zeitgeist these were futile gestures. A second
change in political influence was that the ACL no longer carried the weight it had before in local elections since it
abstained from endorsing or opposing candidates. Indeed, in
the 1920 election it encouraged the vote for Harding, but shied
away from an endorsement, fearing that it would do more harm
than good. An endorsement from the Stadtverband/ACL was no
longer something to be desired by a local politician. However,
by the end of the 1920s local politicians began to make the
trek to German Day celebrations, but that was as far as it
went. Third, the loss of the Cox/Hynicka machine was significant. The ACL could no longer request that German-Americans
receive their fair share of city hall political appointments
from the machine. Finally, the loss of the Natinal German-

American Alliance deprived the local organization of the influence of affiliation with a major national organization. The
loss of such affiliation deprived it political influence locally as well as reginally since Cincinnati had been the seat of
the Ohio Alliance. All local Stadtverbande were thus sheared
of national and regional interrelationships. Although new
national organizations arose in the 1920s, e.g., Steuben
Society of America, the ACL did not associate with any of them.

Most other Vereine, aside from the regionally based mutual
aid societies, survived the war. The major organizations survived, e.g., the Turngemeinde, the German Literary Club and the
German Pionier-Verein, but the struggle was anything but easy.
In late November 1918 the Bavarian Maennerchor considered re-
newing its singing practice sessions, but decided against it in
view of the times. However, it did decide to hold a farewell
fest to the availability of beer with the Badensian Mutual Aid
Society before the prohibition law took effect. The Bavarian
Mutual Aid society reported a surplus in the treasury although
heavy demands had been placed on it, and it had, of course, not
been able to sponsor its annual Sommerfest for some time to
earn new funds. By January 1919 Vereine began to meet again
since "the authorities let up on their harassment of Germans."
For example, the U.S. Marshall removed restrictions against
enemy aliens at Christmas and the grand jury dropped its charges against Judge Hoffman, Sr., for having sung Die Wacht am
Rhein. Also, in December the ACL began to meet again on a
regular basis.(26)

However, the Vereine were cautious publicly. When the
Rev. Haupt advised with respect to the postwar relief work that
the time was not yet right "to take up the work again" he was
in essence speaking in general about any all-German public
affair. In January 1919, for instance, the Hannover Mutual Aid
Society and the Pionier-Verein still refrained from even send-
ing their delegates to the ACL. The president of the Badensian

Mutual Aid Society, Julius Zorn, asked wives to encourage hus-
bands to attend meetings. The Bavarian Mutual Aid Society
reported in October 1919 that it had lost seven members and the
president remarked:

> It was no mean task for me and the other officials to
> hit the right tone at all times, particularly since a
> large number of members showed no understanding
> whatsoever and have not even found it worth their
> while to attend the meetings, so that we, with a
> membership of 177, have barely had a quorum.(27)

The Altenheim survived, but found it advisable to take on
a new name: The Cincinnati Old Men's Home. The constitution
was also changed so that non-Germans could be admitted. The
Protestant Orphan Society attained great success: from 447
members (December 1918) it zoomed to 1,036 (September 1919).
Its treasury showed an excess of $10,237.50. German and Aus-
trian veterans dissolved their group and reorganized in August
1919 as the Cincinnati Kriegerverein which was opened to any
and all former soldiers with honorable service records, an
attempt to gain German-Americans who had served in the world
war. It was especially interested in those "who are not willing to forget their beloved mother tongue." According to
Dobbert, by the fall of 1919 "quite a bit of organized Germandom had furnished evidence of its ability to survive in one
fashion or another."(28)

A major evil to the Vereine was prohibition. The Bavarian
Mutual Aid Society complained that its financial setbacks were
due mainly to prohibition. Fewer and fewer visitors attended
its "dry" festivities. Carl Pletz, local editor of the defunct
Volksblatt, exclaimed in March 1920 that there was no longer a
good draught to be found in Cincinnati, and that "the main attraction for a congenial get-together no longer exists." Dry
society meetings had become the order of the day. "Near-beer"
was considered a poor substitute for the real beverage. The

Pionier-Verein's annual lamented "Moist-happy sessions, jovial festivities are the live nerve for every society, without which in the long run it cannot thrive." Unfortunately, for those who enjoyed a good draught, the wait would be long.(29)

In 1920 Howard Wurlitzer organized the local relief effort, the Society for Needy Children in Central Europe, an indication that public organizational work by German-Americans could now be undertaken. By 1920 many of the Vereine were well on the road to recovery. The three marksmen clubs planned a merger with the advantage of obtaining benefits from one to three of the organizations depending on the amount of dues paid. Among the mutual aid societies the Greater Beneficial Union, formerly the German Beneficial Union, thrived the most successfully with a new chapter being established in Price Hill in July 1920, an indication of the population shift to the west side. To attract second generation Germans, Vereine wisely adapted to the times. The new marksmen club allowed English to be used in its meetings along with the German language. The Haraguri opened its organization to the second generation instead of limiting it only to immigrants. The _Freie Presse_ commented in December 1920 on the comeback being staged by the Vereine:

> In the German societies' world things are moving again. Despair and apathy which during the last year [1919] have invaded so many a society and threatened to estrange quite a few entirely from all things essentially German, have relinquished their place to more hopeful views. Societies and members have begun again to take stock of themselves. And conscious that it can no longer go on like this, the old will to act has reappeared. And it is good so.(30)

The Turngemeinde, a major organization in the nineteenth century, survived the war, but commenced the postwar period with the problem of finances. Its option to buy the land on which the old Turnhalle stood was scheduled to expire soon,

with the distinct possibility of losing what had earlier been
referred to as a "mighty fortress" of German culture. The
amount of $35,000 was quickly needed to buy the land. There-
fore, at the same time money was being collected for needy
children in Germany, the Turners found it necessary to appeal
to the German community to raise $35,000 to save the Turnhalle.
In July 1919 the campaign began, which met in final success,
with close to 30 fund-raising teams.

The Turngemeinde itself reflected the transition of the
Cincinnati Germans from a European immigrant group to an American ethnic group. By 1932 the Verein had 156 members, 110 of
whom were American-born. Official languages for meetings were
German as well as English. It supported the German Sunday
School along with other Vereine and German language classes,
sponsored by the ACL, which were held at the Turnhalle. Among
non-Turners in Turner classes about one-third were German
speaking. The national Turner leadership reflected the transition that was underway locally in Turnvereine. Formerly entitled the Amerikanische Turnerbund, it officially changed its
name to the American Gymnastic Union, a name which gave no
indication as to its German immigrant origin. The national
journal, the Amerikanische Turnzeitung, began the publication
of English language articles. National chairman, Theodore
Stempfel, disapproved of ethnic political activities, a stark
contrast to the political orientation of the Forty-Eighter
founders. In July 1921 the first National Turnfest was held
since the World War had begun. In 1924 the national organization published its new set of Principles which proclaimed the
Turners for:

> Liberty, against all oppression; Tolerance, against
> all fanaticism; Reason, against all superstition;
> Justice, against all exploitation; Free speech, free
> press, free assembly for the discussion of all
> questions, so that men and women may think unfettered
> and order their lives by the dictates of their

conscience -- such is our ideal, which we strive to attain through a sound mind in a sound body.(31)

At least twelve new Vereine were established in the 1918-32 time period. Significantly enough, seven of them were Danube Swabian, a reflection of the immigration from the former Austrian provinces of southwestern Europe. Because of their strong sense of ethnic identity these groups formed their own central organization, the United Banater Societies which met in the Banater-Halle on Logan Street.(32)

German Catholics established the Kolping Society (1923) which became the major German Catholic society in Cincinnati. It held its first Schuetzenfest in 1925. Two new singing societies were formed: the Cincinnati Choral Verein (1918) and the Herwegh Damenchor (1926). The Gyertyamoser Leichenverein, a burial aid society, began in 1918 and gained a sizable membership. The German Theater-Verein aimed at the revival of the German theater in the mid-1920s. This new burst of organizational activity indicated that the Vereine had not only survived, but they were making a successful comeback.

For children the ACL sponsored a Kinderchor while the United Banater Societies also sponsored a Banater Kinderchor. All of the Vereine supported the German Sunday School for local children. However, the most successful future-oriented undertaking was the Cincinnati Club Center directed by Dr. A.F. Morgenstern. Begun in 1926 this organization aimed to collect funds for a Cincinnati Club, i.e., a new German house. It was supported by 45 Vereine with a board of directors including: Heinrich Klehe, Emil Schiele, B.J. Franklin, Frank Rattermann, and F.W. Elven. On 8 February 1927 it held a fest with the main address delivered by Judge Nippert. $22,000 was raised at this event for the Center. By the end of the period plans were well underway for the Center, but not yet executed.(33)

It would be impossible to examine each individual Verein in detail, or to chronicle them here. The focus, therefore, will be on the largest Verein, and the one that represented the widest possible cross-section of the ethnic community, the Pionier-Verein. Founded in 1868 it existed for 93 years until March 1961. It was formed to strengthen old friendships, establish new ones, and to record German pioneer history for future generations. Its national reputation was based on its outstanding historical journal, Der Deutsche Pionier (1869-87), edited from 1874-85 by H.A. Rattermann, a self-taught historian, co-founder and secretary of the German Mutual Fire Insurance Company of Cincinnati. After 1887 it published an annual entitled Vorstandsbericht des Deutschen Pionier-Vereins which contains the proceedings of the Verein as well as obituaries that constitute extensive biographical essays. Because of these yearbooks a wealth of information is available on the Verein in the period under investigation by this study.

The Pionier-Verein, hereafter PV, was not only the largest, most representative, but perhaps the most influential German-American secular organization in the 1920s in Cincinnati. Originally, members had to be German immigrants, male, 40 years or older and residents of Cincinnati for 25 years. In 1930 the requirements were changed so that all U.S. citizens with a command of the German language could join. Although German was used in the yearbooks, English language addresses were delivered increasingly throughout the 1920s by members of the American-born second generation. Membership in the PV grew steadily, but declined in the 1920s with a high point in membership of 1025 for 1925:

Year	Membership	Year	Membership
1890	343	1923	1025
1900	667	1924	1011
1910	865	1925	940
1917	1095	1926	954
1918	1015	1927	918
1920	1004	1928	820
1921	1009	1929	786
1922	957	1930	741
		1931	699 (34)

The PV motto was **Willenskraft-Wege** schafft, or "where there's a will there's a way." The annual calendar of events included monthly meetings, an annual business meeting for the selection of officers, the installation of officers meeting, the Washington Birthday Celebration, and the anniversary celebration, the Stiftungsfest. The latter Fest, usually held in May or June at the Cincinnati Zoological Gardens, became a popular ethnic event, especially since German Day was not celebrated until 1926. Outings were also frequently scheduled to enjoyable places, such as Inwood Park. The pioneers enjoyed festivities, at the center of which was usually an address by a prominent local German-American, and/or the presentation of an original poem or two by a local poet. Monthly meetings included addresses, lectures and talks on a wide variety of topics. While the regionally-based mutual aid societies did not appear to attract the second generation, and indeed substantially declined in number, the PV appears to have attracted more of their number. It included German-Americans from labor, the trades, business and the professions, as can be seen by a reading of their yearbooks.

To place an examination of the PV in historical context the fiftieth anniversary of the Verein in the summer of 1918 will be the point of departure. In 1918 the local police chief provided permission to hold public celebrations only under the condition that the English language wold be used for song- and speechmaking. The fiftieth anniversary celebration, Stiftungs-fest, scheduled for 15 June was almost canceled, but the police chief then granted the necessary permission under the aforementioned conditions. The fest took place under police surveillance so that a German language address prepared by Rev. Andreas Nemenz was, of course, dropped from the program, but printed in the yearbook. The yearbook editor termed the whole fiftieth anniversary affair as "ungemütlich." The address of Andreas Nemenz stated:

> From the moment when our land entered the war there existed only one way for us, it is the way of the pioneer, it is the way of duty and loyalty. It is true, it cut deeply into our heart, to fight the old homeland. However, the time for debate was over ... the majority of the people had spoken through its representatives -- the dice had fallen.

He knew that they would have to endure "accusations, persecutions, and slander" in silence. However, silent suffering would have to be endured even if it meant going "to Gethsemane." (35)

Nevertheless the PV not only survived the war, but attained its highest membership in the 1920s. Perhaps there was safety in numbers, but the society appears to have been one of the most socially acceptable of the Vereine. The ACL did not celebrate its German Day until 1925, and in the intervening years the summer Stiftungsfest took on the status of a community-wide affair. By July 1920 the PV had 1004 members, and reported sixty-eight new ones. The organization was also fortunate to have at its disposal the services of quality officers and directors during the 1920s. They were men from the professions, business and industry, some of them quite successful. Its honorary members in the 1920s were H.A. Rattermann and Dr.

H.H. Fick, the foremost German men of letters in Cincinnati at
that time.   Lectures in the 1920-21 Vereinsjahr were presented
by Emil Schiele; Emil Kramer, a former teacher of German; and
the pastors Andreas Nemenz, Erich Becker, Dr. F.L. Dorn, and
Hans Haupt.   One notes here the active involvement of the Kirchendeutschen in the PV, as opposed to other secular organizations.   Non-members also spoke to the group.   Former Judge
Hugh L.   Nichols spoke on U.S. Grant and was introduced by A.K.
Nippert who was described as "humane judge of liberal views"
and a "friend of German-Americans."(36)

     The Washington Birthday Celebration in February 1921, held
at the Central Turnhalle, offers some insight into Cincinnati
German perspectives on various issues.   The yearbook editor
claimed that the citizen of German descent understands Washington exactly as did Washington the German-Americans and their
patriotism.   Henry Overmann, president of the PV, decried the
false patriotism of the so-called 100% Americans as well as
those who categorized the War of Independence "from the British
yoke" as a mistake.   He then reminded the pioneers that Harding
had been elected "by millions of true Americans," but the mention of the name Harding brought forth such "jubilation" that
it took some time for Overmann to conclude his speech.   The
main address by Alfred Bettinger reveals the depth of sentiment
regarding the war.   The framework of his comments was praise of
the German element's role in the building of the nation.   Particular reference was made to Baron von Steuben, Washington's
all-German bodyguard under the command of Bartholomäus von
Heer, and the German participation in the Civil War.   According
to the speaker, German-American contributions had been generally recognized until the war, German influences on the material, moral and intellectual development of the land had never
been criticized.   Ethnic institutions had only aimed at
preserving "the best" of German culture.   No one had ever ques-
tioned loyalty to the adopted fatherland.   Unfortunately the
war had brought the German name into disrepute.   Houses and

offices were searched, papers and documents had been confisca-
ted in an attempt to locate proof of disloyalty. German Vereine and meeting places stood under the suspicion of being
breeding grounds of treasonous thoughts and deeds.

The German name was brought into such disfavor that the
word "German" was removed by businesses in an attempt to prove
loyalty. Individuals in business and educational institutions
were summarily dismissed from their positions they had held for
years. Old speeches by Americans which praised the German element were disavowed or modified. Street and family names were
changed. "Every reminder of German participation or German
influences on the development of America was eliminated wherever possible." Furthermore, German-American patriotism during
the war was never fully appreciated. According to Bettinger,
there was at least one man who could understand the spirit and
heart of German-Americana, and had demonstrated the courage to
express it: Sen. Warren G. Harding. On 31 March 1917 he had
stated at the Businessmen's Club that he understood the sorrow
of German-Americans at the sight of their homeland and the land
of their choice entangled in the conflict of war. The _Freie
Presse_ reported favorably to the PV's Washington Celebration,
referring to Bettinger as "one of our best," and declared "we
have not sunken so deeply that the celebration of freedom from
British tyranny cannot be celebrated."(37)

In June 1921 a PV member, the poet Jerome Iffland, presented a cycle of his poems entitled "The Pioneer, how he
thinks and feels." It should be noted that no issue of the
yearbook of the PV failed to contain at least several poems,
most of them by Iffland and H.H. Fick. In July officers were
installed with the main address presented by Charles Schmidt,
the popular president of the Combined Singers and the North
American Sängerbund. He stated that the PV represented not
only the male members, but their entire families which amounted
to approximately five thousand people, or one percent of the

city's population. For 53 years the PV had preserved its German-American character and cared for the German language, song, customs and traditions. That this blended well with American patriotism was demonstrated by the annual celebration of Washington's birthday. He observed that peace had finally been concluded with Germany. To the "lying word" of the former President Wilson he dedicated a strophe of verse: "President he became and drove / us into the war, false love of peace / brought him a Nobel Prize / he should be made into mincemeat."(38)

The Stiftungsfest was celebrated at Reichrath's Park, 3720 Spring Grove Avenue. The contrast with the 50th anniversary of the PV was particularly emphasized. Then there were police present and no German language songs or speeches had been permitted. The yearbook editor noted that all three generations of German-Americans were present at the fest and that representatives of many Vereine were present. Near-beer was referred to as "Fern-Bier," or distant beer. The main speech by Charles Schmidt referred to recent events. He stated that the war "brought us Hell with the 100% Americans condemning everything German that had previously been praised and regarded highly. And Uncle Sam's spectacles had been covered with English fog. But in the last election the German-Americans had helped clean his lens so that the lies of the war could be seen." He hoped that the U.S. would see how "war lies" and prohibition were spoiling the character of the American people "which loses all respect for the laws." The U.S. government was losing tax money from beer, wine, and schnapps. Referring to Judge Nippert, he hoped that in spite of his busy affairs in Washington D.C. that he would have time "to speak German with our Uncle Sam." Clearly the U.S. would see that it had no better citizens and friends than the German immigrants and their families. He concluded "All German-America does its duty, following it always, even if it breaks its heart."(39)

The editor of the 1921-22 yearbook commented in the introduction with pride that the PV had survived the blind rage
against everything German, and emphasized that in spite of all
attempts to humiliate and destroy the Germans they would continue to play a leading role. Lectures for the year were presented by Dr. H.H. Fick, Paul Ortmann, Dr. Adolf Morgenstern,
and Pastor Dorn. Dr. Morgenstern spoke of his trip to his
parental home in East Prussia in 1914. He indicated that all
of his brothers were army officers, but that no one over there
had desired war.(40)

The Washington Celebration was held in February 1922 at
the Turnhalle again. With regard to school history textbooks
Henry Overmann, the PV president, declared that they were
splendid for British schools, but of no value for American
schools. The main address was presented by Judge Nippert on
"George Washington and the Demands of the Hour." He maintained
that Washington's advice against involvement in European
affairs had not been heeded, and now the U.S. was up to its
neck "in intrigues, lurking-places, and deceit." The World War
was fought in the name of democracy and freedom, but in actuality there was "now less true democracy and more unfreedom, more
misery and distress" than before the war. A grave had been
shoveled here for truth and beside it had been laid "freedom,
humanity, and justice."(41)

A March 1922 presentation by Dr. K.L. Stoll offered the
Cincinnati physician to recount his experiences regarding his
internment in England from 1915-18. He had been captured by
the British on his way from Cincinnati to Germany in 1915 on a
neutral Danish ship named the United States. After overcoming
"anger, indignation, and vexation" he settled down to life as
an internee with several other physicians for the duration of
the war. Fro 1918-21 he traveled to Germany to assist at various military hospitals. After six years he finally returned
home again to Cincinnati.(42)

In April Carl Pletz, former editor of the now defunct
<u>Volksblatt</u>, presented a lecture on the early German settlers of
the Miami Valley with particular reference to Christian Wald-
schmidt. The Stiftungsfest, held in July 1922, took place at
the Cincinnati Zoological Garden, with the main addresses being
delivered by Dr. H.H. Fick and Charles Schmidt. Fick's
address, a quaint autobiographical piece, essayed his experiences since his immigration 60 years ago. Diplomatically, as
was his custom, he gracefully avoided any mention of the war
which had destroyed the bilingual program he had administered
and devoted his life to. However, he did advise "We must stand
up for ourselves, on <u>the</u> <u>other</u> <u>side</u> they are only too quick and
too willing to misunderstand and belittle us." (Emphasis mine.)
Schmidt greeted the gathering with the verse:

> Grüss Gott zum Fest der Pioniere,
> Vereint im Zoo, dem Park der Thiere,
> Den Schönsten Garten uns'rer Stadt,
> Ein Deutscher angelegt ihn hat!

Schmidt invited all who could sing to join the singing society.
He stated that German-Americans had two important tasks to ful-
fill. First, they must eliminate and enlighten all the misun-
derstandings and false assertions remaining from the war.
Second, they must work to establish good relations between
Germany and America.(43)

The 1923-24 yearbook indicated that the PV membership had
climbed to an all-time high of 1025 members and that 76 new
ones had been obtained. At the installation of officers the
poet Iffland held the main address. He stated that German-
Americans were not ashamed of their origin. "We are proud of
our names, which we will never deny, and we request our descendants to follow the same course, to always step in, when liars
and slanderers misconstrue our intentions, and turn us into
enemies in a hateful manner." He stated that the PV had

survived many a storm and threat but had stood through an evil
time when liars and rascals attempted to eliminate everything
"that spoke German, wrote German and sang German." All that
was desired now was justice, truth and freedom. The PV recognized that the German language had suffered. It had fallen
victim to the war hysteria in churches, schools, newspapers,
the theater, and the societies, according to Iffland. He
noted, however, that the recognition was gaining ground, that
the suppression of everything German had been a blow to cultural progress. He emphasized that the German press, the Vereine
and the churches must be supported.(44)

In October 1923 Rev. R.R. Fillbrandt spoke on the topic of
"Lodge and Church in America." He spoke against the secular
Forty-Eighter spirit in the lodges, but also attacked the
spreading spirit of American Calvinism in German-American churches. In November Rev. Haupt spoke on "New York a Century Ago"
while in December Rev. Erich Becker spoke on "America's Responsibility for the Terrible Consequences of the World War."
Becker referred to the war guilt clause of the Treaty of
Versailles as a "monstrous lie," finding France, Russia and
England as the actual guilty culprits. He discussed the "propaganda of lies" that incited a peaceful America against
Germany. "Our own president Wilson introduced a campaign
against hyphenated Americans, through which the Germandom in
our country ... had to suffer heavily." The U.S. entered the
war to save the millions it had lent to the Allies, according
to Becker. America was responsible that the promise of the
Fourteen Points as the basis for peace had been "contemptuously
broken." America had not protested against the renewed hunger
blockade against Germany which had resulted in 800,000 deaths.
Congress had erred in granting Wilson dictatorial powers during
the war. In Europe the consequence had been disastrous. In
America "a deep split" had been rendered since "the degradation
and unjustice" suffered by German-Americans can not and should
not be forgotten.(45)

Other lectures of the 1923-24 year included Dr. K.L. Stoll
discussing "Eulenspiegel 2200 Years Ago, 700 Years Ago, and
Today"; Dr. F.L. Dorn on "Healing Systems"; Dr. H.H. Fick reading from German-American literature; Emil Kramer on "Petrol-
eum"; Dr. A.F. Morgenstern on his western travels; and Jerome
Iffland on present day German pioneers. Iffland claimed that
"what we want is that no hindrance be placed in our way when we
want to teach our descendants the German language and the
German song ... we want peace and not war." He also remarked
that "Our descendants will see and thankfully remember in later
times that their fathers were not cowards but men who lived in
a difficult time. They will be proud of us, their names and
their ancestry."(46)

The 1924 Washington Celebration, held in the Labor Temple
at 13th and Walnut, was dedicated to the suffering children of
Germany. The main address was delivered by the ever popular
Judge Nippert. He reiterated the central points item by item
from Washington's farewell address, which he claimed, had not
been followed during the war. He noted that it was the 100%ers
in Washington D.C. who spoke now of undesirable immigrants with
chauvinistic phrases. They were "betrayers, hypocrites," and
"thieves." War veterans were being betrayed for millions of
dollars, taxpayers skinned while "the little man is scalped by
the great patriots. And one party is almost as bad as the
other." He closed expressing the hope that a Washington or
Lincoln would emerge in American politics. Charles Schmidt
then spoke, stating that Washington chose Germans as his body-
guards since he knew that they were loyally devoted to him.
Further references were made to Steuben and President Taft's
speech in 1910 at the unveiling of the Steuben monument in the
park across from the White House. Taft had said that the German element was "a great and prominent part of our population"
and had contributed its full part to the building and development of the U.S.(47)

At the 1925 Stiftungsfest Judge William H. Lueders sketch-
ed briefly the history of Cincinnati and its German element.
Then Schmidt spoke with his usual enthusiasm. He was followed
by PV secretary, Conrad Krager. He stated with respect to the
war that the old Alliance had been one of the war's first
victims, falling "on the altar of fanaticism." It had been in
actuality "a true guardian of personal liberty." Hardly was it
dead "than the serpent of prohibition rose its horrible
head..." He commented that "the smashing of an eighty year old
cultural work, the German language instructional program, is
another example of blind destructive rage." Finally Krager
noted that German-Americans had waited, but in vain, for an
apology for the wrongs committed against the German element.
Regardless of past events, he observed that the PV had reached
its goal of one thousand members, and that the Germans were an
invaluable and irreplaceable part of the American nation. Lectures during the year were presented by Hans Haupt, H.H. Fick,
Emil Kramer, Rev. Becker, Georg F. Moser, and Dr. K.L. Stoll,
while the Washington birthdy address was delivered by Hans
Haupt.(48)

The 1926-27 year included lectures by Stoll, Hermann Barnstorff, Adolf Varrellmann, Moser, and Richard Greninger.
Subjects ranged from travel talks to Ohio history. At the 1927
Washington Celebration Haupt gave the main address with a
discussion of German pioneers. He had "much to say on the
Antagonism" which the English had displayed to the German immigrants in the past. Iffland then presented a poem on Cincinnati German history while Dr. Moser of the Freie Presse also
presented a poem. The 1927 Stiftungsfest in the Zoological
Gardens was described as "a great success." Significantly
enough the main address was presented in English and by a member of the second generation. Walter Schwaab, son of Judge
Schwaab, spoke about the PV and the history of the Germans in
Ohio. He called to the youth to follow their forefathers and
their ideals. Schwaab was followed by Rev. Henry Hübschmann

who reminded the younger generation to care for and preserve "the good and beautiful" that their parents had planted and created here.(49)

In March 1928 the PV named the Rev. Hans Haupt as an honorary member for his manifold services for "the furthering of everything good, true and beautiful." At the 1928 Washington Celebration Judge Nippert presented the main address. After ten years the experiences of the war could not be forgotten. He mentioned the persecution and the lies about the Huns. The U.S., he advised, should embrace the principles of Washington's Farewell Address. He referred to prohibition as a threat to freedom. The yearbook editor notes that Nippert's address was enthusiastically received.(50)

The 1928 Stiftungsfest, held at the Zoological Garden, celebrated the 60th anniversary of the PV. Nelson Schwaab, an American-born German and a lawyer, spoke on the necessity of performing "pioneer work" now and in the future. For the German language address the Rev. Erich Becker focused in an important address on what he saw as the basic problem with American society. The essential flaw he identified as a fanatical reforming zeal. He claimed that zealous reform movements resulted usually in prohibitions. "Professional" reformers were responsible for the great evils of the day, especially for the prohibition of the 1920s. He elaborated on the problem of this "fanatic zeal" of the reformers. This, according to Becker, was not a German-American characteristic. German-Americans, he claimed, were not given to such extremes. They worked hard, but they liked to celebrate with gaiety and festivity, and they had a basic right thereto. A cheerful joy of life was as necessary as one's daily bread, according to Becker.(51)

Among the many 1927-28 lectures the most lengthy one reported in the yearbook was that of Becker on "The German Farm in Cleveland." This farm, Die Deutsche Zentrale (the German Central), was in actuality a German house situated on a small piece of land in the country outside of Cleveland. It was open to all in the Cleveland German community and offered a place where festivities, classes, and various programs could be held. This was of special interest because of the Cincinnati Club Center, begun in 1926 by Dr. A.F. Morgenstern, aimed also to construct a center similar to that in Cleveland. By 1928 this group had changed its name to be formally known as the German House Society, an indication that it was no longer necessary to use euphemistic expressions with regard to the German House being planned.(52)

Lecture topics for 1929 included discussions on Christmas customs in the Black Forest and the discovery of the South Pole. At the 1929 Stiftungsfest Erwin G. Schuessler, a lawyer and state legislator, presented the main address extolling praise on German-American "contributions." Present day German-Americans had every reason to be proud of their forefathers and to honor their past. Arthur Schaub, president of the German House Society also spoke. The main speaker at the 1930 Stiftungsfest was Hermann Barnstorff of the _Freie Presse_. The yearbook editor referred to the PV as a "bulwark of the Germandom of the city" and as a "preserver of the old beautiful traditions of its founders."(53)

In the 1930-31 yearbook it was announced that the PV invested $200 in the German House that was being planned for. The editor admonished readers to "preserve and care for the community ... hold together and in unity establish firmly a proud German-America." The editor referred to the recently deceased editor of the _Deutsch-Amerikanische Geschichtsblatter_, Dr. Julius Goebel, who felt that immigrants and their descendants should become familiar with their own history.(54)

At the installation of officers for the 1930-31 year
Charles Schmidt stated that "Our slanderers have fallen silent
in ten years" and the PV had stood the test with honors. Lectures continued on a wide variety of topics, e.g., Jacob Haas
of the Freie Presse spoke on "Experiences as a War Prisoner in
Siberia." At the 1931 Washington Celebration, Dr. K.L. Stoll
spoke on the topic of Frederick the Great. The yearbook also
reported on the demise of Charles Schmidt, a major leader in
the world of the vereine. Schmidt (1851-1930) received a full
two page obituary in the annual. He had been a successful businessman, the founder and president of the still existing
Cincinnati Butchers Supply Co. Since 1898 he had been president of the North American Sängerbund and was known nationally
as the "Sängervater." Locally he was president of the Combined
Singers, a member of the Turngemeinde, the Germanistic Society,
the Altenheim-Verein and was an honorary member of the PV.
Only earlier in the year Schmidt had delivered the main address
during the installation of officers meeting. At the 1931 Stiftungsfest, held at the Zoological Garden, many were in attendance so that the event became "a fest of the Germandom of the
city." President Karl Roling reminded listeners during his
address to speak German with their children and to read the
German language press. The address of Heinrich Klohe from the
Freie Presse was the first that touched directly on the economic crisis of the Great Depression. He felt that the sad
contemporary times were the consequences of the Great War.
Nevertheless, the fest was well attended and the PV dedicated
its new society flag. (55)

The 1931-32 annual indicated that membership had sunk to
681 with only eighteen new members for the year. The editor
stated that the time of economic distress was at hand, but that
all should stand together. Lectures for the year were presented by Haupt, Nippert, Moser, Kramer and others. Because of the
economic situation no public Washington Celebration was held,
but a PV monthly meeting was dedicated to Washington's birth-

day. The 1932 Stiftungsfest was held in July at the Zoological
Garden as usual. Addresses were presented by Rev. R.R. Fillbrandt and E.G. Schuessler. The former stated that the PV had
remained true to its ideals for 64 years in spite of the past
difficult times. Vereine, he declared, were a necessity for
the preservation of German ideals. Once there was a time, he
noted, when German art, scholarship, music, literature, churches and schools had been admired. The purpose of the PV was
to preserve and care for these various splendid possessions.
It had done so in the past and could, therefore, celebrate its
anniversary with pride. Schuessler, the American born speaker,
traced the role of the German-American in American history
since the eighteenth century. He exclaimed that "their patriotism and loyalty can never be brought into question." The
editor closed the annual by observing that the mood of the fest
left nothing to be desired in spite of the absence of beer.
(56) Finally, it should be noted that Volume 64 of the Vorstandsbericht for 1931-32 was the last year the PV published a
substantial annual. It usually ran on the average aproximately
50 pages. One of the most lengthy appeared with Volume 53,
1920-21, which contained 77 pages. However, Volume 64, 1931-
32, contained only 22 pages. Thereafter, only brief four-page
reports were published. The depression along with the rising
costs of printing had obviously contributed to the cutting back
on the issuance of a more lengthy report.(57)

One of the most striking features about the Vereine was
not only their survival of the Great War and their ability to
stage a comeback after the war, but their longevity beyond the
founding immigrant generation, e.g., the Turngemeinde marked
its 75th year in 1923 and the Pionier-Verein its 60th in 1928.
However, there were also several other Vereine which celebrated
their 50th anniversaries in the latter years of the period
under consideration: The German Literary Club, the Cincinnati
Baecker Gesang-Verein and the Teutonia Maenner- und Damenchor.
(58) And by the latter years of the period, Vereine were not

only marking, but were now celebrating their anniversaries with festivals and concerts. The increased activity and festivity of the Vereine found expression in the annual German Day which once again became a popular fest. In 1930 it was moved from the Cincinnati Zoological Garden to Coney Island where its attendance increased substantially. This was partly due to the fact that an amusement park was located at Coney Island, an attraction point for children. Also, the fest was now introduced by a parade of the local Vereine, the Turner and the Jugendchor from the German language school at the Turnhalle. The times had changed since November 1918. According to Jacob Herz, by 1930 Cincinnati's Germandom and the Vereine were again experiencing "an upswing."(59) The total number of people claimed to be represented by the Vereine was ten thousand, or close to the pre-war number of Verein-members.

Religious Institutions

It would be impossible here to examine each individual religious body and congregation, as in the case of the Vereine it was impossible to focus on each individual Verein. An attempt will, therefore, be made to focus on a large Protestant religious body, the German Methodists; and the German Jews and the German Catholics.

The predicament of the German-American Methodists during the Great War had not been alleviated by President Wilson's impetuous question to a Methodist Bishop, "Who are the German Methodists?" His question only served to cast the veil of suspicion upon the ten German Conferences of the Methodist Episcopal Church.(60) During the war the German Methodists were not allowed to preach or pray in German during their religious services. Their journal, Der Christliche Apologete, was forced to file translations of its articles with the local postal authorities so that it decided to publish all war-related or political news in the English language for reasons of safety and security.

The Cincinnati Enquirer announced three days after the 1918 Armistice that the "Hun Tongue" was going to remain in the churches of the German Methodists. Pastors of local Methodist churches declared that German would not be dropped from services, although the Methodist Board of Home Missions and Church Extension recommended that no assistance be granted churches "in which other than the English language is used." Bishop William F. Anderson of Cincinnati had been a strong supporter of this recommendation at the board meeting in Philadelphia. The district superintendent of the Methodist Episcopal Church in Cincinnati expressed the hope that "all German churches soon would be converted into English-language churches." The German Conferences were sub-units of the Methodist Episcopal Church. The majority of the Church's conferences were English-speaking. He claimed that "any other action would indicate more than a protest against a change of language; it would be a protest against Americanism itself." German Methodists faced, therefore, opposition not only from outside the Methodist Episcopal Church, but also from within their own church body. Local German Methodist ministers nevertheless stated that they would not comply with the recommendation of Bishop Anderson since they were financially independent. The Rev. H. Rogatsky, pastor of Spring Grove Avenue German Methodist Church, indicated that "he had not thought of changing the language." Because of the Armistice churches were now free to re-introduce the German language, but the war experience had deeply marked and altered the nature of the German Methodist Conferences.(61)

The war adversely affected German-American Methodism in two ways. First, it "had struck a staggering blow at their faith in Christian brotherhood." This profound sense of demoralization was pervasive, and best expressed by one Methodist leader:

Our preachers lost faith in our leaders. Many of
them were so utterly disappointed that many would
have left the ministry but for the fact that that
would have meant intolerable privations for their
families. The war experiences reduced them to become
bread servants; men, who formerly were most loyal and
enthusiastic ministers of the gospel and patriotic
citizens. (62)

Secondly, the war and its lingering animosities had dealt
a lethal blow to the preservation of the German language in the
German Methodist Conferences. Although banned during the war,
the language was immediately re-introduced after the war.
However, the conclusion could not be escaped that the German-
language mission work, begun by Wilhelm Nast in Cincinnati in
1835, was now in the process of a linguistic transition to English.

A 1924 Report of the Foreign Language Commission to the
Methodist General Conference indicated that in the German Conferences 43% of the congregations reported use of the German
language while 57% had made the transition to English. The
language shift was even stronger within the Central German Conference, to which the Cincinnati German Methodists belonged.
In the Central Conference only 26.9% of the congregations reported use of the German language while 73.1% had made the
language shift to English.

The transition to English was slow, but inevitable. The
process succeeded roughly in the following manner. First,
English would be used in Sunday schools or in the Young People's Society meetings. Next an occasional English church service would be held. As the process continued German services
would be maintained on Sunday morning, but the other services,
with the possible exception of prayer meetings and adult Bible
classes, would shift to the use of the English language. A
final stage would be reached in which all activities of the

church would be conducted in English, with the possible exception of a German Sunday class. Sometimes this plan was varied by offering German services on alternative Sunday mornings or by having the German service follow or precede the English service. The end stage would be when the German language no longer was used in any of the congregational services, classes or activities.

The war in essence created a definite generation gap based on linguistic factors. German Methodist churches became more and more the churches for the older generation. They had more ministers between the ages of 60 and 80 than between the ages of 20 and 40. Young German-American Methodists were increasingly studying at English-language theological seminaries and joining the English-language conferences of the Methodist Episcopal Church. One German Methodist commented that "These young men had lost their linguistic patriotism." Given the nativist nature of the time it is not difficult to understand their loss of such "patriotism." A further hindrance to the German conferences was the fact that their salaries were somewhat lower than those offered by the English conferences. The poor salary situation, therefore, made the German conferences all the more undesirable. (63)

An ecclesiastical administrative dilemma was created due to the fact that the German and English Methodist parishes and conferences overlapped one another, causing numerous duplication of effort problems. Liquidation of the German conferences and merger into the larger English conferences appeared to many to be the only inevitable solution. Nevertheless, it was "a difficult task to be acknowledged by those who loved the German Methodist work with an unsurpassed passion."(64) However, most German Conference churches now held their services in English. Moreover, they could not man their own pulpits or professional education chairs since most young men now entered the English conferences. For example, in 1925 only three of the 25 gradu-

ates of Central Wesleyan College joined into German conferences, the rest entering service in the English conferences. In
1924 the North German Conference became the first of the ten
German Conferences to merge with an English-speaking conference, the Minnesota Conference. A final last-ditch effort to
fight off the liquidation/merger movement was led by the Central German Conference under the direction of Cincinnati German
Methodists.

The opposition to merger was led by John A. Diekmann,
Superintendent of Bethesda Institutions; August J. Bucher,
editor of the _Apologete_; and F.W. Mueller, of the Board of Home
Missions and Christian Extension. The Central German Conference had begun its study of the possibility of merger in 1929
by forming a Committee on Conference Policy. Its report was
presented in 1930 and in 1932 it proposed a petition for an
enabling act to the General Conference. Cincinnati German
Methodists vigorously opposed the merger presenting a widely
disseminated argument against the merger. It argued that in
the majority of the German congregations the merger question
had not been a matter of any interest, nor had it been a topic
of discussion. Moreover, the laity was not pushing for the
merger at all. According to pastoral reports, German congregations would not merge with nearby English congregations but
continue to maintain their own churches. The merger, it was
felt, would lead to a loss of a distinct and valuable type of
Methodism. Also, it would mean that the days of the _Apologete_
would be numbered. However, the protest was futile. In August
1933 the old Central German Conference, including all the Cincinnati German Methodist churches, merged into the English-
speaking Ohio Conference. Emil T. Klotz, Superintendent of the
Ohio District of the Central Conference, wistfully closed the
German-American Conference's last session:

As the time draws near when the name of our dear
Conference is to be wiped from the records of the

Methodist Episcopal Church, a sadness creeps into my heart that I cannot express. You may call this a wedding, and possibly it is, but I have seen tears flow at weddings as well as at funerals. May I close with these words of Saint Paul: Finally, brethren, farewell. Be perfect, be of good comfort, be of one mind, live in peace and the God of love and peace shall be with you. The grace of our Lord Jesus Christ and the love of God and the communion of the Holy Spirit be with you all. Amen.(65)

Der Christliche Apologete reminded its readers not to forget it:

And last but not least, do not forget the _Apologete_. As the last bond which still unites and holds into relationship the German Methodist family in America, Europe, and the world. Defend it, subscribe to it, otherwise it is consecrated to its demise.

The _Apologete_ survived the period investigated by this study. The Methodist Book Concern in Cincinnati published five other German language journals in this period also: _Die Kleine Glocke_, the _Heiden Frauenfreund_, _Der Bibelforscher_, _Deutscher Kalender_, and the _Haus und Herd_. Two were direct casualties of the Germanophobia engendered by the war, two others ceased publication in the 1920s, and only the _Apologete_ and the _Bibelforscher_ survived until 1941 and 1940 respectively. The driving force behind the anti-merger movement in the Central German Conference, and a leading figure among Cincinnati German Methodists, was the American-born John A. Diekmann, President of the Bethesda Institutions of Cincinnati. Within these institutions a Museum of German Methodism was housed and organized by Sister Julia Gross, Curator. In later years it was Diekmann's "determination to preserve the unity and institutions of German Methodism" that kept the _Apologete_ "robust and active." (66)

The historian of the German-American Methodists wrote regarding the conclusion of the merger movement:

The United States had taken to itself the people of
Europe and made them its citizens. They in turn had
contributed their efforts and their culture to the
building of richly pluralistic American culture as
the gift of one of the groups in the polyglot human
structure of the New World. To hundreds of thousands
of German-speaking immigrants, the Methodist Episcopal Church has proclaimed the gospel of a common
Fatherhood, a universal brotherhood, and a common
quest--the forgiveness of human sins by the grace of
God, as Nast said, more abundant than man's
needs. (67)

According to the history, "The immigrant home found a center in
the Church. The Church was ambitious to train the minds of its
youth, hence the progression through the Church to the church
school was natural. American culture was built from the inter-
action of immigrant souls on the national frontiers. From the
immigrant homes flowed the stream of youth to become the sub-
stance of American life." German Methodism "was a part of
America. It helped to make American culture. It joined the
mind, culture, and soul of two continents in the Christian home
and gave to life a purpose which is only created by genuine
faith and conviction." (68)

The Jewish population of Cincinnati in 1918 numbered
approximately 18,000 and was distributed as follows: 56% in the
Over-the-Rhine/downtown district, 22% in Avondale, 9% in Walnut
Hills, 6% in Price Hill, and 2%-3% in Clifton. In 1930 the
Jewish population numbered approximately 20,000, and was distributed as follows: 77% in Avondale, 11% in Price Hill, 5% in
the West End, 5% in the suburbs of Clifton, Hyde Park and Norwood, and 2% in Walnut Hills. Therefore, in the 1920s the
Jewish population shifted almost en masse from the old Over-
the-Rhine downtown sections to Avondale. This out-migration
paralleled that of the rest of the German-American population
out of the central city to the suburbs. (69)

Like the German Methodists, Cincinnati's German Jews had not escaped the Germanophobia engendered by the war. A visible target and one that nativists set their sights on was the learned professor of history and religion at Hebrew Union College, Dr. Gotthard Deutsch. He had not only been actively involved in the activities of the Vereinsdeutschen, but was generally recognized as one of their most articulate spokesmen. As in the case of other community leaders, such as Schwaab and Nippert, Deutsch would fall prey to the negative aspects of the period's Zeitgeist.

The nativist attack on Deutsch was a major affair that would shake Hebrew Union College (hereafter HUC), to its very foundation. During the war "in a highly charged atmosphere of intense patriotism which allowed for litle tolerance of divergent opinion" the patriotism and loyalty of Dr. Deutsch, "the most senior and venerated member of the faculty" came into question so that the board almost dismissed him from his position. Deutsch remained culturally a German, his own children speaking German before they learned English. His own diary was written in German and Hebrew. The 1917 U.S. declaration of war against Germany unsettled Deutsch so that he was unable to conduct the seder and could not attend chapel for six months. His sons joined the U.S. armed forces, but Deutsch was clearly anti-war. He actively became involved in the left-wing pacifist group, the People's Council for Democracy and Peace. On 5 October 1917 he barely escaped a raid by local detectives and the U.S. Secret Service on the anti-war group's meeting. However, the next day the Cincinnati Post listed him as one of the group's leaders. The HUC Board of Governors' Chairman, who had already been receiving police reports on the activities of Deutsch, could no longer ignore the situation. (70)

Edward Heinsheiner, the board president, declared after American entrance into the war in the HUC chapel that any students "who openly expressed disloyalty would be subject to expulsion." That such a warning was made indicates the existence of anti-war sentiment. After warnings Deutsch severed his associations with the People's Council. He specifically was warned that he might be dismissed and was requested to dissociate from the peace group. Then a bombshell incident took place. Deutsch was called to Federal Court as a character witness for a friend's naturalization. The judge asked Deutsch who he wanted to win the war. Considering the question altogether inappropriate to the proceedings at hand, Dr. Deutsch refused to answer. This news received front page coverage in the Cincinnati Enquirer so that Deutsch was again called to the Board of Governors of HUC. A decision was made to publicly display a loyalty statement at the College:

> The Hebrew Union College was founded to have the young men whom it educates for the ministry to preach and teach Reform Judaism and promulgate the American ideas and ideals. Loyalty and patriotism have characterized the institution since its establishment.
>
> This is our country. We know no other fatherland than the land in which we live and no other flag than the flag which floats over it. Our country is at war and all of its citizens must not be passively, but actively loyal and patriotic. No one who does not subscribe to these sentiments is welcome within the walls of the College.

In December the Board voted ten to nine to censure Dr. Deutsch, some favoring outright dismissal. Fortunately, several Cincinnatians (Oscar Berman, Felix Kahn, Alfred Mack, Murray Seasongood and Alfred M. Cohen, the new president of HUC) "were willing to buck public opinion to retain Deutsch. Still a minority of the faculty battled for Deutsch's dismissal, "dredging up new and damaging evidence regarding the extent of his pro-Germanism." Samuel Ach, a member of the board, resigned rather than continue to associate with the College.(71)

The Rev. Madison C. Peters of New York, who came to deliver an address in 1917 at the Sons of Veterans meetings in Cincinnati at Memorial Hall, referred to Deutsch as one of those
"exceptional Jews today [who] are so loud in their traitorous
activities that the American can't hear the patriotic Jew."
Peters claimed that Deutsch had no place in America "no more
... than a weasel in a henhouse ..." and that Deutsch's "place
is in Berlin." The American Israelite carried Deutsch's articles and columns until October 1917, indicating the existence
of some German Jewish reservations with respect to the war.
Leo Wise, publisher, found it necessary, however, to lecture
Deutsch "on the duties of Jews to be superloyal" and requested
him to refrain from writing anything detrimental to England or
beneficial to Germany. Deutsch was forced to drop his byline
and soon severed his connections with the paper. To what
extent Deutsch reflected German Jewish sentiment in Cincinnati
is impossible to ascertain. However, his case certainly illu-
minates the predicament of those who placed a high value on
their German heritage.(72)

Boris D. Bogen, Director of the United Jewish Charities of
Cincinnati, wrote:

> It was a seasoned and well-rooted Jewry that I found
> in this mid-Western city. The leaders spoke English
> with a decided German accent and the prominence and
> the prestige of Cincinnati Jewry was in their hands.(73)

The item to be emphasized here is linguistic. The war had
accelerated the language shift among German-Americans, as was
noted with the German Methodists, and the German Jews were no
exception here. However, in a sense they may have been better
prepared for the cultural shock for two reasons. First, the
German Jews by the 1920s were largely an American-born population. Jewish immigrants to Cincinnati had been mainly from
Germany unti the 1880s. In 1882 the first of the great Russian
exoduses occurred, caused by the persecution of the Czar.

Also, in 1900 persecution had caused the immigration of Rumanian Jews. Therefore, from the 1880s to the 1920s there was no large German Jewish immigration to Cincinnati. By the end of the period under investigation Cincinnati "had one of the most native born Jewish communities in America, largely due to the fact that Cincinnati has had practically no immigration since 1902, and that in 1931 the cessation of immigration to these shores of the U.S. has become practically complete." (74) Second, Cincinnati's German-American Jews stressed the German tradition of assimilation. This has been the central thrust of Reform Judaism. The form and spirit of Judaism which Isaac M. Wise had advocated "were an organic adaptation to the American scene." He called himself an American born in Bohemia and defined American Judaism accordingly: "Judaism, reformed and reconstructed by the beneficent influence of political liberty and progressive enlightenment, is the youngest offspring of the ancient and venerable faith of Israel. The old soul is found in a new body; that majestic palm tree is but transplanted into a more fertile soil and invigorating clime ..." Many were imbued with the "strongest and most perennial cravings ... for complete political identification with America, to be an American of the Israelitish faith." According to Hermann Eliassof, "they were quickly imbued with the American spirit of self help, of courage and of daring. They soon became Americanized." Hence, the German Jewish population had already acclimated itself and the war can be said most likely to have accelerated a language shift that was already underway before the war. (75)

Nevertheless, three factors contributed to a strong sense of identity among Cincinnati's German-American Jews. First, they were actively involved in the various Vereine and their numerous activities, and thus constituted "an active element in the whole life of the German-American community." (76) They were not only an integral part of the German community, but often contributed ethnic leadership to the various Vereine,

e.g., the Cincinnati Club Center, later the German House Society. Second, the non-German Jewish immigration to Cincinnati
created a stronger sense of in-group identity in relation to
the new immigrants. The East European Jews were soon at odds
with the reformers since they emphasized the need of returning
to a conservative, Orthodox Judaism. This resulted in the
development of two distinct Jewish communities in Cincinnati,
the German Jewish and the East European Jewish. A third factor
was that many German Jews who spoke of "Americanization" meant
political allegiance to the U.S., rather than Anglicization.
"While they strove to Americanize themselves they still
remained true Jews and loyal to their German culture, they fostered the German language in their homes and in their syna-
gogues."(77) A thread running through German-American Jewish
history is their love of the German cultural heritage in the
areas of art, music and literature. References abound to the
works of Mendelssohn, Lessing, Kant, Goethe and Schiller. A
recent commentator noted something in common about Cincinnati
German Jewish homes:

> There are always some original works of art, always
> some books and virtually always a piano. Splashy
> fabrics and decorator schemes have no place, but the
> past is omnipresent. It's rare that someone can't
> pull out a scrapbook showing pictures of a Cincinnati
> ancestry that stretches back a hundred years, or at
> least tell stories that reach as far. (78)

The Cincinnati German Jews were thus a group that was well
acclimated culturally, politically and linguistically by the
1920s, but one that nonetheless maintained a particular sense
and pride of its own identity.

This identity was preserved by several institutions, at
the center of which was HUC, "the first permanent rabbinical
seminary in America and today the oldest and largest anywhere
in the world." Its president until 1921 was Kaufman Kohler,

born in Furth, Bavaria in 1843. He studied the Talmud with the better known traditional scholars in Germany (Jacob Ettlinger and Samson Raphael Hirsch). His doctoral dissertation incorporated the latest in biblical criticism. His rabbinical career in the U.S. included service in Detroit, Chicago and New York. In Cincinnati he participated in the feste of the Vereine. In 1910 he presented the main address at the Washington Celebration of the Pionier-Verein on the topic, "The Influence of Germandom in America." His best known work was entitled Jewish Theology: Systematically and Historically Considered. His Weltanschauung could be summarized as follows. Faith was founded in the universal God of prophetic Judaism known by a progressive process of revelation. A special task has been assigned for God's chosen people: to bring divine truths to mankind. Customs and practices are not commandments and unless they serve a specific religious purpose can be replaced. Judaism must be flexible in its structure and practices and be open to the world. Kohler believed in continual human moral progress, the achievement of the human mind and the ability of Reform Judaism to draw the messianic age closer. This perspective translated into an acclimation to American life and culture.(79)

HUC, according to Kohler, must have "a positive Jewish character." However, it "should have a thorough American character," he states elsewhere. Students should strive to be imbued with the American spirit, he advised. The HUC student body doubled to 120 students from 1919 to 1929. Julian Morgenstern succeeded Kaufman Kohler as president of HUC in 1921. Born in 1881 in St. Francisville, Illinois to a German Jewish family, Morgenstern studied at HUC and in 1902 went to Germany where he completed a doctorate in Semitic Languages (summa cum laude) at Heidelberg. He served as a rabbi in Lafayette, Indiana before coming to HUC as an instructor of Bible and Semitic Languages. In his view, he "saw Judaism as gradually extricating itself from the primitive notions and superstitions to

which it had been exposed in the Near East." This was, therefore, an evolutionary religious philosophy and one that implied
a progressively better understood religious message. (80)

Morgernstern added several competent scholars to HUC. In
1921 Jacob Mann replaced Gotthard Deutsch, who had died that
year. Mann represented the dispassionate scholarship of Wissenschaft des Judentums "in its most minute and exacting form."
He was an erudite and careful scholar who read "his fact-packed
lectures from note cards." He purposely abstained from broad
generalizations and fanciful theories in the classroom no less
than in his publications. Other quality scholars were also
added to the staff of HUC by Morgenstern, such as Abraham Cron-
bach, professor of Jewish Social Studies and a lifelong
pacifist. Especially noteworthy were two new professorial
appointments in the 1920s: Jacob Marcus, with a Berlin doctorate, was appointed assistant professor of Jewish History (1926)
and Nelson Glueck, who had also studied abroad, became instructor in Hebrew Language and Bible (1928). Students were in the
main American-born or East European, and included all possible
perspectives, e.g., "Zionists or non-Zionists, theists or hu-
manists, conservatives or socialists, pacifists or non-
pacifists." Student activites included the production of
plays, such as Stefan Zweig's _Jeremiah_ and Richard Beer-
Hoffman's _Jacob's Dream_. (81)

The Wall Street crisis caused the stagnation of the Reformed movement in the U.S. The number of United American
Hebrew Congregations fell by 13% from 1929-35. Some ceased to
exist, others merged and some fell deep into debt. By 1932
some rabbis were "literally on the verge of starvation" and
were compelled to depend on charity. In Cincinnati there were
five Reformed congregations, one Conservative, and three Orthodox congregations. The old Isaac M. Wise T.K.K. B'nai Yeshurun
fared the economic stress well. Membership there rose steadily: 451 (1918), 543 (1925), to 784 (1932). (82)

Rabbi James Heller succeeded Dr. Louis Grossman as rabbi of the congregation in 1921. Among his innovations were the publication of a congregational bulletin and a Yearbook. Also, women became eligible for service on the Board of Trustees and the rabbi was made an ex officio member. Because of space problems, land was acquired on the southwest corner of Reading Road and North Crescent Ave. for a new Isaac M. Wise Temple Center (1924), and the new center was dedicated 24 April 1927 with greetings extended by the Mayor, Murray Seasongood. A new constitution stated, "Judaism, under the beneficent influence of religious liberty, lighting the way for human progress, is the highest conception of the ancient and venerable faith of Israel. It is this conception of American Reform Judaism, fostered and developed by the revered Dr. Isaac M. Wise, for which Congregation B'Nai Yeshurun stands." In December 1932 the ninetieth anniversary was celebrated. (83)

The German Jews remained active in the various Vereine, especially the Pionier-Verein and the German Literary Club. Dr. Adolf Morgenstern led the Cincinnati Club Center, later the German House Society, and as a member of the Literary Club presented several papers in the 1920s on such topics as the World War, Oswald Spengler, art, the American West, and the Maya Indians. Dr. Deutsch presented only one paper before the Literary Club before his death in 1921. The Phoenix Club was reserved for the German Jewish elite. It cultivated the arts, music and literature. Up to the year 1882 all business transactions and minutes of the Phoenix Club were in German. By the time of the First World War membership in the club was lagging. In an attempt to attract more members a branch was formed, the Phoenix Hill Country Club (1917), located in Bond Hill. In 1918 it seceded from the downtown Club to become the independent Hillcrest Country Club, located at Reading and Seymour Ave. Nevertheless, the old downtown club celebrated its 75th anniversary in 1931. Another German Jewish Verein was the Losantiville Country Club, established in 1902, which became "the

center of social life for the Jewish elite." Another group was
the Wednesday club formed before World War I by local German
Jewish intellectuals "for the purpose of discussing Jewish
cultural affairs." Each month a paper would be presented by a
member on a specific topic. There were also several other
social, cultural and fraternal organizations, and musical
societies, most of which were small in terms of membership.(84)

In conclusion to the discussion of the German Jews, several points could be made. First, they had also been targets of
the Germanophobia engendered by the war. Second, the language
shift was not a forced affair caused by the war, but was most
likely already underway since at least the turn of the century
as a result of the German tradition of assimilation into the
surrounding cultural milieu. This may have tempered somewhat
the cultural shock caused by the war and its aftermath. Third,
German-Jews were largely an American-born population by the
time of the period investigated by this study. Fourth, German
Jewish institutions and organizations survived the war fully
intact and did not disappear as a result of the war. Fifth, as
in the case of the German Methodists, the war caused a de-
emphasis on the German ethnic component in the 1920s. It indeed appears to have not been an agenda item for consideration.
In the case of the Cincinnati German-American Jews is seen a
case of successful ethic survival by the process of the German
tradition of assimilation. Blending into this tradition, however, was the reality of organizational and community organizations which structured, maintained, and fostered German Jewish
identity.

The main characteristic of German Catholicism in the Twen-
ties was the survival of a subdued German ethnicity within the
framework of parochialism. The term "parochial" is used here
not in a negative sense to connote narrow-mindedness, but in
its positive sense to refer to the centrality of the local
parish in the life of the German Catholic. This was, of

course, a transplantation from Europe where religious life
revolved around one's own particular parish. The solution to
ethnic differences in nineteenth century Catholic church life
had been the establishment of national parishes for the various
ethnic groups. The national parish "became the trademark of
German American Catholicism; as a church within a church it
satisfied their unique religious needs and reinforced their
group consciousness." German immigrants from various regions
of Europe were united by "their common Catholic heritage and
the sense of Das Deutschtum that they had developed in a
strange new world." According to Jay Dolan, "the workingman's
religious life was centered around the parish church. It was
the setting for the liturgical reenactment of Christian life,
and the immigrants fostered the same devotions that their ancestors had practiced in Germany." The parish church was "a
beehive of activity" with literally thousands of communions,
baptisms, confessions, services, and other functions and activities. The church was "a religious oasis in the city" which
enabled German Catholics to define their own individual identity.(85) German Catholics had constructed ecclesiastical institutions complete with schools, bookstores, publications and
Vereine. Although the Zeitgeist of necessity required a new
orientation, the organizational structure of German Catholicism
survived intact. The parochialism of the 1920s reflected to a
great extent life in German hometowns, but also it was a reflection of the forced inward-turning caused by the anti-German
hysteria of the war.

Leading Cincinnati German Catholics into the new decade
was Cincinnati's first German-American archbishop, Henry Moel-
ler, born in Cincinnati in 1849. Both of his parents were from
Westphalia. He attended St. Xavier College, the American
College in Rome and was ordained in 1876. After service at
Bellefontaine, Ohio,; Mt. St. Mary's Seminary in Cincinnati,
and at Vincennes, Indiana, Moeller in 1880 became secretary to
Archbishop Elder of Cincinnati. In 1900 he was appointed

bishop of Columbus and in 1904 became the Archbishop of Cincinnati.   His administration laid particular stress on the building of a quality parochial school system. From 1904-21, 28 new
parishes were added to the diocese.   Also, a number of new
religious communities were added during his administration,
such as the Sisters of St. Ursula, with a convent on McMillan
Street.(86)

The war had been no more pleasant for German Catholics tha
for other German-Americans.   The most obvious sign that they
too must adapt to the needs of the time was the pronounced language shift from German to English.   Each year the diocese
found it increasingly difficult to locate priesthood candidates
who would either be conversant in German or who were interested
in studying the language.   The Vatican allowed Germans to join
English-speaking congregations, but did not allow the reverse
situation of the English-speaking joining the German parishes,
even when services were held in English.   German-American
priests protested this, but English-speaking churches then
charged the German parishes in attempting to take away members
from their folds.   Before the war Moeller planned to redefine
and reclassify all parishes, especially German churches no longer using German as the central language of worship.   Such
churches were to be reclassified as English.   This plan let
loose a storm of protest.   The English churches opposed it and
Germans "assailed Moeller for anglicizing their parishes and
warned him that the Church would lose countless German youths
in the process." Surprisingly enough, Moeller stated that he
did not believe that "the Faith is bound up in the language, an
that if the language goes the Faith will go with it."   His
basic view here differed from Henni's belief that language
serves faith.   In 1919 he complained of "confusion" and "wrang-
ling" in the archdiocese.   The feuding between English and
German parishes continued for several years. Apparently German
parishes did not desire to be reclassified as English parishes,
but at the same time desired the opportunity of accepting non-

Germans as members and also the privilege of holding English language services. However, it is absolutely clear that they were staunchly and firmly opposed to the elimination of their classification as German churches. Understandably, they had made the language shift, or offered services in both languages, but they desired the maintenance of their own unique identity. In 1921 Rome permitted Moeller "to abandon the old ethnic division of the diocese into German and English parishes and to establish territorial lines for all the parishes which no longer had a separate and distinct ethnic or racial constituency." What this did was to take away the ethnic classification of churches as national parishes, but to in effect recognize them and grant them a degree of territoriality. German parishes in this manner survived and acquired geographical definition.(87)

Catholics maintained their own school system from the primary on through to the university level. In 1919 in the entire archdiocese of Cincinnati there were 33,960 pupils at 123 schools. In 1921 pastors of eleven local parishes met to plan for the establishment of one central Catholic high school in the city, Purcell High School. In 1923 Mt. St. Mary's Seminary moved to Norwood Heights to become the major seminary of the archdiocese. In 1920 the College of St. Xavier became St. Xavier University. In all these educational institutions English was, of course, the language of instruction. Nevertheless, German Catholics had a separate educational system for their children, and one that maintained their own sense of identity.(88)

German Catholic Vereine numbered approximately 80, with a total membership of 12,000 members, all of whom affiliated with the local German Roman Catholic Zentralverband, the local branch of the Central-Verein. This paralleled for German Catholics the organizational structure of the secular National Alliance with its various local Stadtverbande. However, German Catholic Vereine were strictly non-political, but "true to the traditions and the free spirit of the German Fatherland," according to a local history. The programs of the Central-Verein were publicized in its numerous German and English language publications and pamphlets on various social questions. Its journal was entitled the Central-Blatt, a publication which in 1909 became the bilingual Central-Blatt and Social Justice Review. It remained a German-English publication until 1940 when it made the language shift to its present form as the Social Justice Review. From 1908 until 1952 the Central-Verein was wisely led by Friedrich Kenkel. The organization's survival was made possible by the language shift in the 1920s. In 1924 the Verein changed its name to the Catholic Central Union of America and the proceedings of its meetings were published henceforth in English, as were many of its publications. For example, in 1925 the Verein distributed in a three month time period 85,000 pamphlets in English and only roughly 2,000 in German. Kenkel's strategy was particularly designed to attain the goal of ethnic survival. Even though the necessary linguistic concessions were made the going was still not easy. Two years after the war the Verein requested all Catholics to cease using the terms "Boche" and "Huns." Kenkel stated that he had "scant reason" to feel "overly friendly" to Catholic coreligionists because of "attacks on Things German ..." He noted that he would never forget that American Catholics and the American Federation of Catholic Societies hadn't defended them during the war "when every wretched Know-Nothing in this country considered it brave and honorable to vent his spleen on all Americans of German blood." By 1930 a survey of all the state branches of the Verein indicated that English had become a primary language. Most of the local organizations affiliated with the Verein were benevolent aid societies similar to the secular mutual aid societies. The Verein was especially interested in the formation of programs to prepare young German Catholics for active involvement in public life and in the various trades and professions. It supported the rights of labor to organize and to form Catholic workingman societies similar to those in Germany. (89)

The major German Catholic Verein in Cincinnati in the 1920s was the Kolping Society which was established in 1923. It maintained close contacts with the dioceses of Dortmund and Osnabrück, the homes of many of its members. It also sponsored a popular summer festival, the Schützenfest. The Verein was patterned after the organization founded in Elberfeld, Germany in 1845 by Father Adolph Kolping. It was conceived of as a Catholic journeyman's society with a special emphasis on social activities. The German statutes point out that the general vocation of the journeyman was to become a faithful Catholic, an efficient worker, and an ideal father for his family. Members were to foster the spirit of brotherhood, assist in Sunday devotions like brothers, and to promote one another's welfare. Other Kolping Societies were formed elsewhere in the U.S., and in 1923 the first national convention was held and the foundation laid for a national organization known as the Kolping Society of America. All members receive the monthly journal entitled The Kolping Banner. The Kolping Society became a major German Catholic organization of Cincinnati, and also one of the strongest German-American organizations. It became a focal point for German Catholic families in Cincinnati and has maintained its own clubhouse on its extensive grounds on Winton Road. (90)

During the period under investigation by this study there were four German Catholic publications in Cincinnati: Der Cincinnati Hinkende Bote, the Sodalist, the Sendbote, and the St. Franziskus Bote. These and other German language publications were available at the local parish and the various Catholic bookstores in the city. (91)

In the case of the German Catholics there is, as has now been seen with other religious groups, a retreat to subdued

ethnicity behind the organizational structure of the particular
religious body. The language shift to English was an obvious
necessity. In spite of this ethnic retreat it would be incor-
rect to state that the German Catholics were a case of ethnic
disappearance, but rather of survival via submergence.

Summary

The German element was substantial: In the immediate
postwar period it was roughly one-half of the population of the
city of Cincinnati, and the German-speaking element was one-
third of the city's population. German immigration continued
in the 1920s, especially from the former provinces of the now
defunct Austro-Hungarian Empire, a casualty of the war. These
German-speaking immigrants, known as Danube Swabians, were
known for their strong sense of ethnicity which exerted a positive influence on the Cincinnati Germans after the demoralizing
experience of the war. A smaller number of immigrants also
came from Weimar Germany during the same period. During the
19th century as the German element grew, it of course expanded
beyond the narrow confines of the tiny Over-the-Rhine district,
the original site of the German community in the previous century. Although German-Americans settled throughout the city,
they concentrated especially on the west side, resulting in a
socio-cultural division that is evident even today between the
west and east sides of Cincinnati.

The German community was fortunately blessed with some
excellent ethnic leaders. Judge John Schwaab set the basic
tone of adopting not only a strategy of subdued ethnicity, but
also attempting to make German-American institutions appear as
low-key and invisible as possible. Here he had two goals in
mind. First, this strategy aimed at the maintenance and survival of German-American institutions. Second, it aimed to remove such institutions from public attention so that they would
not become a target of the anti-German element. A second im-

portant leader was Judge A.K. Nippert, who although he was not
an elected leader, was a publicly important person in Cincinnati, and articulated many of the feelings of German-Americans.
A third leader was Dr. H.H. Fick who functioned as a cultural
philosopher by setting an example in thought, word and deed
which may be viewed as the Cincinnati German Weltanschauung of
the time.

German-American secular institutions survived the war,
except for the smaller societies which could not survive the
anti-German hysteria, the enactment of prohibition, nor the
economic setbacks emanating from the depression. The era had
the effect of changing German-American societal structure from
one of many societies with small memberships to one of fewer
societies with larger memberships. It should be noted that the
German-American Alliance continued by merely changing its name
to the American Citizens League. In the case of religious institutions none was a casualty of the war, but as with the
Vereine, they adapted to the needs of the time by adopting a
greater use of English language in their services. This contributed to the developing German-American bilingual, bicultur-
al synthesis. As a German Methodist observed, the Methodist
Church "joined the mind, culture, and soul of two continents in
the Christian home." German Jews actively involved themselves
in the community, especially in the Cincinnati Club Center,
later the German House Society, and the German Literary Club.
German Catholics in the 1920s saw their parishes defined geographically so that they were given a degree of territoriality
to their ethnic parishes.

In conclusion, the German-American community along with
its various institutions survived the war almost fully intact,
but was altogether much less vocal and visible than before the
war. German-American ethnicity was redefined to meet the
demands of the time by the adaptation of a new strategy of
ethnic survival which entailed making German-American institu-

tions as low-key, subdued, and publicly invisible as possible. This was a realistic strategy and one that succeeded in its goal of ethnic survival, and in keeping younger generations within the fold. It was of course not a time of public ethnic pride in the German heritage. That would have to be deferred to a later time and generation.

CHAPTER II

CULTURAL LIFE AFTER THE GREAT WAR

It was the good old Cincinnati with its artistic
traditions from which the strong German strain
after all would not allow itself to be erased ...

--The Freie Presse commenting on a postwar
performance in the Music Hall (1)

Education

Before the war Cincinnati had been called "the original
home of German-English education" since it had been first introduced there in 1840.(2) Commenting on the fact that the
Official Bulletin of the Cincinnati Public Schools had been
printed in a special German language edition, Fick concluded in
prewar days that this was "certainly the best proof of the high
position of German language instruction." Superintendent Richard Boone in the same edition stated "German instruction is an
organic basic part of our public school system. It deserves
all reasonable support. The school administration will continue its endeavor to bring the quality of the teachers in German
instruction to the highest level."(3)

Before the war all 47 schools at the elementary and inter-
mediate level had special German language instructional
classes. Even one of the black schools had German instruction
which had been instituted on request by "prominent colored
citizens."(4) The amount of time devoted to German instruction
varied from five to nine hours per week. The textbooks used
were those authored especially by Supervisor Fick for the program. So successful was the program and the textbook series
that it became nationally known as the "Cincinnati Plan."

In September 1917 the German Textbook Censoring Committee, appointed by the School Board, removed all materials deemed unworthy from the public schools. From a prewar high of over 17,000 students, enrollment in German classes plummeted to 7,546 in September 1917. From a prewar high of 250 the number of German teachers had dropped to 72. In February 1918 the Board of Education decided to eliminate the German program, and in May Dr. Fick tendered his resignation as Supervisor of the German Department. In July "Hun Tongue" teachers were stricken from the payrolls of the public schools. The Ohio Ake Law made German language instruction below the eighth grade illegal in public and parochial schools from 1919-23. In spite of this state law Alexander Thomson continued his crusade against the evils of German language instruction, and presented a pamphlet to the Ohio State Legislature entitled History of German in Cincinnati Public Schools. In April 1919 an attempt was made to remove Judge John Schwaab from his positon as a member of the Union Board of High Schools because he had been a staunch supporter of German instruction as well as a well-known ethnic leader. Along with the bilingual program went all the local teacher organizations: the German High School Teachers Association (est. 1860), the German Teachers Association (est. 1878), and the Harmony Society of German Women Teachers (est. 1908). Needless to say, along with them went the careers of the teachers.

Since German instruction below the eighth grade was illegal until 1923 it is not at all surprising that it was not reintroduced into the public schools during the period investigated in this study. After 1923 Danube Swabians established a German-English parochial school at the St. Joseph of Nazareth Church on Liberty Street in Over-the-Rhine. This was apparently the only parochial elementry school which offered a German-English bilingual program during the period investigated here. In 1930 the Citizens League established a German language Saturday school in the Turnverein with six teachers under the direction of a Mr. Varrelmann. Also, two German language children's choirs were established by the Vereine to promote the language, as was a German language Sunday school.(5) Only in 1926 was German reintroduced into the high schools of Cincinnati, and only after being petitioned by the graduate faculty of the University of Cincinnati. Louis T. More, dean of the Graduate School, transmitted the following recommendations to the Board of Education:

> Gentlemen -- members of the Faculty of the University have long felt the unfortunate effects of not having German taught in the high schools. The embarrassment to the University is due to the fact that any advanced work in scholarship absolutely requires a reading knowledge of German, as in many fields the most important work is published in that language and not available in translations; also many students who come to the University wish to learn German either for the sake of its own literature or as a tool for other collegiate work, but they are prevented from obtaining that language for either of these uses and are forced to begin German in the University, which does not give them time for a mastery of the subject.
>
> At a recent meeting of the Graduate Faculty of the University I was asked to send you the following petition with the request that you consider the matter carefully and if possible comply with the desire of this body of scholars:
>
> "Since the knowledge of the German language is highly important for the scholarly work of university students and since the elements should be acquired before entering a university, the Graduate Faculty of the University of Cincinnati, consisting of the heads of all departments, of all the Colleges of the University, urgently requests the Board of Education to reinstate instruction in German in the High Schools of the city."
>
> Very sincerely yours,
> LOUIS T. MORE,
> Dean of the Graduate School(6)

In September, 1926 a course was approved by the Union Board of High Schools, and resulted in the enrollment of approximately five percent of the high school students. Fourteen classes with 418 students had been formed at Hughes, Withrow, and Woodward High Schools. Thus, after an absence of eight years German language instruction returned to the public schools of Cincinnati, at least at the high school level.(7)

At the university level things appeared a bit brighter in the area of German instruction because of the arrival of a new young professor of German who became chairman of the Department of Germanic Languages and Literatures at the University of Cincinnati, Edwin Hermann Zeydel. Born in New York in 1893, Zeydel arrived in Cincinnati in the mid-1920s to take a position in the Department. His father had been on the staff of the New Yorker Staats-Zeitung, America's oldest German language newspaper still in publication, and he had grown up in a "genuine German home atmosphere where the cultivation and enjoyment of the German language and literature were a family concern."(8) In 1915 Zeydel published a monograph in the yearbook of the German-American Historical Society of Illinois entitled "The German Theater in New York City, With Special Consideration of the Years 1878-1914."(9) He was both a product of and a student of the German-American community. He became an active member of local societies, such as Schlaraffia and the German Literary Club, and wrote for the local German langauge press. Later he edited two important periodicals: The German Quarterly and Modern Language Journal. It was Zeydel who "brought to Cincinnati an ever-increasing number of serious students and earned his department a national and international reputation."(10)

In 1928 Zeydel published an article on "Germanistic Activity in America 1918-1927" in which he attempted to overview the activities of teachers of German. He wrote:

As America entered the World War on the side of the Allies, it announced through its President the high ideals it allegedly represented, but at the same time

introduced a propaganda campaign not only against
German militarism and Kaiserdom, but also against
German scholarship and music, indeed even against the
German language and literature. This campaign, carried on under the cloak of Public Information, was
executed most cleverly ... This campaign against German finally had the result that the German language
was forbidden not only as a subject in the public
schools, but also as a colloquial language. These
narrow-minded, hating enactments on the part of
mature, responsible people will unfortunately always
remain a stain on America's honor, an eloquent witness to the intellectual level of the U.S. at the
beginning of the 20th century. (11)

Elsewhere, Zeydel commented about this period stating "Events
occurred of which fair-minded, level-headed Americans will
always be ashamed." (12)

Regarding German instruction at the University level in
America, Zeydel noted the difference in post- and prewar times.
According to him, four-fifths of the German classes at the
college/university level were actually not university level
courses. Since German had been banned from the public schools
at the elementary level many students now came to American
universities with little or only high school German knowledge.
This required teaching beginning German at American colleges
and universities. Zeydel estimated that sixty percent of the
university students in German classes were beginners. Such
conditions forced American Germanists to devote a great deal of
time to elementary German, which had previously been taught in
elementary schools, rather than to more advanced topics in language and literature. This resulted, according to Zeydel, in a
weaker knowledge of recent German literature, especially since
Heine, among American Germanists. In the scholarly publications in the area of German studies from 1918 to 1926 Zeydel
only found several dissertations and a few books worthy of mention. He noted that American Germanists were especially interested in the Goethe Centennial planned for 1932 which would

deal with the role Goethe had played in the literary and cultural life of America. Of special importance for the Cincinnati German community was the celebration of the 250th anniversary of the founding of the first permanent German settlement in America, Germantown, Pennsylvania, in 1933.

It should be remembered that Zeydel was an American-born German-American and that he not only played an active role in the local German community, but was also well acquainted with German-American history. It was, therefore, not surprising that he should undertake to coordinate the local celebration of the 250th anniversary of the founding of Germantown. The anniversary, the Pastorius Celebration, took place 29 October 1933 in Emery Auditorium. As the main speaker Prof. Albert B. Faust from Cornell University, the major German-American historian of the day, had been invited. His address, published in 1934 by the Carl Schurz Memorial Foundation, Inc., was introduced by an unsigned foreword, most likely written by Zeydel. It stated that "Cincinnati has always been known for its large, progressive and enterprising German population. One hundred years ago Cincinnati repeated the historical function of Germantown, Pennsylvania, by becoming the distributing center for German immigrations moving westward and southward." The foreword went on briefly to trace the history of the Cincinnati Germans, noting various industrial influences, the Sängerfeste and musical activities, the German theater, the involvement in the Civil War, local historian Heinrich A. Rattermann and other cultural influences. The local community "fought a successful battle for liberal influences and the German language in the schools." The Pastorius Celebration was an occasion "when American citizens of German ancestry, men, women and children, united in a memorable social event ..." It "was an evidence of pride in their not-to-be forgotten German traditions." In his address Prof. Faust remarked:

> German-Americans ... have had their share of failure
> and success, of trial and triumph, of labor and
> honest effort in the building of the American nation.
> They are privileged to love and cherish America as
> rightful partners, as owners in common with other
> great European stocks that compose the American peo-
> ple. The study of our history makes us better Ameri-
> cans, secure in traditions of service, true in devo-
> tion to national ideals.

In a filiopietistic manner Faust went on to sing the praises of
the contributions of the Germans to the building of America.
Perhaps this could be understood as an antidote to the rhetoric
of the war/postwar era. Faust admonished his listeners that
"we should consider it our privilege and duty to retain or acquire that German cultural background along with the American
foundations upon which we stand." Concluding his address, he
termed the Pastorius Celebration a "milestone of German-
American history." The importance of a Pastorius Celebration
was that it indicated that the German heritage had finally
again attained a semblence of respectability, and that the war/
postwar era was finally over. It also signified that Prof.
Zeydel was inheriting the position that Dr. Fick had enjoyed in
the German community as the foremost local German man of
letters. (13)

In conclusion, what can be said about the status of German
language instruction as it relates to the German community in
the 1920s? As Joshua Fishman has pointed out in an essay on
ethnic language maintenance, it is the home and ethnic community "that provides, preserves and directs its language maintenance contributions ..." this means that "the flow of language
maintenance influence is much greater from home-and-community
into the school than from the school into the home." In short,
the maintenance of an ethnic language cannot be said to be in
any case primarily dependent on an external secondary institution, such as the public school. According to Fishman, speech

communities speak mono- or bilingually on the basis of reward systems requiring the use of speech:

> The rewards involved are social (enforcing and recognizing membership in the family, community, in the society, in the people), fiscal (jobs, promotions, raises, bonuses), political (awards, contracts, appointments, public acclaim), and religious, etc.

Schools' reward systems consist of grades, promotions, prizes, and approval. Fishman terms schools secondary reward systems, which is a "social reward system ... generally weaker than--and subservient to--primary reward systems." Primary reward systems are constituted by the family and ethnic community. It is these primary systems that ethnic mother tongue maintenance is dependent on, not on the public school, a secondary reward system.(14)

What the loss of German language instruction in the Cincinnati Public Schools meant was that a secondary reward system had been eliminated that would have supported the primary reward systems within the German community. This translated into the absence of any external support for ethnic mother tongue maintenance outside the ethnic community. The preservation of the German language, hence, would have to rely completely on the primary institutions of the home and the institutions of the ethnic community. The loss of the bilingual program was a definite loss from the point of view of the German community, but it did not necessarily mean that the German language could not be sustained without it. That the German community was attempting to address these issues is apparent by its establishment of a German-English Catholic parochial school, Saturday school, and various children's choirs. Also, German language instruction did stage a comeback at the high school and university levels by the end of the 1920s. The basic point here is that although the loss of the bilingual program was disastrous, it did not necessarily mean the cessation of the maintenance of the German language in the primary institutions of the home and the institutions of the ethnic community.

Joshua Fisham poses the basic question with respect to ethnic mother tongue maintainence and the public schools: "Are our schools to be partners in the building of a culturally democratic America or are they to imply that only a linguistically and culturally Anglified American is a true American?" (15) To members of the German community in Cincinnati in the 1920s the answer was clear.

The German Language Press

World War I constituted the darkest hour in the history of the German-American press since it was dealt a staggering blow by the anti-German hysteria. However, it certainly was not a knock-out blow, but there were nonetheless many casualties. The press, like German language instructional programs in the public schools, offered an obvious target for nativist hostilities. Across the land the German language press struggled for its very existence during the war. In October 1917 the first federal law in American history was enacted to establish controls on the foreign language press. All war-related news would have to now be submitted to the local postmaster for censorship purposes. After the loyalty of the publication had been established by the local postmaster a permit would be granted to the foreign language publication exempting it from the costly and time-consuming efforts of translating and filing news with the postmaster.

A complicating issue at the local level was the Germanophobia of the day. Advertising boycotts were organized against the German language press and newspaper stands also refused to carry German-American publications. In Kentucky German papers were banned. It was not uncommon for newspaper offices to be raided by federal agents in the search of some piece of incriminating evidence, although none was ever found. By 1918 many German language publications were either closing business, or converting to bilingual, or English language publications. German-American publications declined from 537 in 1914, to 278 in 1920, and to 201 in 1930. A major effect on the editorial policy of German-American newspapers, which was a direct result of the war, was that the press "no longer was active politically and tried to avoid controversial issues."(16)

In Cincinnati there were fifteen German language publications in the period 1918 through 1932. Of these, five ceased publication in 1918-19 as direct casualties of the war-engendered Germanophobia. Three others closed shop in the 1920s so that by the end of 1932 the number of publications had been cut to six. The press, as a "mirror" of the community, reflected the structural diversity of the German community. As the community subdivided basically into the Kirchen- and Vereinsdeutsche, so too the press can be categorized into the religious and the secular press.

In the area of the religious press the Cincinnati German Methodists were a major force with a total of five publications in the period. It should be noted that the German Methodist professors, editors, and preachers were quite active in the publication of "many scholarly books and some creative didactic literature." The publications of the German Methodists were published and distributed through the Methodist Book Concern located in Cincinnati. It should be remembered that the German Methodists were organized into German conferences within the broader framework of an Anglo-American Methodist Church, and were thus in a minority position within their church body.(17)

From 1897 to 1918 German Methodists published a Sunday School monthly for children entitled Die kleine Glocke. In

1912 it enjoyed a circulation of 6,300, but by war's end the Sunday School journal had become a "1918 war casualty."(18) The content of such publications was not so important as the fact that they were printed in the German language. From 1886 to 1926 German Methodists published the Heiden Frauenfreund, a women's missionary paper. A quarterly journal dealing with Biblical research was Der Bibelforscher, published from 1871 to 1940, with a peak circulation of 42,000 in 1912. Each issue contained ca. 24 pages and was edited by the noted German-American author Heinrich Liebhard. The proceedings and annual reports of the Southern German Conference of the Bishopric of the Methodist Church were published from 1866 to 1926 as Deutscher Kalender. Verhandlungen und Berichte der ... Jährlichen Sitzung der Südlichen Deutschen Konferenz der bischöflichen Methodistenkirche. It varied from 100 to 208 pages, and was richly illustrated with portraits and tables pertaining to church history. One of the finest of the German Methodist publications was its monthly family-oriented journal entitled Haus und Herd.

Haus und Herd, which commenced publication in 1873, was finely illustrated with steel engravings and woodcuts; one volume, for example, contained twelve of the former and 210 of the latter. It was considered "an excellent paper for family reading, rather than a religious periodical."(19) A volume of Haus und Herd displays a diversity of reading material: biography, history, natural history, travel sketches, stories, poetry, Biblical commentaries, psychology, ethics, current events, lists of church meetings and conventions, etc. Each issue also contained a poem of song set to music. Under the rubric of "Am Büchertisch" the reader found reviews and references to recent publications of interest to German Methodists. In 1918 it was decided that, because of the difficulties emanating from the war, the publication of the journal would cease, although its circulation as late as 1915 had stood at 8,500. Rather than completely end the fine journal it was finally decided to merge

Haus und Herd into another German Methodist newspaper, Der
Christliche Apologete. A leading member of the German Methodists wrote with reference to the demise of Haus und Herd:

> The war throws its waves on all shores. Its disturb-
> ing influence is felt in few areas so seriously as in
> the field of publications. A large number of newspa-
> pers of all languages have fallen its victim all over
> the land.(20)

The Apologete was a pioneer German-American newspaper
which had commenced publication in 1839 in Cincinnati to "champion the cause of orthodoxy and to take issue with a growing
rationalism." Basically, it was a German Methodist family-
oriented newspaper of exceptionally high quality, but it also
at times contained learned discussions relating to theological
matters. Its editorial position before American entrance into
the Great War was opposition to "militarism and resolution of
international disputes by war ..." In its editor, Albert J.
Nast, there was a complete self-identification "with those
peace movements and that social activism of the day which
awaited the imminent dawn of the kingdom of God in the democratic and socialist movements of the nineteenth century." In
October 1917 the U.S. Congress passed a law requiring all war-
related reports to be filed with the local postmaster in a true
English translation, and the Apologete eventually received its
permit. The paper announced to its readers in an article sur-
rounded by 110 American flags:

> On the 6th of October a law was signed by President
> Wilson which places strong controls on all non-
> English language newspapers and other publications in
> so far as they deal with the government of the U.S.
> or any of the other nations involved in the war ...
>
> In this connection we would like to inform our rea-
> ders that, beginning with the next issue, we will be
> printing the brochure "How the War Came to America."

This is an authentic presentation, published by the "Committee on Public Information" which every American should own. (21)

In January 1918 the _Apologete_ announced the establishment of the War Council by the Methodist Episcopal Church at the Wesley Episcopal Church at the Wesley Building in Philadelphia. The Council "identified the Gospel with political freedom, and America's cause with that of the Church." An appeal by the bishops to the church "parallels their own call for salvation of the world with General Pershing's cry for Germany's defeat." On 15 May 1918 the _Apologete_ published in English an article entitled "Methodism and Americanism -- A Patriotic Deliverance by the Book Committee." According to the article the Committee had charge of:

... the dissemination of moral and religious principles of justice, righteousness, and democracy and the
spread of Christianity ... directs that there be
placed on its records this solemn declaration of its
inimpeachable and unswerving loyalty to the President
of the United States in this most pregnant hour of
our national existence ...

Methodists may well recall their invariable devotion
to their flag, their steadfast allegiance to the government throughout nearly one hundred and fifty years
of national life, and their swift and constant support of the government in every national crisis ...

We therefore place all of our resources, especially
our many periodicals ... at the disposal of the government ... for the Americanization of men and women
of other lands who ... have not yet been fully pos-
sessed by the American spirit.

Sickened in soul by hypocrisy, foul blasphemies, the
wanton destruction of sacred places and conscience-
less diplomacy, angered by unbelievable brutalities,
daily practiced, the cries of outraged, starving,
dying children and of women enslaved, the sanctioned
treatment of conquered territory, and the exploita-
tion of helpless inhabitants ... and, believing in
God, America, and in victory, we pledge the support
of 'the people called Methodists' to our country and
our allies for the holy task of winning the war and
the redemption of the world. (22)

The Americanism and patriotism of the <u>Apologete</u> and its editor Nast were impeccable, but that apparently was not good enough. In January 1918 certain vague allegations began to surface about the "pro-German" sentiments amongst the leadership at Baldwin-Wallace College in Berea, Ohio. In March the Board of Trustees of the college decided to accept Nast's resignation as president of the board. Nast, hence, began to see the handwriting on the wall. His father Wilhelm Nast had founded and edited the <u>Apologete</u> for 56 years and Albert Nast was now in his twenty-third year of service as editor. He wrote:

> What excellent progress it has been able to report! What difficult battles it has survived. And today there is no lack of dark clouds rising on the horizon of the New Year! What might not we have to report all this year of 1918? We do not know, but our German work and our German Weekly stand in God's hand. We trust in the Lord of Lords. We wish all our readers the best gift of all gifts in the new year -- the noble peace of God. And we ask from your side your hearty support in earnest petition and in true friendship! (23)

On 23 January 1918 the church's publishing agents reprimanded Nast for his supposed editorial disloyalty:

> Since the United States declared war with Germany the Publishing Agents have felt that the policy of the Editor of <u>Der Christliche Apologete</u> was not in full harmony with the spirit of the church and of the country ...
>
> The Agents distinctly and sincerely regret that the <u>Apologete</u> has not been outspoken in its support of the United States and our Allies ... and in opposition to the war spirit ... of Germany ...
>
> There can be but one attitude consistent with the American and Methodist spirit ...
>
> The Agents have, therefore, felt obligated to make such arrangements for the editorial conduct of the <u>Christliche Apologete</u> as will relieve it of all criticism of its patriotism. Henceforth it will

> sound a clear note for the utter defeat of Germany
> and its despotic military system and rulers, and for
> the complete victory of the United States ... There
> shall be no half hearted or divided allegiance.

Although Nast and his assistant editors signed a statement
agreeing with the publisher's agents, it was clear that he
would be replaced. On 13 March it was announced that an associate editor for war matters had been appointed, although he
had in actuality already been at work in place of Nast. A week
later Frank Wilson, the U.S. publicity officer, praised the
patriotism of the Apologete's Feb. 20 issue. On 1 May 1918
Nast resigned and despite his efforts "all German-language
materials for younger children were discontinued and the decision was made to merge the weekly Apologete with the monthly
Haus und Herd. Nast wrote in his 'farewell word,'"

> We must not forget that we live in abnormal cir-
> cumstances, and we must reckon with them ... the
> position which the Christliche Apologete took in its
> very first issues after the declaration of war, and
> its position since then is known to all of our rea-
> ders. It was and is a position of most unambiguous
> and decisive loyalty to our country and our govern-
> ment.

> In disregard of this, our loyalty has been
> questioned, despite the fact that the paper was fully
> and totally accepted by the government several weeks
> ago ...

> We can be thankful that in these abnormal
> circumstances the Book Committee has provided for the
> continuing existence of [our papers].

After the resignation of Nast in May 1918 the editorship
of the Apologete was assumed by the Rev. August J. Bucher who
edited the paper until 1936; the publication finally concluding
publication in 1941. Its circulation remained fairly steady in
the 1920s until the arrival of the Great Depression: 1920:
9,847; 1923: 10,742; 1926: 9,798; and 1930: 7,380. According

to Wittke, the paper was "a household necessity of many German Methodist homes." Although it survived the war, it is clear that "the darkest hour" had dealt a solid blow to German Methodist publications. (24)

Six other German language publications were issued in the 1918-32 period that belong to the area of the religious press. Five of these publications were German Catholic. All of them were small monthly or annual publications of a strictly religious nature in contrast to the large general interest religious newspaper of the Methodists, the Apologete. The Benzinger Brothers published Der Cincinnati Hinkende Bote from 1836-1927. It was a German Catholic almanac containing news on weather, folklore, stories, poetry etc. The German Catholic St. Francis Church published Der Sodalist from 1884-1938. It was a small Roman Catholic monthly printed in German and English. Der Sendbote was another German Catholic monthly religious periodical, published since 1873. The German Evangelical Protestant Church published a religious monthly entitled the Armen- und Krankenfreund from 1904 to November 1918.

Crossing over to the area of secular publications one finds special interest journals as well as the larger general interest newspapers. Two special interest publications of the period were the Brauer-Zeitung and the Vorstandsbericht of the Pionier-Verein. The former, a brewery workers' journal, was published in German by the International Union of Brewery, Flour, Cereal and Soft Drink Workers of America. Under the editorship of Julius Zorn (1917-27), a staunch member of the local Vereine, the Brauer-Zeitung took a vigorous stand against Prohibition. It maintained use of the German language until 1934 when it became the Brewery Worker. An extremely valuable yearbook for Cincinnati German history is the Vorstandsbericht of the German Pionier-Verein, published from 1886 to the 1960s. Each issue contained news and information regarding the society

and its membership, as well as rather extensive obituaries of
members who had died in the past year.

Of the three major newspapers serving the German community: the Deutsch-Ungarischer Bote, the Volksblatt and the Freie
Presse, only the latter survived into the 1920s. The Bote,
edited primarily for Germans from Hungary, commenced publication in 1905. It was a weekly newspaper which attained a
prewar (1915) circulation of 9,400. (25) The circumstances emanating from the war atmosphere proved, however, to be too much.
By late 1918 circulation had shriveled to 630, and the Bote
became another war casualty. In 1919 a major newspaper, the
Volksblatt, also ceased publication.

The Volksblatt, which had commenced publication in May
1836, had throughout the nineteenth century been one of the
major German-American newspapers of the West, but the war with
advertising boycotts, refusals of sale at newsstands, and raids
by federal agents had hit the newspaper exceptionally hard.
After the war it made a gallant, but futile attempt to rebuild
its business. However, its task was complicated by the fact
that it had to compete with the other general interest newspaper that was in exactly the same predicament, the Freie Presse.
It attempted to build pride again in the German heritage.
Hence, it pointed with pride to the many returning soldiers
with German surnames. It complained that the U.S. Census "with
its category of native-born of native parentage, was purpose-
fully obscuring the achievements of early immigrant generations
such as the Pennsylvania Dutch." It rejected as absurd the
Germanophobia of the day, and asked whether mathematics would
be abolished as German had been. In June 1919 it supported the
now-defunct Alliance for its efforts to recruit volunteers for
the army and its attempts to encourage Liberty Bond sales. It
condemned all attempts to associate the Communists with the
Germans, since they were conservative, eager to own property,
and they viewed the public holding of property as theft. It

asserted that to now abandon the German heritage would be to substantiate "the nativists' claim as to the treachery of the Germans who under the guise of cultivating their culture were carrying on all kinds of treasonable activities until stopped by the patriotic leagues." However, the Volksblatt recognized a no-win situation with regard to the state law against German language instruction. It maintained that it was senseless to fight against the elimination of German in the public schools of the state of Ohio. It also appeared to editor Charles Krippendorf that it no longer made any sense to struggle to continue publication of the newspaper. On 5 December 1919 it published its last issue after having been sold to the publisher of the Freie Presse for $7,500.(26)

The Freie Presse, which was established in 1874 and has continued publication to the present time in its successor the Amerika-woche, thus became in December 1919 Cincinnati's only general interest German language newspaper. Its job now was to represent "German interests in their totality" according to the editor of the Pionier-Verein's yearbook. Publisher F.W. Elven staffed the newspaper with several professional journalists, including Dr. George F. Moser, who had also worked as an editor with the Louisville Anzeiger, and Dr. Fritz Witte who replaced Richard Greninger after his death in 1928. Witte's journalistic experience had begun with the Ullstein press in Berlin for which he had also served four years as a correspondent in China. Also employed by Elven as a contributor was Dr. H.H. Fick, former Supervisor of the German Department of the Public Schools.(27)

The Freie Presse had, besides its daily edition, a Sunday edition: the Sonntagsblatt der Cincinnatier Freie Presse (1874-1930), and the evening edition: the Tägliche Abend-Presse (1877-1930). In 1921 the circulations for the daily and the Sunday editions was 23,342 and 22,281 respectively. By 1930 the circulation of the daily was 12,318, while the Sunday

edition by that date was 18,720.   From these statistics it can
be deduced that many readers were canceling the daily   edition,
but holding onto the Sunday newspaper.   The economic depression
caused   the cessation of the evening edition in 1930.   The depression   was hard on the _Presse_,   therefore.   Already   before
this   economic   crisis   it had been operating with   a   deficit
($8,173 in 1919 and $9,938 in 1920).   Finances improved   until
the   onset   of the depression which caused further cutbacks   in
the area of the evening edition.(28)

Given   the circumstances,   the _Freie Presse_ commenced   the
postwar   era   realizing it had an uphill   climb,   stating   "The
present   is filled with portents of storms and uncertain is the
future."   Nevertheless, it attempted to re-establish the prewar
influence and prestige of the German-Americans and to regain as
much lost ground as possible.   A general aim was to raise American respect for German-Americans and to dispel hatred for   all
things   German.   Several   methods were used to   achieve   these
aims.   One tactic was to cite examples of the virtue of German
character   and   the vices of the Allies.   The campaign for   a
respected   German   element began with the enthusiastic support
for   the Victory Loan in the spring of 1919.   The _Presse_ contained full page advertisements and appeals to local   citizenry
to   buy the bonds.   This was followed by a series of   articles
which aimed to demonstrate how the stories of German atrocities
came into being, and to prove that many of them were false.
The _Presse_ maintained that many of the stories circulated about
Germans and German-Americans during the war were the basest   of
lies   and propaganda.   Another method was to publish long letters   of American soldiers who were in the American   occupation
army in Germany.   These letters from overseas soldiers commented on the cleanliness of the Germans,   the motherliness of   the
Hausfrau,   and the kindliness and cordiality of the German soldiers   toward   the Americans.   The newspaper reported on   the
celebrations   of   Christmas Day by Germans and   Americans,   and
also   the   friendships between both peoples   along   the   Rhine.

Quotations from the German press about the fine conduct of American soldiers of the Army of Occupation were also published, as were frequent references to the stories of captured Americans who were treated well by their German captors. George Creel and Hans Rieg, chief of the Foreign Language Division of the Treasury Department, were quoted frequently with their supportive comments about the foreign populations of the U.S. during the war.(29)

In 1919-20 the Presse devoted a series of articles to the subject of the future of the Vereine. The basic assumption was that the future of the German community and the Vereine were all linked together. It lamented the divisiveness that existed between some of the Vereins- and Kirchendeutschen, stating:

> Had their federations not only included the societies of a purely social nature but stayed in even closer touch with the entire German-speaking population and the religious one in particular, they could have made themselves into the leaders and saviors of the German population in the crisis which had that time broken over its head.

The Presse considered the formation of the old Alliance "an unfortunate undertaking." It claimed it was "deficient in the loftiness of its aims" and that its leaders are not capable of providing "any loftier goals." This apparently was a criticism of the national organization, rather than the local Stadtverband, since the newspaper admonished its readers:

> We have friends, let us join them. We have leaders, let us follow them. We have societies, let us develop them; let us give them firm, valid goals. This for the near future must be one of our great tasks.(30)

With regard to international affairs the negative stance of the Freie Presse concerning the Versailles Treaty and the

League of Nations has already been noted. In the area of national politics it has been noted that in all the U.S. presidential elections from 1920-32 the _Freie_ _Presse_ endorsed Republican candidates. In local elections the Republicans were
favored over the Democrats, although the _Presse_ carried heavy
advertising from both parties at election times.

Finally, a word should be said about how the German language press viewed its role in relation to the German community
in the 1920s. In 1920 F.W. Elven, publisher of the newspaper,
expressed the thought that the German language press should be
the appropriate leader of the German ethnic group. This was
not only a critique of the old National Alliance, but also an
attempt to fill the void its demise had created. Furthermore,
there was a need for responsible representation of the German-
American element. According to him, it was the duty of the
German press to prevent "persons who lack every qualification
of leadership to force themselves into prominent positions and
by their blunders compromise the cause of the German element."
Elven claimed that ethnic group political activity would be
unwise: "We have our hands full at present to make amends for
the sins of men of German blood who do not take their oath of
allegiance too seriously and refuse to recognize the fact that
we are not living in a German colony." The German press,
therefore, regarded itself as the responsible commentator,
voice, and representative on social, economic and political
affairs for the German element. This task was facilitated by
the able and qualified staff of journalists with the _Freie_
Presse. (31)

Finally, focus should be placed on the various obstacles
which the German language press had to overcome in the period.
First, was the very basic struggle for existence during the
war. Second, in the postwar era there was the problem of
rebuilding one's business, and at the same time competing with
other publications within the framework of a rather well-

defined market. Third, there was the very sizable loss of advertising revenue from local beer breweries due to the advent of prohibition. Fourth, there were the continuing vestiges of the nativist antipathies engendered by the war. In spite of the considerable losses in the face of these factors, it cannot be said that the German language press did not survive the war and that it disappeared.

Literature

The First World War can in no way be said to have led to the disappearance of German-American literature in Cincinnati. Rather than to chronologically annotate the individual works from the 1920s, the focus here will be on the work of the three most prolific German-American authors of the period: H.H. Fick, Edwin Zeydel and Ralph C. Wood. The latter two were American-born, Zeydel a second-generation and Wood a fifth-generation German-American.

H.H. Fick had been a widely published author of literary, historical and educational materials since the latter decades of the nineteenth century, and one may have thought that his writing period would be over, but not so. The postwar era proved to be his most productive years of all. Because of the loss of his position in the public schools, Fick found employment as a contributor to the Apologete and Freie Presse in Cincinnati and the Abendpost in Chicago. All of these newspaper contributions were carefuly collected by Fick into scrapbooks which are now located in the German-Americana collection at the University of Cincinnati Blegen Library. (32)

Fick's journalistic contributions included essays on topics from American history, such as: Benjamin Franklin; literary topics, e.g., Negerpoesie; discussions of trips to historic sites in the region, such as Trappists in Kentucky and New Harmony. He also wrote a series of articles on historical points of interest in Cincinnati entitled Historische Spuren in Cincinnati und der Umgegend. All of these individual and smaller pieces of journalistic work must, however, be considered as Fick's minor contributions. His major works of the period consisted of several full-length book manuscripts that appeared in the German press of Chicago and Cincinnati throughout the 1920s, as well as two unpublished book-length manuscripts. It is apparent that Fick used the journalistic opportunity to record and document an era of German-American history.

Deutsche Dichter und Dichtung in Cincinnati (121 pp.) is a history of German-American literature in the Queen City which contains numerous literary examples of poetry collected by Fick from the local German press. After noting in his introduction that German-American literature does not have a Lessing, Schiller, Goethe or Heine, Fick observes that neither does Anglo-American literature have a Shakespeare or a Milton. He then begins his discussion of local German literature starting in 1820 with Christian Burkhalter, the former secretary of Prince Blucher. A more personal and anecdotal work is Fick's Meine deutsch-amerikanischen Poetenbekanntschaften (55 pp.) which contains discussions of the life and work of the various literary acquaintances of Fick's. Of exceptional importance is Fick's unpublished bio-bibliographical reference work on German-American literature entitled "Bibliographie der deutsch-amerikanischen Schon-literatur." It contains data on 378 authors. In it Fick inserted numerous autographs, pictures and letters of dozens of German-American poets. (33)

Fick's biographical collection of articles on German-Americans, Wir in Amerika, fills four scrapbook volumes. Another four scrapbook volumes are filled with his collection of travel essays entitled Ausflüge ins romantische Amerika. His unpublished autobiographical manuscript entitled "Im Rahmen von sechs Jahrzehnten" (132 pp.) was completed in 1924. He appears to have based two other autobiographies on this work:

<u>Wie</u> <u>es</u> <u>so</u> <u>kam</u>: <u>Lebenserinnerungen</u> (67 pp.) and <u>Zwischen</u> <u>Anfang</u> <u>und</u> <u>Ende</u>:   <u>Mein</u> <u>Leben</u> (53 pp.). The latter work, written late in the 1920s, is perhaps the best of the three autobiographical works.   It consists of 27 chapters detailing chronologically the course of his life and work.

In terms of the genre of poetry, for which Fick had been primarily known in the prewar era, there is little to be found authored by him in the 1920s.   All of his energies appeared to have been devoted to the aforementioned historical works.   The few poems which he wrote in the 1920s were published in the yearbook of the Pionier-Verein, and dealt exclusively with the theme of the German pioneer.   The following was the most popu- lar poem, often reprinted and set to music:

THE SONG MY MOTHER SANG

At an early age I had to leave my home
From my parents, dear and true;
I was driven from one place to another,
I heard the sound of foreign language;
But in life's busy activities,
which bound their fetters around me,
Above all will remain precious to me,
The song my mother sang.

When I as a child tired of play,
turned to my mother's lap
and quickly calmed by the song,
Now carefree closed my eyes,
then I felt how the simple melody
Penetrated powerfully deep into my heart:
No song, if loud or soft, affects me
As the song my mother sang.

Since then if I listen in my mind to the song
It absolves me of every sharp pain,
And silent sadness, sweet peace
Moves then into my soul.
How oft, when I in gloomy hours
Battled with cares and heavy concerns
Have found comfort and calm
In the song my mother sang.

So may it hover over me for evermore
On the wandering path of my existence,
Until once the toilsome life

Has found its conclusion,
When the tired eyes are closed,
No mournful choir, No sound of the bell!
Sing to me as the last song here below,
The song my mother sang.(34)

The products of Edwin H. Zeydel's pen can be divided into works of a literary and a non-literary nature. In the first category were works in the field of German Languages and Literatures. In the period under investigation Zeydel completed seven books dealing with German language instruction: grammars, readers and courses on written and spoken German. His An Elementary German Reader (1926), for example, aimed "to supply a sufficient quantity of easy reading-matter for the use of beginners in German."(35) These books were directed at college and university students, in contrast to Fick's textbook series which was for elementary school children. In 1918 Zeydel published a monograph on the image of Germany in German literature entitled The Holy Roman Empire in German Literature in which he described the old Empire as "a great and powerful institution built around a wonderful system of ideals" and one which "has after all left behind it on earth a noble heritage." He cites others who describe it as the "most signal instance of the fusion of Roman and Teutonic elements in modern civilization." Other works included The Ludwig Tieck-Freidrich von Raumer Letters (1930) and Ludwig Tieck and England (1931).(36)

In the non-literary category are a number of works which Zeydel edited and/or translated for publication. In 1919 he edited an edition of documents entitled Constitutions of the German Empire and German States which consisted of an alphabetically arranged collection of the constitutions of the German states.(37) In 1921 he translated Dr. Hans Wehberg's The Limitations of Armaments. A Collection of the Projects Proposed for the Solution of the Problem, Preceded by an Historical Introduction.(38) In 1928 he translated Hermann Oncken's Napo-

leon III and the Rhine. The Origin of the War of 1870-1871, a
work which claimed that the French policy with regard to Germany had for centuries consisted of the following objectives:
First, "to conquer or control all the German territory up to
the left bank of the Rhine," and second, "to keep the German
states disunited and thereby subject to French control." It
claimed good relations were dependent on mutual self-respect
and equality, but warned that should nations:

> ... be unable to divorce themselves from an evil tra-
> dition and stubbornly adhere to a policy, by virtue
> of which each couples with its own triumph the sub-
> jection of the other, we may be sure that all elated
> talk about reconciliation and peace is but empty
> prattle and self-delusion.(39)

In 1930 Zeydel translated Wilhelm Kiesselbach's Problems of the
German-American Claims Commission which offered "a brief survey, from the German point of view, of the problems which had
to be solved by the Mixed Claims Commission at Washington in
connection with the establishment of the American claims
arising from the World War." With respect to the Treaty of
Versailles the book commented "It must be stated at the outset
that the 'legal' foundations of the Treaty of Versailles as
such are not worthy of any comment."(40) In the same year
Zeydel translated Alfred von Wegerer's A Refutation of the
Versailles War Guilt Thesis which stated as its central thesis
"that the Versailles verdict concerning the responsibility for
the war is false ... and that a revision of this verdict is
necessary in order to restore Germany's good name and to take
the discordances between the nations which have arisen out of
the false verdict on the outbreak of the World War ..." The
author claimed the Versailles verdict would have to be set
aside for the sake of "self-respect and in order to establish
the necessary moral foundation for a revision of the Treaty
..."(41) In 1931 Zeydel translated another work by Wehberg:

The Outlawry of War which consisted of a series of lectures   on
the topic by the author.   Wehberg maintained:

> Illness will not cure illness, and to the sober judg-
> ment of peace-time the futility of "war to end war"
> is apparent.   Internationalist, statesmen, the man in
> the street, have come to the realization that the
> only effective and permanent solution of this,   the
> greatest of the world's problems, is to place war
> completely outside the pale of the law.   The goal is
> plainly visible, and the ways and means of reaching
> it are being evolved with a heartening measure of
> success. (42)

Some of Zeydel's translation work appears to reflect an adherence to the revisionist perspective prevalent in the 1920s
regarding the outbreak of the First World War.   By the end of
the 1920s all this revisionist historical writing had contributed, according to Selig Adler, to the fact that Germany again
"enjoyed a decent respect in the opinion of mankind." (43)

Recently deceased in Emmendingen, West Germany, after a
long career as a professor of German at Lehigh University in
Bethlehem, Pennsylvania, was the third and perhaps the most
interesting German-American author of the period: Ralph Charles
Wood.   A fifth-generation American of German descent in spite
of his non-German surname, Wood, born in 1905, attended the bilingual schools of Cincinnati and studied German at the University of Cincinnati under the direction of Zeydel.   Wood completed his M.A. thesis in 1930 on the history of the German
theater in Cincinnati entitled Geschichte des deutschen Theaters in Cincinnati, a study based on extensive use of the
German language press. (44)   In 1932 he moved on to Cornell University to study under the foremost German-American cultural
historian of the time, Albert B. Faust. There he expanded on
his earlier study to complete a comprehensive history of the
Cincinnati German theater entitled Geschichte des deutschen
Theaters von Cincinnati, a work which not only traces the his-

tory of the theater, but also indexes all plays performed in Cincinnati to the time of the Great War. After publishing his dissertation in the yearbook of the German-American Historical Society of Illinois, Wood obtained a position in the German Department at Lehigh University, after which time he devoted himself to the study of Pennsylvania Germanica.(45) It was within this field that he was to distinguish himself in later years. His early works are of special interest not only for their historical research value, but because of the fact that they were written in the German language by a fifth-generation American.

Finally, a number of other works were produced in the 1920s in Cincinnati which reflect the continuing interest in German literary traditions. In 1926 Alma S. Fick, the daughter of H.H. Fick, edited Theodor Storm's classic _Immensee_ for Macmillan's German Series.(46) Also, the local poet Jerome Iffland should be mentioned. All of his work appeared in the local press and in the yearbooks of the Pionier-Verein, and were usually written for specific occasions, i.e., _Gelegenheitsgedichte_. At many community events in the 1920s Iffland was present to read one of his original poems. Perhaps the finest translation of the 1920s was Bertha Fiebach Markbreit's translation George Elliston's work entitled _Sonnenglanz_. Her translation of the poem regarding the attainment of Franco-German understanding, an appropriate contribution to the time, concluded that we are all "Kam'raden:"

> Du bist ein Franzose, ein Deutscher bin ich,
> Sind Landsleute dennoch getreu.
> Träume diselben bewegen uns hier,
> Im Lande das alt und doch neu.
>
> Uns're Gedanken, der Wünsche Endziel,
> Sie finden uns friedlich vereint.
> Lass' uns nicht hadern um Blutsunterschied
> Da uns derselbe Mond bescheint.

Illustration from the 1927 Festschrift of the German Literary
Club of Cincinnati. From a volume in the German-Americana
Collection, Blegen Library, University of Cincinnati.

Du bist kein Franzman mehr, kein Deutscher ich,
Ansässig im fredlichsten Land;
Kam'raden sind wir; im Sinne des Wort's,
Der Achtung von festem Bestand. (47)

Intellectual Life

German-American intellectual life in the 1920s in Cincinnati revolved around the activities of the German Literary Club which had been founded in 1877. A high point in the period under investigation was the celebration of its 50th anniversary in 1927. In honor of the occasion the Freie Presse published a special issue as a festschrift which was entitled Fünfzig Jahre: Deutscher Literarischer Klub von Cincinnati 1877-1927, and the club itself published its own Festschrift zum goldenen Jubiläum des Deutschen Literarischen Klubs von Cincinnati 1877-1927 which was authored by Hermann Barnstorff. (48) Honorary president of the club, H.H. Fick, provided an introduction for the latter work in which he likened the club's history to the course of a traveler, who having traversed a long, troublesome uphill course, could now stop to look around and orient himself. At this point the wanderer:

> ... then probably measures the accomplished distance, rests perhaps a bit, and strives, happy at the view to far and near, defying every phase of weather, towards the longed-for goal. A joyous call spurs him on; derogatory glances and words he leaves unnoticed; trouble and hindrances are easier forgotten in the knowledge of coming nearer to the destination.

The club had faced "adverse conditions," but according to Fick, "neither age nor the senseless war-hysteria could vanquish the club." (49)

The organizational purpose of the club was "to care for and further German Literature in the close social circle" of the society, but as its president, Hans Haupt noted it served a broader purpose since it was the "only place in the city at which educated German men of all occupations met together." It attracted as members various clergymen, professors, editors and some members of the elite, such as Nippert and former mayor Spiegel. Barnstorff claimed the club was "founded by intellectually high-standing men who almost all, next to their occupations, showed an interest for literature, art and learning, and for the most part were also literarily active." The books written by members over the years formed "a stately library." Indeed, Rattermann had viewed the purpose of the society to stimulate members to literary activity and "through the exchange of opinions, friendly discussion and critiques to elevate the form and the intellectual context of their work." One could be either an active or a passive member, active members all being required to present a paper as part of the club's lecture series. Meetings were held every other week after the war, but then it was decided to place meetings on a weekly basis with every other week being a "free evening," i.e., without a lecture. Also, an occasional Damenabend was held to which wives and lady friends were invited. President Haupt noted in the Festschrift that at various times the different words in the name of the group had been emphasized. It was "German," it was "Literary," but it was also a "Club."

However, this club had "nothing in common with an American club .. by which one immediately thinks of cushioned armchairs, finest Havana cigars, and great lamp-shades." To Haupt, the German Literary Club brought other things to mind: Gemütlichkeit, pipes, tankards, humor, wit, and Geselligkeit. Moreover, the German Literary Club was not imbued with a desire to engage in a self-righteous puritanical crusade to recast the individual, society and the world into its own image. As Haupt stated the society "was no Reform-club and does not desire to reform anywhere. That we leave to the know-it-all." According to him, the members of the club wanted to entertain themselves while learning, and to learn while they were entertaining one

another. They "strove for a life-happy continuous development,
for concrete comprehension of intellectual questions, for a
clearer understanding of the world and humanity. What unites
us is this striving and the German language."(50)

Before the war the club met at the Ernst Koch Halle on the
southwest corner of 12th and Walnut. Since this was located in
the stately Germania Building owned by Rattermann the meeting
place came to be known as the Rattermann Halle.(51) Here the
club met and also housed its library which consisted in works
presented by members to the club, such as Ratterman''s Gesammelte ausgewählte Werke. It also contained a fine edition of
the works of Schiller presented by Kaiser Wilhelm II. After
U.S. entrance into the war, the meetings of the society continued until 1918:

> but the anti-German atmosphere ... did not lack in
> exerting its influence and effect on the German Lit-
> erary Club. Many members stayed away from the meet-
> ings out of fear that they would fall prey to a
> police raid, as other German societies had experienc-
> ed it.

On 3 April 1918 it was decided to postpone meetings indefinitely "So one closed the doors behind oneself and left the meeting
place without great hope for a swift renewal and early
revival."(52)

Barnstorff observed that after the war, the Versailles
Treaty concluded, and Warren G. Harding had become president,
"then one dared also again to think on the forelorn Germandom
in the U.S." A meeting was called for 7 September 1921 after a
respite of three and a half years. A first meeting was held at
Mecklenburg's Biergarten, located on University and Highland
Ave. After the confusion of the war and the location of a new
meeting place it was discovered that the club's fine little
library consisted now of little more than some bookshelves.

However, by the second meeting things seemed back in "the old navigable water." Fick composed a prologue for the reopening of the lecture series and Dr. Deutsch presented the first paper in the series on the topic of the history of the Renaissance age in which he critiqued the ideas of Savonarola and Machiavelli. Plans were made to attract more new members, especially among recently arrived immigrants, by publicizing in the press the forthcoming presentations by Haupt and Dr. Morgenstern. Finally, it was decided that a new home for the club had been found at Grammer's Restaurant, 1470 Walnut St.(53)

On 22 November 1921 the first foundation fest was held in the postwar era with presentations on the group's history by Fick and Charles Schmidt, president of the local Combined Singers and the North American Sängerbund. Julius Zorn, editor of the Brauer-Zeitung, spoke on the topic of "Our Gifted Writers" while Carl Pletz, editor of the now defunct Volksblatt, spoke on suffragettes. In the same year special memorial services were held in honor of the learned Hebrew Union College professor, Dr. Gotthard Deutsch. In 1922 the Sommerfest celebrated the fifteen hundredth meeting of the society at Philippi's Garten in Westwood with delegates of six other societies present.

In 1923 Prof. J.C. Leichtle from the Volkschochschule in Heilbronn spoke regarding Germany and its people, and also in Fichte. Some of the lectures were held in larger quarters, such as the St. Peter's or Zion's Church. A Mr. Konner from the German Foreign Office spoke about the publication of the official German war documents pertaining to the war. On 17 October 1923 a special memorial service was held in St. Peter's Church in honor of the passing of the most prolific German man of letters in the history of the city: H.A. Rattermann. the main funeral orations were delivered by Fick, Morgenstern, and Pletz. Even a poem for the occasion had been composed and sent to Cincinnati by Wilhelm Müller in Germany.(54) In 1924 Prof. R.R. Schmidt from the University of Tubingen spoke on the topic

of German antiquities. In conjunction with a paper by Morgenstern (27 February 1924) a special ceremony was held to commemorate the one hundredth anniversary of the death of the philosopher Immanuel Kant. The club actively supported the efforts
of the Cincinnati Club Center, later known as the German House
Society, which was chaired by a club member, Dr. Morgenstern.
In early October 1926 the 75th birthday of Charles Schmidt was
celebrated, and followed later in the month by a Beethoven
Celebration. In February 1927 Nippert sponsored a reception in
the Gibson Hotel for the new German consul, Dr. Borchers. In
the summers trips were made to the home of club member George
A. Katzenberger in Greenville.(55) The club also cooperated
with and co-sponsored events with the Germanistic Society.

According to the club's officers "our boundaries are those
of human knowledge." An examination of the list of lectures
held in the 1920s indicates that club members were interested
in a wide range of topics. Barnstorff spoke on German lyric
poetry, Theodore Dreiser, Shaw, Anatole France, Cecil Rhodes,
Brigham Young and other historical topics.(56) Rev. E.W.
Becker spoke on the emancipation of women, the Goethe-Schiller
Monument in Cleveland, German travel impressions and other
related subjects. Sol. Einstein discussed the theory of rela-
tivity, German currency, and his views on traveling in Germany.
Fick spoke on German-American literature, dialects in German-
American literature, Thomas Jefferson, the Haymarket Riot, John
Brown, American women writers and other literary aspects. Rev.
Haupt presented papers on a wide variety of topics, including:
Buddha, Dostojewski, Werfel, Napoleon I, Schiller and Goethe.
Morgenstern discussed the World War, Spengler, the American
West, the Mayan Indians and other topics relating to the far
west. Dr. Moser from the _Freie Presse_ delivered half a dozen
papers on various topics such as Walt Whitman, General U.S.
Grant, Lafayette and Carl Follen. David Rosenthal discussed
the impact of the war on art. Sängerbund President Schmidt
spoke naturally on the topic of Sängerfeste, but also on such

diverse topics as Thomas Münzer and eating habits.   Prof. Zeydel understandably presented a paper about the German language
in the American instructional system.   And Julius Zorn, editor
of the Brauer-Zeitung, discussed economic matters and the Dawes
Plan. These are but a few of the subjects which were then presented as paper topics by members of the German Literary Club
in the 1920s.

    Concluding the club's 1927 Festschrift was a selection of
seventeen poems contributed by nine members: H.H. Fick, Fred
W. Noak, Hans Haupt, Hermann Barnstorff, Oscar Braun, Edwin
Zeydel and Erick W. Becker.   The subject matter dealt with in
these poems ranged from the Goethe-Schiller Monument in Cleveland,   a translation of Poe's "The Raven," German song, the
immigrant, to the topic of humor.   As an American-born author
Zeydel contributed a poem entitled "To the One Born Here" in
which he addressed the American-born as follows:

Be proud of your ancestors, O do not be ashamed of them,
Their countenance is reflected in your face.
They gambled goods and possessions, their life,
In order to fight for freedom here, since liberty was their
   goal.

No illusion of splendid treasures drew them into a distant
   land,
No thoughtless haste tore the bond to their homeland,
No, more noble was their striving! In spite of many a
   spiritual torment
They followed heartily this high ideal.

And work, work, work that was their watchword
So that gradually they raised their deeply concealed
   treasure:
The fortune in the new homeland, the courage to fresh action,
Rejuvenated the joy of existence and the harvest of one's
   seed.

O scorn them not, the faithful, they were always there,
When it was necessary to protect this land from grim tyranny,
Be proud of your ancestors, O do not be ashamed of them,
Their desire for freedom is reflected in your countenance.
                                                        (57)

It is apparent that in spite of the 1918-21 respite, the war in no way can be said to have led to the disappearance of German intellectual life in Cincinnati in general and to the disappearance of the German Literary Club in particular. Both survived.

Theater

A basic strength of the German theater in America was that it appealed to a cross-section of the German community, but the other side of the coin was that it could claim no one area of the ethnic community as its institutional and financial sponsor. Because of this rather precarious financial position the German theater of Cincinnati acquired the reputation of a Schmerzenskind, or child of sorrow, since it was viewed as a step-child in the community. This tenuous foundation was complicated by the circumstances of the First World War.

At the outset of the war there were two theatrical organizations which sponsored competing theatrical groups: the Theaterverein, established in 1890, and the German Theater Co., founded in 1913. The latter, which was under the direction of Dr. Karl L. Stoll, was praised by the Volksblatt in April 1914 for its "artistic successes." It claimed that it "offered good things in the area of the drama and the very good in comedy, and what concerns the operetta, presentations were performed which New York and Milwaukee would envy us for." On 4 October 1914 the Theater Co. opened its last theatrical session. Its plays, however, were so well received that the acting group received invitations from Pittsburgh, Indianapolis, Fort Wayne, Cleveland and Toledo. Then on 20 November director Willy Dietrich announced from the stage that the company and the acting group were going their separate ways because of impending financial difficulties. (58)

The theatrical group then turned to Otto Ernst Schmid who had been directing German plays at the Grand Opera House and had also directed for the Theaterverein. It was he who had been responsible for what Wood views as the high point of the Cincinnati German theater: the presentation of Wilhelm Tell in the Music Hall on 30 April 1905. Under Schmid's direction the theatrical troupe attained in 1915-16 "one of its artistically most successful years." The group fortunately now received the financial support of the Theaterverein. This group's members included those who were prominent in the elite and the Vereine, such as Leopold Markbreit, Max Burgheim, Henry Hauck, and Charles Schmidt. In retrospect the founding of a competing organization, the German Theater Co., in 1913 must be viewed as a mistake given the difficulty in financially supporting a German theater. It appears that the older Theaterverein had a great deal more potential for community-wide support. Its presidents included Adolf Sander, Albert Mühlhauser and Judge John Schwab. In 1915-16 Schmid's group performed plays by Schiller, Hauptmann, Sudermann, Schiller, Ibsen, Lessing, Freitag, and Lehar. Because of the support of the Theaterverein and the good attendance the deficit of the theater was reduced from $8,000 in the 1915 16 season to zero by May 1917. However, now other problems presented themselves. (59)

It "was the service of the Cincinnatians of German descent that more than once the house was almost sold out." Still, the first season into the war was not a success for several reasons: First, there was the harsh winter of 1917-18 which kept theater-goers at home. Second, financial support from the Theaterverein was no longer forthcoming, and a deficit of $4,000 had been registered. It should be remembered that a great amount of money at the time was channeled into humanitarian war-relief projects, and there was most likely no excess funding available for the theater which in the context of the war situation may have appeared a luxury item. Finally, there was the nativist spirit of the time. According to Wood, "the

anti-German propaganda became daily more vehement." Cn 28
April 1918 three members of the theater group were arrested as
enemy aliens, thus causing the closing of the theater.(60)

In 1924 the Sport- und Spielklub Edelweiss established a
special department in its society devoted to the monthly presentation of German language plays. A group of actors, under
the direction of Dr. Werner Bertram, presented Alt Heidelberg
on 4 October 1925, the first German language play in seven
years in the Queen City. The Edelweiss group gradually grew
into a separate organization, the German Theater Society which
was under the direction of Heinrich Klohe, a leading member of
the Cincinnati Club Center/German House Society. Dr. Bertram
continued to direct the Society's acting group. The Society
sponsored German plays on a monthly basis in Emory Auditorium,
and held weekly meetings each Friday in the Odd Fellow Temple,
located on 7th and Elm Sts. Among the many plays that were
produced were: Faust, Wilhelm Tell, Der Trompeter von Säck-
ingen, Die Menschen-Freude, Im weissen Rossl, and Die Spanische
Fliege. In honor of the fiftieth anniversary of the German
Literary Club the German Theater Society presented Ludwig
Fulda's Die verlorene Tochter on 16 November 1927. The rebirth
of the German theater was obviously a point of pride to those
interested in German cultural life and letters. The 1927 festschrift of the Freie Presse dedicated to the 50th anniversary
of the German Literary Club contained an article by Dr. Moser
on music and the German stage in Cincinnati, and one by Dr.
Bertram entitled "Unser deutsches Theater."(61)

It should be remembered that the rebirth of German theater
in Cincinnati was no easy task. First, there was the need of
establishing a new organization to sponsor German theater.
Second, there was the concomitant crisis emanating from the
Great Depression in the latter years of the period investigated
by this study. Third, there was the appearance of two recent
phenomena which seemed to be attracting the interest of a great

many Americans: the radio and the movies. The German theater in Chicago, for example, "fell victim to the competition of the movies in 1931."(62) In spite of these various obstacles it is remarkable that the German theater not only revived in 1925, but that it survived throughout the entire period.

Music

The effects of the war were also to be felt in the realm of music. Across the U.S. the "works of German composers disappeared from symphony programs; German artists were denied the use of concert halls," for example.(63) In Cincinnati two aspects of musical life internal and external to the German community can be examined: First, the German-American Gesangvereine, or singing societies, and, second, the May Festival and the Cincinnati Symphony Orchestra. The former were an integral component part of German community life, whereas the latter represented broader community-wide institutions, but ones in which German-Americans and German musical traditions played significant roles.

Cincinnati was the home of the North American Sängerbund, established in 1849 by German and Swiss singing societies from Kentucky, Indiana and Ohio. Thereafter, numerous Gesangvereine had been formed which contributed to sponsoring large national Sängerfeste in the Queen City in 1851, 1867, 1870, 1879, and in 1899 (the 50th, or golden anniversary). Theodore Thomas remarked in his autobiography that music seemed to be a part of everyday life in Cincinnati.(64) Indeed, German song and music was the very reason for existence for the various Gesangvereine, of which there were eleven at the outbreak of the war in Cincinnati. All of them were affiliated with a local umbrella organization, the Vereinigten Sänger, known as the Combined Singers. All of these groups of course belonged also to the local Stadtverband. President of the Combined Singers was Charles Schmidt, who was also national president of the Sängerbund, a fact which made Cincinnati national headquarters for the singing societies of the Midwest. During the war the singing societies grew silent, at least in public because of the local police orders against German language public meetings which were enforced by occasional police raids. The possibility of a Sängerfest was, hence, totally out of the question until after the war. Some societies merely postponed meeting indefinitely. After the war Gesangvereine resumed their meetings and singing activities. There were no casualties among the Gesangvereine as a result of the war. All eleven societies and the Combined Singers' umbrella organization survived the Great War. Also, two children's choirs were established, one by the Citizens League and one by the Danube Swabians. The former was under the direction of the talented and popular director William Kappelhoff. A former president of the Herwegh Singing Society, which met in the Workmen's Hall on Walnut St. near Mercer, recalled that the Herwegh Singers:

> ... met every Thursday night for rehearsal. And we belonged to districts. Our district included Indianapolis, Dayton, and Columbus. Once a month we'd meet somewhere in the district for a concert, dinner and dancing.
>
> And every four years we would have a national concert ... There were three-day long occasions in St. Louis, Pittsburgh, New York, Rock Haven, Conn., Rochester, N.Y., and Minnesota.
>
> It was beautiful. We rehearsed some songs for years. The women wore formals and the men, dark business suits, white shirts and black bow-ties. The music, the friendships ... it was sacred to me. (65)

No national Sängerfest was held in Cincinnati until 1952. Nevertheless, the evidence seems to indicate that the singing societies weathered the storms of the Great War.

In the area of the May Festival/Cincinnati Symphony Orchestra the effects of the war were felt. CSO conductor Dr. Ernst Kunwald was an Austrian citizen and reservist of the Austrian-Hungarian army. He and many CSO members had familial ties to Germany and to Austria-Hungary. Mrs. Charles P. Taft, president of the Orchestra Committee, admonished the group that "they would keep their thoughts on harmony at home rather than discord abroad." It should be remembered that local German-American societies were protesting to Charles P. Taft, publisher of the Times-Star, because of what they viewed as the publication's "one-sided pro-British war reporting." Protests were being made about "the malicious Anglo-American press." For the 1916 May Festival Kunwald scheduled the American premiere of The Alpine Symphony by Richard Strauss, a difficult endeavor "because Germany -- with Strauss and his music -- was sealed off from the rest of the world by war." Fortunately, the score was obtained through the U.S. Embassy in Berlin so that the American premiere could take place in Cincinnati.(66)

After Wilson asked congress for a declaration of war (2 April 1917) a war resolution was passed on 6 April that placed the U.S. in a state of war with Germany and Austria-Hungary. This meant that the citizens of these countries were enemy aliens. Dr. Kunwald, who had stated that his heart was on the other side, was arrested one night at his home, taken to a jail in Dayton, and later interned at Ft. Ogelthorpe for the duration of the war; he, of course, resigned his position as the CSO conductor. After the war he moved to Germany, but fled in the 1930s, stating "I got into trouble in Cincinnati for being too German, but I got into trouble in Berlin for not being German enough."

Significantly and symbolically, the successor to Kunwald was a Belgian, Eugene Ysaye, a well known concert violinist. He was a charming, affable "party person" especially popular now as a man without a country. That the U.S. was engaged in a

war was a fact he "never let Cincinnatians forget ..." Chorus-
master Alfred Hartzell was brought from his army post to per-
form in uniform at the May Festival, and Ysaye performed his
composition entitled Exile. The Funeral March of Beethoven's
Eroica Symphony was played by a standing orchestra in memorial
to the heroes on the battlefield. May Festival profits were
turned over to the YMCA and the Red Cross.(67)

A de-emphasis on works by German composers during Ysaye's
period of direction could be noted. The programs were "heavily
loaded with French and Belgian music ..." Among the non-German
works presented was Edgar Stillman-Kelley's The Pilgrim's Progress. However, Ysaye was not a man given to detail, methodical
practice, and punctuality, which were necessities for conducting and practicing with large numbers of people for the May
Festival. Local critics even observed "that the artistic level
was dropping." In 1919 the conductor returned to Belgium with
an invitation from Mayor Galvin to King Albert and Queen Eliza-
beth to visit Cincinnati. The 1920 May Festival was disappointing since "the patriotic fervor Ysaye formerly whipped up
was gone and the season was considered dull."(68)

Already in late 1919 there had been a few positive signs,
however. In October 1919 the Cincinnati Public Library allowed
German books dealing with chemistry and music to be returned to
the library shelves. And on 13 November Fritz Kreisler performed for a large audience in the Music Hall, and the Freie
Presse commented:

> It was the good old Cincinnati with its artistic tra-
> ditions from which the strong German strain after all
> would not allow itself to be erased ... The Kreisler
> evening was the brilliant triumph of majestic art
> over mean hate, and hence it will be unforgettable to
> those who were so privileged to experience it.   (69)

After Ysaye's resignation in 1922, the Orchestra Committee obtained the services of Fritz Reiner from the Royal Dresden Opera, an indication of a return to the prewar tradition of German conductors. A Times-Star critic wrote, "the improvement in the playing of the orchestra is so remarkable that absolute perfection is nearer at hand than is generally believed." Such praise was due to the fact that Reiner conducted strenuous. and arduous rehearsals which apparently "cured the leisurely habits of the orchestra ..." Reiner served as conductor until 1931. Succeeding Ysaye as Musical Director of the May Festival was a German-American, Frank van der Stucken who served 1923-27.(70)

Van der Stucken was a popular figure who has been affectionately described:

> ... a gold watch chain emphasized his generous girth, his bald dome had a halo of short gray curls, his blue eyes squinted a twinkle through his small, gold-rimmed glasses and even when he was angry, he had a benevolent look about him. He looked like the Social-Security-aged director of a Cherubim choir. (71)

Mr. Van, as he was called, introduced Cincinnati to Bach's St. John Passion and in the 1927 May Festival he did Beethoven's Missa Solemnis. In 1929 Frederick Stock succeeded Van der Stucken as the Festival's Musical Director, coming from the position of Director of the Chicago Orchestra (the Theodore Thomas Orchestra). From 1931-46 an Englishman, Eugene Goosens, served as Festival Musical Director, and as CSO conductor from 1931-47. "After nearly sixty years of directors in three German accents, and one in French, the May Festival was rehearsed in an Olivier-type British accent." Some felt he had "a British chill about him," but he told amusing stories in a Cockney or Lancaster accent that apparently proved to be endearing to many. In his 1931 repertoire were, moreover, the works of continental composers such as Bach and the Symphony of a Thousand by Mahler. A critic commented "If there is such a thing as a

perfect program" it had been realized by Goosens. He apparently was more successful in synthesizing the older musical
traditions than Ysaye.(72)

The appointments of Reiner and Van der Stucken in 1922 and
1923 respectively and the repertoire of Goosens reflected a
greater degree of continuity with Cincinnati's German musical
tradition than had the years under the direction of Ysaye. The
Great War in no way can be said to have caused the disappearance of German musical tradition in the area of the Gesangvereine, nor in the area of the May Festival and the Cincinnati
Symphony Orchestra. However, it would be difficult to disagree
with the observation that the war had not caused an accomoda-
tion to the needs and demands of the 1920s Zeitgeist:

> German composers dominated the 19th century, and
> until World War I German musicians determined the
> course of American classical music, as well. They
> served as models and pedagogues for our composers;
> they played in our orchestras and, not least, they
> were the best-known conductors, worldwide. The First
> World War began to disrupt all that ...   (73)

Art

A discussion of art during and after the war must focus on
the art establishmen in Cincinnati, namely the Cincinnati
Museum Association which maintained the Cincinnati Art Museum
and the Cincinnati Art Academy. A list of the Association's
136 shareholders in 1919 reveals that approximately one-fourth
were German-surnamed, e.g., Alms, Doepke, Fleischmann, Geier,
von Steinwehr, Windisch, and Wurlitzer. Also, approximately
one-fourth of the annual members of the Association were
German-surnamed. Of the Art Academy's ten teachers, three bore
German names. Thus it must be concluded that Americans of German descent were included within the ranks of the local art
establishment.(74)

The involvement of this local establishment in the World War I effort was remarkable. The 1919 trustees' annual report indicates that the impact of the war was great. Ten of the employees of the Association joined the service, or took positions in some war industry. Nearly all of the young men attending day or night classes enlisted, or found work in one of the war industries. The sharply diminished enrollment caused a substantial decline in tuition received at the Art Academy.

Despite financial shortages, the Director of the Academy, J.H. Gest, observed in his 1919 annual report that "Educational institutions everywhere were subordinated to the winning of the war."(75) The Art Academy was certainly no exception. It responded in several interesting ways: It supplied the demand for war posters in Cincinnati; produced great numbers of surgical dressings, and its members knitted many sweaters and other woolen garments. Large landscape paintings were produced to serve as targets at artillery training schools. In cooperation with the Cincinnati Hospital, special instruction was given to young women interested in working in hospital occupational therapy. The Librarian reported that large numbers of prints had circulated in the public schools as illustrations of English composition. It also circulated periodicals, such as Colliers, the Literary Digest, and the Red Cross Magazine.

As in the area of music, there is a noticeable de-emphasis on the Germanic and an emphasis on that which is French. For example, in 1918 there was a lecture on "French Art of the 18th Century." Artists and art students contributed to the Zoo Fete for the Fatherless Children of France by producing paper crepe flowers "which added greatly to the pictorial charm of the occasion and also added to the exchequer." Women artists designed and produced twelve banners for the Exposition of War Trophies in Music Hall also. In 1918 special art courses were offered, including one on the art of Flanders and northern France. A 1918-19 course on the history of art throughout the

world subsumes a discussion of German art under the lecture title "Painting in the North." Other countries are clearly spe-
cified in the titles of the lectures. Other exhibits which
related to the war effort included a display of 99 war lithographs by Joseph Pennell.

A major loss for the Germanic art tradition in Cincinnati
was the demise of Frank Duveneck on 3 January 1919. His loss
at the Museum and the Academy was deeply felt. In April a
group of his students met in the Deveneck Memorial Room to
honor his memory. A special exhibit of his work was also held
at the Museum. Although no single artist of the 1920s emerged
of Duveneck's stature, it must be said that he did leave behind
a significant legacy as well as a following of students.(76)

It is not until the end of the period 1918-32 that the art
of the "North" again seems to be prominent and acceptable. In
January 1931 the Cincinnati Art Museum held an exhibit of engravings, woodcuts, and etchings by early German masters including works by Lucas Cranach, Hans Holbein the younger, and
Aldegrever Hirschvogel.(77) In late 1931 the Museum's Bulletin
carried an article on the topic of European art museums with
favorable comment on German museums. It claimed that German
museums had "initiated an eduational policy which was designed
to make the publicly owned collections really public." It
noted that since the war "contacts between America and Europe
have been closer than ever before." German museums, especially
those in Frankfurt am Main, Berlin, Dresden and München, are
praised as inaugurators of moderm museum techniques.(78) Thus,
the period closes in the area of art with the beginnings of a
rediscovery of interest in continental art and museum techniques.

Summary

German-American cultural life was blossoming again by the mid-1920s, but several casualties had been incurred by the war. Nativists in Cincinnati had succeeded in destroying one of the nation's finest German-English bilingual programs which dated back to 1840, and along with it the career of many a fine teacher. German-Americans established a bilingual Catholic parochial school, a Saturday German school, and several children's choirs, and continued to advocate the desirability of German language instruction, but the nativist ban enacted during the war continued in place against the wishes of the German element. Only in 1926 was German reinstated in the public schools of Cincinnati, and then only at the high school level. Moreover, this was not accomplished in response to the desires of the German community, but rather at the request of the University of Cincinnati graduate faculty. At the university a guiding force was Professor Edwin Zeydel, Chairman of the German Department, who established a reputation for the Department as a center of study and research in the field. Zeydel himself was actively involved in the German community, especially with the German Literary Club, and was closely associated with the former supervisor of the German bilingual school program, Dr. H.H. Fick. With regard to German instruction for German-American children, however, it should be noted that this became a family responsibility confined to the home.

The German language press was highly visible since it served as a mirror of the German community, and as such became an easy target for anti-Germans, and, hence, received a harsh blow. Of the fifteen German newspapers and journals published in the postwar period one-third ceased publication as direct casualties of the war-engendered Germanophobia. The struggle for survival in the area of the German press can certainly be viewed as a Darwinian struggle for the survival of the fittest. A major paper, such as the _Volksblatt,_ which dated back to

1836, could not survive the raids, harassment, boycotts, etc., so that the Freie Presse emerged as the general newspaper of the German community. Several other special interest publications also survived, but the only other major newspaper was the German Methodist Christliche Apologete.

In the area of literature there were numerous publications in the postwar period, most coming from Dr. H.H. Fick, Prof. Edwin Zeydel, and Ralph Wood, the latter two being American-born. Fick's writings provide an important document of German-American cultural and literary life in Cincinnati. Zeydel contributed numerous books to the areas of German instruction and German historical and literary studies. Ralph Wood was only beginning his long and productive career as a German-American literary and historical scholar. Also there were a number of lyric poets who contributed regularly to the pages of the German language press.

German-American intellectual life revolved around the activities of the German Literary Club which had resumed its functions in 1921. It stressed that it was interested in the exchange and discussion of ideas, and contrasted itself with the reform clubs which aimed at recasting society into their own doctrinaire puritanical images.

In the area of the arts German culture was making a comeback by the mid-1920s. In 1918 the German Theater had closed. Not until 1925 was a German play presented again in Cincinnati, and this time under the newly formed German Theater Society which sponsored German plays and performances. In the area of music all of the German singing societies survived and resumed their activities as before the war. Furthermore, several children's choirs were formed to foster the German language. In the area of Cincinnati's musical institutions the war caused the works of German composers to be swept from the programs and the hiring of non-German directors, but by the mid-1920s German music had been returned, and German-American conductors hired in 1922 (Fritz Reiner) and 1923 (Frank van der Stucken). As with music, the local art institutions de-emphasized what was Germanic, and emphasized art from France and the low countries. By the end of the 1920s interest in German art, referred to as the art of the North, was re-emerging.

Cultural activities are fragile and susceptible to a number of social, economic and political influences, and it took until the mid-1920s before German cultural life and influences again were getting back on their feet, and being enjoyed and appreciated. However, the German language press had been especially hard hit by the war and its aftermath, and the outstanding German bilingual program in the public schools had been scuttled by nativists.

134

Richter Alfred K. Nippert,

der sich durch sein furchtloses, unparteiisches Auftreten in Verteidigung
der gerechten Sache die ungeteilte Achtung und Liebe seiner
deutsch-amerikanischen Mitbürger erworben hat.

Judge Alfred K. Nippert, who has acquired the undivided respect
and love of his German-American compatriots through his fearless, non-partisan representation in defense of the just cause.
From August B. Gorbach, <u>Deutscher Vereins-Wegweiser</u> (1915), a
volume located in the German-Americana Collection, Blegen Library, University of Cincinnati.

CHAPTER III

MAJOR POLITICAL ISSUES

... it is the pro-German forces and the other forces
that showed their hyphen during the war that are now
organized against the treaty ... There is no organized
opposition to this treaty except among the people who
tried to defeat the purpose of this Government in the
war. Hyphens are the knives that are being stuck into
this document. (1)

--Woodrow Wilson

Establishing Peace with Germany

The major issue in the field of foreign affairs which was
of concern to German-Americans in the 1920s was the re-estab-
lishment of peace with Germany. Slowly and cautiously individuals spoke out again with respect to the issues. The Armistice
made it safe and possible for German-Americans to discuss
foreign affairs again without fear of retribution. Some spoke
guardedly on all questions related to the war, but the time had
come when a journalist and editor for the German-language press
could again "begin to call his soul his own again and express
his real views." (2) The expression of these "real views" in
the German language press of Cincinnati reflects the depth and
intensity of the pent up feelings of the community.

The Volksblatt rejoiced that the German people had come to
realize that they had been ruled by fools and hoped that 1918
would accomplish what 1848 had not. It sharply denounced the
Kaiser, the Crown Prince, and the Junker, but especially the
Kaiser who was accused of carrying all the state papers into
exile that might be used to establish the war guilt of his
regime. The armistice terms were rightly forecast since all
knew Germany must yield, but the Volksblatt felt the Allies
should be more lenient with the new German Republic, and that a

just peace, based on Wilson's Fourteen Points, would be established. (3)

Sympathy was expressed for the new Republic, although the
Volksblatt designated Liebknecht as Germany's greatest foe.
The paper claimed Germany was on probation, that she should
faithfully maintain internal order and prevent any Soviet form
of government. The Freie Presse proposed a mild policy toward
Germany, which it felt should become a western European bulwark
against the Bolshevik menace.

Wilson's trip to Europe to take personal charge of his
peace program was supported in the Cincinnati German press.
The trip was regarded as essential to ensure a peace so that
American boys "shall not have died in vain." The press called
to his readers to "stand by the president." The Volksblatt
rejoiced that the Senate Foreign Relations Committee had rejected Sen. Cummins' resolution to send a committee of senators
to Paris. Clearly, German-Americans hoped that the president
would aid in establishing a just peace with Germany. The Freie
Presse recognized that the U.S. would be the only unselfish
power at Versailles, and anticipated friction with the Allies.
Nevertheless, Wilson was expected to gain a permanent peace.

France was opposed since she desired a peace based on
force rather than justice, but it was hoped that the "iron will
of Woodrow Wilson will win in the end, and compel the other
nations to live up to their agreement." With reference to the
treaty, the Freie Presse stated that Danzig was a German city
and that a fair plebescite in eastern parts of Prussia would
result unfavorably for Polish annexation plans. Other editorials claimed that Schleswig-Holstein had always been German and
had never been torn from Denmark. The Freie Presse pleaded
also for the right to self-determination for Germans in Bohemia. Sentiment for the addition of Austria to the new Republic
was also expressed. Immediately with the signing of the Armis-

tice, the press campaigned to arouse humanitarian support for the defeated Germany. The Volksblatt believed that the blockade against her should be lifted immediately as a matter of justice, and to help maintain the new government of Germany.

Criticism of the peace proceedings increased steadily in the Cincinnati German press. The Freie Presse noted that the treatment of the Jews by the Rumanians and the Poles "evidently proves that all peoples, even though they may be associated with the Allied cause, do not yet understand the real meaning of democracy." Also, the Abend-Presse noted, "Where Polish troops move in, peace leaves." The Abend-Presse publicized the Rumanian policy towards the Germans in Transylvania, a policy aimed at prohibiting the use of the German language. Negative comments are reserved for Italy and Gabriel D'Annunzio's "Roman Peace." France, according to the Abend-Presse, underestimated the wartime aid of the U.S., and has always been ungrateful. After Wilson received from King Albert of Belgium a volume of La libre Belgique, the only paper Germany could not suppress, the Abend-Presse suggested that the president reciprocate with a volume of American newspapers dealing with Belgian atrocities in the Congo. The Japanese, criticized for their machinations in China and Korea, were also criticized for their autocratic form of government. Also, the press refers to some future "Yellow Peril" the U.S. will have to face. However, the harshest criticism of all was reserved for England. The right of self-determination was advocated for the Boers of the old Orange Free State. The Abend-Presse observed in relation to the desire of Lloyd George to bring the Kaiser to trial, that the premier must have forgotten that Kitchener brought back the title "the Butcher" from his Sudan and South African adventures and also that British planes struck a funeral procession in Freiburg, Germany and that it was a French professor who made the first poison gas bomb.

Strong opposition to British propaganda was voiced. The
Freie Presse warned of English propaganda in the U.S. schools
and American textbooks. Professor Albert Bushnell Hart was
criticized for stating that American colonists were well
treated at the time of the American Revolution. Reference was
made to assertions that England and France were saved by U.S.
intervention. Displeasure was expressed at the appointment of
a former foreign secretary as British ambassador to the U.S.

The League of Nations was enthusiastically supported by
the Volksblatt. It rejected all objections as to the constitu-
tionality of the League, maintaining disarmament was the major
issue, and asserted that the League was the only hope for
peace. It maintained that the League would apply the Monroe
Doctrine to the world and held that such a League would have
staved off the Great War.

The Volksblatt argued for ratification of the covenant
without amendment and believed countries should be forced to
accept the decrees and mandates of the League, but wasn't disturbed by the fact that England had more votes than the U.S.
By August, the Volksblatt recognized that the ratification
could not be secured without some reservations. The Freie
Presse favored the League with a degree of skepticism, maintaining it required an international police force to enforce
decrees of the League Council. It recommended also that Germany be admitted into the League, but by the fall of 1919 became
critical of the League, stating it would not be a misfortune
were the League to fail altogether.

Cincinnati German newspapers claimed that any peace not
based on the Fourteen Points would be regarded as a violation
of a sacred promise to a defeated country. The delay and hostility to Wilson's program was credited to France, whose Clemenceau was viewed as an exponent of Louis XIV's policy. The
imperialistic claims of France caused the Abend-Presse to

observe that if the conference desired to grant all the territorial demands it should create another world. Attention was
also called to the fact that it was claimed that the blockade
maintained after the armistice had caused the death of 800,000
children in Germany. Herod's murder of Bethlehem's babies was
amateurish compared to this, the Freie Presse declared.

The Volksblatt approved dismantling of the forts of Kiel
and Helgoland, but held similar steps should be taken in all
strategic straits and waterways. Bitterness with the peace
caused the Freie Presse to remark that Germany was fortunate
that the Allies did not impose prohibition on her. The loss of
the coalfields of the Saar Valley and Upper Silesia was viewed
as disastrous. The Shantung clause of the treaty was attacked:
"anatomy is a curious thing. We cut China's throat in order to
save the heart of the world."

The press of Cincinnati regarded the treaty as a failure
with reference to the freedom of the seas problem. Articles
from American and English periodicals that criticized the
League were reprinted in full. For example: General Smuts'
statement on his refusal to sign the treaty; Arthur Henderson
on the peace treaty; Dr. Bullitt's resignation from the American Peace Commission; and "The Betrayal."

Clemenceau was considered the arch-conspirator against
Wilson's peace plan based on the Fourteen Points. Passages of
the treaty arc cited without comment to call attention to their
inconsistency with Wilson's peace plans. The Freie Presse felt
that Wilson was dissatisfied with the peace but powerless to
change it. The Volksblatt felt that Wilson and Secretary Lansing were ignorant of European diplomacy. Eventually, commen-
tary about the treaty becomes increasingly bitter and the peace
is seen as a curse.

After his return, Wilson was criticized for his rational-
ization of treaty provisions and the peace conference. The
Austrian treaty was viewed as worse than the German treaty.
The proposed separate alliance between England, the U.S. and
France was denounced as contrary to the spirit of the League
and as a dangerous alliance. Local editors urged the U.S.
Senate to ratify the treaty and the League so that peace could
be re-established. Wilson was criticized for labeling opponents of the treaty "pro-German."

Ultimately, the Cincinnati German press viewed the peace
settlement with Germany a failure, and one that was inconsistent with Wilson's Fourteen Points. The Volksblatt, at first a
supporter of the League, stated that German-Americans did not
regard the League at all as important, and that they cared
nothing about the treaty. "Opposition to it was the one issue
on which all Germans, regardless of party or class agreed."(4)
Here again a war-related issue served to accentuate the commun-
ality of the various segments of the community.

Trade was resumed with Germany in July 1919. Although
relations gradually improved, they remained somewhat ambiguous
since the U.S. had not ratified the Treaty of Versailles. Formally the country remained at war until August 1921 when the
Treaty of Berlin took effect. The Freie Presse felt that "the
path of reconciliation was now open." This peace finally
lifted officially the U.S. declaration of war (6 April 1917)
against Germany. The favorable reaction of the Freie Presse
reflects the strong German-American desire for the re-estab-
lishment of peaceful relations between Germany and America.
The war was finally over. Diplomatic relations resumed in
November 1921 and in May 1922 the first German ambassador, Dr.
Otto Wiedfeldt, arrived in Washington D.C. The first U.S.
ambassador, and one who could even speak German, Alanson B.
Houghton, arrived in Berlin. In 1923 President Harding ordered

the return of the U.S. Occupation Army from Europe. By 1926
Germany was admitted to the League of Nations.

Relief

We have carried the burden of love for two years,
thousands have gone through private suffering to
help those abroad and they will continue to do so.(5)

A postwar activity which reflects the survival of the
German-American community was the war relief work conducted in
Cincinnati on behalf of the suffering in Germany. Here, as
elsewhere, German-Americans moved slowly and with caution in
emerging from the war-engendered cocoon. The Rev. Hans Haupt,
secretary of the pre-war German-Austrian-Hungarian Aid Society,
was asked in August 1919 if the Aid Society would again coordinate fund raising to assist the starving children of Germany.
He responded, "The time to take up the work again is not yet
come." Conditions did not as yet "permit us to start a campaign for publicity without rendering the overall outcome of
the affair highly questionable, even if done in the name of
mercy." Haupt, therefore, suggested the relief be carried on
an individual basis with contributions going to the needy,
lists of which could be obtained from the priests, ministers
and mayors of German villages and cities. The Freie Presse
advised that the old country should be swamped with war relief
packages. It was, therefore, still not advisable to organize a
relief program publicly in Cincinnati. Given these conditions
it is understandable that the Herwegh Männerchor tabled a petition to join an international organization to aid the starving
children of Germany in August 1919.(6)

A year after the Armistice the time appeared to have come
to take up the relief work again. According to the Freie
Presse, German-Americans "need no longer to raise the brotherly
hand" to aid in the destruction of the old country:

> Today we are only their brothers, sisters and daugh-
> ters; nothing keeps us today from giving free rein to
> our natural bent of extending them our helping hand
> ... How easy will it be for us to extirpate all
> possible anger and distrust against us and to reopen
> the ways for the cordial relations of former days. (7)

Individual aid efforts began in late summer and early fall 1919 with the _Freie Presse_ functioning as an unofficial collection agency for the community. In November an all-German benefit fest was organized by women at the Central Turnhalle, an event that was highly successful. The _Presse_ was astonished that the Halle was filled to the "last nook and cranny."(8) During 1919 very few names of donors were listed in the _Presse_ since such humanitarian efforts were monitored by A.H. Tarvin's tabloid, _Comment, One Hundred Percent American_. Donors, therefore, hid behind initials, or indicated that the donation was from a friend, an unknown friend, or that the source was unknown. Contributions ranged from $25 to $300. No organizations involved themselves in war relief in 1919.

In January 1920 Howard Wurlitzer, who had been active in pre-war relief work, organized the local chapter of the Society of Needy Children in Central Europe. In sixteen months a total of $52,334.84 was raised by the Cincinnati chapter. The project was compared with the pre-war relief work, which the _Freie Presse_ described as "the only gratifying and pleasing ray of light in the history of the World War." It had been a source "of honor and pride to the Germandom of this country." In January the Rifle Association held a relief bazaar, which the _Presse_ recommended to its readers should become "one of the glorious pages in the history of this city's Germandom." German-Americans were advised to contribute so that those in Europe would not succumb "to the hate of the Allies." At a benefit bazaar sponsored by the Badensian Mutual Aid Society in February Rev. Frederick L. Dorn maintained that "We have a wrong to make right with our blood brethren." He claimed that

"every little bit of aid will arouse their awareness that one
has not forgotten them, and will inspire them with confidence
and a new will to live." The Presse wrote of the positive
effects of giving on the German-American: "It is in his activity of rendering aid to the unfortunate homeland which keeps
alive in him love, the heart's more noble passion." The
various war relief bazaars and projects provided the community
with a new focal point and a means to aid in the postwar comeback. (9)

Amongst the Kirchendeutschen the generosity of the German
Methodists was especially noteworthy. The German relief fund
in Cincinnati, coordianted by Der Christliche Apologete, A.K.
Nippert, and J.A. Diekmann, collected more than a half million
dollars. Contributions reportedly poured in in such a volume
"that recording facilities broke down." As soon as it was possible the Methodist Episcopal Church of America cabled funds to
Switzerland to purchase food and clothing in Switzerland so
that the first relief train of three freight cars could be sent
into Germany. The first shipment included: 1000 pounds of
tea; 1000 pounds of coffee; 1500 pounds of cocoa; 16,200 pounds
of corned beef; 21,600 pounds of bacon; 30,000 bars of soap;
7200 cans of syrup; 600 cases of fats; 96,000 cans of evapor-
ated milk; 48,000 cans of condensed milk; 1000 women's coats;
2520 suits of children's underwear; and an unspecified number
of shoes, suits, stockings and overcoats. German Methodists
purchased "Vacation Certificates" at $10 each which entitled a
needy child to a month's rest paid for by an American family.
Mite boxes were distributed to families for the collection of
daily sacrifices. Sunday School classes made their contributions and special offerings were made at Christmas. A central
Methodist European Relief Office was opened in New York City to
coordinate these various relief projects.

It is impossible to estimate how much money was sent by
individuals abroad, but it most likely equaled the $50,000

donated in the prewar relief period. The total collected for postwar relief work amounted to: individual donations: $50,000 (estimated); society for Needy Children in Central Europe: $52,334.84; German Methodists: $500,000. Postwar relief, therefore, totaled $602,334.84 which compares to the prewar collection of $426,382.88. The German community had given substantially more after than before the war. Looking back in 1920 on the war relief work, Rev. Haupt observed:

> ... our English Cincinnati newspapers did not report what the conditions in Europe were, refused to accept and publish letters stating the needs of the suffering children and did not offer their columns to advertise any of the benevolent efforts ... but rather worked against them by continuing to call the Germans and their offspring "Huns." Now our time has come for rejoicing, for the 100 per cent American has awakened! Hoover has written to the "Literary Digest" and there is on foot a great movement to arouse the spirit of the sympathetic Americans in favor of the starving children and women of Central Europe. Thank God! When we are almost at the end another source of help is opening up. But there is one thing that is lamentable. These people begin their campaign by belittling what has been done by the Americans of German blood during these last two years. That is neither fair nor noble. We have carried the burden of love for two years, thousands have gone through private suffering to help those abroad and they will continue to do so. We desire no thanks from those who called us "Huns" yesterday, but we feel that in works of charity all competition should be honest and not carry the ugliness of slander nor the Newspaper language of a political American campaign. (10)

Had the German community disappeared there would have been no war relief program.

Local Politics--Reform as Nativism in Cincinnati

The better, the real Cincinnati took the driver's seat in 1924 and proceeded to prove its quality. The new regime showed so complete a reversal of form from the old that it left observers dazed.(11)

In local politics the ethnic political machine forged by Boss Cox was pitted in conflict with WASP reformers after the First World War. "The conservative bias of many progressive reformers could be most clearly seen in their attacks on the boss and the machine while their real intentions were frequently obscured." The reformers spoke of the "people" and "fundamental democracy" but it was not made clear that "by the people they meant not the huddled masses in center cities but solid citizens with sensible views and sober habits who had previously abdicated in favor of the bosses and their benighted clients." Behind the crusaders' call for fundamental democracy was "the progressive call for the politically vanquished to return to the fray armed with new weapons."(12)

The death of Boss Cox in May 1916 did not lead to the sudden demise of the machine he had forged since the 1880s. His lieutenants assumed control of the machine apparatus with Rudolph "Rud" Hynicka at the helm. Hynicka, a Pennsylvania German born in 1858 in Meyerstown, Pennsylvania, enjoyed a middle-class upbringing, acquired social graces, and developed an ability for public speaking and writing. Until 1926, a year before his death, he held the powerful position as chair of the Hamilton County Republican Committee. Whereas Cox had been a laconic loner, Hynicka was gemütlich, ebullient, and an excellent social mixer. He dined with his cronies in the elegant Sinton Hotel dining room. "Frequently, he staged meetings there and delivered stirring speeches to his followers." Whenever problems with the machine arose one went to the "compassionate Crown Prince." As one individual noted, "Rud Hynicka is my friend; he takes care of me."(13)

Hynicka, realizing that the days of the autocratic urban boss were fading, recognized that deference must be accorded to the reformers within the Republican Party. He, therefore, cleverly reorganized the hierarchy of the party locally to include such reform elements in positions of authority, although he himself remained firmly in charge regardless of the organizational chart. Also, the machine remained solidly in place at the City Hall and the County Courthouse. In the wards and precincts machine men dominated. It should be noted that "there were no blatant cases" of graft but that the occurrence of petty privileges persisted, e.g., payoffs and kickbacks. In 1917 Hynicka moved to New York City to run his Columbia Amusement Co., a firm consisting of forty theaters in the U.S. and Canada. However, he remained as an absentee boss in contact with the machine via telephone and telegraph. Before each election he would ritualistically arrive a week or two in advance to coordinate the election and then cast his ballot. Under the Cox machine Hynicka had been well known for the maintenance of a card catalog with information on Hamilton County voters.(14)

An excellent innovation was Cincinnati's first Home Rule Charter of 1917. This provided for a large council of 32 members. The city was divided into 26 wards, each of which elected a councilman, while six more were elected at large. This type of system held distinct advantages for ethnic and racial groups in assuring the possibility of representation from various wards. Each neighborhood had a councilman it could turn to as its elected representative.

The central organization for reformers in the postwar period was the Cincinnatus Association, organized in 1920. Its prime founder, ironically, was a second-generation German, Victor Heintz, who had been serving since March 1919 as a political organizer for the Republican National Committee for the mid-American region. In February 1920 during a stay in Cincinnati he called together a meeting of about 20 men, mostly Republicans but including Democrats and independents, for a meeting at the University Club. In social standing most were representatives of the "better sort." This meeting marked the beginning of the Cincinnatus Association, an elitist WASP civic organization. Membership was limited to 100. "A small militant body -- this was a more efficient and effective reform instrument, and it should be non-partisan," according to an organizational history. This group aimed to provide a forum for discussion of vital issues of the day and should also "assist in awakening a public consciousness and would develop a means through which members of the younger generation could give affect to their aspirations for a higher sense of civic duty and for a better local government." The seed planted by Heintz was cultivated by other local reformers.(15)

Leadership passed to John B. Hollister, first president of the Cincinnatus Association. Hollister, born in 1890, was a native Cincinnatian with local roots reaching back to 1789, but his ancestral origins derived from Vermont and New Jersey. His New England heritage was "solidly American." He attended St. Paul's preparatory school (Concord, New Hampshire), Yale (1911) and Harvard Law School (1915). He served in World War I as a commander of a battery of artillery. He returned to Cincinnati in 1919 after aiding Hoover in relief programs in Poland, Lithuania and Latvia. A study of Cincinnatus' members when it was organized reveals a striking degree of resemblance with the background of Hollister:

> ... they represented almost a perfect "WASP grouping -- i.e., white, Anglo-Saxon Protestants. Twenty-six were college graduates, with Yale leading the way (thirteen) and Harvard a distant second (five). Almost one-third (sixteen) were business executives. there were nine lawyers, five insurance salesmen, three real estate brokers, two architects and one minister. In religion, they were heavily Episcopalian (eighteen). The Presbyterians stood next with five. Over half (twenty two) made their homes in the better residential districts of the "Eastern Hills" (Hyde Park, Walnut Hills and Indian Hill). About

> one-third resided in the four remaining "prestige"
> districts: Mt. Auburn, Clifton, Avondale, or Glen-
> dale. All were Caucasian. (16)

It should be noted that the Association adhered to an unwritten
rule which excluded non-Caucasians.

At this point it is well to focus on the linkage of the
machine to the ethnic community. As the history of the Cincinnatus Association observes:

> The Germans are essential to our story for one rea-
> son: many acquired citizenship and, by extension, the
> right to vote.   They soon became the nexus between
> failure and success for the two main political par-
> ties.   Capture the German vote and you win the city
> and county -- this became an axiom of politics in
> Cincinnati in the post-Civil War era. (17)

Cox permitted, it will be remembered, the taverns to be open on
Sunday, explaining that since more than one third of the city
was composed of Germans and that they demanded that privilege,
he felt that the German vote was a major factor at election
time. In the machine it was part of the job of August Hermann
to function as an ambassador of good will of the machine to the
German community.   He often attended local picnics, festivals,
and other community events and celebrations.

Reformers felt that the machine had transformed ethic and
racial elements into automatons:

> It was the common practice of both major parties to
> instruct the mass of illiterate voters in the slum
> wards of the Basin -- and this group usually repre-
> sented the margin of victory in most elections -- to
> vote for the party symbol rather than for the men
> listed in the column below. Since the days of Cox,
> the Republicans had been more adept at this practice
> than had the Democrats. They skillfully "petty-
> favored, wheedled and trained to the point of automo-
> tism" the large German-American and Negro elements of

the electorate to vote for the "chicken with the
short legs and with pants on," i.e., the eagle.
Those who faithfully adhered to the instructions were
properly rewarded; and each time they voted, there
was an appropriate reward!(18)

Since, it was felt, the immigrants lacked an understanding of
the apparatus of American government they could be easily in-
fluenced with joviality, beer and wurst.

Members of the machine were contrasted sharply and unfavorably with the reformers. Machine "toughs" shared "in common, boorish social habits, the ethical outlook of highwaymen,
and a pronounced antipathy for 'blueblood' reformers."(19) A
contrast can be seen in a report regarding a debate between a
member of the machine, Judge Joseph Woeste, and a member of the
Cincinnatus Association, Russell Wilson. The debate took place
before the Association in 1920. Judge Woeste of Municipal
Court, a Hynicka supporter, was soundly defeated by Wilson who
delighted in annihilating opponents in forensic debate.
Woeste, in an attempt to win sympathy because of his humble
origins, stated, "Well, I'm not a graduate of Princeton. I'm a
graduate of the school of hard knocks.", Wilson thereupon sar-
castically replied, "Well, at that you're hardly an honor to
your alma mater." Both represented different origins. Woeste
had risen via the machine. In October 1924 Cincinnatus presented a three-act farce, but one not devoid of lightly veiled
nativism. One lackey named Adolph Kxmmxr replies to another
lackey in mock seriousness: "Don't forget, Henry, dat Rud's
got sumting else again to do but run dis City. He's got to
look out for his burlesque interest."(20)

Cincinnatus hammered haid at the machine with the issue of
the poor condition of downtown city streets apparently as its
central issue. This was a tangible issue that could be
exploited for political purposes since local citizens were

familiar with street conditions. Reformers advocated the abolition of Cincinnati's mayor-council system and the adoption of a new charter with a city manager system. Murray Seasongood, of German-Jewish descent, became the leader of the anti-machine forces. Born in 1878 in Cincinnati he had attended local public schools, Edgeborough School (Guildford, England), Harvard and Cambridge. In 1909 he commenced his legal career with the firm of Paxton and Warrington.(21)

In 1924 a non-partisan group of reformers, the City Charter Committe, wrote a new charter which was passed by voters, and in January 1926 the first Council under it took office. "The old machine was utterly routed, smashed, and macerated, never to rise or be seen again in politics." The machine was "overthrown and an era of 'good government' was instituted." The long reign of Cox and his "evil allies" may have seemed inexplicable in a city as "cultured and intelligent" as Cincinnati, but Alvin Harlow observed that "In the most advanced of cities, there is, always has been and will be ... a great mass of uninformed, thinkless voters; and inertia's clammy hand will long continue to hold motionless, as in the past, many folk who should know better."(22)

The new charter provided: First, that the City Council would be small and consist of nine members, who themselves would elect one of the nine as mayor. Second, Council members would be elected by proportional representation from the city at large, rather than from a district ward. Third, a city manager would be hired by the council to run the city's business and carry out the council's policies. Fourth, all city employees would be required to take a civil service examination for city jobs.

This charter would be critiqued at several points. First, citizens lost the opportunity to directly elect their own mayor, that right being granted to the city council. Second, individual neighborhoods and districts lost the opportunity of electing local representatives. Substituting "at-large" city wide elections for local ward elections rendered it difficult for neighborhoods to attain direct representation.(23)

Cincinnati's government was completely overhauled. There were numerous excellent reforms and improvements: streets were repaired, signs posted on street corners; parks expanded and improved; recreation facilities were expanded. the police and fire departments were modernized; the auditor's office system of bookkeeping was streamlined; a civil service system was instituted; municipal contracts were placed on a fair bid basis; a city newspaper was created; services increased and the tax rate decreased; the city gained the right to fix its tax rate and free itself of county control, etc. However, progressivism did not address iself to ethnic community concerns. Certainly none of the issues and concerns of the local German community appeared on the local reform agenda, e.g., the issue of nativism during and after the war in Cincinnati. Indeed, posting new signs on street corners was the closest reformers came to touching on an issue related to a recent nativist act: the changing of street names by city ordinance.

Presidential Elections

After the war years the German-American community was basically cautious in expressing itself on any controversial issues. Although publicly reticent, German-Americans silently expressed their political resentment in the polling booth, as well as through the columns of the German language press.(24)

Of the four presidential elections from 1920-32 no other election stirred the emotions and feelings of German-Americans as did the 1920 election. The old Stadtverband, now the Citizens League, did a solid about-face on the issue of woman's suffrage. Previously, it had opposed woman's suffrage, but it now recognized the power of the German-American woman vote. It appealed to women to go to the polls and vote for Harding in the 1920 election. It, however, avoided an open endorsement, stating that this "would more hurt than benefit the candidate." Nevertheless, it declared bitterly "the time will come, and is no longer far away, when we are going to speak up, and ears will be ringing among the German haters."(25)

In April 1920 the _Freie Presse_ expressed the general feeling of discontent:

> If we went to war to make the world safe for democracy, we have to book a dismal failure. Ireland is in chains, India and Egypt ruled by the bayonet. Shantung is enslaved and Korea cries out in its deadly peril of oppression. In Europe imperialism rules wherever one goes.

All those who had spoken for the war with the pretext of "fighting the devil, have let Hell loose on Earth." Basic rights had been threatened:

> We have witnessed how a weak, stubborn, old and vain man is destroying the work of the Jeffersons, Adamses and Franklins. More than 60 laws are on the books which in one way or another aim at making us into a nation of serfs ... and most of them have been approved by the tribunal which we were wont to consider as our strongest bulwark against tyranny.

The newspaper could only ask:

> ... when we look sadly across the waters, oh brothers, to the fields of France where 80,000 of those magnificent boys are moldering, then one cannot possibly keep back one's tears and suppress one's sobbing as one is forced to cry out loud: My God, was it all worth it?(26)

By 1920 the German-Americans had seen the various pledges, promises and proposals for peace made during the war either "neglected, refused, or compromised at the conference table."(27)   The publication of the harsh Treaty of Versailles had been a bitter disillusionment to them since their faith in Wilson to establish a just peace had been sincere. The 1920 election offered Cincinnati's German-Americans the chance to settle scores at the ballot box, and gave them their first opportunity to pass judgment on Wilson's work.

The German-American press was unanimous in its denunciation of Wilsonism and all that it implied. The press began early in the campaign to show an uncompromising and bitter opposition to Wilson's foreign policy. Press editors expressed the old anti-British and anti-French attitudes, and argued that unrestricted warfare had been justified and would perhaps be used by France and England in the next war. The *Freie Presse* dared to say that the U.S. entered the war to protect American capitalists and industrialists.(28)

Hiram Johnson appeared to be the favorite at first for the Republican nomination, mainly because of his opposition to the Treaty of Versailles, the League Covenant and also because of his progressive record. Hoover was considered too British, although he was of German ancestry. Leonard Wood was utterly impossible. When the *Freie Presse* learned that Harding's nomination was opposed by the pro-British press the wisdom of the Republican convention in selecting him was without question.(29)   After the nomination the vehement denunciation of Wilson began.

The *Freie Presse* said that the U.S. entered the war to make the world safe for democracy, and then surrendered all its principles at the peace conference.(30)   On 31 October, 1920 it published an article on the administration entitled "The Despot of the White House." Of course, the League was totally rejected since it would give the British control of the world forever, and would "most likely furnish American cannon-fodder for the British Empire."(31) The _Presse_ also insisted that the German vote in 1920 would be Republican, because the Democrats had deceived the German-Americans in 1916 with the slogan, "He kept us out of war."(32) Moreover, the administration was accused of extravagance, autocracy, interference with constitutional rights and unfounded distrust of the German element.

The German-Americans were advised to mobilize against Gov. Cox, the Democratic nominee for the presidency, and present a united front. The April 1919 message of Governor Cox's speech to the Ohio Legislature was recalled, in which he charged the presence of German propaganda in the public schools and used his influence to end the teaching of German in the schools of Ohio. The words of Cox were quoted repeatedly. Voters were urged to grant the governor the appropriate response, and the _Freie Presse_ considered this message the focal point for the anti-Cox movement amongst German-Americans.(33) An appeal signed by editors of the _Freie Presse_ and the _Cleveland Waechter und Anzeiger_ was reprinted throughout Ohio widely. It summoned all German-Americans to strike at Cox via the ballot box. The _Freie Presse_ called for vengeance on all who called German-Americans "Huns" during the war.(34) It quoted the _Milwaukee Herold_ as follows:

> The German-Americans stood the test during the war, and not only made every sacrifice to be expected form any citizen, but a much greater sacrifice, for their hearts bled when their sons stood opposite to their brother in battle. They suffered, but remained faithful.(35)

The editorial claimed that all German-Americans were opposed to Wilsonism and would solidly oppose Cox.

The _Freie Presse_ was critical of Cox's estate near Dayton, Ohio and refers to Cox as Sir James Trailsend. Attempts were made to link Cox to big business and the pro-British press (The _New York Times_ and the _New York Evening Post_).(36) When Cox was forced to rest his voice for several days because of the strain of the campaign, the _Freie Presse_ remarked that the doctor who advised Cox to save his voice was the wisest Democrat possible.(37)

The _Freie Presse_ claimed that Cox was a threat to Catholics and to German-Americans in particular. According to the _Presse_, the Democrats had opposed Catholic parochial schools "wherever possible." With reference to former Gov. Cox of Ohio the _Presse_ noted that he had

> ... revealed himself as a fervent hater of Catholics and a fanatic Germanophobe. Besides he is a regular weathercock and a miserable schemer without honor and without principles. Therefore, our slogan for the election must be: Down with the Democrats. They are only exploiters of the people ... yes, even traitors to the peoples cause, but not representatives, not leaders, not servants, of the people.(38)

The press hatred of Cox was especially vitriolic. The _Presse_ stated "the man who in many public speeches has blasphemed them [the Germans] and slandered them is Cox." Until Harding was nominated the _Presse_ advocated the formation of a third party, an indication of the degree to which alienation was felt towards the major political parties. In sharp contrast to the image of the Democratic candidate was the German-American view of Harding, as reflected in the press. His apparent rejection of the League, his motto "America First," his declaration for an immediate peace with Germany and the prompt removal of the American Occupation Army from the Rhine, won the German-Americans. The _Freie Presse_ advocated adherence to Harding's slogan and rejected the "Rule Brittania" watchword of the Democrats.(39) Effort was expended to show that Harding was a friend of the German-Americans. Harding's father-in-law was of German stock, spoke fluent German and had visited Germany. All of these factors reflected well on the candidate from the German-American perspective. Republican campaign managers exploited the situation to their advantage. Campaign literature was issued in the German language and the Republicans advertised heavily in the German language press. One advertisement, "What the German Language Press Has to Say About the Two Candidates for President" carried statements from German-American editorials across the state of Ohio, and an extract from an article by former Secretary of Labor, Charles Nagel.(40) All of them, of course, endorsed Harding. In spite of the situation, the Democrats attempted to win some German-American votes. They stated that Cox had been misrepresented, and that he actually supported German admission to the League of Nations. However, the press turned a cold shoulder to all the Democratic attempts to woo the German-Americans. The only trouble encountered in the attempt to line up the German-Americans for Harding came from an attempt to inject the wet and dry issue into the campaign. The Freie Presse received numerous questions about Harding's views on prohibition, and raised the issue of whether prohibition was not really the leading question of the campaign. If so, German-Americans would even vote for Cox. But the Freie Presse assured that Harding's views on prohibition were satisfactory, that Cox could not be trusted, and that in any event no German-American could sell his self-respect for a four cent beer.(41) The 1 November issue of the Freie Presse carried the headline, "Stimmt fuer Warren G. Harding."

Election results for Hamilton County indicated that James M. Cox had been decisively defeated by Warren G. Harding. The Republican candidate had received 112,590 votes to 77,598 for the Democratic candidate. Only 6,778 voted for candidates in the "other" category.

The Republican landslide brought forth the utmost jubilation from the German press in Cincinnati. The _Freie Presse_ remarked, "The free people of America have crushed the snake of Wilsonism."(42) It also reported a rumor that as a consolation Cox would recieve a high British honor or decoration. Henry Overmann, President of the Deutscher Pionier-Verein, looked forward to March 4, when Harding would take office. In his speech at the Washington Birthday Fest on 21 Feb. 1921, the mention of the name "Harding" brought forth such jubiliation that the speech could hardly be continued. Albert Bettinger's speech at the same fest declared that among the few who understood the predicament of the German-American was Warren G. Harding. Bettinger quoted Harding's speech of 31 March 1917 at the Business Men's Club in which he declared that he could understand the sorrow that German-Americans must feel to see their new and old homelands at war with each other, and he wished he could spare them the conflict between duty and sympathy. The yearbook of the _Pionier-Verein_ for 1920-21 printed the full text of his speech in German translation.(43)

On 16 February 1921, a five-man delegation of the German-American Citizens League (the national organization), including George Sylvester Viereck, visited Harding urging him to evaluate German-American achievements when making his cabinet appointments. The visit of course resulted in making it impossible for Harding to appoint a German-American because of the anti-German spirit of the time. The League, however, continued to press Harding in the fall of 1921 for a German-American appointment to the position of ambassador to Austria. Viereck's pressure politics alienated German-Americans, but especially the editors of the German-American press. Viereck's story constitutes a separate chapter in German-American history, but his conflicts with the press over political issues relate to Cincinnati German affairs.

German-Americans divided as a result of Viereck's pursuit
of political power. Editors adopted a quiet, low-key approach.
With the anti-German hysteria fresh in mind they "preferred to
limit the public display of German ethnicity to cultural and
social affairs such as German Day celebrations, bazaars, and
benefit concerts." They sought political goals through private
negotiations and discussions. Elven supported the behind-the-
scenes approach to politics rather than the abrasive approach
of Viereck. Because of this Viereck attacked Elven and other
editors with similar views in a series of articles denouncing
them as "renegade Judases," of "supine docility," and "bovine
passivity." Viereck's American Monthly also attacked cliques
in New York and Cincinnati for creating the impression in Harding's mind that German-Americans were hopelessly divided.(44)

The 1924 Election

In the 1924 election the German-American press expressed
solid support for the Republican candidate, Calvin Coolidge.
Advertisements in the Freie Presse asked the question of readers, "Coolidge or Chaos?"(45) The Freie Presse quoted former
vice-mayor of Cincinnati, Gilbert Bettmann, who had been temporary chairman of the Ohio State Republican Convention,
listing what the Republicans had accomplished for the state.
The Freie Presse endorsed a solid Republican ticket from the
local, state to the national level. Special emphasis was
placed on a speech by Charles Nagel, former Secretary of Commerce and Labor. The speech, delivered in St. Louis, was
significant in that Nagel was perhaps the most widely respected
German-American involved in public affairs at the time. The
article was entitled "Charles Nagel's Last Word." It urged
German-Americans to support Coolidge in the forthcoming presidential election. LaFollette was rejected as being too
radical. This endorsement assured Coolidge the support of
numerous German-American newspapers.

The caution of German-Americans is reflected in the on-going debate between press editors and George Sylvester Viereck. In 1924 Elven feared a repeat of Viereck's political strategy during the 1920 presidential election. He, therefore, published a lengthy editorial criticizing the "flagrant· tact-lessness" of the national Citizens League with its abrasive policy of concessions and demands. Elven proclaimed the German language press as the legitimate, responsible and appropriate institution to lead the German-Americans as an ethnic group. Although he did not mention him by name, Elven's editorial was clearly aimed at Viereck, and those who advocated his particu-lar political approach to the issues. Viereck responded with an attack on Elven charging that the Freie Presse and other German-American newspapers had been bribed with political advertisement contracts by the Republican national commit-tee.(46) The debate, an aside to the 1924 election, indicates that the Cincinnati German press did not identify at all with the political style of the controversial Viereck.

Election returns for Hamilton County for the 1924 presi-dential election indicated a Republican landslide: 115,950 voted Republican; 34,916 voted Democrat, and 40,163 voted "other." The high vote in the "other" category indicated that a substantial number of local voters had voted for LaFollette on the Progressive ticket. John W. Davis, the Democrat candi-date, was literally overwhelmed in Cincinnati.

The 1928 Election

In the 1928 presidential election Republican candidate Herbert C. Hoover faced Democratic candidate Alfred C. Smith. The election returns for Hamilton County reflect another solid Republican victory with Hoover receiving 147,534 votes against 110,151 for Smith. A mere 1,007 votes can be found in the "other" category. Endorsements of Hoover in the Freie Presse

prior to the election by prominent German-Americans indicated
that the Republican candidate held the edge.

The _Freie Presse_ in late October published a telegram of
Judge Nippert to the Republican meeting in Carnegie Hall. The
highly respected and influential judge stated:

> I would deem it a privilege to endorse in person the
> candidacy of Mr. Hoover for President ... I am
> especially interested in Mr. Hoover's candidacy for
> the reason that nine years ago when no one dared to
> come to the rescue of the millions of starving women
> and children in Germany, it was Herbert Hoover who,
> with courage and determination, lifted the food
> blockade of Central Europe and forced the Allies to
> permit millions of tons of food to be transported
> into Germany, Austria and Hungary, and thus saved
> these nations from starvation and all of Europe from
> the menace of Bolshevism.(47)

Republican advertising in the _Presse_ emphasized that after the
First World War Hoover had been good enough "to help our old
homeland."(48) Hoover's postwar relief work was obviously a
positive factor that appealed to German-Americans. As during
the 1924 presidential election, the _Freie Presse_ again carried
a position statement by Charles Nagel, former Secretary of Commerce and Labor, who was described as "the greatest and most
important" contemporary German-American. Nagel identified the
three central issues of concern to German-Americans as prohibition, immigration restriction, and foreign affairs. Although
not entirely in accord with all aspects of any candidate, Nagel
endorsed Hoover because of his extensive experience, his metho-
dological approach, and because he seemed to present a more
definite set of plans for the future than his opponent during
the campaign.(49) Advertisements in the _Presse_ announced "This
is a Republican Year."(50)

The _Freie_ _Presse_ also carried Democratic advertising on behalf of its candidate, Alfred C. Smith. One advertisement proclaimed "Prosperity for All! Freedom for All!" and announced that Smith supported changes in the current prohibition law. It also stated that Smith was a "ray of light of American democracy" against the "dark forces of the KKK and their invisible whispering allies of reaction, the chauvinists, the bigots and the narrow-minded nativists."(51) Here was a direct appeal to two issues of concern to German-Americans: prohibition and nativism. Smith also won some notable nationally known endorsements from the former Republican Congressman Richard Bartholdt (Missouri), Theodore Hoffmann (Steuben Society), Charles Korz (Catholic Central-Verein), Val Peter (Omaha Tribune), baseball players Babe Ruth and Lou Gehrig, and even the Baltimore sage H.L. Mencken. It should be noted that some German-Americans still regarded Smith's party as the party of Wilsonism and prohibition. None of the campaign rhetoric and endorsement on behalf of Smith could stave off the Republican victory locally. The German Methodist periodical, _Der_ _Christliche_ _Apologete_, celebrated the election of a "dry" by honoring the new president with the publication of a full-page portrait after the election.(52) The _Freie_ _Presse_ referred to the election's results as "Herbert Hoover's Glorious Victory."(53)

The 1932 Election

In late October before the 1932 presidential election Hoover visited Cincinnati and the _Freie_ _Presse_ reported that "Thousands Greet President Hoover."(54) He was greeted by a committee that included Robert A. Taft, Joseph Assel, Lincoln Mitchell, William Hess, John Hollister, and Julius Fleischmann. Alice Roosevelt Longworth was also in attendance. The _Freie_ _Presse_ maintained that economic conditions resulting from the depression were improving, and that President Hoover had taken a better course than what was being suggested by Governor Roosevelt. It also praised Hoover for freeing Germany from the pressure of war reparations since he had announced a one-year moratorium in 1931 on reparations and war debts. (55) Endorsements by local Republicans proclaimed "Every Crisis Produces its own Master" and advised readers to hold fast to Hoover. (56)

A cartoon in the _Presse_ portrayed Roosevelt as stating to voters "I'll promise you anything just so you vote for me." However, Democratic advertising by the German-American Division of the Democratic National Committee hit hard at the issues of the day. It announced unequivocally that FDR was for the repeal of the 18th Amendment and noted that this was desired by citizens of German descent. It claimed that a vote for Roosevelt would be "a step forwards to justice for you and your countrymen." (57)

Elven, in the _Freie Presse_, endorsed Hoover for re-election. Endorsements for the Republican tickets included George Puchta, A.K. Nippert, Elmer Hunsicker, Edward H. Lillie, B.H. Kroger, Edward H. Schorr, Fred E. Wesselmann, A. Otis Graeser, Frank H. Waesman and others. Advertisements advised German-Americans to "Hold Fast to Hoover." (58) An endorsement came from a prominent Cleveland German, Otto L. Fricke, advising "Americans of German Origin Vote All for Herbert Hoover." (59) Other endorsements for Hoover came from Victor Heintz, Max Stern, Ralph Holterhoff, Stanley Rowe, and Charles P. Taft II. (60) The election results for Hamilton County indicate that Roosevelt defeated Hoover by a vote of 123,109 to 118,804; only 7,163 belonging to the "other" category. The _Freie Presse_ announced that the "Democratic Victory was Complete." (61)

Summary

The major political issues in the postwar period were the establishment of peace with Germany, postwar relief for Germany, local politics, and the presidential elections. With regard to the peace settlement German-Americans were naturally

concerned that a just and fair peace based on the Fourteen
Points of Wilson be established. The imposition of a harsh and
vengeful Treaty of Versailles caused Cincinnati Germans to view
the Treaty as a failure and one not in accord with the Fourteen
Points.

After the war Cincinnati Germans carried out a labor of
love in raising substantial sums of money for the sick, needy,
orphaned, war wounded, and starving in Germany. The war relief
work was considered "the only gratifying and pleasing ray of
light" emanating from the war and a source of honor and pride
in the German community.

In the area of local politics Cincinnati Germans saw the
ethnic political machine forged by Boss Cox on the defense
against the local WASP reformers. These so-called progressive
reformers spoke at length about "the people" and "fundamental
democracy" but established a system of city government that
deprived citizens of the right to elect their mayor and deprived neighborhoods of the right to elect a councilman to
represent their own specific neighborhood.

In presidential elections from 1920 to 1928 German-Americans consistently voted Republican, the party seen as most
supportive and reflective of German-American interests.
Although publicly reticent, their viewpoints could be found
reflected in the columns and editorials of the German language
press. Especially the 1920 election was seen by German-Americans as a chance for them to settle scores at the ballot box
for the war, the Treaty of Versailles, Wilsonism, and all that
the latter represented. In 1924 German-Americans voted for
Coolidge, although some votes were siphoned off by LaFollette,
while in 1928 they solidly supported Hoover. However, in 1932
because of the depression FDR narrowly carried the area, an
indication of the concerns of the economic crisis, as well as
the tempering of feelings since the Great War.

The   end of the postwar period brought a mixed picture   of
positive and negative perceptions with regard to local, national,   and   international affairs.   The Treaty of Versailles was
seen as a complete failure,   but Cincinnati Germans were justi-
fiably   proud of the relief work they carried out for the   suffering in postwar Germany.   Locally they saw the WASP reformers
install   a new form of city government,   and one that   was   not
conducive   to neighborhood representation.   In national   politics,   they   rejoiced   at the defeats received by the party   of
Woodrow Wilson in the 1920s.

CHAPTER IV

THE POSTWAR WAR AGAINST THE GERMAN HERITAGE

We Are Waiting

But the first step has to be taken by those who have
sown hate and fostered discord, who have heaped us
with suspicion and slander, who have persecuted us
with lies and meanness, who have tortured us and
tormented our souls in a fashion as no human beings
who have loyally fulfilled their duties have ever
been suspected, slandered, persecuted and tormented
... We are ready to forgive, but they must ask to be
forgiven; for it is not we but they who have sinned.
—The _Freie_ _Presse_ after the Great War(1)

Nativism in the 1920s

The war "bequeathed to the 1920s a heritage of hatred and
hysteria that permeated and disturbed every aspect of life and
thought."(2) Few eras in American history "have been so rife
with cultural conflict as the 1920s. It was a time ... that
the bitter brew of ethnic and religious hostility, which had
been simmering for years, finally boiled over."(3) John Higham
refers to the 1890-1924 period as one of "repressive waves of
nativism and racism."(4) Although "most nativists were Anglo-
Saxon Protestants," not all WASPs, of course, were necessarily
imbued with nativist sentiments.(5)

Two expressions of the 1920s nativist atmosphere were immigration restriction legislation and the Ku Klux Klan. The
Immigration Act of 1921 limited immigration from countries to
three percent of a country's foreign stock in the U.S. in 1910;
the 1924 Johnson Act lowered the quota to two percent and
pushed the base year back to 1890, excluding Oriental immigration altogether; the "national origins" system which became
operative in 1929 further reflected the trend to limiting the

immigrations. The total number of immigrants permissible from outside the western hemisphere was 150,000. In comparison to the 1924 plan the British quota was doubled, whereas those of Germany, Scandinavia and the Irish Free State were reduced. The quota assigned to Britain exceeded the total combined for all the countries of northwestern Europe, a fact which caused critics to refer to the National Origins Law as the "British Origins Law." Its supporters hailed the new plan "as a way to preserve the cultural composition of the American population as it existed in 1920, and prevent any further dilutions, but enforcing qualitative selections among those who wanted to come." (6)

The new Klan by 1924 claimed a national membership of five million. It was not only anti-black, but also anti-Semitic, anti-Catholic, and anti-immigrant. Its membership was drawn from the lower middle class old American Protestant stock. The Klan gained members outside the south, especially in Indiana. In July 1923 75,000 Ohio Klansmen met at Buckeye, near Columbus, for their first state convention. Plans were made "for the advancement of Klankraft in this section of the country where the order is already of great strength." It aimed to "save our people from inoculation of false ideas, peoples and Gods." (7)

U.S. Senate hearings reflected and supported nativist sentiments. In 1919 the Senate Subcommittee on the Judiciary submitted its report on **Brewing and Liquor Interests and German and Bolshevik Propaganda**. Here, conveniently lumped together by nativists were brewers, Germans and Bolsheviks. This Senate document reflects the intolerance of the time. In it all segments of the German-American community were charged with disloyalty. Brewers, certainly some of the most prominent members of the German-American elite, were described in uncomplimentary terms:

The organized liquor traffic of the country is a vicious interest because it has been unpatriotic because it has been pro-German in its sympathies and its conduct. Around these great brewery organizations owned by rich men, almost all of them of German birth and sympathy, at least before we entered the war, has grown up the societies, all the organizations of this country intended to keep young German immigrants from becoming real American citizens.

It is around the saengerfests and saengerbunds and organizations of that kind, generally financed by the rich brewers, that the young Germans who come to America are taught to remember, first, the fatherland. (8)

The club Germans were viewed as separatists from American society:

In addition, these Germans and German-Americans have maintained a system of social segregation through numerous local societies and organizations which come under the general head of vereins and verbunds, the object and purpose of which have been to preserve the language and customs of Germany and to bind together those of German lineage. Many of these various societies and associations are subsidiary to or part of the German-American Alliance, a national organization incorporated by act of Congress of the United States, the charter of which has, however, been revoked by act of Congress since the United States entered the war. This organization, with its 1,300 local vereins and verbunds, claimed to have at the time of the outbreak of the European war a membership of approximately 2,000,000 persons. The members of the alliance never concealed their main aim, which was to keep their own nationality separate from that of their fellow citizens in the United States, and by means of the dissemination of literature by the National Alliance, as well as by the State alliances and local societies, their objects were accomplished.

The church Germans, especially the Lutherans, were addressed by the Senate Subcommittee on the Judiciary:

It is in evidence before the committee that certain branches of the Lutheran Church were particularly active in defending the German cause during the
period of neutrality, not only by means of religious
teachings, but by work through the secular societies,
especially the subsidiary organizations of the
German-American Alliance.

The German language press was not overlooked:

There had been built up in the United States a
German language press with ramifications in practically every part of the country, which German language press was represented by large dailies in the
principal cities of the United States. This German
language press was supplemented by a vast number of
periodicals and magazines printed in the German language and widely distributed, the official newspaper
directories showing that upward of 1,100 German
language publications were in existence in the United
States at the outbreak of the European war.

The committee felt that the foreign language press was in many
instances inspired with the purpose of discouraging assimilation and had been used for political and propaganda purposes.
The Committee held:

Foreign-language newspapers are a danger to the
country unless they are utilized to assist in the
assimilation of the alien element and to aid in the
process of Americanization which is essential to the
healthy development of the population into a homogen-
eous whole. This much-sought-for Americanization
would be impeded by either depriving the alien of the
educational value of a newspaper in the only language
he can read or by withholding from him proper aid and
facility for learning the English language and fail-
ing to encourage him to acquire the educational
advantages incident to the mastering of the language
of his adopted country. With this in mind, therefore, this committee recommends legislation to
control and regulate the printing of foreign-language
publications in this country.

With general reference to the citizenry of German descent the
Committee observed that:

Of this vast number it is in evidence that a
considerable part maintained and designedly perpet-
uated the language, customs, and racial ideals of
Germany, and through and by means of the introduction
and maintenance of the German language in the common
schools of the various States and in the parochial
and religious schools, seminaries and colleges, in
conducting religious services in their churches in
the German language, in the wise dissemination of
German literature through the German language press,
and in the publication, both in Germany and in this
country, of books and writings in the German language, this portion of our population has been
educated along lines of German thought.(9)

In the U.S. Senate report on brewers, Germans and Bolsheviks the nativist hostility of the 1920s Zeitgeist received
clear expression. The major segments of the German-American
community had been referred to in no uncertain terms. According to Arthur Marwick, one of the psychological implications of
the war was the strengthening of in-group feelings and of hostility to out-groups. Alongside the solidarity for the war
effort there coexisted "a heightened sense of solidarity within
classes and groups accompanied by intensified feelings of hostility toward other groups within the nation."(10) It is within this context of a spirit of intolerance that a discussion of
the nativist Kulturkampf against the Germans in Cincinnati
should be placed. Nativism, as it pertains to the Cincinnati
Germans, derived from local, regional, and national sources.
The focus in this chapter will be on several of the major incidents and occurrences of nativism as they relate to the Cincinnati Germans from Armistice through 1932. The _Freie_ _Presse_
demanded an end to all persecution under an editorial, "We are
Waiting:"

But the first step has to be taken by those who
have sown hate and fostered discord, who have heaped
us with suspicion and slander, who have persecuted us
with lies and meanness, who have tortured us and
tormented our souls in a fashion as no human beings
who have loyally fulfilled their duties have ever

been suspected, slandered, persecuted and tormented
... We are ready to forgive, but they must ask to be
forgiven; for it is not we but they who have sinned.(11)

The Freie Presse looked forward to better days in January
1919. "The coming of peace casts its shadow farther and farther before it. Liberty Cabbage is again known as sauerkraut,
and tastes as fine as ever."(12) On November 13, 1919 Fritz
Kreisler played for a large audience in the Music Hall and the
Presse noted:

It was the good old Cincinnati with its artistic
traditions from which the strong German strain after
all would not allow itself to be erased ... the
Kreisler evening was the brilliant triumph of majestic art over mean hate, and hence it will be unfor-
gettable to those who were so privileged to
experience it.(13)

A.H. Tarvin published a tabloid, Comment: One Hundred
Percent Americans (1918-19) which expressed an aim to expose
German spy networks in Cincinnati. It printed lists of Americans who had purchased German war bonds. The tabloid published
an article on the former German consul containing an expose of
spy networks and undercover facilities. He was accused of
practicing the avocation of photographing young ladies au natural. Furthermore, his apartment was draped with Oriental
hangings which "gave the needed atmosphere for licentious or-
gies that made the host the envied of his kind and the 'hero'
of the sort of moral rottenness that is characteristic of the
people of Germany." With regard to the question of assimilation of foreigners the publication states, "To us it seems that
Americans might do well to now devote their energies, through
individual effort and organized demand, to the suppresson of
those things we have learned to understand are menaces to national safety."(14)

The Academy of Medicine

Seven days after the Armistice, 18 November 1918, the Academy of Medicine passed the following resolution:

BE IT RESOLVED by the Academy of Medicine in Cincinnati that it disapproves of the use of German quotations or translations of German quotations in its proceedings, that it will not keep German literature in its archives; that the Academy of Medicine of Cincinnati will not admit anyone of pro-German sentiment to its membership; that it will not permit the presence of portraits of German scientists or medical men or women; that this society will neither purchase nor use anything made in Germany, and that it thoroughly disapproves of medical students at educational institutions in Germany.(15)

The _Enquirer_ announced, "Boche Literature Banished by Academy of Medicine." A sub-headline indicated "Cincinnati Physicians Resolve Not to Purchase Anything Made in Country of Huns." The resolution was introduced by Dr. B. Merrill Ricketts, who had just received word several days prior to the resolution's adoption by the Academy that his son, Corporal Langdon Laws Ricketts, had been killed in action on the French front. His resolution received a unanimous vote. Hence, "The German nation with its scientific literature" would be "a scientific pariah to the physicians of Cincinnati. Anathema was pronounced by the Academy of Medicine against the Huns ..." according to the _Enquirer_.(16) The Academy, therefore, purged itself of German literature in its archives, German quotations or translations from German in its proceedings, portraits of German scientists, and pro-Germans as well as materials from Germany. A motion by Italian-born Dr. Ravogli to table Ricketts' motion found no one to second it.

The nativism of the Academy of Medicine is significant since it represents not the action of a rabid nativist mob but

the action of a professional institution of several hundred
physicians in Cincinnati. It demonstrates the pervasiveness of
the hostilities engendered by the war. That such sentiments
were not transitory is evidenced by an event occurring five
years later. In November 1923 a letter soliciting "a collection to be taken for the benefit of German physicians, many of
whom were at the present time close to starvation" was sent to
523 physicians. Only 35 contributed a total of $495 to the
funds. Dr. Ricketts complained in a letter that "the wild rush
of harmony and of speed with the forgetfulness that is indulged
for the Germans is appalling." He wrote,

> Rude in their manner and laconic in their speech,
> barbarous in their virtues, morose in their joys.
> Like the Ionians, they have lived among holidays;
> they can do nothing without song and dance, or like
> the Romans under Nero who went down fiddling, dancing
> and dissipating in all that is wrong, disregardful in
> all that is good.

Bitterly he stated,

> Surely those who have lashed themselves into a glow
> of admiration for Germans or Germany have not nour-
> ished with their blood, the poppies on the graves of
> the fields of Flanders, the daisies that grow upon
> those of Roumaine, the hollyhocks on those on the
> banks of the Dardanelles, the sweet Narcissus on
> those in the valley of Fiume and that which has made
> red the blue waters of the high seas.(17)

Community Leaders

It would be impossible to list those who were harassed,
demoted, or fired from jobs because of their involvement in the
German community as officers in the societies, but those listed
in August Gorbach's _Deutscher Vereins Wegweiser_ (1915) became
prime candidates. This was a guide to local societies, an address book of the officers with brief histories of the Vereine.
It offered the nativist an ideal "hit-list." More well known,

however, was the symbolic attack on the two major German-American ethnic leaders. Judges Schwaab and Nippert had been for
some time the two foremost representatives and spokesmen of the
German community, a fact which made them visible, obvious and
likely targets of nativist hostility.

In March, 1919 a petition was filed by the patriotic So-
ciety of Cincinnati protesting against the reappointment of
Judge John Schwaab as a meber of the Union Board of High
Schools at the expiration of his term in April. The protest
was based "on the fact that Mr. Schwaab was a Vice President of
the National German-American Alliance and President of the Ohio
German-American Alliance, on statements said to have been made
by him in a speech at Akron, Ohio, after the sinking of the
Lusitania; also, because of his objection to Dr. Charles W.
Dabney, President of the University of Cincinnati, when an effort was made to have Dr. Dabney ousted because of the attitude
he took toward Germany in the early part of the war."(18)

Schwaab claimed the petition was "due to a wet and dry
fight," but later claimed, "I don't think the wet and dry fight
is the real cause behind the protest." He asserted the real
issue was based on a personal matter between himself and another member of the board, Mr. Malcolm McAvoy. Col. Edward Colston and James G. Stewart, members of the executive board of
the Patriotic Society, claimed the wet and dry issue was in no
way involved in the matter and had not the slightest basis for
the protest. Colston claimed it was, however, true that McAvoy
had told him that Schwaab's term would expire in April, but
that McAvoy had no connection with the protest or the Patriotic
Society of Cincinnati. Colston asserted that he "prepared the
charges solely on the ground of the man's pro-German sentiments, as expressed before this country's entering the war."
Schwaab stated that since he was an attorney he would represent
himself and said "It is perfectly absurd to doubt my patrio-

tism. I can bring hundreds of witnesses of American stock to
vouch for it."(19)

Judge Frederick Hoffmann, presiding judge of the Common
Pleas Court, to whom the petition was given, called a special
meeting on April 22 to consider the protest. It was noted also
that no other candidate besides Schwaab had filed for the position on the Union Board of High Schools. The Patriotic Society
pressed its demand for the rejection of Schwaab's candidacy and
filed a statement with the Common Pleas judges responding to
some of Schwaab's remarks. Accompanying their communication
was an affidavit from the well known anti-German Gustavus Ohlinger, a Toledo attorney and a captain in the Military Intelligence Department of the U.S. Navy. The document contained
his translation of Schwaab's speech as published in the official bulletin of the Alliance. Schwaab claimed that the statements were "disconnected" and "misconstrued." The Patriotic
Society felt that the remarks demonstrated that Schwaab was
"thoroughly saturated with pro-Germanism." In the speech he
had said, "When we emerge victorious from this war ..." This
implied identification with the victory in Germany. Schwaab
also said, "If we are shaking the edifice of this great republic as we have been accused of doing then our countrymen should
mark well that the German tears down only when he expects to
erect something in its place." Schwaab also claimed in the
speech that he never read English language newspapers since
they contained "gruesome lies." Schwaab denied making none of
these remarks.(20) Ohlinger was well known as the German-American author of two pieces of anti-German propaganda, Their True
Faith and Allegiance (New York: Macmillan, 1916) and The German
Conspiracy in American Education (New York: Doran, 1919).
Ohlinger had been the principal witness against the German-
American Alliance during the Senate hearings in 1918.(21)

By April 1, the Patriotic Society was joined in its protest by the Business Men's Club. On April 22 the judges voted

five to nine in favor of the reelection of Schwaab. The Enquirer reported, "Candidate's Loyalty Sustained Unanimously."
The judges held an open session on the charges, but no one appeared for or against the charges, although the Patriotic
Society now was supported by the Business Men's Club, the
Kiwanis Club, the Hyde Park Business Club, the Norwood Club,
the Women's Club, and the Daughters of the American Revolution,
and by "diverse and sundry individuals." Judge Hoffmann announced that he had received letters nominating others for the
position, including former mayor Edward Dempsey. Judge Cald-
well referred to a patriotic speech made in 1915 in the Third
Ward by Schwaab, encouraging all aliens to become citizens and
also claimed that Schwaab had done everything to have his son,
Major Walter Schwaab, sent to France after American entrance
into the war. Judge Darby stated that Schwaab had urged the
deportation of all aliens who refused to become citizens, had
made numerous patriotic speeches after American entrance into
the war, had bought Liberty Bonds, and war savings stamps. He
declared there was nothing to indicate disloyalty on the part
of Schwaab and felt for them to sustain the charge would be "an
unwarranted stain upon his name and the name of his soldier
son."(22)

The four Democratic judges claimed the vote had divided on
party lines, and that Schwaab had been sustained by the Republican majority. Upon hearing the decision Schwaab said, "I am
very thankful to the judges, especially for their declaration
concerning my loyalty. It is not my intention to try to have
German put back in the schools. The people do not want it, and
that settles it." Col. Colston maintained that Schwaab felt
that pro-Germanism was consistent with loyalty to the U.S., and
obviously others felt the same way. He also charged that the
local Alliance, now the American Citizens League, had put itself on record to the effect that "the teaching of German in
public schools and the use of the German language in the family
must be maintained." The central issue, according to him, was

whether he should be appointed to the high position on the board whose "pro-German sentiments" were so pronounced "as those entertained by Mr. Schwaab." Schwaab's reelection to the Union Board of High Schools had been a small victory in spite of the fact that he asserted that he had no intention of trying "to have German put back in the schools." (23)

The Hyde Park Businessman's club set its sights on a prominent member, A.K. Nippert. Already in March 1919 the Club had gone on record in a letter to the School Board stating that German language instruction was "a criminal waste of time and money" and an insult to patriotic, intelligent citizens. (24) It also opposed the local publication of German language newspapers in its letter. In July the Club focused on Judge Nippert. This movement was initiated by Col. F.W. Galbraith who had just returned from Europe with French, Belgian and U.S. military decorations (U.S. Distinguished Service Cross). An investigation was requested regarding certain statements Nippert made in New York in early July 1919. The purpose of the investigation would be to either clear Nippert of the matter or dismiss him from the Club. In July and August Nippert wrote two letters to the club indicating that he would appear before a board of inquiry if the investigation would be limited to his remarks made in New York in July. Since the statutes of Ohio did not specify the procedures to be followed for such an investigation by a voluntary organization, several procedures were recommended for the hearings. It was planned to have a member of the Club prepare and present evidence, recommend the calling of witnesses, cross examine the witnesses and then prepare all the evidence for a presentation to the Club's board. Judge Nippert was to be allowed to be present and cross examine witnesses. In return he was to agree to resign should the board vote against him.

The verdict was a foregone conclusion. Judge Nippert wrote to the Club that he would not submit himself "to a public

inquisition without any specific or definite charges and speci-
fications preferred against me by any responsible person or
party and at whch inquiry by your grace I am permitted to be
present." Deprived of the opportunity of a kangaroo court in-
quisiton against Nippert, the Club's president, H.G. Frost,
informed Nippert in the Annual Report for 1920 that he was no
longer welcome at the Club:

> If there are at present any members of the club who
> have been so shortsighted, or so pro-alien, as to
> show, by word or act, that they love some other coun-
> try more than the United States, the laws of the
> state relating to corporations at the present seem to
> preclude us from properly disciplining them by can-
> celing their membership. But we can, and do now, let
> them know that their presence in the Club is not
> desired.

The president, when he read these remarks to the Club's membership, was given a standing ovation as the "staid businessmen
cheered and shouted: 'That's the stuff, good boy, Henry!'"

Frost went on to say that time might bring changes, but
that for now and the immediate future, "We must be on guard
against those who were proved to be dangerous and who betrayed
our hospitality in our time of trial and danger from within and
without." He said that although the German classics might not
be lost forever the "feelings and sentiments of our countrymen
who went abroad and those who remained here [in readiness] to
give their all for the preservation of our country against
subtle serpentile attacks of Culture must be respected." Frost
claimed:

> The despicable and damnable hypocrisies of the Hun
> and his awful barbarous and unspeakable methods of
> warfare are still too fresh in our minds to tolerate
> at this time the revival of either German opera or
> the German theater -- that time may come, gentlemen,
> but it is not here yet. (25)

Schwaab's membership on the Union Board of High Schools and Nippert's membership in the Hyde Park Club were symbolic points at which local nativists could harass well known German-American community leaders. Such attacks on ethnic leaders could only serve to intimidate members of the ethnic community. In their opposition to them, local nativists revealed their opposition to many aspects interrelated with the German community, e.g., German language instruction, the literature, music and theater of Germany, etc. All of these are bound up, in the view of the nativist, with the "subtle serpentine attacks of Culture" from the nation of the "Huns."(26)

Governor Cox and the Postwar War

Impetus and legitimation to the postwar war against German-Americans in Ohio was provided by Gov. James M. Cox of Ohio. On 1 April 1919 he delivered his "Special Message for the Teaching of German in the Elementary Schools." Although addressing the issue of the solution to the problem of German language instruction in the schools of Ohio, Cox in actuality discussed a variety of issues that related to the nativism against German-Americans. In February he had spoken to the Ohio General Assembly on the subject of the teaching of German in elementary schools -- public, private and parochial. As a result the House passed H.R. 37 on 24 February:

> Be it resolved, That this House does most respectfully petition the Governor to be, by him, placed in possession of facts showing in what manner and to what extent disloyalty and treason have emanated from or been fostered by the subjects taught in the schools of Ohio, and what class of schools, whether parochial, private, or public, have been most productive of existing evils, for the correction of which a remedy is demanded.(27)

Cox's 1 April address to the General Assembly aimed to find a solution to "existing evils." He maintained that the

German language instruction was "a distinct menace to Americanism" which was part of an international conspiracy concocted in
Berlin by the German government.   To support his argument he
offered what he termed "three definite accusations."   Apparently proof was not necessary.   First, he claimed "The German
government maintained agencies in America for the exclusive
purpose of holding en bloc, Americans of German birth or
ancestry, in order as expressly stated to preserve Germanism in
our country." Second, the method for the consummation of this
international plot was German language instruction. Third, the
texts of the schoolbooks for German language instruction were
clearly treasonable.   Relieving himself of the responsibility
for providing evidence for these fantasies, Cox claimed that
any unprejudiced person would be informed of the Prussian conspiracy and "knows full well that the recent world war was its
direct result."

    Cox exclaimed "We have communities in this country which
are not only distinctly German in their ancestry, but they live
and feed on no tradition, historical or national, except that
of the fatherland."   He, therefore, felt that "As Germanism
dies, Americansim lives and grows ..." To obtain the death of
"Germanism" Cox had a specific proposal in mind, but first he
discussed German instrutional materials being used in Ohio
schools.   In these textbooks Cox found not only "songs of the
fatherland" but also "adulation of the kaiser."   Moreover,
teachers of German were usually of German origin with hearts
"full of Prussian poison."   Hundreds of them invested in German
war bonds and many had uttered treasonable remarks, he asserted.

    To bolster such outlandish charges he cited an innocent
textbook entitled <u>Hier</u> <u>und</u> <u>Dort</u> which had been published by the
Supervisor of German in the Cincinnati Public Schools, Dr. H.H.
Fick. Cox claimed that the 1916 textbook discriminated against
Washington by emphasizing the role of Baron von Steuben during

the American Revolution. In an article on Christmas, Cox asserted that the author had discussed German Christmas customs only. The reader was left with the impression that "we should have no Christmas trees now if the Germans had not brought the custom here with them." In another slightly veiled reference to Dr. Fick, Cox recoiled that "men have been given yearly salaries for the purpose of exclusively dedicating themselves to the task of supervising these text-books and seeing to it that the spirit of Germanism is kept alive." What then was the end solution to be? Cox proposed "that it be made unlawful for anyone anywhere in this state to teach German to the children in the grades, whether they attend public, private or parochial schools ..." Non-public schools must be included since they provided "sequestered places where German propaganda will be sheltered by the arm of the law." Cox further recommended loyalty oaths for teachers by statutory direction. The governor concluded "We have had our bitter experiences, and love for our children compels us in common prudence, to protect them from the 'wolf in sheep's clothing.'" (28)

The Ohio Legislature, upon the recommendation of the governor, passed the Ake Law in May 1919 which stipulated that (1) all studies below the eighth grade in the public schools be taught in English language only, and that German should not be taught as a separate study in these grades; and (2) that all private and parochial schools below the eighth grade also be in the English language. Gov. Cox scuttled an alternative bill by Republican legislators that permitted German instruction in private and parochial schools. This would have, according to Cox, created "preserves of treason" in Ohio. "If any person in Ohio wants his child indoctrinated with Prussian creeds, let our safeguards be such that he must go elsewhere." (29)

Test cases from Ohio, Nebraska an Iowa were brought to the U.S. Supreme Court which ruled in June 1923 that all laws:

... relative to the teaching of foreign languages, or
the use of foreign languages as a medium of instruction, are unconstitutional, as violating Const. U.S.
Amend. 14, providing that no state shall deprive any
person of liberty without due process of law.(30)

The Court observed that no emergency had "arisen which
renders knowledge by a child of some language other than English so clearly harmful as to justify its inhibition with the
consequent infringement of rights long freely enjoyed."(31)
The Ohio, Nebraska and Iowa laws were all reversed. However,
from May 1919 to June 1923 German language instruction below
the eighth grade in private, parochial an public schools was
illegal in the state of Ohio because of the Ake Law, a law
which had been upheld by the Ohio Supreme Court in 1921. The
U.S. Supreme Court, therefore, can be credited with having
brought an end to the movement to eliminate and/or restrict
non-English language instruction in public, private and parochial schools.

German Language Instruction in Cincinnati

The bilingual program had been dropped from the curriculum
of the Cincinnati Public Schools beginning with the fall term
of 1918, scuttling a program dating back to 1840. In spite of
its demise, nativists continued to beat a dead horse. This
reflects the depth of anti-Germanism. In March 1919 the Hyde
Park Businessmen's Club wrote to the Board of Education stating
"that the teaching of German in the elementary schools is a
criminal waste of time and money and an insult to the patriotism and intelligence of our citizens ..."(32) Alexander Thomson, the leader of opponents to German language instruction in
Cincinnati, presented a pamphlet in March 1919 to the Ohio
State Legislature entitled "History of German in Cincinnati
Public Schools." He attacked German language instruction as "a
waste of the time of children to the neglect of the three R's,

and a serious handicap in their study of English. A means of
propagating German influence to the weakening of American citizenship."(33)   Interrelated to the attacks on German language
instruction was the attempt in March-April 1919 to remove Judge
Schwaab as a member of the Union Board of High Schools.
Schwaab earlier had been, as a member of the School Board,
entrusted with the supervision of the German program until Dr.
Fick had assumed this responsibility in 1901. Although Schwaab
had won his case, he had felt required to state that he had no
intention of trying "to have German put back in the
schools."(34)   After the enactment of the Ake Law in May 1919
no further attacks on German language instruction in Cincinnati
were made.   Nativists had attained their goal of the destruction of the bilingual program. The continued agitation against
Geman instruction after the Armistice reflects the continuance
of war-engendered hostilities.

German Books at the Public Library

After the Armistice, some German books began to find their
way back to the shelves in the public library.   On 20 November
1919, books on religion, natural science, fine arts, and history were returned to the collection, with the exception of
those books under the "830" classification section for German
literature and those under the "914.3" classification for descriptions of German, and "940" which dealt with German history.   By August 1919, the Secretary of War had authorized
replacing books dealing with explosives, and in September Mr.
Hodges, the librarian, gave his permission to renew subscriptions for the German technical periodicals.   Permission to
return the German dictionaries to the shelves was granted in
January 1920.   Another year passed before the rest of the
German collection could be restored to the collection for general circulation.(35)

On 4 February 1921 the _Enquirer_ announced "Veterans to Combat Movement to Return German Language Books to Library." Members of the American Legion, the Disabled American Veterans of the World War and other military organizations of Cincinnati had been "quietly making plans to combat a reported movement among Germans in Cincinnati to have German language books replaced on the shelves of the Cincinnati Public Library and its branches ... " Delegations of these groups planned to file protests with the Library Board. However, complaints had also been received because of the absence of the German book collection. According to one member of the board, "We have received a number of complaints about not having the books in circulation and a number of requests for their return, and probably will take up the question at our next meeting." The member explained that the board declared that the books "could be returned when the war is over, and we have been holding off, because peace has not been formally declared ..."(36)

Two members of the library board, Charles Handman and James A. Green, were opposed to restoring the books: according to Green, "When the library took the books from the library shelves many of the books were so un-American and so thoroughly detrimental to the interest of the country that I considered it to be an act of the highest patriotism to put them out of circulation" Green explained that German sympathizers kept placing German books "filled with propaganda" on library shelves so that there was no alternative but to "abolish such books." Cincinnati had "suffered much from the ill-advised efforts of certain Germans in Cincinnati who did not realize that this country is America." Green felt in sympthy with the removal of all German books from the library shelves and was "thoroughly in sympathy with what has been done to make Cincinnati 100 percent American." At the meeting of 9 Feb., the board declined to resolve the issue of the German collection, but did read five communications from members of the public relating to the matter. Four letters were in favor, and only one was against. The _Enquirer_ reported that "German language books which might be used in the promulgation of the arts and sciences and those pertaining to belles-lettres will be readmitted to the shelves of the Cincinnati Public Library soon."(37) However, "those which pertain to politics, economic, or international issues or what could be termed controversial subjects, stand no chance of being restored, at least for the present."(38) According to the _Enquirer_, only one request per week had even been registered for German books, but that there were many more for technical materials.

Frederick Elven, writing in the _Freie Presse_, declared that the board's action of banning the German collection had been "inexecusable, even during the war, and intolerable after the war." Another community member, Howard Wurlitzer, had written Green, president of the board, stating, "You claim to be 100 per cent American, so why don't you stop circulating the British books. I cculd name quite a few British in Cincinnati who are un-American." With reference to the attempts to have the German collection reshelved, Green remarked:

> So far as any attempt of forcing the board to replace the books, I will vote for their elimination until doomsday. If there was one center of deceit before the war, it was in Cincinnati, for here the German propagandists sought to make the city divided against itself. They did their best to make it a bilingual city and they spent thousands of dollars to further their propaganda through its schools. I feel that Cincinnati was never as American as it is now.

Finally, on 23 February 1921 the Board of Trustees resolved to return all the German books to the shelves with the exceptior. of such books as the librarian "sees fit to place upon restricted shelves."(39) In 1923 the library began to purchase German books again. Finally in January 1925 it resumed its subscription to the _Cincinnati Freie Presse_ more than five years after the Armistice.

Prohibition

The 1919 U.S. Senate report on <u>Brewing</u> <u>and</u> <u>Liquor</u> <u>Inter-</u><u>ests</u> <u>and</u> <u>German</u> <u>and</u> <u>Bolshevik</u> <u>Propaganda</u> referred to the "liquor traffic" as "a vicious interest" that "has been unpatriotic because it has been pro-German in its sympathies and conduct." It also demonstrated that the National German-American Alliance had been generously financed not by Berlin, but by the brewers in America.(40) In light of these assertions prohibition became associated with the hysterical superpatriotism of the time. To a great extent the Eighteenth Amendment was a legacy of the wartime hysteria since it identified prohibition with patriotism. Prohibition was linked not only to an aversion to drunkenness, and its associated evils, but "to the immigrant drinking masses."(41) According to Richard Hofstadter, "When the crusading debauch was over, the country's chief inheritance from the Yankee-Protestant drive for morality and from the tensions of the war period was prohibition." It was "a grim reminder of the moral frenzy that so many wished to forget, a ludicrous caricature of the reforming impulse of the Yankee-Protestant notion that it is both possible and desirable to moralize through public action."(42)

The Cincinnati Stadtverband had historically opposed all prohibiton laws. On 1 August 1914 it had opened its campaign against prohibition with a mass meeting, and its president, Judge John Schwaab, declared that "prohibition is a fight against the Germans." The Ohio Alliance, of which Schwaab was also president, presented on the same day, to the secretary of state of Ohio a petition with 290,000 signatures against prohibition. At the outbreak of the war the Alliance treated prohibition as a British import. Its national publication, the <u>Mitteilungen</u>, in September 1914 spoke against the intolerance, the hypocrisy, the hatred of the Germans and the Puritanism "that have been implanted here by the English." Judge Schwaab claimed in July 1915 that "The drink question is forced upon us by the same hypocritical Puritans as over there are endeavoring to exterminate the German nation." According to him, English influences aimed at the destruction of Germany in Europe and of German influences in the U.S.(43) The Volstead Act of 1919 prohibited the manufacture and sale of any beverage more than one-half of one percent alcohol in content. From the German-American perspective the prohibition law was viewed as an extension of the anti-German hysteria of World War I. Before prohibition went into effect, the local Alliance, now the German-American Citizens League, sponsored a huge beer fest, "a brilliant wake," to the end of beer.

Prohibition deprived German social life of an essential element. The Bavarian Singers explained, "Our losses were mainly due to the unmentionable prohibition, bringing with it a decline of visitors to our celebrations and a corresponding loss in revenue and surpluses." Carl Pletz, former editor of the now defunct Volksblatt, lamented that "there is no longer a good draught to be had, and the main attraction for a congenial get-together no longer exists."(44) Also the Stammtisch "had almost completely disappeared from many an inn." Most societies would agree with the observations of the Pionier-Verein that dry society meetings were "unthinkable" and that the near-beer was a mediocre substitute for the real beer. Under prohibition "the minutes ar read, the secretary replying monotonously: absent. After a good half hour it is time to go home. Such is the course of business," according to the secretary of one society.(45)

Throughout the 1920s German-Americans of Cincinnati voiced opposition to prohibition. Charles Schmidt, president of the North American Saengerbund and the Vereinigte Saenger of Cincinnati, spoke 12 July 1921 at the 53rd Foundation Festival of the Pionier-Verein, and expressed the hope that the new president, Harding, would see the evil of prohibition. According to him, beer, wine and schnapps had earlier brought in tax money for the government, but now nothing. Now one had to be sick in order to get something to drink. However, beer was more than a tonic, according to Schmidt, it was "Teutonic." Moreover, all the products used for brewing were American grown, and those who brewed and drank it were "good Americans."(46)

At the 49th Foundation Festival of the German Literary Club in 1926 prohibition provided the basis for satire in song:

> Wir sind fuer feuchte Planke,
> Verflucht sei der Gedanke:
> Entalkoholisiert.(47)

Most societies had no choice but to accept prohibition, while longing for its conclusion. The main speaker, Alfred K. Nippert, at the Washington Fest of the Pionier-Verein, 23 February 1928, described prohibition as a threat to personal liberty. At another Foundation Festival of the Verein, in 1928, Erich Becker referred to the reform movement as the basic flaw in America. This reform movement has led to the evil known as prohibition, according to him. He noted that just as the repulsive war was over the German-Americans had been blessed with prohibition.(48)

Prohibition was difficult to enforce in Cincinnati. In 1929, 490 bootleggers were arrested and the town was honeycombed with home brew parlors, speakeasies and private clubs. Some of the brewing companies were forced out of business. The Moerlein Co. closed its plant in May 1919, and the Hauck Brewing Company followed suit in March 1927. By 1933 all breweries had ceased the production of beer except Bruckmann's which produced near-beer. In March 1933 the production of light wine and 3.2 beer was allowed, and Ohio revoked its Prohibition Act and the city council passed an emergency ordinance legalizing the production of beer. In April 1933 beer was legal again in Cincinnati. Bruckmann's swiftly ran out of all its beer so that some had to be imported from Louisville, Chicago and Colorado. Some brewers decided to start again after 13 years of prohibition, but only three pro-prohibition brewers survived: Hudepohl, Foss-Schneider, and Schaller Brothers. By 1935, 1,114,000 barrels of beer were being produced.(49)

H.S. Mencken wrote, "Prohibition went into effect on January 16, 1920 and blew up at last on December 5, 1933 -- an elapsed time of twelve years, ten months and nineteen days. It seemed almost a geologic epoch while it was going on, and the human suffering that it entailed must have been a fair match for that of the Black Death or the Thirty Years War ..."(50) The years left their mark on Cincinnati. Gone were the family beer gardens, sitting rooms and nickel beer which had brought people together in the community. No longer would they serve as centers of social, civic and business life. They were replaced by a new institution, the dimly-lit tavern. Grammer's and Mecklenburg's were among the few remaining restaurants and beer gardens. Over-the-Rhine had lost an elemental flavor and atmosphere with the loss of many restaurants, concert halls and beer gardens. No longer would there be family Sunday afternoons in the beer garden accompanied by the little bands playing strains of Strauss and oom-pah music.

The Cincinnati Home Guards

Another aspect of the continuation of the war-engendered nativism was the intimidating factor that the Cincinnati Home Guards, established in 1917, was maintained until 1929. It was organized 8 May 1917 as a war emergency measure and consisted of six battalions of 24 companies with close to 1700 men and officers. In May 1917 City Ordinance 202-1917 had included the provision for private policemen and authorized the Director of Public Safety to commission 5000 of them. Such policemen would serve without compensation and were to be subject to the orders of the mayor and chief of police. All rules regarding private

policemen were to be obeyed as they were established by the
Director of Public Safety. Guardsmen were to be on call at all
times and were entitled to all powers held by patrolmen with
respect to arrests for offenses against the laws of the city of
Cincinnati, the state of Ohio and the U.S.(51)

The city ordinance 202-1917 was to be an emergency measure
designed for the immediate preservation of public peace and
safety during the war. Home Guard companies were recruited
from the various neighborhoods, e.g., sixty-five men from Bond
Hill and an entire company from Avondale.(52) The Guardsmen
engaged in rifle practice and drilled in Burnet Wocds.(53) In
the spring of 1918 they even staged a minstrel show in Emery
Auditorium. Strangely enough the Cincinnati Home Guard remained in existence until they were disbanded in 1929. In 1926
the guard had 1,445 men and officers.(54)

The organizational force behind the Home Guard was A.
Clifford Shinkle, president of the Chamber of Commerce, who
financed the group and made the Chamber of Commerce's facilities available as the headquarters of the Guard. Shinkle, who
resided in Walnut Hills, was also president and chairman of the
board of Central Trust Co., as well as president of the Covington and Cincinnati Bridge Co. During the war he served as
treasurer of the Cincinnati chapter of the Red Cross and also
as Inspector in Ohio of the American Protective League.

Subscriptions in the 1920s paid off the loan Shinkle had
made to the Guard to get it established, and by 1926 the group
held a surplus in its bank account. During and after the war
the guard did not engage in battle with any Kaiserists, but did
assist during the local flood (January-February 1918), the
police strike (September 1918), and the firemen's strike (April
1919). Nevertheless, the organization continued its rifle
practice at Camp Proctor. Fear of the "Huns" now appeared to

be replaced by fear of the Bolsheviks. On 25 March 1919 Mayor John Galvin thanked the Guard for its service, stating:

> I cannot speak too highly of the officials, the rank and file of your organization. They have not only brought honor to themselves, but to our great city, and have shown to the country at large that we have here in good old Cincinnati, an organization of men of so high a standing, that at a moment's call they are willing to put aside all business and social engagements of any kind whatsoever, in order to stamp out any movement that might cause a blot upon the fair name of the Queen City of the West. (55)

In 1929 there apparently was no longer felt to be any need for the maintenance of the Home Guard, and it was disbanded. In April 1930 plans were announced to schedule the group's first reunion during the summer. The mere creation of this organization must be regarded as an expression of the nativist spirit. Although established as a war-emergency measure in 1917, it lasted twelve years, almost as long as prohibition. (56)

Summary

The war bequeathed to the postwar period a heritage of nativism so that it is not surprising that the Germanophobia engendered by the war continued well after the signing of the November 1918 Armistice. Nationally Germanophobia was encouraged by the 1919 Senate Subcommittee on the Judiciary Report, Brewing and Liquor Interests and German and Bolshevik Propaganda, which essentially was an across-the-board attack against the German element, rather than merely a report on German-American brewers.

In Cincinnati a nativist tabloid, Cincinnati: One Hundred Percent Americans, was published from 1918 to 1919. From 1918 to 1923 the Academy of Medicine demonstrated that its membership feelings against Germans had not subsided. The nativist

attacks against the recognized leaders of Cincinnati's Germandom, Schwaab and Nippert, were symbolic, and could only serve
to intimidate local German-Americans. In 1919 Gov. Cox of Ohio
gave state sanction to Germanophobia by calling for legislation
against German language instruction in the public, private and
parochial schools of the state of Ohio, the Ake Law which was
in effect until it was declared unconstitutional in 1923 by the
U.S. Supreme Court.

     Public institutions were obviously viewed as vehicles of
anti-German expression. Nativists had destroyed the German
bilingual program in the Cincinnati public schools in 1918, but
continued nevertheless with agitation against German instruction well into the year 1919, an indication of the depth of
such hostility. Likewise the public library was viewed as a
vehicle for the suppression of the German heritage. Not until
1921 did the public library return all German books to the
shelves with the exception of those books the librarian "sees
fit to place upon restricted shelves."

     To German-Americans prohibition was a nativist piece of
legislation directed against them. As Richard Hofstadter has
observed it was "a ludicrous caricature of the reforming impulse" of WASP reformers and progressives that it was desirable
and possible to legislate and governmentally regulate the individual. The prohibition era ended an important social institution in the ethnic neighborhood: the family style beer garden.
Finally, it should be noted that the Cincinnati Home Guards,
established in 1917, were maintained until 1929.

     In conclusion, Germanophobia continued well after the 1918
Armistice, and from the point of view of the German community
can only be regarded as having drawn to a close with the
lifting of prohibition in 1933, although the peak period can be
dated from 1917 to 1923.

CONCLUSION

> ... every community is established with a view to
> some good; for mankind always act in order to obtain
> that which they think good.
>
> Aristotle(1)

> ... Cincinnati Germans have maintained their May and
> Oktoberfests, their German bilingual school, and
> several parishes with German ethnic identity ... they
> have spread throughout the city and the suburbs on
> both sides of the river. It was not a set of
> buildings that made a Cincinnati German culture. It
> was a people.(2)

Introduction

LaVern J. Rippley has written that ethnic groups emerged
from the Great War confused, and hence "sought shelter both in
anonymity and in political isolationism."(3) The War, therefore, formed a turning point in German-American history, and
one in which German-Americans redefined their ethnicity in
accord with the Zeitgeist. The war marked the close of the
pre-war period, but the beginning of a new one.

Anti-Germanism After the Great War

From the perspective of the German community the nativism
which commenced with the Great War can only be said to have
officially drawn to a close in 1933 with the repeal of prohibition, although overt acts of hostility had long since ceased to
occur. Indeed, the years from 1919 to 1923, when the German
language was illegal in public, private, and parochial schools
in Ohio, may be regarded as the peak postwar years of the postwar war against the German element. After 1923 there were
apparently no instances of an overt act of nativism in relation
to the German heritage. Nevertheless, as Dr. Fick wrote in the
late 1920s:

> The war has been over for years. The uproarious de-
> famation of the Germans may have abated in public and
> the evil word "Hun" may not be heard often any more.
> Brutal attacks and bodily harm belong to the past and
> yet often an unfriendliness makes itself heard in an
> unpleasant manner.(4)

Moreover, the Cincinnati Home Guards, established in 1917 to protect Cincinnati from foreign powers, was maintained until 1929. It is, therefore, clear that the Germanophobia engendered by the war did not subside almost concurrently with the signing of the 1918 Armistice, or soon thereafter, but lingered on for most of the decade.

The 1923 U.S. Supreme Court declaration of the Ake Law of the state of Ohio as unconstitutional and the 1933 repeal of prohibition are important markers in the cessation of the war-engendered Germanophobia, but references must be made to the institutionalization of nativism in Cincinnati. Nativist inspired actions became elemental aspects of a new status quo with respect to the German element. For example, Woodrow Street remained Woodrow Street in the 1920s since the April 1918 Cincinnati ordinance changing street names stood in place as law, and was not repealed. German instruction was not re-introduced, nor was a new supervisor of German hired by the Cincinnati Public Schools. In short, there was a definite end to overt acts of anti-Germanism, but some of the negative aspects and results of the nativism against the German element lingered on as institutionalized segments of the new status quo.

Ultimately, the nativist Kulturkampf was a failure since German-Americans as an ethnic group with community institutions survived the war. The war not only did not weaken, rather it strengthened and united the German community as never before, but its long-range impact was to eliminate or limit the avenues through which the German heritage could be preserved and maintained. The years spent in defense of the old country followed by postwar years of nativism solidified German-American identity, but the Zeitgeist brought with it the suppression and persecution of the heritage, especially the German language. The individual who identified strongly "with the norms and behavior of his community found his natural tendencies reinforced in a defensive reaction to anti-German sentiments, even though the wartime repression limited his freedom of expression and behavior."(5) Those who identified least strongly as German-Americans found it most likely difficult to be both German and American, although nativism had accentuated individual ethnic awareness. German-American identity and unity were, therefore, heightened, but the tragedy of the war greatly "diminished opportunities for ethnic self-expression."(6)

Ethnic Survival

German-Americans had survived the war, but they had been deeply hurt by the experience. This resulted and culminated in a redefinition of German-American ethnicity in accord with the spirit of the time. Several factors should be considered as a part of this redefinition.

First, there was the factor of status deprivation for German-Americans who had been involuntarily removed by the war from the status of one of America's most desirable to one of her least desirable ethnic elements. This status loss was complicated by the fact that a stigma had been placed on everything German as a result of the war. Indeed, the ethnic slur "Hun" was common in the English language press, as well as in American slang during and after the war. Although its usage tapered off and faded out of use by the end of the 1920s, its mere usage and acceptability in the years immediately after the war reflected the loss of status. Fortunately, by the end of the decade there appeared some beginnings of a return to normalcy. Zane Miller notes that "Many Cincinnatians in the period boasted of our German musical heritage ... and the comprehensive city plan of 1925 listed the city's legacy of skilled workmanship and its pool of German immigrants as advantages." Also a 1927 Cincinnati history identified Germans "in their numbers and nationality ... the most important ingredient of the community." In a section on "The German People" the history claimed that "no class ... have contributed more in brains, sinews, labor, and money, toward building up Cincinnati and making it what it is today. And no class deserves greater credit."(7) These comments come close to the words of praise for the German element found in pre-war Cincinnati histories, and are an indication that by the end of the 1920s the status of the German element was again on the rise.

A second factor was the privatization of the German heritage. As a result of the anti-Germanism of the time ethnicity became largely a private affair confined to the home, family, and various ethnic institutions. It is not, therefore, surprising that to external observers the Germans appeared to have become "invisible ethnics." Community organizations and institutions, however, provided the framework within which such a subdued ethnicity could be maintained. Moreover ethnic leaders adopted a strategy of subdued public ethnicity for the purpose of the maintenance of ethnic institutions, as well as removing these institutions and organizations from public visibility so that they would not become the targets of nativists in the years immediately following the war.

Third, there was the factor of ethnic group politics. Regardless of the obscure motives of the WASP reformers of the 1920s, it is clear that their reforms resulted in the dilution of ethnic group politics in Cincinnati. German-American political influences were diminished by the severance of the connections with City Hall via the machine. Also, the ACL no longer endorsed or opposed political candidates, and its constitution specifically excluded organizations that engaged in

political activities. Publicly German-Americans adopted a low
profile with regard to politics. They were cautious in general
about expressing themselves on controversial issues, except
within the safe confines of the ethnic community. As a result
they seemed publicly apathetic and apolitical, but they were
not. They merely confined their political expressions and
resentments to the ballot box. Working to the advantage of the
German element politically were two factors. First, it could
by no means be written off from consideration since it formed
the major ethnic element. Second, the Republican party, the
former machine party, was the one endorsed by the German press
and prominent members of the community and was the party German-Americans historically had affiliated with. These connections and affiliations were strengthened by the basic
opposition to the party of Woodrow Wilson.

A fourth factor to be considered was that of the 1920s
language shift. Two factors contributed to this. First, there
was the nativism of the time which resulted in the state law of
1919-23 against the German language in schools in Ohio. It is
not difficult to imagine the effect this ban might have had on
children of German descent. The German language itself "once
the second tongue in the United States, suffered an almost mor-
tal blow with World War I ... German was reduced to a poor
fourth in languages studied in the United States."(8) A second
factor contributing to the language shift was the fact that the
German element was in the process of transition from a Euro-
pean-born to an American-born ethnic group. The leadership of
Cincinnati German secular and religious organizations and
institutions wisely shifted from German to acceptance of both
English and German, a bilingual approach that contributed both
to ethnic survival and also to keeping the younger American-
born with the fold. It also meant that German-American ethnicity was no longer to be associated or equated with an all-
German speaking community structure, but with a bilingual one

in which the English language was becoming the major medium of expression.

All of these aforementioned factors blended together for a redefinition of German-American ethnicity. At the same time ethnic leaders were adopting a philosophy of ethnic survival that consisted in a cultural course of action within the framework of ethnic group institutions and organizations. Ethnicity was in a sense, therefore, driven underground, or at least from public view. One defined one's German heritage in relation to family, home, Verein or religious institution. German-Americans participated in politics as individuals, but ethnic group politics were avoided. The group's viewpoints were confined to the ballot box and to the pages of the German language press, as well as to speech-making at the functions of the Vereine. These factors converged to bring about the public submergence of German-American ethnicity. To the external observer beyond the institutional framework of the ethnic community, German-Americans certainly appeared to be less visible than before the war, but this was due to their redefined ethnicity in accord with the Zeitgeist. The times dictated a German-Americanism far different from that of pre-war days. The German element after the war has been referred to appropriately as "the great white whale, a stolid and often lethargic creature which moves in the deeps of the national consciousness and regards itself politically as 'moderate,' 'middle of the road,' expressive of middle-class attitudes."(9)

Enveloping this new definition was the institutional structure of the ethnic community. The survival of these institutions enabled German-Americans to define themselves in terms of their own particular religious or secular organizations or institutions, and also ensured ethnic survival. As has been seen, the survival of those institutions and organizations through the war was substantial. Moreover, a number of new organizations were established in the 1920s, such as the Kolping Society and the German Theater Society.

Implications for the Future

Although this work focuses on the postwar period from 1918 to 1932, it does have a number of long-range implications. Already in the 1920s the myth of the melting pot came into question. American society was slowly moving to a new understanding of the nature of ethnicity as it related to the diversity of the American people. In the 1930s Franklin D. Roosevelt "accepted group identity along ethnic lines as an inescapable fact of American life.(10) The German-American experience during and after the war no doubt contributed to this growing understanding of the nature of American society.

Another long-term implication was that the German heritage, because of its survivability and the fact that it had weathered the storm of the war, came to be regarded as one of the very basic and elemental aspects of the Greater Cincinnati area. It has been observed that "so many aspects of the German character have become an organic part of the standard definition of 'American' that it is often impossible to distinguish one from the other ... German-American ethnicity is, in fact, 'American' ethnicity."(11) Edwin Zeydel, the late chairman of the University of Cincinnati German Department, observed that in his generation "the role assumed by German culture in America is well nigh impossible to analyze so much has it become part of the very woof and fabric of that life."(12) The German heritage became recognized not only as one of the most enduring and generally well known characteristics of the area, but also a source of pride. All of these factors greatly contributed to healing the wounds of war over the years. Now the German heritage is commonly lauded and praised in the local press, especially at the time of the German Day celebration, as well as by local elected officials.

It will have to be the focus of another book to trace the history of the Cincinnati Germans from where this work leaves off up to the present, but suffice it to say that today there is a great sense of pride and interest in local German-American history and culture, as well as an appreciation of the many strong family ties and friendships that exist between Cincinnati and the Federal Republic of Germany, Austria, and Switzerland. Indeed, the German heritage has become so popular that it has become commercialized and packaged as an attraction point to the city of Cincinnati. Each year the city's Downtown Oktoberfest attracts hundreds of thousands to a weekend of Frohsinn and Gemuetlichkeit at one of the country's largest such fests. Advertising invites those near and far to "Zinzinnati." All of these factors and events are predicated on and are some of the long term implications of the fact that the German heritage survived and adapted to the hard time during and after the Great War, as has been described in this study.

With regard to any "historical lessons" forthcoming from the German-American experience during the period described by this work at least several points can be made. First, as one historian has observed, "The real problem, at least at certain crucial times, is how to keep the majority, silent or otherwise, from wreaking its often mindless will on minorities, ethnic, political, or generational."(13) Second, the Cincinnati German experiences demonstrate that there is a model for ethnic group survival during and after a time of crisis. Third, it demonstrates that during such a crisis period that the individual's strongest support is to be found within the framework of that individual's own community.

Finally, it should be noted that the German-American experience in the first half of the century has been described as a heritage deferred, and that only in the second half of the century is it becoming a heritage fulfilled. Present day Cincinnatians of German descent, like German-Americans else-

where, "have much time to make up, much ground to regain." A
recent commentator observed that it cannot be said that German-
Americans have suddenly caught up or even made up for lost
time, but there are signs that they have been stimulated to
explore their roots" and tell their story.(14) An important
chapter in that story is to be found in the years after World
War I.

NOTES ON SOURCES

The sources used for this book can be found in the foot-
notes in the following pages. With regard to secondary
literature the reader should consult my German-Americana. A
Bibliography (Metuchen, N.J.: Scarecrow Press, 1975). General
surveys of German-American history, literature, and culture can
be found in my America's German Heritage (Cleveland: German-
American National Congress, 1976), as well as my German-
American Literature (Metuchen, N.J.: Scarecrow Press, 1977). A
basic introduction to various aspects of Cincinnati German
history can be found in my Festschrift for the German-American
Tricentennial Jubilee: Cincinnati 1983 (Cincinnati: Cincinnati
Historical Society, 1982).

Among local depositories the German-Americana Collection
at the University of Cincinnati Blegen Library is especially
valuable for the history, literature, and culture of the German
element. At the Cincinnati Historical Society is the Louis and
Ida I. Nippert Memorial Library of German Methodism, as well as
other important source material on Cincinnati history.
Significant holdings of the German language press are to be
found at the Public Library.

NOTES

INTRODUCTION

1
The U.S. Census provided information regarding ethnic ancestry for the first time in 1980. Prior to that information was available only on the foreign-born and their children, the foreign stock. I have estimated the German element for the pre-1980 statistics, since I am interested in the totality of the population of German descent, including German-speaking immigrants and their descendants from Austria, Switzerland, and other German-speaking sections of Europe, and not merely the first and second generation. Statistics cited here and elsewhere are drawn from the U.S. Bureau of Census, Census Reports (Washington, D.C., 1820-1980). Regarding the 1980 Census see "Ohio's German Heritage Certified: Ethnic Group is State's Largest," Cincinnati Enquirer (19 May 1985) and Don Heinrich Tolzmann, "The 1980 Census and the German Element," Society for German-American Studies Newsletter, 5:2 (1984):2. Below are census statistics together with my estimates:

Total Population of Cincinnati	Foreign Stock: First and Second Generation: From Germany, Austria, and Switzerland	German Element: All Cincinnatians of German Descent (my estimate)	
363,247	121,719	181,795	(1910)
401,247	98,762	200,623	(1920)
451,247	80,018	225,623	(1930)

2
For an overview of Cincinnati German history see Tolzmann, Festschrift, esp. pp. 2-9, 92-102, and also Don Heinrich Tolzmann, "Survival of an Ethnic Community: The Cincinnati Germans, 1918 Through 1932," (Ph.D. diss., University of Cincinnati, 1983). For a general history of German-America see Don Heinrich Tolzmann, America's German Heritage (Cleveland: German-American National Congress, 1976). Further references to the German immigration and German-American history can be found in Don Heinrich Tolzmann, German-Americana. A Bibliography (Metuchen, N.J.: Scarecrow Press, 1975).

3
Works Projects Administration, Writers Program, Ohio. The Ohio Guide (New York: Oxford University Press, 1940), p. 79.

4
   Regarding the first Germans in Ohio and Ziegler see
Tolzmann, America's German Heritage, pp. 49-50, 56-57, 82-88.

5
   Don Heinrich Tolzmann, "The German Image of Cincinnati
Before 1830," Queen City Heritage 42:3 (1984): 35.

6
   Ibid.

7
   Ibid, p. 36.

8
   Friedrich Gerstacker, Wild Sports in the Far West
(London: Geo. Routledge & Co., 1854), pp. 119-20.

9
   Heinrich A. Rattermann, Gesammelte ausgewahlte Werke, Bd.
12 (Cincinnati: Selbstverlag des Verfassers, 1911), p. 526.

10
   Guido Andre Dobbert, The Disintegration of an Immigrant
Community: The Cincinnati Germans, 1870-1920 (New York: Arno
Press, 1980), p. 38.

11
   Armin Tenner, Cincinnati Sonst und Jetzt (Cincinnati: M.
& R. Burgheim, 1878), p. 81.

12
   Carl Wittke, The Germans in America. A Student's Guide
to Localized History, Localized History Series (New York:
Teachers College Press, 1967), p. 11.

13
   Tenner, Cincinnati, p. 82.

14
   Tolzmann, Festschrift, p. 4.

15
   Ibid, p. 10.

16
   Ibid, pp. 10, 21.

17
   Gordon A. Craig, The Germans (New York: G.P. Putnam's
Sons, 1982), p. 24.

18
For a more detailed history of the pre-war Cincinnati German community see Tolzmann, "The Survival of an Ethnic Community," pp.. 43-103.

19
For a more detailed history of the anti-German hysteria, see Tolzmann, "The Survival of an Ethnic Community," pp. 104-38, and also Tolzmann, Festschrift, pp. 94-95.

20
Writers Program of Ohio, Cincinnati. A Guide to the Queen City (Cincinnati: Wiesen-Hart, 1943), p. 95.

21
Moses Rischin, Immigration and the American Tradition (Indianapolis: Bobbs-Merrill, 1976), p. xxxvi.

22
For a review of the literature of American history on German-America during World War I see Tolzmann, "The Survival of an Ethnic Community," pp. 1-42. Also see Tolzmann, German-Americana. A Bibliography, pp. 87-96.

NOTES

CHAPTER I

1

Vorstandsbericht des Deutschen Pionier-Vereins, 63 (1930-31): 9-10.

2

Anna Reichrath, Die Donauschwaben in Cincinnati, Ohio (Cincinnati: Verein der Donauschwaben, 1974), p. 64.

3

See Geza C. Peikert, The Danube Swabians (The Hague: Martinus Nijhoff, 1967).

4

Anton Kremling, ed., Die Donauschwaben in den Vereinigten Staaten von Amerika. Festschrift zur Zwanzig-Jahr-Feier des Verbandes der Donauschwaben in den USA e.V. (Cleveland: Verband der Donauschwaben in den U.S.A. e.V., 1977), p. 23.

5

See Gordon Craig, Germany, 1866-1945 (New York: Oxford University Press, 1978) and Koppel Pinson, Modern Germany. Its History and Civilization (New York: Macmillan, 1966).

6

LaVern J. Rippley, "The German Element in Minnesota," In: Paul A. Schons and Edward W. Gerstner, eds., Minnesota AATG Resources Directory (St. Paul: St. Thomas College, 1978), pp. 1-5.

7

Glen E. Gilbert, "Origin and Present Day Location of German Speakers in Texas: A Statistical Interpretation," In: Joseph Wilson, ed., Texas and Germany: Crosscurrents, Rice University Studies, 63:3 (Houston: Rice University, 1977), p. 32.

8

George M. Henzel, "Over-the-Rhine U.S.A.," Cincinnati Historical Society Bulletin 40 (1982): 7-62. Regarding the east/west side split in Cincinnati see Donna Vonderhaar, "So Say Something Nice About the West Side," Cincinnati Enquirer (15 May 1983) and Molly Kavanaugh, "For East Side West Side, the Twain Shall Meet," Cincinnati Post (17 June 1983).

9

Henzel, "Over-the-Rhine U.S.A.," p. 61.

208

10
     Maxine Seller, To Seek America. A History of Ethnic
Life in America (Englewood, N.J.: Ozer, 1977), p. 146.

11
     Regarding   Schwaab   and   Nippert   see   Dobbert,
Disintegration, pp. 306-10. An obituary of Schwaab appeared in
the Cincinnati Times-Star (30 March 1933). See also his
biography in William M. Morris and E.B. Krieger, The Bench and
Bar of Cincinnati: Commemorating the Building of the New
Courthouse (Cincinnati: New Court House Publishing Co., 1921).
For a biograhy of Nippert see National Cyclopedia of American
Biography, Vol. 46, pp. 267-68; obituaries of him appeared in
the Cincinnati Enquirer (7 August 1956), the Cincinnati Post (7
August 1956), and the New York Times (8 August 1956).
Regarding Fick see Don Heinrich Tolzmann, German-American
Literature (Metuchen, N.J.: Scarecrow Press, 1977), pp. 273-84.

12
     Volksblatt   (1 June 1916).   Also see Verhandlungen   der
Deutschamerikanischen Konferenze in Chicago den 28. und 29. Mai
1916 (n.p., n.p., 1916).

13
     Tolzmann, "The Survival," p. 83.

14
     H.H. Fick, Zwischen Anfang und Ende. Mein Leben, p. 48.

15
     Max Griebsch, "Dr. H.H. Fick," Monatshefte 27 (1935):
193.

16
     Ibid.

17
     Fick, Zwischen Anfang und Ende, p. 48.

18
     The Living Webster Encylopedia Dictionary of the English
Language, p. 962.

19
     Hermann Barnstorff, Festschrift zum goldenen Jubiläum
des Deutschen Literarischen Klubs von Cincinnati 1877-1927
(Cincinnati: Deutscher Literarischen Klub, 1927), p. 4.

20
     "Letzte Ehren für Dr. H.H. Fick: Würdige Trauerfeier in
der Kapelle des Spring Grove Friedhofes," Cincinnati Freie
Presse, an undated newspaper obituary appended to H.H. Fick,
Zwischen Anfang und Ende.

21
"Letzte Ehren für Dr. H.H. Fick."

22
Satzungen der Amerikanischen Buergerliga (Cincinnati, 1936).

23
German-American Citizens League, 50. Jubilaumsfeier der Deutsch-Amerikanischen Buergerliga, 1908-1958 (May 3, 1958), (Cincinnati, 1958), p. 1.

24
Dobbert, Disintegration, pp. 427-28.

25
Greninger was city editor of the Freie Presse; Albertz, former secretary of the Stadtverband and the Ohio Alliance, operated a printing company located at 1308 Walnut St., which specialized in German-English printing. Glöcker was in the restaurant, König in the meat industry.

26
Dobbert, Disintegration, p. 411.

27
ibid, p. 414.

28
Ibid, pp. 415-16.

29
Ibid, pp. 417.

30
Ibid, p. 428.

31
Ueberhorst, Turner unterm Sternebanner, p. 203. Also see Cincinnati Central Turners, Gems in Gymnastics, 1848-1941 (April 20, 1941) (Cincinnati, 1941).

32
See United Banatai Societies, Silver Jubilee, 1927-1952 (June 29, 1952) (Cincinnati, 1952) and also its Benatar Volks-Kalender (Cincinnati, 1935).

33
Freie Presse, 27 October 1927.

34
See the Vorstandsbericht 22-64, 1890-1932.

35
  Ibid, 50, 1917-18, 29.

36
  Ibid, 53, 1920-21, 19.

37
  Ibid, pp. 21-34.

38
  Ibid, p. 35.

39
  Ibid, pp. 35-39.

40
  Ibid, 54, 1921-22, 16-19.

41
  Ibid, pp. 20-21.

42
  Ibid, pp. 21-22.

43
  Ibid, p. 30.

44
  Ibid, 56, 1923-24, pp. 16-19.

45
  Ibid, pp. 19-23.

46
  Ibid, p. 29.

47
  Ibid, pp. 29-33.

48
  Ibid, 57, 1924-25, 26.

49
  Ibid, 59, 1926-27, 13-14.

50
  Ibid, 60, 1927-28, pp. 12-14.

51
  Ibid, pp. 15-18.

52
  Ibid, p. 20.

53
   Ibid, 62, 1920-30, 10-18.

54
   Ibid, 63, 1930-31, 9-10.

55
   Ibid, pp. 11-22, 30-31.

56
   Ibid, 64, 1931-32, 9-13.

57
   The last yearbook the author has seen is   Vorstandsbericht 88, 1955-56. In possession of the author.

58
   See Barnstorff, Festschrift, and Teutonia Maenner- und
Damenchor, Jubiläums-Konzert, 1872-1932 (April 10, 1932) (Cin-
cinnati, 1932).

59
   German-American Citizens League, 50. Jubiläumsfeier, p.
1. German Day in the 1930s rose to a peak attendance of 30,000.

60
   Paul Douglass, The Story of German Methodism (Cincinnati: Methodist Book Concern, 1939), p. 189.

61
   Cincinnati Enquirer, 14 November 1918.

62
   Douglass, The Story of German Methodism, p. 211.

63
   Ibid.

64
   Ibid, p. 212.

65
   Ibid, p. 219.

66
   Ibid., p. 219, v. John A. Diekmann was born in
Sandridge, Illinois, a village southeast of Chicago, in 1872.
His family belonged to the first German Methodist Episcopal
Church in Chicago. He attended German Wallace College in
Berea, Ohio and the Nast Theological Seminary and did
postgraduate work at Drew Theological Seminary. After serving
in three pastorates he was elected President of the Bethesda
Institutions in Cincinnati in 1922. Diekmann "kept alive the

evangelical passion in the true tradition of German Methodism
and the spirit was contagious in all the many works in which he
was concerned. A platform lecturer, a camp-meeting preacher, a
Bible student, after-dinner speaker, and conversationalist, he
loved the personalities and traditions of German Methodism with
a passion unsurpassed by any German Methodist of his
generation." Douglass, The Story of German Methodism, p. 148.

67
    Ibid, p. 219.

68
    Ibid, p. 270.

69
    Barnett R. Brickner, "The Jewish Community in
Cincinnati, Historical Descriptive, 1817-1933," (Ph.D. diss.,
University of Cincinnati, 1935), p. 25.

70
    Michael A. Meyer, "A Centennial History," in Samuel E.
Korff, ed., Hebrew Union College-Jewish Institute of Religion
at One Hundred Years (Cincinnati: Hebrew Union College, 1976),
p. 78.

71
    Ibid, p. 80-81.

72
    Dobbert, "Ordeal," pp. 130-31.

73
    Boris D. Bogen, Born a Jew (New York: Macmillan Co.,
1930), p. 72.

74
    Brickner, "The Jewish Community in Cincinnati," p. 27.

75
    James G. Heller, As Yesterday, When it Was Past: A
History of the Isaac M. Wise Temple (Cincinnati: Isaac M. Wise
Temple, 1942), pp. 3-4.

76
    Rudolf Glanz, Studies in Judaica Americana (New York:
KTAV Publishing House, 1970), p. 206.

77
    Herman Eliassof, "German-American Jews," Deutsch-
Amerikanische Geschichtsblätter 14, 1914-321.

78
    Polk Laffoon IV, "Cincinnati's Jewish Community," Cin-

cinnati (April 1977), 46-52.

79
Meyer, "Centennial History," pp. 7, 52-78, 81-96, 290-99.

80
Ibid, pp. 63-67.

81
Ibid, p. 119.

82
Heller, As Yesterday, p. 229.

83
Ibid, p. 196.

84
Brickner, "The Jewish Community in Cincinnati," p. 296.

85
Jay Dolan, The Immigrant Church: New York's Irish and German Catholics, 1815-1865 (Baltimore: Johns Hopkins University Press, 1975), pp. 71-85.

86
John H. Lamott, History of the Archdiocese of Cincinnati 1821-1921 (New York: Frederick Pustet Co., 1921), pp. 92-96.

87
James H. Campbell, "New Parochialism: Change and Conflict in the Archdiocese of Cincinnati, 1878-1925" (Ph.D. diss., University of Cincinnati, 1981), pp. 166-67.

88
Lamott, History of the Archdiocese of Cincinnati, pp. 273-316.

89
Philip Gleason, The Conservative Reformers. German-American Catholics and the Social Order (Notre Dame: University of Notre Dame Press, 1968), pp. 173-, 47-48, 204-220, 176-78.

90
National Convention: Catholic Kolping Society of America, Cincinnati, Ohio August 30-September 2, 1974 (Cincinnati: Catholic Kolping Society of America, 1974).

91
The German language press will be discussed in greater detail in the next chapter.

NOTES

CHAPTER II

1
Cited in Dobbert, Disintegration, p. 409.

2
Rattermann, Gesammelte ausgewählte Werke, Vol. 12, p. 107, and Ford, History of Cincinnati, pp. 134-35.

3
H.H. Fick, "Im Rahmen von sechs Jahrzehnten," Unpublished autobiographical manuscript, German-Americana Collection, University of Cincinnati Libraries, p. 123.

4
See my "The Last Cincinnati German Poet: Heinrich H. Fick," in German-American Literature (Metuchen, N.J.: Scarecrow Press, 1977), pp. 273-84.

5
Wood, "Geschichte des deutschen Theaters von Cincinnati" (Ph.D. diss., Cornell University, 1932), p. 8.

6
Cincinnati Board of Education, Official Proceedings, 25 Jan. 1926, pp. 6-7.

7
Cincinnati Enquirer, 25 September 1926.

8
Gottfried Merkel, ed., On Romanticism and the Art of Translation: Studies in Honor of Edwin Hermann Zeydel (Princeton: Princeton University Press, 1956), p. 6. Regarding Zeydel see my "Musenklange aus Cincinnati," in my Festschrift for the German-American Tricentennial Jubilee: Cincinnati 1983 (Cincinnati: Cincinnati Historical Society, 1982), pp. 53-65.

9
Deutsch-Amerikanische Geschichtsblätter 15 (1915): 255-309.

10
Merkel, On Romanticism, p. 6.

11
Edwin H. Zeydel, "Die germanistische Tätigkeit in Amerika 1918-1926," Euphorion 20 (1928), pp. 239-49.

12
    Edwin H. Zeydel, "German Instruction in Cincinnati," In Tolzmann, _Festschrift_, p. 88.

13
    See Albert B. Faust, _Francis Daniel Pastorius and the 250th Anniversary of the Founding of Germantown_ (Philadelphia: Carl Schurz Memorial Foundation, Inc., 1934), pp. 3, 5.

14
    Joshua A. Fishman, "Minority Language Maintenance and the Ethnic Mother Tongue School," _Modern Language Journal_ 64, 1980, 168.

15
    Ibid, p. 70.

16
    Carl Wittke, _The German-Language Press in America_ (Lexington: University of Kentucky Press, 1957), pp. 262-282.

17
    John Sinnema, "German Methodism's Ohio Roots," _Journal of German-American Studies_ 7 (1974): 80.

18
    Karl J. Arndt, _The German Language Press of the Americas_ Volume I: History and Bibliography 1732-1968; United States of America (München: Verlag Dokumentation, 1976), p. 448.

19
    Ibid, p. 436.

20
    Douglass, _Story of German Methodism_, p. 228.

21
    James A. Dwyer, "Der christliche Apologete: German Prophet to America, 1914-1918," _Methodist History_ 15:2, 1977, 85.

22
    Ibid, pp. 89-90.

23
    Ibid, pp. 91-92.

24
    Wittke, _William Nast, Patriarch of German Methodism_ (Detroit: Wayne State University Press, 1943), p. 83.

25
Arndt, The German Language Press of the Americas, p. 442.

26
Volksblatt, 5 December 1919.

27
Arndt, The German Language Press of the Americas, p. 444.

28
Ibid, and Dobbert, Disintegration, p. 429.

29
Carl Wittke, "Ohio's German Language Press and the Peace Negotiations," Ohio Historical Quarterly 29, 1920, 49-74.

30
Dobbert, Disintegration, p. 429.

31
German-American World 7 (1924): 280-81.

32
See Robert E. Ward, "The German-American Library of H.H. Fick: A Rediscovery," German-American Studies 1, 1969, 49-68; 2, 1970, 2029. Also see "Collection of German-Americana Established," Candid Campus (University of Cincinnati) (29 May 1974).

33
One article written about a letter inserted into this bibliography is Edward P. Harris & Don Heinrich Tolzmann, "An Unpublished Letter of Konrad Nies to H.H. Fick," German-American Studies 8, 1974, 86-88. This letter sheds light on the poetry journal entitled Deutsch-Amerikanische Dichtung which was edited and published by Nies.

34
The author's translation.

35
Edwin H. Zeydel, An Elementary German Reader (New York: Knopf, 1926), p. v.

36
Edwin H. Zeydel, The Holy Roman Empire in German Literature (New York: Columbia University Press, 1918), pp. 1, 120; his The Ludwig Tieck-Freidrich von Raumer Letters (New York: Columbia University Press, 1930) and his Ludwig Tieck and England (Princeton: Princeton University Press, 1931).

37
Edwin H. Zeydel, Constitution of the German Empire and German States (Washington, D.C.: Government Printing Office, 1918; reprint ed., Wilmington, Del.: Scholarly Resources, 1974).

38
Washington, D.C.: The Carnegie Endowment for International Peace, 1921.

39
Hermann Oncken, Napoleon III and the Rhine. The Origin of the War of 1870-1871 (New York: Knopf, 1928), pp. ix, xxiii.

40
Wilhelm Kiesselbach, Problems of the German-American Claims Commission (Washington, D.C.: The Carnegie Endowment for International Peace, 1930), p. 1.

41
Alfred von Wegerer, A Refutation of the Versailles War Guilt Thesis, Introduction by Harry Elmer Barnes (New York: Knopf, 1930), pp. v, xvi.

42
Hans Wehberg, The Outlawry of War (Washington, D.C.: The Carnegie Foundation for International Peace, 1931), p. v.

43
Selig Adler, "The War-Guilt Question and American Disarmament, 1918-1928," Journal of Modern History 23, 1951, 10-23.

44
Ralph Charles Wood, "Geschichte des deutschen Theaters in Cincinnati," (M.A. Thesis, University of Cincinnati, 1930),

45
Ralph Charles Wood, "Geschichte des deutschen Theaters von Cincinnati," (Ph.D. diss., Cornell University, 1932). This dissertation was published under the same title in Deutsch-Amerikanische Geschichtsblätter 32, 1932, 411-523. Regarding his work on Pennsylvania German history see Ralph C. Wood, ed., The Pennsylvania Germans (Princeton: Princeton University Press, 1942). Among his contributions to German-American literature the following should be consulted: his novel on German-American community life entitled Klumpendal. Ernstes und Heiteres aus dem Leben einer deutschen Gemeinde in den USA (Wolfshagen-Scharbeutz: Franz Westphal Verlag, 1955) and his masterful translation into the Pennsylvania German dialect of the Gospel of Matthew: Es Evangelium vum Mattheus aus der griechischen Schprooch ins Pennsilvendeitsch iwwersetzt (Stuttgart: Steinkopf, 1957). Also see an anthology of Pennsylvania

218

German literature which he co-edited with Fritz Braun entitled
Pennsilfaanisch-deitsch: Erzählungen und Gedichte der Pennsyl-
vaniadeutschen, Pfälzer in der weiten Welt, 6 (Kaiserslautern:
Heimatstelle Pfalz, 1966). Also see his brief discussion of
German-American literature: "German-American Poetry," American
German Review 23:4, 1957, 3. Since most of Wood's work falls
outside the period under consideration by this study, they are
not examined.

46
        Theodor Storm,   Immensee.   Edited by Alma S.   Fick (New
York: Macmillan, 1926).

47
        George Elliston,   Sonnenglanz,   Gedichte aus George
Elliston's Bright World.   Deutsch von Bertha Fieback Markbreit
(Cincinnati: S. Rosenthal & Co. Press, 1928), p. 15.

48
        Fünfzig   Jahre: Deutscher   Literarischer   Klub   von
Cincinccinnati 1877-1927 (Cincinnati: Cincinnatier Freie Presse,
1927) and Barnstorff, Festschrift.

49
        Barnstorff, Festschrift, p. 4.

50
        Ibid, pp. 7, 10, 18, 5 and Vorstandsbericht 60, 1927-
28, 12-14.

51
        Regarding   Rattermann   see   Henry   Willen,   "H.A.
Rattermann's Life and Poetical Work," (Ph.D. diss., University
of Pennsylvania, 1939); Sister Mary Spanheimer, "Heinrich
Rattermann, German-American Author, Poet and Historian, 1832-
1923," (Ph.D. diss., Catholic University of America, 1937), and
Fred Karl Scheibe, "Heinrich Armin Rattermann: German-American
Poet, 1832-1923," in my German-American Literature, pp. 240-44.

52
        Barnstorff, Festschrift, pp. 32-33.

53
        Ibid, pp. 33-35.

54
        Regarding the work of Müller see Wilma Guyot, "William
Mueller, Writer," in my German-American Literature, pp. 216-
219.

55
Katzenberger authored a number of articles, several of
them pertaining to Cincinnati German history, including "Major
David Ziegler," Ohio Historical Quarterly 21, 1912, 127-74 and
"Martin Baum," Ohio Historical Quarterly 44, 1935, 204-19.

56
Among Barnstorff's other publications see "German and
American Interest in Schiller," German Quarterly 13, 1940, 92-
100 and "German Literature in Translation Published in Poet
Lore," Modern Language Journal 25, 1941, 711-15.

57
Barnstorff, Festschrift, p. 72.

58
Wood, "Geschichte des deutschen Theaters von Cincinnati," pp. 101-02.

59
Ibid, p. 103.

60
Ibid.

61
See George F. Moser, "Musik und deutsche Bühnen," in
Fünfzig Jahre: Deutscher Literarischer Klub von Cincinnati:
1877-1927 pp. 19-20 and Werner Bertram, "Unser deutsches Theater," In: Ibid, p. 73.

62
Conzen, "Germans," p. 417. German theater had not only
to compete with English language radio and movies, but also beginning in 1929 with German language radio broadcasting in
Cincinnati.

63
Wittke, The German-Language Press in America," p. 269.

64
Regarding the 1899 Sängerfest see Stanley Matthews,
"Aftermath of a Golden Jubilee," Cincinnati Historical Society
Bulletin 16, 1958, 143-50. Regarding Thomas see his A Musical
Autobiography. Edited by George P. Upton. New Introduction by
Leon Stein (New York: DaCapa Press, 1964).

65
"Sounds of the Herwegh Singing Society are Sacred Memory
for Martha Nadoud," The Cincinnati Post (20 December 1977).

66
Sylvia Sheblessy, 100 Years of the Cincinnati May Festival, pp. 53 and Gorbach, Hilfswerk, pp. 61, 73.

67
Sheblessy, 100 Years, pp. 55-56.

68
Ibid, p. 56.

69
Dobbert, Disintegration, p. 409.

70
Sheblessy, 100 Years, pp. 57-59.

71
Ibid, p. 57.

72
Ibid, p. 63.

73
John Rockwell, "A Romantic Leap from Leipzig," New York Times (18 July 1982).

74
Cincinnati Museum Association, Thirty-Eighth Annual Report (1918): 52-56.

75
Ibid, p. 20.

76
Frank Duveneck, 1848-1919. (Cincinnati: Cincinnati Museum Association, 1919).

77
Bulletin of the Cincinnati Art Museum 2:1 (1931): 17-19.

78
Walter H. Siple, "Changing Conditions in European Museums," Bulletin of the Cincinnati Art Museum, 2:4 (1931): 111-20.

NOTES

CHAPTER III

1
Cited in Lloyd E. Ambrosius, "Ethnic Politics and German-American Relations after World War I: The Fight over the Versailles Treaty in the United States," In: Hans L. Trefousse, ed., Germany and America: Essays on Problems of International Relations and Immigration. Brooklyn College Studies on Society in Changes, No. 21 (New York: Columbia University Press, 1980), p. 30.

2
Wittke, German-Americans and the World War, p. 197.

3
This section on the peace settlement is drawn from Carl Wittke, "Ohio's German Language Press and the Peace Negotiations," Ohio Historical Quarterly 28 (1920): 49-74.

4
Hans Gatzke, Germany and the United States: A Special Relationship? (Cambridge: Harvard University Press, 1980), p. 80.

5
Hans Haupt, "Our English Language Newspapers," The Bridge, No. 20 (November 1920), n.p.

6
Freie Presse,, 19 August 1919.

7
Ibid, 23 August 1919.

8
Ibid, 17 November 1919.

9
Dobbert, Disintegration, pp. 421-22.

10
Haupt, "English Language," n.p.

11
Alvin F. Harlow, The Serene Cincinnatians (New York: Dutton, 1950), p. 415.

12
Bernard Bailyn et al., The Great Republic. A History of the American People. Vol. 1. (Lexington, Mass.: D.C. Heath & Co., 1977).

13
Louis Leonard Tucker, Cincinnati's Citizen Crusaders: A History of the Cincinnatus Association, 1920-1965. (Cincinnati: Cincinnati Historical Society, 1967), p. 50. Also see Miller, Boss, p. 86.

14
Regarding Hynicka see Cincinnati Enquirer, 22 Feb. 1927; Cincinnati Times Star, 22 Feb. 1927; and the Cincinnati Post, 25 February 1927.

15
Tucker, Cincinnati's Citizen Crusaders, p. 66.

16
Ibid, p. 69. See Rowland P. Dietz, "Amateurs in Politics," (Ph.D. diss., Columbia University, 1962) for an analysis of the membrship. Also see William Kent Woods, "A Late Bloom of Progressivism in Cincinnati. A Study of Cincinnati Municipal Reformers of the 1920s," (M.A. thesis, University of Cincinnati, 1965).

17
Tucker, Cincinnati's Citizen Crusaders, p. 5.

18
Ibid, p. 131.

19
Ibid, p. 135.

20
Ibid, pp. 83, 127.

21
See William Archer Baughin, "Murray Seasongood: Twentieth Century Urban Reformer," (Ph.D. diss., University of Cincinnati, 1972).

22
Harlow, Serene, pp. 413-15.

23
A copy of the charter is reprinted in Robert I. Vexler, ed., Cincinnati. A Chronological & Documentary History, 1676-1970. (Dobbs Ferry, New York: Oceana Publications, Inc., 1975), pp. 98-100. Also see Martha Louise Brand, "The Growth nd Defects of the Council-Manager Plan in Cincinnati," (M.A. thesis, University of Cincinnati, 1950). On proportional representation see Leander Clark, "Proportional Representation in Cincinnati," (M.A. thesis, University of Cincinnati, 1927). For the civil service system reform see Mildred Louise Rose, "The Civil Service System in Cincinnati," (M.A. thesis, Univer-

sity of Cincinnati, 1934) and also Edwin Merrill Scott, "An Analysis of the Cincinnati Civil Service Classification Plan," (M.A. thesis, University of Cincinnati, 1941).

24
The election statistics in this section are from Edgar Eugene Robinson, The Presidential Vote, 1896-1932 (Stanford: Stanford University Press, 1934).

25
Freie Presse, 12 September 1920. Regarding the local suffrage movement see Lee Ann Rinsky, "The Cincinnati Suffrage Movement," (M.A. thesis, University of Cincinnati, 1968).

26
Dobbert, Disintegration, pp. 429-30.

27
Louis Gerson, The Hyphenate in Recent American Politics and Diplomacy. (Lawrence: University of Kansas Press, 1964), p. 99.

28
Freie Presse, 5 September 1920.

28
Ibid, 5 September 1920.

29
Ibid, 16 June 1920.

30
Ibid, 23 September 1920.

31
Ibid, 22 October 1920.

32
Ibid, 19 September 1920.

33
Ibid, 26 October 1919.

34
Ibid, 4 October 1920.

35
Ibid, 18 October 1920.

36
Ibid, 15 August 1920.

37
Ibid, 20 September 1920.

38
Ibid, 1 November 1920.

39
Ibid, 2 November, 1920.

40
Ibid.

41
Ibid, 7 June 1920.

42
Ibid, 3 November 1920. Regarding Cox see James E. Cebula, "James M. Cox, Journalist and Politician" (Ph.D. diss., University of Cincinnati, 1972).

43
Vorstandsbericht des Deutschen Pionier-Vereins 53, 1920-21, 21, 31.

44
Frederick C. Luebke, "The Germans," In John Higham, ed., Ethnic Leadership (Baltimore: Johns Hopkins University Press, 1978), pp. 73-74, 76.

45
Freie Presse, 2 November 1924.

46
German-American World 7 (1924): 280-281.

47
Freie Presse, 31 October 1928.

48
Ibid, 4 November 1928.

49
Ibid, 3 November 1928.

50
Ibid, 4 November 1928.

51
Ibid, 1 November 1928.

52
Der Christliche Apologete, 90 (1928): 1083.

53
  Freie Presse, 7 November 1928.

54
  Ibid, 28 October 1932.

55
  Ibid.

56
  Ibid, 30 October 1932.

57
  Ibid, 1 November 1932.

58
  Ibid, 2 November 1932.

59
  Ibid, 5 November 1932.

60
  Ibid, 6 November 1932.

61
  Ibid, 10 November 1932.

NOTES

CHAPTER IV

1
Dobbert, Disintegration, p. 416.

2
Writers Program of Ohio, Cincinnati: A Guide to the Queen City (Cincinnati: Wiesen-Hait, 1943), p. 95.

3
Arthur S. Link and William B. Catton, American Epic. A History of the United States Since 1900. Vol. I. (New York: Alfred A. Knopf, 1980), p. 235.

4
Don S. Kirschner, "Conflicts and Politics in the 1920s: Historiograhy," Mid-America 48 (1966): 228.

5
John Higham, Strangers in the Land. Patterns of American Nativism, 1860-1925 (New York: Atheneum, 1975), p. 21.

6
Carl Wittke, We Who Built America. The Saga of the Immigrant (Cleveland: Case Western Reserve University Press, 1964), p. 529.

7
H.E. Evans, "Imperial Wizard Outlines Klan Objectives Before Immense Gathering in Ohio," The Imperial Night-Hawk (18 July 1923).

8
U.S. Congress. Senate Subcommittee on the Judiciary. Brewing and Liquor Interests and German and Bolshevik Propaganda. Report and Hearings of the Subcommittee on the Judiciary, U.S. Senate. Washington, D.C.: Government Printing Office, 1919, pp. 1-2.

9
Ibid, pp. 6-7, 43, 4-5.

10
Arthur Marwick, War and Social Change in the Twentieth Century. A Comparative Study of Britain, France, Germany, Russia and the United States. New York: St. Martin's Press, 1974, pp. 80-81.

11
Cited in Dobbert, Disintegration, p. 416.

12
Freie Presse, 7 January 1919.

13
Cited in Dobbert, Disintegration, p. 409.

14
Comment: One Hundred Percent American, 14 December 1918.

15
Cincinnati Academy of Medicine, Minutes, 18 November 1918.

16
Cincinnati Enquirer, 19 November 1918.

17
R. Merrill Ricketts, "A Reply to a Committee Appointed by the President of the Cincinnati Academy of Medicine Dec. 12, 1923 to Solicit Funds to Aid German Scientists and Particularly German Physicians in their Distress Resulting from a War Which They So Cruelly Waged and Lost," Letter to the Academy of Medicine, 15 December 1923. Cincinnati Academy of Medicine.

18
Cincinnati Enquirer, 20 March 1919.

19
Ibid, 22 March 1919.

20
Ibid, 24 March 1919.

21
See U.S. Congress, Senate Subcommittee on the Judiciary, National German-American Alliance: Hearings (Washington, D.C.: Government Printing Office, 1918)

22
Cincinnati Enquirer, 23 April 1919.

23
Ibid.

24
Cincinnati Board of Education, Minutes, 24 March 1919.

25
"President's Annual Report," The Optimist 7 (1920): 3.

26
Ibid.

228

27
Cited in Smith, Ohio Reader, p. 242.

28
Ibid, pp. 242-48. Cox later wrote that he had requested the Ohio legislature to squeeze "every germ of Prussian poison out of the organic law of Ohio." James M. Cox, Journey Through My Years (New York: Simon & Schuster, 1946), p. 212.

29
James K. Mercer, Ohio Legislative History. Vol. 3 (Columbus, Ohio, 1920), pp. 71-89.

30
See Pohl and Bohning v. State of Ohio. 262 U.S., 404 (1923). The test case from Ohio came from two Cleveland teachers, H.H. Bohning and Emil Pohl, both of whom had been convicted of teaching German below the eighth grade in a parochial school of the Lutheran Church - Missouri Synod. The Synod brought the case to court and was represented by Timothy S. Hogan and Frank Davis Jr., both of Columbus. In 1921 the Ake Law was upheld by the Ohio Supreme Court in Pohl and Bohning v. State of Ohio 102. O.S. 474 (1921). It should be noted that Hogan was the former Irish-American Ohio Attorney General, who is described by Wittke as especially popular as a speaker at German gatherings in Ohio. See Wittke, German-Americans and the World War, p. 25. Also see Charles M. Hogan, Timothy S. Hogan: Ohio's Crusading Attorney General: (1911-1914). (Cincinnati, Ohio, 1972), especially pp. 158-60.

31
Cited in Luebke, "Legal Restrictions on Foreign Languages," p. 15.

32
Cincinnati Board of Education, Minutes, 24 March 1919.

33
Alexander Thomson, History of German in the Public Schools. Pamphlet Submitted to the Ohio Legislature March 1, 1919. (Cincinnati, 1919).

34
Cincinnati Enquirer, 23 April 1919.

35
Ibid, 4 February 1921.

36
Cincinnati Enquirer, 4 February 1921.

37
Ibid.

38
Cincinnati Enquirer, 19 February 1921.

39
Ibid. Regarding public libraries during the war, see Carol Ulrich, "The Role of the Library in Public Opinion Formation During World War I," MNU Bulletin 2:4, 1971, 91-104.

40
German and Bolshevik Propaganda, pp. 1-2.

41
Hofstadter, Age of Reform, pp. 287-88.

42
Ibid.

43
Mitteilungen des Deutschamerikanischen Nationalbundes (September 1914): 3.

44
Freie Presse, 21 March 1920.

45
Ibid.

46
Charles Schmidt, "Unser 53. Stiftungsfest: Die Festrede," Vorstandsbericht des Deutschen Pionier-Vereins 53, 1920-21.

47
Barnstorff, Festschrift, p. 40.

48
"Sechzigstes Stiftungsfest," Vorstandsbericht des Deutschen Pionier-Vereins 60, 1927-28, 17.

49
See Downard, Cincinnati Brewing Industry.

50
H.L. Mencken, A Choice of Days. Essays from Happy Days, Newspaper Days and Heathen Days. Selected and with an introduction by Edward L. Galligan. New York: Knopf, 1980, p. 307.

51
Cincinnati Commercial Tribune, 9 May 1917.

52
Ibid, 12 and 14 June 1917.

53
Ibid, 13, 22 and 27 June 1917.

54
See Cincinnati Home Guard, *Cincinnati Home Guard Minstrels, Emery Auditorium, May 3rd and 4th, 1918* (Cincinnti: n.p., 1918) and S.S. Stewart, *A Narrative of the Organization and Activities of Company "O", Cincinnati Home Guard.* (Cincinnati, 1923).

55
Lewis A. Leonard, *Greater Cincinnati and Its People: A History* (New York: Lewis Historical Publishing Co., Inc., 1927), p. 389.

56
Cincinnati Times Star, 20 April 1930.

NOTES

CONCLUSION

1
   Aristotle, _Aristotle on Man in the Universe_, Edited by Louis Ropes Loomis. (Roslyn, NY: Walter J. Black, Inc., 1943), p. 249.

2
   "Another View from Over-the-Rhine," _Cincinnati Post_, 26 April 1983.

3
   LaVern J. Rippley, _The Immigrant Experience in Wisconsin_ (Boston: Twayne, 1985), p. 115.

4
   Fick, _Zwischen Anfang und Ende_, p. 49.

5
   Nelson, _German-American Political Behavior_, p. 79.

6
   Carl Chrislock, _Ethnicity Challenged: The Upper Midwest Norwegian-American Experience in World War I_ (Northfield, MN: Norwegian American Historical Association, 1981), p. 144.

7
   Zane L. Miller, "Cincinnati Germans and the Invention of an Ethnic Group," _Queen City Heritage_ 42:2 (1984): 17.

8
   A. Leslie Wilson, "Entering the Eighties: The Mosaic of German Literatures," _World Literature Today_ 55 (1981): 552.

9
   O'Connor, _The German-Americans_, p. 457.

10
   Richard Weiss, "Ethnicity and Reform: Minorities and the Ambience of the Depression Years," _Journal of American History_, 66:3 (1979): 568.

11
   Robert Bishoff, "German-American Literature" In: Robert J. DiPietro and Edward Ifkovic, eds., _Ethnic Perspectives in American Literature. Selected Essays on the European Contribution_. (New York: Modern Language Association of America, 1983), p. 43.

12
   Tolzmann, _Festschrift_, p. 102.

232

13
Roger Daniels, Concentration Camps USA: Japanese Americans and World War II. (New York: Rinehart & Winston, Inc., 1972), p. 173.

14
Clarence A. Glasrud, ed., A Heritage Fulfilled: German-Americans/Die erfüllte Herkunft (Moorhead, MN: Concordia College, 1984), p. 7.

Part Four

From Ethnic Survival to Ethnic Revival

Cincinnati's German Heritage in the Twentieth Century

by Don Heinrich Tolzmann

German-American community life at the turn of the century reflected to a great extent home town life in the Fatherland. Residents of German home towns were noted for their sense of community, strong local pride and their *Geselligkeit,* or sociability which found expression "in their pleasure in family and community feasts and frolics, in the celebration of anniversaries and namedays and in activities of the innumerable organizations to which they belonged — church, societies, choirs and instrument groups, skat and skittle clubs, and the like."[1] The customs, traditions and values were transplanted to Cincinnati by immigrants from Germany, Austria, Switzerland, and other German-speaking sections of Europe.

Although the old Over-the-Rhine district had served as a center of the German community in the nineteenth century, by the time of the First World War Cincinnati's Germans were fairly evenly distributed throughout all the wards of the city. In 1917 the German-speaking population was estimated at 127,000, or 34.9% of the total population of Cincinnati. The German element thus constituted more than a full third of the city.[2]

Religious institutions represented the various faiths: Independent Protestant, German Evangelical Synod of North America, Lutheran Church-Missouri Synod, the Presbyterians, the Methodists, the Baptists, the German Reformed Church, the Catholics and the Jews. Many of the religious bodies held religious services in the German language and published their own books, newspapers and periodicals in German. Cincinnati's first German congregation was the St. Johannes-Kirche whose old building is located at 12th & Elm. Cincinnati was the home of German Methodism, the creation of Wilhelm Nast whose Trinity Church stands across from the Music Hall. The Methodists published a high quality family newspaper, *Der Christliche Apologete,* from 1839 to 1941. This pioneer paper championed the cause of orthodoxy and took issue with nineteenth century rationalism. The Queen City also was the home of Reform

---

[1]Gordon A. Craig, *The Germans.* (New York, 1982), p. 24.
[2]August B. Gorbach, *Das Hilfswerk und Cincinnatis deutsche Vereine.* (Cincinnati, 1917), p. 9.

Judaism. Isaac Meyer Wise became rabbi of the congregation Ben Yeshurun in 1854, a position he held for 46 years. He founded *The Israelite* along with its German language supplement *Die Deborah,* published from 1855 to 1902. In short, there was a wide variety of religious institutions available to meet the spiritual needs of the German community.

For those interested in societies and organizations there were over one hundred Vereine to choose from before the Great War. There were 12 singing societies, 12 trade unions, 59 mutual aid societies, 3 marksmen clubs, 3 Turnvereine, 13 cultural organizations, 7 charitable organizations, and 3 central organizations. Local Vereine affiliated with the Stadtverband, commonly known as the German-American Alliance. It was a branch of the Ohio German-American Alliance which in turn belonged to the National German-American Alliance. Local Stadtverband president, Judge John Schwaab, was also president of the Ohio Alliance and a vice-president of the National Alliance.

Best known of the local Vereine was the largest one, Der Deutsche Pionier-Verein von Cincinnati. It had been founded in 1869 to renew old friendships, establish new ones and to preserve the history of German pioneers for future generations. Before the war, it had close to a thousand members. The Pionier-Verein celebrated various Feste, such as Washington's Birthday. It's publications provide a lasting contribution. From 1869-87 it published the historical journal entitled *Der Deutsche Pionier* which is a veritable mine of historical information on nineteenth century Cincinnati German history. It also published an annual *Vorstandsbericht* in later years which contained extensive biographical information on members who had passed away during the year. The Verein's honorary president was Carl Schurz and its members included Christian Moerlein, Karl L. Nippert, Jakob Seasongood, Friedrich S. Spiegel, Gustav Tafel, Isaac Meyer Wise and others.

German-English bilingual instruction had been available in Cincinnati's public schools since 1840. By 1915 there were 175 teachers of German with 17,000 students of the language. Supervisor of the program was Dr. H. H. Fick who had authored a series of textbooks for use in the program that came to be known nationally as the "Cincinnati Plan." A typical textbook of Fick's was *Neu und Alt* which attempted to synthesize the best from the Old and the New Worlds. Such school books contained readings by and about Schiller, Goethe, Franklin, Washington, Lincoln and German pioneers.

Many special interest German language publications were

available, such as the *Brauer-Zeitung* for brewery workers, but the two major newspapers were the *Volksblatt* and the *Freie Presse.* Both had a combined aggregate circulation of 92,000 in 1910. Both issued daily, weekly and Sunday editions. The press informed readers on the social, political and economic conditions of the land and instructed them on their duties, privileges and rights as citizens. It contributed to a preservation of the immigrant heritage by the use and cultivation of an exemplary German and through the encouragement of the retention of German customs and traditions, and by reporting on events from the old country. It also aimed to serve as the mouthpiece of the German community.

Well over 200 German language books had been published by Cincinnati German authors prior to the first World War, making these publications one of the largest branches of German-American literature. The local German Theater presented plays by Lessing, Grillparzer, Schiller, Goethe, Shakespeare and others. For German immigrants it kept alive a familiarity with their native literature while for the American-born it transmitted an understanding of the land of their forebears. To non-Germans it provided a knowledge of the German drama. In 1906 the Schiller Celebration culminated in the performance of *Wilhelm Tell* in Music Hall, a high point in the history of the local German theater.

The advent of war in Europe in 1914 struck many an American like a bolt of lightning from a clear blue sky. The German element was naturally as "pro-German" as Anglo-Americans were "pro-British" in the 1914-17 neutrality period. Cincinnati Germans concentrated and focused their sympathies on humanitarian war relief projects. Altogether a total of $426,382.88 was collected for the widows, orphans and the suffering in Europe. The U.S. declaration of war on Germany in April 1917 resulted in a tragic display of hysteria directed against everything and anything German. Although carried on by nativist extremists, the majority silently approved, or at least did not speak out against the nativist hysteria.

In July 1918 "pink slip" day occurred as "Hun tongue" teachers were stricken from the payroll of the public schools, thus destroying a bilingual program dating back to 1840. In September the Academy of Medicine formed a committee to address the issues of the day, called The Academy of Medicine Against the Huns. A noted community leader, Dr. Gotthard Deutsch, a learned professor at Hebrew Union College, was censured for his outspoken views. At the University of Cincinnati Prof. Martin Ludwich, who taught German in the College of Engineering, was dismissed since he had failed to become a citizen. The Philosophy Department's Prof. Tawney was accused of being pro-German, but was not dismissed. The statue of Germania in the Germania Building on Walnut Street was "Americanized" into Columbia. The Father Jahn Manument in Inwood Park became the target of vandalism. Tar and featherings occured and two attempted lynchings of German-Americans were reported. The offices of the German press were raided by local officers and federal agents, although nothing incriminating was ever found. In 1918 the entire German collection of the Public Library was removed to the sub-basement. The *Cincinnati Enquirer* headlined, "Kultur of the Kaiser's Kind Not Promoted Through Library."

Name-changing became the rage. The German Mutual Insurance Company became the Hamilton County Insurance Company and the German National Bank the Lincoln National Bank, for example. On 9 April 1918 the Cincinnati City Council passed an ordinance changing street names "which commemorate political and military places and persons" in Germany and Austro-Hungary. Among those changed were: Bismarck to Montreal St.; Berlin to Woodrow St.; Bremen to Republic St.; Brunswick to Edgecliff Pt.; Frankfort to Connecticut Ave.; Hamburg to Stonewall St.; Hanover to Yukon St., etc. Symbolically, German Street was renamed English Street.

Dr. Ernest Kunwald, conductor of the Cincinnati Symphony Orchestra, was imprisoned as an enemy alien for stating his heart was on the other side. Prof. Emil Heermann, orchestra concertmaster, was also arrested, but released to the custody of the College Conservatory of Music. Three members of the German Theater were arrested, causing the Theater to close. Under local police orders only English language public meetings could be held. Many Vereine decided to postpone meetings until the war's end.

Nativism against the Germans continued into the 1920s. In 1919 the State of Ohio passed the Ake Law which forbade German language instruction in public, private or parochial schools below the eighth grade. The law, supported by the Supreme Court of Ohio, fortunately was declared unconstitutional in 1923 by the U.S. Supreme Court. Two major spokesmen of the German community came under nativist attack. A movement was begun to remove Judge Schwaab, president of the Citizens League, formerly the Stadtverband, from his position as member of the Union Board of High Schools, but the attempt failed. The Hyde Park Businessmen's Club declared that Judge A. K. Nippert was no longer welcome, nor were any other "pro-aliens." In 1921 the

German books removed from the Public Library's shelves were finally returned with several exceptions. By the mid-1920s, therefore, the Germanophobia engendered by the war was finally subsiding. Unfortunately, it had not subsided immediately with the November 1918 Armistice.

Another remnant of the war hysteria was the enactment of Prohibition. The 1919 U.S. Senate report on *Brewing and Liquor Interests and German and Bolshevik Propaganda* described brewers as pro-German, unpatriotic and supporters of the older German-American Alliance. In the light of these assertions Prohibition became associated with the hysterical superpatriotism of the day. In Cincinnati, Prohibition meant the loss of the family-style beer gardens. After repeal they were replaced by the dimly-lit taverns of a new day. Among the few old style beer gardens today are Mecklenburg's and Forest View Gardens.

In the 1920s societies revived again, festivals were held again, and many churches continued to hold German-language services. Nevertheless, the war had been a definite turning-point in German-American history. Parts of the German heritage had been lost, some of them irretrievably. Several German language publications had died, including the prestigious *Volksblatt,* published since 1836. The bilingual program was gone and the results of the name-changing hysteria were irrevocable: German St. remained English St. Still, new societies were formed such as the Kolping Society. Attempts were made to revive the German Theater and in 1927 the 50th anniversary of the German Literary Club was celebrated. Edwin Zeydel, the new chairman of the German Department at the University of Cincinnati, succeeded in attracting students at the university level. He also authored numerous books, articles, reviews and essays in the field of Germanic languages and literatures. Therefore, in spite of wartime losses much of the German heritage survived.

The 250th anniversary of the founding of Germantown, Pennsylvania was celebrated at the Pastorius Celebration in Cincinnati on 29 October 1933 in Emery Auditorium. The main speaker at the celebration was the well known German-American historian Albert B. Faust, Professor of German, Cornell University. He stated that:

> German-Americans . . . have had their share of failure and success, of trial and triumph, of labor and honest effort in the building of the American nation. They are privileged to love and cherish America as rightful partners, as owners in common with other great European stocks that compose

the American people. The study of our history makes us better Americans, secure in traditions of service, true in devotion to national ideals.

To the future descendants of Germantown, Pastorius dedicated about 20 lines of Latin verse which were later translated by the American poet Whittier in his poem entitled, "The Pennsylvania Pilgrim." Faust read Whittier's translation, which Pastorius had entitled "Salve Posteritas!". It is especially of interest to re-read during this Tricentennial year of 1983:

Hail to Posterity!
Hail, future men of Germanopolis!
Let the young generations yet to be
Look kindly upon this.
Think how your fathers left their native land,—
Dear German-land! O sacred hearths and homes!
And, where the wild beast roams,
In patience planned
New forest homes beyond the mighty sea,
There undisturbed and free
To life as brothers in one family.
What pains and cares befell,
What trials and what fears,
Remember. And wherein we have done well
Follow our footsteps, men of coming years!
Where we have failed to do
Aright, or wisely live,
Be warned by us, the better way pursue,—
And knowing we were human, even as you,
Pity us and forgive!
Farewell, Posterity!
Farewell, dear Germany!
Forevermore farewell![3]

By 1935 the number of German societies stood at 64. In 1938 German Day at Coney Island attracted 38,000 people. In 1939, 600 new citizens of German origin were presented at German Day by Councilman Charles Taft. Main speakers for the fest were Mayor James J. Stewart and Dr. Karl L. Stoll. Although German language instruction was not re-introduced in the public schools at the elementary level, German instruction was sponsored by the Vereine by six teachers in the Central Turnhalle. A youth choir

---

[3]Albert B. Faust, *Francis Daniel Pastorius and the 250th Anniversary of the Founding of Germantown.* (Philadelphia, 1934), p. 17.

was directed by William Kappelhoff, father of actress Doris Day. Also, childrens' choirs were formed as well as a German language Sunday School for children. In 1935 fifteen churches still offered services in German. The major publications at the time were the *Freie Presse,* the Methodist *Apologete,* and the Catholic *Sendbote.* The *Brewery Worker,* a trade publication for the brewing industry, appeared with German and English language articles.

The tragedy of the Third Reich and World War II caused two large immigrations to come to Cincinnati. A substantial number of German Jews fled the Third Reich in the 1930s. Many contacted local relatives, requesting that they become sponsors, enabling the refugees to obtain a visa to freedom. After the war, large numbers of Germans were "displaced" from their homes in southeastern Europe by Soviet forces, thus causing the last great wave of German immigration to Cincinnati, the Danube Swabians.

Between the end of the war and 1956 it is estimated that the number of German women who married American G.I.'s and immigrated to the U.S. was about one-half million; some of them no doubt came to Cincinnati. Immigration in the last several decades has continued and included individuals and families from the former eastern German provinces, such as Pomerania and Silesia; the German Democratic Republic; the Federal Republic of Germany as well as from Austria and Switzerland.

Postwar immigrants acclimated to American life quite swiftly, most motivated by the desire to get ahead as quickly as possible. The postwar immigrants came from all walks of life: a cross-section of all the professions, trades, and occupations have been represented. It would be impossible to list all the businesses, companies, stores, and shops they have established. However, many a neighborhood has a local bakery, meat market or shop which is owned and operated by recent immigrants. Some immigrants became involved in the building trades, forming construction companies which have built a large number of homes, apartments and other buildings, especially on the west side of town. Among the highly educated are a number of well known scholars at local institutions of higher learning, such as the University of Cincinnati. In short, the postwar immigrants have made a definite contribution to the social, cultural and economic life of the city. Their acclimation to American life was aided considerably by the fact that recent immigrants usually have learned some English in schools in their home towns before coming to America. Some upon arrival have purposely refused to read, speak, or write German until they have mastered the

English language. One recent immigrant from the Schwarzwald, for example, spent all his free time at the Public Library reading all varieties of books to master the English tongue. In their zeal for acclimation recent immigrants demonstrate their desire to swiftly become involved in the mainstream of American life. Except in the cases of the Danube Swabians and the East German refugees, the main reason for immigration in the postwar era has been economic, rather than political.

As after World War I, Cincinnati's German community raised funds for humanitarian relief work projects on behalf of Germany. The American Relief for Germany Committee raised $44,000 and 20,000 pounds of clothing for the needy in Germany. A 1950 concert in Music Hall by the Combined Singers raised $10,000 alone for the German-American relief effort.

In 1952 the 41st National Sängerfest of the North American Sängerbund was held in Cincinnati, and in 1952 the National Song Festival of the Federation of Working Singing Societies was held here. The German Day celebration was again held at Steuben Park at Sterling and Simpson Avenues in North College Hill. In 1956 the first Danube Swabian Day was celebrated by the recently formed Verein der Donauschwaben. Another new society was the Germania Society, which originated and sponsors the popular Oktoberfest each year in Harvest Home Park. Another well attended local fest is the Schuetzenfest of the Kolping Society, held each year at Kolping Grove. In 1975 three Vereine celebrated centennials: The Goodfellow Sängerchor, the Swabian Beneficial Society and the Bavarian Beneficial Society. In 1976 German Day at Kolping Grove attracted its highest attendance in decades with over 10,000 people. The Downtown Oktoberfest, sponsored by the Downtown Council in cooporation with community organizations, attracts hundreds of thousands each year to a weekend of Frohsinn and Gemütlichkeit. Today there are more than a dozen German societies and the following maintain their own clubhouses: the Verein der Donauschwaben, the Germania Society, the Kolping Society, the Steuben Park Society, and the Cincinnati Turners.

German music is offered several times weekly on local radio stations. The *Freie Presse* was succeeded by the *Cincinnati Kurier* and then by the *Amerika-Woche*. Other German language papers which circulate in Cincinnati are the *New Yorker Staatszeitung und Herold* and *Aufbau,* both published in New York. Among the literary publications edited in Cincinnati are the *Lessing Yearbook,* currently edited by Edward P. Harris of the University's German Department, and the *Zeitschrift fur*

Verein der Donauschwaben at 4290 Dry Ridge Rd., Cincinnati, Ohio 45247 — celebrating "Kirchweih".

The German Culture Center, Home of the Germania Society, on West Kemper Rd., Cincinnati, Ohio. Since incorporation in 1964, Germania Society members have been actively involved in the German-American activities of the area.

deutschamerikanische Literatur, which was published by the Association of German Language Authors in the early 1970s.

German instruction has been offered in public and parochial schools. An evening class at Hughes High School was offered by the Swabian Beneficial Society in the early 1960s. In 1968 the Tri-State German-American School Society was founded. It conducts classes for all interested in the German language on Saturdays throughout the school year. The school is currently directed by Auguste Kent. In 1968 the German FLES program in Cincinnati began under the leadership of Dr. Gottfried Merkel of the U.C. German Department. Classes were offered on a voluntary basis after school in various schools, but later introduced into the school day. Enrollment rose from a few hundred to 800 in 1974. In the same year a German-English bilingual public school program was established at Fairview and Schiel Elementary Schools. In the first grade alone there were 240 pupils. The program is open to those interested in German-English bilingual instruction, and is currently directed by Dr. Frederick Veidt.

Some students of Tri-State German-American School of Cincinnati.

In 1976 an extension office of the Goethe House New York was established at the University of Cincinnati, the current Representative of which is Christel Kronenberg. Lectures, films, exhibits, musical events, and informational materials are all part of the cultural programs offered through the local office. The University, of course, has been a center of study and research in the field of Germanic Languages and Literatures. The German Department faculty enjoy an international reputation in their respective fields of publication. The department is the international headquarters of the Lessing Society which publishes the Lessing Yearbook. The University Libraries maintain an excellent collection in Germanic Languages and Literatures. In 1974 the Fick Collection of German-Americana was established on the basis of the library of Dr. H.H. Fick, former Supervisor of the German Department of the Public Schools of Cincinnati. Because of the Collection, a Symposium on Immigrant Literature and German-Americana was held at the University in 1976. The Symposium, which attracted many German-American historians and literary scholars, was held in conjunction with the celebrations for the American Bicentennial. Also taking place in 1976 was the Public Library's exhibit entitled "Prosit Cincinnati" which dealt with the history of the Queen City's German heritage.

Several local churches still offer German language church services, such as Concordia Lutheran Church and Old St. Mary's, but most churches founded by the immigrants have long since shifted to the English language. According to the 1970 U.S. Census, 55,000 Cincinnatians claim German as their mother tongue. One can still hear a wide variety of German dialects spoken, but most Cincinnatians of German descent are speakers of American English, rather than of German.

Part of the German tradition has no doubt been diluted or lost as a result of two world wars, but much still remains. Indeed, so much of it has become a part of everyday life that people are unconscious of German origins. As Edwin Zeydel has written, "In our generation the role assumed by German culture in America is well-nigh impossible to analyze, so much has it become a part of the very woof and fabric of that life."[4] The Germans that have been arriving since 1788 have impressed "a distinct Teutonic flavor on the Queen of the West, which has enriched this beautiful inland community and become inculcated forever into its milieu."[5]

---

[4] Quoted in Don Heinrich Tolzmann, *America's German Heritage*. (Cleveland, 1976), p. 104.
[5] Prosit Cincinnati. (Cincinnati, 1976), n.p.

Part Five

Bibliographical Sources

Facsimile copy from: Don Heinrich Tolzmann, **Catalog of the German-Americana Collection, University of Cincinnati.** (München: K.G. Saur, 1990), Vol.1, pp. 295-325.

3.3.9. Ohio-Cincinnati

1843.
Allgemeiner Deutscher Bäcker Gewarbe-Verein, Cincinnati. Beamten für das Jahr 1941. (Covington, Ky.: Wolff, 1941). 4 pp. WC 2
>   Lists officers for 1941

1844.
Allgemeiner Deutscher Bäcker Gewarbe-Verein, Cincinnati.   Diamond Jubilee 1861-1936.   October 31. 1936. (Covington, Ky.: Wolff, 1936). 48 pp. WC 1
>   For a history of the Verein see pp. 8-13 and a list of the members, p. 14.

1845.
Allgemeiner Deutscher Bäcker Gewarbe-Verein, Cincinnati. Officers for the Year 1942. (Covington, Ky.: Wolff, 1942). 4 pp. WC 3

1846.
Allgemeiner Deutscher Bäcker Gewerbe-Verein, Cincinnati. Offi-
cers for the Year 1943.   (Covington, Ky.: Wolff, 1943),   4 pp.
WC 4

1847.
Alte,   Der.   "Zwei   amerikanische   Culturbilder   (1852),"   Der
Deutsche Pionier 7 (1875): 171-72.   E184.G3D5
    Two   poems written in Cincinnati in 1852,   one of which   is
entitled   "Over   the Rhine," and was written in response   to   an
article   in the Cincinnati Daily Times about the German district
which   was described as "where the hogs,   dutch   and   souerkrout
dwell in peace and harmony together, ... "

1848.
"Das   alte Heim des Schützenvereins von Cincinnati "   (illustration), New Yorker Staats-Zeitung und Herold, n.d.   NC108A
    Illustration of the meeting place of the Verein.

1849.
"Ein   amerikanisch-deutscher   Verein," Der   Deutsche   Pionier   6
(1874): 6768.   E184.G3D5
    On the German Club in Cincinnati.

1850.
"Die   Aufhebung der Sonntagsgesetze in Cincinnati," Der Deutsche
Pionier 6 (1874): 66-67.   E184.G3D5
    On Sunday laws in Cincinnati.

1851.
Baecker Gewerbe Unterstützungs-Verein, Cincinnati.   Konstitution
des   Baecker Gewerbe   Unterstützungs-Verein.   (Covington,   Ky.:
Wolff, 1944).   56 pp.   WC 5
    The Verein's constitution in German and English.

1852.
Banater Deutscher Frauen Kranken-Unterstützungs-Verein,   Cincinnati.   Konstitution. (Covington, Ky.: Wolff, 1948).   12 pp. WC 6
    The Verein's constitution.

1853.

Banater Deutscher Frauen Kranken-Unterstützungs-Verein, Cincinnati. Silver Jubilee 1923-1948. Covington, Ky.: Wolff, 1948. 8 pp. WC 7

   The Verein was formed 28 October 1923 with 57 charter members.

1854.

Banater German Men's Sick Beneficial Society, Cincinnati. Silver Jubilee 1924-1949. May 14, 1949. Covington, Ky.: Wolff, 1949. 12 pp. WC 9

   The Verein was formed 1 May 1924 with 70 charter members.

1855.

Barnstorff, Hermann. Festschrift zum goldenen Jubiläum des Deutschen Literarischen Klubs von Cincinnati 1877-1927. Cincinnati: Deutscher Literarischer Klub, 1927. 79 pp.   F535.G3C6 1927

   The history of the German Literary Club of Cincinnati.

1856.

Bayerischer Unterstützungs-Verein, Cincinnati.   Bavarian Society. 75th Anniversary 1875-1950. July 15, 1950.   Covington, Ky.: Wolff, 1950. 16 pp. WC 12

   For a history of the Verein see pp. 2-3.

1857.

"Der Bericht der städtischen Wasserwerke von Cincinnati," (illustration), New Yorker Staats-Zeitung und Herold, n.d. NC108E

   An illustration of the report of the Cincinnati Water Works which was printed in German.

1858.

Bohlman, Theodor. In memoriam Dr. Frederick Forchheimer. Cincinnati: n.p., 1913. 12 pp. FPC 4

   An address on a Cincinnati medical doctor.

1859.
Brühl, Gustav.   "Reden...,"   Der   Deutsche Pionier   2   (1879):
Beilage 1-8.   E184.G3D5
      Speech of Brühl at second foundation festival of the
Pionier-Verein.

1860.
Burgheim, Max.   Cincinnati in Wort und Bild.   Cincinnati: Verlag
von M. & R. Burgheim, 1888.   604 pp.   FCA 21
      A history of the Cincinnati Germans which contains a bio-
graphical directory of local citizens.   Burgheim was a Cincinnati publisher and owner of a German bookstore.

1861.
Burgheim, Max.   Cincinnati in Wort und Bild.   Mit zahlreichen
Illustrationen   Cincinnati: Burgheim Publishing Company, 1891.
558 pp.   F499.C5B94
      A later edition of the previous work.

1862.
Burgheim, Max.   Der Führer von Cincinnati.   Cincinnati: M. & R.
Burgheim, 1875.   288 pp.   F499C5B95 R.B.
      A guidebook to the sites and history of Cincinnati.   Ward
53.

1863.
Busch, Moritz.   "Cincinnati Germans Anno 1851," American-German
Review 9.1 (1942): 28, 30.   E183.8G3A6

1864.
"Die Centennial-Austellung in Cincinnati," Der Deutsche   Pionier
18 (1886): 338-39.   E184.G3D5
      Centennial exhibit in Cincinnati.

1865.
"Christian Köhler,"   Der Deutsche Pionier 17 (1885):   297.
E184.G3D5
      A Cincinnati pioneer; came in 1837.

1866.
"Christopher F. Hanselmann," <u>Der</u> <u>Deutsche</u> <u>Pionier</u> 6 (1874): 180-
83. E184.G3D5
    First president of Pionier-Verein.

1867.
"Cincinnati (Eine historische Skizze)," <u>Der</u> <u>Deutsche</u> <u>Pionier</u> 1
(1869): 4-9, 38-44, 75-79, 138-42, 166-69. E184.G3D5
    Survey of Cincinnati German history.

1868.
"Cincinnati in Wort und Bild," <u>Der</u> <u>Deutsche</u> <u>Pionier</u> 17 (1885):
203, 389-90. E184.G3D5
    Reviews Burgheim's book.

1869.
"Cincinnati in Wort und Bild," <u>Der</u> <u>Deutsche</u> <u>Pionier</u> 18 (1886):
294-95. E184.G3D5
    Reviews Burgheim's book.

1870.
"Cincinnati vor 50 Jahren," <u>Der</u> <u>Deutsche</u> <u>Pionier</u> 3 (1871): 22-
23. E184.G3D5
    Cincinnati in early 1800s.

1871.
Cincinnatier Allgemeiner Deutscher Kranken-Unterstützungs-
Verein. <u>Statuten</u> ... . Covington, Ky.: Wolff, 1945. 42 pp. WC
13
    The Verein's constitution in German and English.

1872.
Cincinnati Baecker Gesang-Verein. <u>Konstitution</u> <u>und</u> <u>Nebengeset-</u>
<u>ze</u>. Covington, Ky.: Wolff, 1947. 14 pp. WC 15
    The Verein's constitution.

1873.
Cincinnati Baecker Gesang-Verein. <u>Souvenir</u> <u>zur</u> <u>Feier</u> <u>des</u> <u>Gold-</u>
<u>enen</u> <u>Jubiläums</u> <u>1881-1931.</u> <u>November</u> <u>8,</u> <u>1931</u>. Covington, Ky.:

Wolff, 1931. 56 pp. WC 14
     For the Verein's history see pp. 32-34.

1874.
Cincinnati Baecker Gesang-Verein. Souvenir. Seventieth Anni-
versary Concert, 1881-1951. November 18, 1951. Covington, Ky.:
Wolff, 1951). 32. pp. WC 16
     For a history of the Verein see p. 1.

1875.
Cincinnati Central Turners. Gems in Gymnastics 1848-1941.
April 20, 1941. Covington, Ky.: Wolff, 1941. 24 pp. WC 17A
     A Turner program booklet, including the article by Anthony
H. Hug, "Why go to Gym?", p. 24. For a comment on the import-
ance of the German press see the Freie Presse advertisement "Der
Ernst der Zeit," p. 22.

1875.1
Cincinnati Central Turners.   "Years of American Turnerism and
More," n.p., n.d., pp. 22-27. WC17B
     A history of the Cincinnati Turngemeinde, now the Cincinna-
ti Central Turners; last date listed is 1941.

1876.
Cincinnati Kurier.   "German Picnic ... Sunday, July 19th, 1964,
at Coney Island." Poster. FCA147A

1877.
Deutsch-Ungarischer Damen Kranken-Unterstützungs-Verein, Cincinnati. Konstitution. Covington, Ky.: Wolff,1 945. 25 pp. WC
27
     The Verein's constitution in German and English.

1878.
Deutsch-Ungarischer Jugend Kranken-Unterstützungs-Verein, Cincinnati. Konstitution. Covington, Ky.: Wolff, n.d. 18 pp. WC
28
     The Verein's constitution.

1879.
"Der Deutsche Pionier und Herr Karl Knortz," Der Deutsche Pionier 6 (1874): 35-37.   E184.G3D5
    On the Pionier and its editor.

1880.
Der Deutsche Pionier-Verein.   "An unsere Abonnenten und Gönner," Der Deutsche Pionier 7 (1875): 200-204.   E184.G3D5
    About the Verein's journal.

1881.
Der Deutsche Pionier-Verein.   "Fest des Pionier-Vereins zu Ehren der Damen-Excursionisten," Der Deutsche Pionier 14 (1882):   372-76.   E184.G3D5
    Fest for women of the Verein who had just returned from a trip to Germany.

1882.
Der Deutsche Pionier-Verein.   "Das Pionierfest am 27. Mai," Der Deutsche Pionier 5 (1873): 119-26.   E184.G3D5
    The Verein's annual fest.

1883.
Der Deutsche Pionier-Verein.   "Das Stiftungsfest des deutschen Pionier-Vereins," Der Deutsche Pionier 6 (1874):   106-15.   E184.G3D5
    Fest of the Verein.

1884.
Der Deutsche Pionier-Verein.   "Das 7. Stiftungsfest des deutschen Pionier-Vereins," Der Deutsche Pionier 7 (1875):   112-25.   E184.G3D5
    On the Verein's fest.

1885.
Der Deutsche Pionier-Verein.   "Das 8. Stiftungsfest des Deutschen Pionier-Vereins," Der Deutsche Pionier 8 (1876):   107-28.   E184.G3D5
    Contains a lengthy address by Rattermann on the role of the

Germans in the discovery and building of America, and focuses on Ohio and Cincinnati, pp. 109-27.

1886.
Der Deutsche Pionier-Verein.   "Das 9. Stiftungsfest des Deutschen Pionier-Vereins," Der Deutsche Pionier 9 (1877):   130-41. E184.G3D5
   Verein's annual fest.

1887.
Der Deutsche Pionier-Verein.   "10. Stiftungsfest des Deutschen Pionier-Vereins," Der Deutsche Pionier 10 (1878):   123-32. E184.G3D5
   On annual fest of the Verein.

1888.
Der Deutsche Pionier-Verein.   "11. Stiftungsfest des Deutschen Pionier-Vereins," Der Deutsche Pionier 11 (1879):   163-67. E184.G3D5

1889.
Der Deutsche Pionier-Verein.   "12. Stiftungsfest des deutschen Pionier-Vereins," Der Deutsche Pionier 12 (1880):   99-121. E184.G3D5

1890.
Der Deutsche Pionier-Verein.   "13. Stiftungsfest ...," Der Deutsche Pionier 13 (1881): 122-27.   E184.G3D5

1891.
Der Deutsche Pionier-Verein.   "14. Stiftungsfest ...," Der Deutsche Pionier 14 (1882): 117-20.   E184.G3D5

1892.
Der Deutsche Pionier-Verein.   "15. Stiftungsfest ...," Der Deutsche Pionier 15 (1883): 134-36.   E184.G3D5

1893.
Der Deutsche Pionier-Verein.   "16. Stiftungsfest ...," Der

<u>Deutsche</u> <u>Pionier</u> 16 (1884): 120-28. E184.G3D5

1894.
Der Deutsche Pionier-Verein. "Das 17. Stiftungsfest ...," <u>Der</u>
<u>Deutsche</u> <u>Pionier</u> 17 (1885): 194-99. E184.G3D5

1895.
Der Deutsche Pionier-Verein. "18. Stiftungsfest ...," <u>Der</u>
<u>Deutsche</u> <u>Pionier</u> 17 (1885): 385-88. E184.G3D5

1896.
Der Deutsche Pionier-Verein. "20. Stiftungsfest ...," <u>Der</u>
<u>Deutsche</u> <u>Pionier</u> 18 (1886): 389-91. E184.G3D5

1897.
Der Deutsche Pionier-Verein. "Eine Washington's Geburtstagsfeier
des deutschen Pionier-Vereins," <u>Der</u> <u>Deutsche</u> <u>Pionier</u> 7 (1875):
499-07. E184.G3D5
. On a fest of the Verein.

1898.
Der Deutsche Pionier-Verein.   "Die Washington's Geburtstags-
Feier des Deutschen Pionier-Vereins," <u>Der</u> <u>Deutsche</u> <u>Pionier</u> 9
(1877): 36-48. E184.G3D5
On the Washington celebration of the Verein.

1899.
Der Deutsche Pionier-Verein. "Washington's Geburtstagsfeier des
Deutschen Pionier-Vereins von Cincinnati," <u>Der</u> <u>Deutsche</u> <u>Pionier</u>
11 (1879): 75-77. E184.G3D5
The Verein's Washington fest.

1900.
Der Deutsche Pionier-Verein. "Washington's Geburtstagsfeier...,"
<u>Der</u> <u>Deutsche</u> <u>Pionier</u> 16 (1884): 458-63. E184.G3D5

1901.
Der Deutsche Pionier-Verein. Washington-Geburtstagsfeier...,"
<u>Der</u> <u>Deutsche</u> <u>Pionier</u> 17 (1885): 276-83. E184.G3D5

1902.
Der Deutsche Pionier-Verein. "Washington's Geburtstagsfeier...,"
Der Deutsche Pionier (1886): 295-99. E184.G3D5

1903.
Der Deutsche Pionier-Verein. "Zur Geschichte des Deutschen
Pionier-Vereins," Der Deutsche Pionier 1 (1869):   26-27.
E184.G3D5
     History of the Verein, established in 1868.

1904.
Deutscher Literarischer Klub.   Deutscher Literarischer Klub von
Cincinnati. Cincinnati: S. Rosenthal & Co., 1885.   21 pp.
PN21.D4
     The club's constitution and lists of members, programs and
lectures. ·

1905.
Deutscher Literarischer Klub. Geschichte des Deutschen literar-
ischen Klubs von Cincinnati, Erinnerungsschrift für das zehnte
Stiftungsfest 26. November 1887. Cincinnati: S. Rosenthal &
Co., 1887. 125 pp. PN21.d4 1887
     A history of the Klub with a collection of original songs.

1906.
Deutscher Literarischer Klub.   Vorträge gehalten im Deutschen
litterarischen Klub von Cincinnati. Festgabe zum 20. Stiftungsfest, 24. November 1897. Cincinnati: S. Rosenthal & Co., 1897.
43 pp. PN21.D4 1897
     A list of lectures presented at the Klub.

1906.1
Doane, Kathy. "Does Our German Image Still Fit," Cincinnati
Enquirer, Tristate Magazine, 8 Sept. 1985. FCA134B
     Critical assessment of the German heritage.

1907.
Dobbert, Guido Andre. The Disintegration of an Immigrant Community: The Cincinnati Germans, 1879-1920. Chicago: University of

Chicago Library Department of Photoduplication, 1979. 442 pp. Microfilm 804, Langsam Library.

1908.
"Dr. Benjamin Ehrmann," Der Deutsche Pionier 17 (1885): 275-76. E184.G3D5
    A Cincinnati physician.

1909.
"Dr. J. Th. Frank," Der Deutsche Pionier 18 (1886): 289. E184.G3D5
    Cincinnati medical doctor.

1910.
"Drei deutsche Pionierinnen gestorben," Der Deutsche Pionier 6 (1874): 405-06. E184.G3D5
    On three Cincinnati German women.

1911.
Ernst, Heinrich Ernst. "Erinnerungen aus alter Zeit," Der Deutsche Pionier 1 (1869): 241-43. E184.G3D5
    Remembrances of a German who came to Cincinnati in 1805.

1912.
"Das erste deutsche Frauen-Kränzchen in Cincinnati," Der Deutsche Pionier 4 (1872): 210-14. E184.G3D5
    On first German-American women's group in Cincinnati.

1913.
"Der erste Kunstgärtner von Cincinnati," Der Deutsche Pionier 2 (1870): 3-5. E184.G3D5
    On first landscape gardener in Cincinnati.

1914.
"Der erste Mayor Cincinnatis ein Deutscher," Der Deutsche Pionier 1 (1869): 11-15. E184.G3D5
    On David Ziegler, first mayor of Cincinnati.

1915.
"Ferdinand Bodmann," Der Deutsche Pionier 6 (1874): 186-88.
E184.G3D5
    Obituary of a councilman and member of many Vereine.

1916.
Fick, H. H. "Historische Spuren in Cincinnati und der Umgegend." Newspaper articles. FPC 51
    Deals with historic sites in and around Cincinnati.

1917.
"Frau Anna Molitor," Der Deutsche Pionier 9 (1877): 365-68.
E184.G3D5
    Wife of Stephan Molitor, editor of the Cincinnati Volks-
blatt.

1918.
"Fünfzig Jahre Deutscher Literarischer Klub von Cincinnati,
1877-1927," Cincinnati Freie Presse, 6 November 1927.   80 pp.
PT21f.D4C5
    A festschrift published by the Presse on the 50th
anniversary of the Cincinnati German Literary Club which
contains articles on Cincinnati German history, literature, and
culture.

1919.
"General Grants letzter Besuch in Cincinnati," Der Deutsche
Pionier 17 (1885): 370-401.   E184.G3D5
    Grant's last visit in Cincinnati.

1920.
"Georg Alexander, Sr.," Der Deutsche Pionier 17 (1885): 112.
E184.G3D5
    Resident of Camp Washington in Cincinnati.

1921.
German-American Citizens League, Cincinnati. "German Day.
Deutscher Tag. Sunday, August 5, 1951." Poster. FCA31A

1922.
German-American Citizens League, Cincinnati.   50 Jubiläumsfeier
der Deutsch-Amerikanischen Bürgerliga.   1908-1958.   May 3, 1958.
Covington, Ky.: Wolff, 1958.   24 pp.   WC 31B
    See Jacob Herz, "Die Geschichte des Deutschtums und der
Deutsch-Amerikanischen Bürgerliga von Cincinnati," pp. 1-2 and
English translation, pp. 3-4.

1923.
German-American Citizens League, Cincinnati.   Deutscher Tag.
August 3, 1958.   Covington, Ky.: Wolff, 1958.   6 pp.   WC 32
    See Martin Mayer, "Zum Deutschen Tag 1958," p. 1.

1924.
German-American Citizens League, Cincinnati.   Deutscher Tag.
August 11, 1963.   Covington, Ky.: Wolff, 1963.   4 pp.   WC 33
    A German Day program.

1925.
German-American Citizens League, Cincinnati.   Deutscher Tag.
69. Jubiläums-Programm.   August 14, 1964.   Covington, Ky.:
Wolff, 1964   8 pp   WC 34
    A German Day program.

1926.
German-American Citizens League, Cincinnati.   70th Anniversary,
1895-1965.   Tag der deutschen Einheit. Festschrift.   Deutsch-
Amerikanischer Tag, 1895-1965.   August 15, 1965.   Covington,
Ky.: Wolff, 1965.   12 pp.   WC 35
    A German Day program.   See Martin Mayer, "1895-Der Deutsche
Tag-1965," p. 2.

1927.
German-American Citizens League, Cincinnati.   75. Jubiläumsfeier. Festschrift. Tag der deutschen Einheit. Deutsch-amerikanischer Tag.   Covington, Ky.: Wolff, 1970.   24 pp.   WC38
    A German Day program.   See Martin Mayer, "1895 - Zum 75.
Deutschen Tag - 1970," p. 3.

1928.
German-American Citizens League, Cincinnati.   79. Anniversary.
Tag der deutschen Einheit. Festschrift. Deutsch-amerikanischer
Tag. 1895-1974. August 16, 1974.   Covington, Ky.: Wolff, 1974.
22 pp.   WC36
   A German Day program.

1929.
German-American Citizens League, Cincinnati.   Deutsch-Amerikanischer Tag. 1895-1976. Cincinnati: n.p., 1976.   22 pp.   WC 37
   See Don Heinrich Tolzmann, "Das Deutschtum von Cincinnati,"
p. 25, a brief description of the German heritage.

1930.
German-Hungarian Trade Beneficial Society, Cincinnati.   Official
Program. Fiftieth Anniversary 1910-1960. January 31, 1960.
Covington, Ky.: Wolff, 1960.   28 pp.   WC39
   The Verein's anniversary festschrift.

1931.
"Das Germania-Gebäude in Cincinnati, Ohio (illustration)," New
Yorker Staats-Zeitung und Herold, n.d.   NC108B
   Rattermann's building in Cincinnati which housed his
Deutsche Gegenseitige Versicherungs-Gesellschaft von Cincinnati.

1932.
Germania Society of Cincinnati.   "Oktoberfest program booklets,
1973-76."   FCA144A

1933.
Geschichte des Deutschen Altenheims. vom Beginn bis zum 1. April
1908. Cincinnati: Roessler Bros., 1908.   32 pp.   HV1471.C5D4
   A history of the German Old Men's Home in Cincinnati, located on Burnet Ave.   For a description of architecture see Tolzmann (1982): 19.

1934.
Giorg, Kara.   "Johann Georg Hagen," Der Deutsche Pionier 2
(1870): 353-55.   E184.G3D5

On one of the founders of the German Society of Cincinnati.

1935.
Goethe House of New York at the University of Cincinnati.   1983
Calendar of Events.   37 pp.   FCA 41
    A calendar of events for the German-American   Tricentennial
in Cincinnati.

1936.
Gorbach, August B.   Deutscher Vereins-Wegweiser von Cincinnati,
Ohio.   Erste Ausgabe. Im Auftrage des Stadtverbandes von Cincin-
nati.   Cincinnati: S.   Rosenthal & Co., 1915.   274 pp.
F499.C5G648y
    A directory of Cincinnati's German societies.

1937.
Gorbach, August B.   Das Hilfswerk und Cincinnatis deutsche Vereine. Zweite Ausgabe.   Cincinnati: S. Rosenthal & Co., 1917.
207, LV pp. F499.C5G65
    Regards the war relief for Germany and Austro-Hungary
before American entrance into World War I.

1938.
"Die Gründung der deutschen Gesellschaft von Cincinnati," Der
Deutsche Pionier 5 (1873): 41-46   E184.G3D5
    On the establishment of the German Society of Cincinnati.

1939.
H., H.   "Jacob Gülich," Der Deutsche Pionier 1 (1869):   35-38.
E184.G3D5
    On an early 19th century Cincinnati German associate of
Martin Baum.

1939.1.
Harlow, Alvin F.   The Serene Cincinnatians.   New York: Dutton,
1950.   442 pp.   F499.C5H35 Langsam Library

1940.
"Heinrich Kress," Der Deutsche Pionier 18 (1886): 320. E184.G3D5

Ran boarding-house in Cincinnati.

1941.
"Heinrich Möser," Der Deutsche Pionier 17 (1885): 349-50.
E184.G3D5
A Cincinnati pioneer; came in 1852.

1942.
"Heinrich Roedter," Der Deutsche Pionier 1 (1869): 130-33.
E184.G3D5
On the editor of the Cincinnati Volksblatt, and a community
leader in the first half of the 19th century in Cincinnati.
Ward 242.

1943.
"Eine Hermannsschlacht in Cincinnati," Der Deutsche Pionier 1
(1869): 250-53. E184.G3D5
An eyewitness account of a nativist attack on a Cincinnati
German Jaeger-Companie.

1944.
Ein Himmelsbrief von Gott gesandt.   Gedruckt, den 12. November
1942. WC50
Bearers of this Himmelsbrief will not be captured or harmed
by enemies, nor will they be wounded; apparently intended for
Cincinnati German-American soldiers during World War II.

1945.
The History and Story of Findlay Market and the Over the Rhine
Community Center Dedication Day, June 9, 1974.   Cincinnati:
n.p., 1974. n.p. FCA 144C
Contains brief history of the Market and information on the
1974 dedication.

1946.
"Im Plauderstübchen mit einem viel gewanderten Pionier," Der
Deutsche Pionier 4 (1872): 73-76, 109-114. E184.G3D5
Conversation with a peddler in Cincinnati.

1947.

"J.M. Memmel," Der Deutsche Pionier 17 (1885): 64.   E184.G3D5
     First postmaster in Mt. Airy, Treasurer of Green Township,
and active in German-American affairs in Cincinnati.

1948.

"Johann   Nordheim," Der Deutsche Pionier 17 (1885):   299.
.E184.G3D5
     Active with the Cincinnati Zoo.

1949.

Jones, Wilbur D.   "Some Cincinnati German Societies a Century
Ago," American-German Review 18:1 (1951): 22-24.   E183.8G3A6

1950.

"Karl Volz," Der Deutsche Pionier 4 (1872): 319-25.   E184.G3D5
     Head of Cincinnati Water Works and local businessman.

1951.

Katzenberger, Geo. A.   Mayor David Ziegler, Biography of the
First Mayor of Cincinnati.   Columbus: F. J. Heer, 1912. 50 pp.
GC 118

1952.

Kelly, Mike.   "Zinzinnati in Cincinnati: Long, Proud Heritage,"
Cincinnati Post (8 October 1983). FCA134C
     Deals with Cincinnati's German heritage, and focuses on the
1983 Tricentennial.

1953.

Klauprecht, Emil.   Deutsche Chronik in der Geschichte des Ohio-
Thales und seiner Hauptstadt Cincinnati ins Besondere ...
Cincinnati: G. Hof and M. A. Jacobs, 1864. 198 pp. GC 122
     History of the Ohio Valley with particular emphasis on the
Cincinnati Germans; the author resided in Cincinnati. Ward 155.

1954.

Kohlenberg, Karl F.   Das kleine Trapperbuch. Mit Zeichnungen von
Kurt Wendlandt.   Stuttgart: Union Verlag, 1966. 79 pp.

F516.K65

Deals with the life of Ludwig Wetzel, a trapper and Indian fighter well known in the Cincinnati and Kentucky area.   Also see R.C.V. Meyers' work.

1955.

Kotz, A. L. "Samuel David Gross, M.D., D.C.L., LL.D.," Pennsylvania German Society Proceedings and Addresses 39 (1931): 5-20. F146.P23 v. 39

Born in 1805 in Forks Township, Northampton County, Pennsylvania, Gross became a surgeon and was later elected to the chair of Pathological Anatomy in the Medical Department of the Cincinnati College in 1835; authored a two-volume work entitled Elements of Pathological Anatomy in 1839. Afterwards he occupied a number of chairs at various medical institutions. He died in 1884.

1956.

"Louis Ballauf," Der Deutsche Pionier 18 (1886): 337-38. E184.G3D5

On Sen. Ballauf of Cincinnati.

1957.

"Ludwig Rehfuss," Der Deutsche Pionier 1 (1869): 226-30. E184.G3D5

On one of the co-founders of the German Society of Cincinnati (1834).

1958.

Meyers, R. C. V. Life and Adventures of Lewis Wetzel, the Renowned Virginia Ranger and Scout. Comprising a thrilling history of this celebrated Indian fighter, with his perilous adventures and hair-breadth escapes, and including other interesting incidents of border-life. Largely compiled from authentic records hitherto unpublished. With illustrations. Philadelphia: John E. Potter and Company, 1883. 414 pp. F517.W4M4

The biography of a well-known trapper and Indian fighter in the Cincinnati and Kentucky area. See also the work of Karl F. Kohlenberg.

1958.1
Miller, Zane L. Boss Cox's Cincinnati: Urban Politics in the Progressive Era. New York: Oxford University Pr., 1968. 301 pp. F499.C5M52 Langsam Library
  Valuable for pre-World War I political history.

1959.
"Namenlose Pioniere," Der Deutsche Pionier 4 (1872): 246-49, 270-72, 312-16, 416-19. E184.G3D5
  On early unknown pioneers.

1959.1
Parry, Dale. "The German Spirit in Cincinnati," Cincinnati Enquirer 5 Sept. 1986. FCA134E
  Scries of articles on the Cincinnati Germans, and the annual Oktoberfest.

1960.
Pieper, Charlotte. Wooden Shoe Hollow. A Novel. New York: Exposition Press, 1951. 243 pp. PS3531.I29W6
  A novel dealing with the Cincinnati Germans.

1961.
Polt, H. K. "Lewis Wetzel," American-German Review 8.6 (1942): 23-26. E183.8G3A6

1962.
Public Library of Cincinnati and Hamilton County. Germans in America 1683-1983. n. pag. FCA 69
  A reading list prepared for the 1983 Tricentennial.

1963.
R., C. "Denkschrift für C.F. Adae," Der Deutsche Pionier 1 (1869): 259-61. E184.G3D5
  A banker in Cincinnati who served as consul for Württemberg and several other German states.

1964.
R., C. "Ernst Friedrich Kurfiss, Der Deutsche Pionier 3 (1871):

49-51, 83-86.   E184.G3D5
    On community leader in Cincinnati before the Civil War.

1965.
R., C.   "Heinrich Flinchbaugh," Der Deutsche Pionier 3 (1871):
133-137.   E184.G3D5
    On a pre-Civil War Cincinnati German.

1966.
R., C.   "John A. Röbling," Der Deutsche Pionier 1 (1869): 194-
201.   E185.G3D5
    On the builder of the Cincinnati Suspension Bridge and the
Brooklyn Bridge.   The former has now been renamed in honor   or
Roebling.

1967.
R., C.   "Philipp Reiss," Der Deutsche Pionier 2 (1870): 355-59.
E184.G3D5
    Reiss came to Cincinnati in 1831.

1968.
R., C.   "Skizze des Lebens von Jacob Schroeder," Der   Deutsche
Pionier 2 (1870): 226-30.   E184.G3D5
    On a Cincinnati pioneer (d. 1864).

1969.
Rattermann, H. A.   "Adolph Strauch," Der Deutsche Pionier 15
(1883): 428-34, 489-97; 16 (1884): 39-45, 62-71.   E184.G3D5`
    Also published separately as the next item.

1970.
Rattermann, H. A.   Adolph Strauch, der Begründer der landschaft-
lichen Friedhöfe.   Eine biographische Skizze.   Cincinnati:
Mecklenborg & Rosenthal, 1884.   34 pp.   SB470.S7R3
    A biography on the founder of landscape cemeteries,   Adolph
Strauch, who designed Spring Grove Cemetery in Cincinnati.

1971.
Rattermann, H. A.   "Albert Böhmer," Der Deutsche Pionier 15

(1883): 210-12. E184.G3D5
    Painter in Cincinnati.

1972.
Rattermann, H. A. "Alte deutsch-amerikanische Dokumente. 6,"
Der Deutsche Pionier 13 (1881): 142-53. E184.G3D5
    Heckewelder's 1792 description of Cincinnati.

1973.
Rattermann, H. A. "Andreas Gross," Der Deutsche Pionier 15
(1883): 219-26. E184.G3D5
    Owner of Exchange Coffee House in Cincinnati.

1974.
Rattermann, H. A. "Anekdote von Hauptmann David Ziegler, dem
ersten Mayor Cincinnati," Der Deutsche Pionier 7 (1875): 76-77.
E184.G3D5
    Anecdote on Ziegler.

1975.
Rattermann, H. A. Chronik des Deutschen Literarischen Clubs von
Cincinnati. Humoristischer Vortrag zum dritten Stiftungsfeste
des selben. Cincinnati: Mecklenborg & Rosenthal, 1881. 20 pp.
FPC 133
    A history of the German Literary Club of Cincinnati in
humorous verse.

1976.
Rattermann, H. A. "Deutsch-Amerikanische Künstler. Der Pionier
der Landschafts-gärtnerei," Der Deutsche Pionier 10 (1878): 82-
93. E184.G3D5
    On A. Strauch.

1977.
Rattermann, H. A. "Deutsche Bilder aus der Geschichte der Stadt
Cincinnati," Der Deutsche Pionier 9 (1877): 6-17. E184.G3D5
    On the Cincinnati Water Works.

1978.
Rattermann, H. A. "Deutsche Bilder aus der Geschichte der Stadt Cincinnati," Der Deutsche Pionier 10 (1878): 3-12.   E184.G3D5
    On David Ziegler.

1979.
Rattermann, H. A. "Deutsche Bilder aus der Geschichte der Stadt Cincinnati," Der Deutsche Pionier 10 (1878): 42-48.   E184.G3D5
    On Martin Baum.

1980.
Rattermann, H. A. "Eine deutsche Pionier in Cincinnati's gestorben. Frau Elisabeth Siefert," Der Deutsche Pionier 7 (1875): 419-20.   E184.G3D5
    On a Cincinnati pioneer; came to Cincinnati in 1834.

1981.
Rattermann, H. A. "Dr. August Ferdinand Mosterts," Der Deutsche Pionier 13 (1881): 204-05.   E184.G3D5
    A physician in Cincinnati.

1982.
Rattermann, H. A. "Dr. med. Georg Holdt," Der Deutsche Pionier 13 (1881): 251-57.   E184.G3D5
    A medical doctor in Cincinnati.

1983.
Rattermann, H. A. Festrede gehalten beim Pflanzen der Bismarckeiche in Cincinnati. Ostersonntag, den 10. April 1898. Cincinnati: n.p., 1898. 5 pp.   FPC 135

1984.
Rattermann. H. A. "Franz Helfferich, sen.," Der Deutsche Pionier 12 (1880): 125-27.   E184.G3D5
    Innkeeper in Cincinnati.

1985.
Rattermann, H. A. "Eine Frauen-Temperenz-bewegung vor dreissig
Jahren," Der Deutsche Pionier 6 (1874): 33-35.   E184.G3D5
    On prohibition movement led by women.

1986.
Rattermann, H. A. "Ein Froschgeschichte aus Cincinnati's Ver-
gangenheit," Der Deutsche Pionier 7 (1875): 198-200.   E184.G3D5
    On Cincinnati in the 1820s.

1987.
Rattermann, H. A. "Gesellige Unternehmen der Deutschen Cincinnati's vor dreissig Jahren," Der Deutsche Pionier 7 (1875): 280-
83.   E184.G3D5
    Cincinnati German social life in the 1850s.

1988.
Rattermann, H. A. "Heinrich Brachmann," Der Deutsche Pionier 14
(1882): 379-88, 473.   E184.G3D5
    Deals with a Cincinnati German and Cincinnati politics
before the Civil War.

1989.
Rattermann, H. A. "Heinrich Rasche," Der Deutsche Pionier 7
(1875): 210 14   E184.G3D5
    Rasche, born in Ohlenburg, came to the U.S. in 1841, and
settled in Cincinnati, where he was active in German Catholic
affairs.

1990.
Rattermann, H. A. "Jakob Hust," Der Deutsche Pionier 12 (1880):
465-66.   E184.G3D5
    Member of Cincinnati City Council in mid-19th century.

1991.
Rattermann, H. A. "Johann Bast," Der Deutsche Pionier 12
(1880): 4-9.   E184.G3D5
    Came to Cincinnati in 1837; was an architect and builder.

1992.
Rattermann, Heinrich A. <u>Johann</u> <u>Bernhard</u> <u>Stallo.</u> <u>Denkrede</u>
<u>gehalten</u> <u>im</u> <u>Deutschen</u> <u>Litterarischen</u> <u>Klub</u> <u>von</u> <u>Cincinnati,</u> <u>am</u> <u>6.</u>
<u>November</u> <u>1901.</u> Cincinnati: Verlag des Verfassers, 1902.   54 pp.
CT275.S688R3
    An address on Stallo, a well-known politician, lawyer,
philosopher and author in Cincinnati; was U.S. minister to Italy
in 1885. This copy is dedicated to the University of Cincinnati
Library by the author.

1993.
Rattermann, H. A.   "Johann Christian Becker," <u>Der</u> <u>Deutsche</u> <u>Pio-</u>
<u>nier</u> 8 (1876): 394-98.   E184.G3D5
    Becker was active in the Pionier-Verein; first came to
Cincinnati in 1838.

1994.
Rattermann, H. A.   "Johann Meyer," <u>Der</u> <u>Deutsche</u> <u>Pionier</u> 7
(1875): 436-41.   E184.G3D5
    On an early pioneer in Cincinnati (1793-1875).

1995.
Rattermann, H. A.   "Johann Michael Pfau," <u>Der</u> <u>Deutsche</u> <u>Pionier</u>
12 (1880): 284-88.   E184.G3D5
    Owner of Hotel Pfau in Cincinnati.

1996.
Rattermann, H. A.   "Das neue Pionierbild," <u>Der</u> <u>Deutsche</u> <u>Pionier</u>
7 (1875): 156-62.   E184.G3D5
    On a photograph of the Pionier-Verein; provides biographi-
cal information on individual members.

1997.
Rattermann, H. A.   "Nikolaus Höffer," <u>Der</u> <u>Deutsche</u> <u>Pionier</u> 6
(1874): 419-26.   E184.G3D5
    On a Cincinnati German community leader.

1998.
Rattermann, H. A.   "Die Pionier-Turngemeinde Amerika's," <u>Der</u>

Deutsche Pionier 7 (1875): 178-87.   E184.G3D5
    On the Cincinnati Turnverein.

1999.
Rattermann, H. A.   "Politisches Bestreben der Deutschen Cincin-
nati's vor 30 Jahren," Der Deutsche Pionier 6 (1874):   189-95.
E184.G3D5
    On German-American politics in the 1840s.

2000.
Rattermann, H. A.   "Eine Reliquie," Deutsch-Amerikanisches Magazin 1 (1887): 620-24.   AP31.D44
    Deals with Heinrich Rödter.   Ward 242.

2001.
Rattermann, H. A.   Theodor Sittel.   Deutsch-amerikanischer Arzt
und Physiologe.   Denkrede, gehalten im Deutschen literarischen
Klub von Cincinnati, am 18. Oktober 1905.   Cincinnati: Verlag
des Verfassers, 1911.   173 pp.   FPC 141
    Biography of a Cincinnati physician from Trier an der
Mosel.

2002.
Rattermann, H. A.   "Die Weiber-Whiskey-Wuth," Der Deutsche
Pionier 6 (1874): 31-33.   E184.G3D5
    On prohibition, and the support of the movement by women.

2003.
Reichrath, Anna.   Die Donauschwaben in Cincinnati, Ohio.   Cincinnati: Verein der Donauschwaben, 1974.   96 pp.   F500.G3R4 copy
2
    An illustrated history of the Danube Swabians in Cincinna-
ti.   An expanded second edition was issued in 1984 for the
Verein's 30th anniversary: Anna Reichrath, Die Donauschwaben in
Cincinnati, Ohio.   Cincinnati: Verein der Donauschwaben, 1984.
110 pp.   FCA141

2004.
Röllecke, Heinz.   "A Letter From Cincinnati's Committee for the

Needy in Germany to Jakob Grimm," Journal of German-American Studies 5 (1972): 163-68.   E184.G3G315 v. 5
   The letter informs Jakob Grimm that a sum of $2774.57 has been collected.   More detailed instructions are to follow in a subsequent letter.

2005.
Rümelin, Karl.   "Ansprache ...," Der Deutsche Pionier 13 (1881): 409-15.   E184.G3D5
   On his trip to Europe, 1881.

2006.
Rümelin, Carl.   "Geschichtliche Skizze eines amerikanischen Township," Der Deutsche Pionier 18 (1886): 164-75, 244-61. E184.G3D5
   On Green Township.

2007.
Schmadel, Donna.   "Oktoberfest Old World, New World," Cincinnati Enquirer Magazine 9 Sept. 1984.   FCA134D
   Compares Cincinnati's Oktoberfest with that of Munich.

2008.
Sell, Rainer.   "Der Deutsche Pionier-Verein von Cincinnati, Heinrich Armin Rattermann, and Der Deutsche Pionier: A Nucleus of Nineteenth Century German-America," Yearbook of German-American Studies 20 (1985): 49-60.   NC293

2009.
Sell, Rainer.   "The German Language: Mirror of the German-American Struggle for Identity as Reflected in Der Deutsche Pionier (1869-1887) and the Activities of Der Deutsche Pionier-Verein von Cincinnati," Journal of German-American Studies 11:3-4 (1976): 71-81.   E184.G3G315 v. 11:3-4.
   A history of the Pionier-Verein and its publications.

2010.
"Skizzen bekannter Pioniere," Der Deutsche Pionier 4 (1872): 267-70, 308-12, 330-33, 386-92.   E184.G3D5

Well-known Cincinnati pioneers.

2011.

Smith, Clifford Neal. <u>Early</u> <u>Nineteenth-Century</u> <u>German</u> <u>Settlers</u>
<u>in</u> <u>Ohio</u> (<u>Mainly</u> <u>Cincinnati</u> <u>and</u> <u>Environs</u>), <u>Kentucky,</u> <u>and</u> <u>Other</u>
<u>States:</u> <u>Part</u> <u>I</u>. (German-American Genealogical Research Mono-
graph Number 20.) McNeal, Arizona: Westland Publications, 1984.
36 pp. F499.C59G37 1984 pt. 1
        An index to the 900 obituaries which appeared in <u>Der</u>
<u>Deutsche</u> <u>Pionier</u>, published by the German Pioneer Society of
Cincinnati. Although focused on the Cincinnati area, the obituaries of German-Americans in other states are also included.

2012.

Stationery. 15 items. WC48
        Stationery of various German-American organizations in
Cincinnati and the Freie Presse, 1940s-50s.

2013.

Tenner, Armin. <u>Cincinnati</u> <u>Sonst</u> <u>und</u> <u>Jetzt</u>. <u>Eine</u> <u>Geschichte</u>
<u>Cincinnati's</u> <u>und</u> <u>seiner</u> <u>verdienst-vollen</u> <u>Bürger</u> <u>deutscher</u> <u>Zunge,</u>
<u>mit</u> <u>biographischen</u> <u>Skizzen</u> <u>und</u> <u>Portrait</u> <u>Illustrationen</u>. Cincin-
nati: Mecklenborg &rosenthal, 1878. 448 pp. F499.C513
        A history of the Cincinnati Germans with a biographical
directory.

2014.

Tickets. 67 items. WC49
        Tickets to various functions of Vereine in Cincinnati,
1940s-1950s. Also includes membership cards.

2015.

"Die todte Sache unter den deutschen Pionieren Cincinnati's,"
<u>Der</u> <u>Deutsche</u> <u>Pionier</u> 5 (1873): 18-25. E184.G3D5
        Cincinnati German politics, 1820-40s.

2016.
Tolzmann, Don Heinrich.   Cincinnati German   Biography   Index.
Cincinnati: University Libraries, 1984.   2 pp.   FCA 291A
Name indexes to Nrs. 1861 and 2013.

2017.
Tolzmann, Don Heinrich.   "Deutsche Vereine im Raum Cincinnati,
Ohio," New Yorker Staats-Zeitung und Herold, n.d.   NC108F
List of Vereine in Cincinnati in 1977.

2018.
Tolzmann, Don Heinrich.   Festschrift for the   German-American
Tricentennial Jubilee.   With an Introduction by Christel Kronen-
berg.   Cincinnati: Cincinnati Historical Society, 1982.   105 pp.
F499.C5F5 copy 4
     Contains essays on the German community, architecture,
August Willich, German societies, customs, saloons and the
brewing industry, literature, philosophy, German instruction,
and bibliographical sources.

2018.1
Tolzmann, Don Heinrich.   "The Survival of an Ethnic Community:
The Cincinnati Germans,   1918 through 1932," Ph.D. diss.,
University of Cincinnati,   1983.   405 pp.   c.u.151.83T65
     Langsam Library and another copy in Archives and Rare
Books.

2019.
"Two Centuries: Bicentennial of the First German Settlement in
America," a newspaper article.   FPC 175
     About the Bicentennial celebration of the founding of
Germantown, Pennsylvania which was held in Cincinnati's Music
Hall in 1883.

2020.
United Banater Societies, Cincinnati.   Silver Jubilee 1927-1952.
June 29, 1952.   Covington, Ky.: Wolff, 1952.   20 pp.   WC 47
     Includes a list of the UBS's delegates.

2021.

"Unsere erste lithographische Zeichnung," Der Deutsche Pionier 1
(1869): 9-11. E184.G3D5
    First lithograph of Cincinnati is discussed.

2022.

"Urtheil der Presse über unsere Zeitschrift," Der Deutsche
Pionier 18 1886): 268-69, 295. E184.G3D5
    Reviews of the Pionier.

2023.

Verein der Donauschwaben. Einladung zum VIII. Donauschwabentag,
Cincinnati. July 7, 1963. Covington, Ky.: Wolff, 1963. 4 pp.
WC 30
    Advertisement for the 8th Danube Swabian Day in Cincinnati.

2024.

"Das vierte Jahresfest des deutschen Pionier-Vereins," Der Deutsche Pionier 4 (1872): 152-59. E184.G3D5
    Fourth annual fest of the Verein.

2025.

"Vor fünfundzwanzig Jahren," Der Deutsche Pionier 4 (1872): 20-
24, 69-73, 106-09, 149-52, 186-88, 214-18, 243-44, 279-82, 305-
08, 358-64, 392-95, 410-16. 5 (1873): 25-28, 51-52. E184.G3D5
    Cincinnati in the 1840s.

2026.

Ward, Robert E. "Bibliographical and Genealogical Data in the
Publications of the German Pioneer Society of Cincinnati," Journal of German-American Studies 13·4 (1978): 113-16. E184.G3G315
v. 13:4
    Discusses the Verein's annual report and its historical
journal, Der Deutsche Pionier.

2027.

Warden, R. B. "Umgang eines Nicht-Deutschen mit deutschen
Pionieren," Der Deutsche Pionier 1 (1869): 277-81. E184.G3D5

About Heinrich Roedter, community leader and editor of the Volksblatt.

2028.
Warden, R. B. "Vater Cist und die deutschen Pioniere," Der Deutsche Pionier 1 (1869): 367-70. E184.G3D5
    On a Pennsylvania German and his importance for early Cincinnati history.

2029.
Weier, Ernst A. "Das Hecker-Denkmal im Washington Park zu Cincinnati, Ohio," Der Deutsche Pionier 17 (1885): 49-56, 98-102. E184.G3D5
    On the Hecker monument in Washington Park.

2029.1
White, Joseph Michael. "Religion and Community: Cincinnati Germans, 1814-1870." Ph.D. Diss., University of Notre Dame, 1980. Ann Arbor, Mich.: University Microfilms, 1981. 363 pp. BR560.C5W5 Langsam Library

2030.
"Wielerts Pavillion ... im Cincinnati (illustration)," New Yorker Staats-Zeitung und Herold, n.d. NC108C
    A well known saloon in Over-the-Rhine before World War I.

2031.
Wise, Isaak M. "Rede ..." Der Deutsche Pionier 7 (1875): 32-35. E184.G3D5
    Address at the Pionier-Verein; deals with German-American achievements.

2032.
Zipperlinl, Adolph. "Meine Reise nach Amerika," Der Deutsche Pionier 9 (1877): 89-94, 150-57, 212-15, 245-51, 268-75, 318-23, 359-64. E184.G3D5
    An author's trip to America; author was a prominent Cincinnati surgeon, and author of occasional verse.

2033.

"Zwei neue deutsche Asyle begründet," Der Deutsche Pionier 13
(1881): 204. E184.G3D5

 On widow's and old people's homes in Cincinnati and Baltimore.

2034.

"Zweihundertjärhrige Jubelfeier der Landung der ersten deutschen
Ansiedler in den Vereinigten Staaten," Der Deutsche Pionier 15
(1883): 215-16. E184.G3D5

 On Cincinnati's German-American Bicentennial Committee.

Part Six

Newspaper Sources

Facsimile copy from: Karl J.R. Arndt and
May E. Olson, **The German Language Press of
the Americas: Volume 1: History and
Bibliography, 1732-1968: United States of
America**. (München: Verlag Dokumentation,
1976), pp. 433-59.

CINCINNATI

Tägliche Abend-Post : Mar. 3, 1877—Dec. 1880.

Daily, morning except Sunday. For weekly edition, see CINCINNATI WÖCHENTLICHE POST. For morning edition, see CINCINNATI TÄGLICHE POST. For Sunday edition, see CINCINNATI SONNTAGS-POST. Circulation: 1880, 4700. Edited by Gustav Hof, & published by Jeup & Wahle, 1877—80. See *Rowell, 1878—80; Ayer, 1880; Mink; Groen.*
OC: 1877—80.

Tägliche Abend-Presse : Aug. 1? 1877—Feb. 28, 1930.

Independent daily, evening except Sunday, the evening edition of CINCINNATIER FREIE PRESSE. Title varies: CINCINNATIER ABEND-JOURNAL: Jan. 3—8, 1920; other slight variations in title.

Circulation: 1880, 5000; 1890, 15,300; 1900, 27,110; 1910, 36,119; 1915, 47,000. Established by Alexander Torges, Jr., Aug. 1877, as a one-cent daily. See *Rowell, 1878—85; Ayer, 1880—1920; Mink; Groen.*
OCHi: [1882—Feb. 28, 1930].
OHi: Aug. 30—Sept. 3, 1918 [May—Sept. 1919].

Die Abend-Zeitung : 1859?—1880?

Edited & published by August Becker & Godfried Becker. See *Groen; DER DEUTSCHE PIONIER,* Oct. 1871.

Der Alte Hickory : Aug. 30—Sept.? 1852.

Democratic campaign paper. The editor is not named, but *Groen* states that it was Dr. Wilhelm Albers; published in the office of the TAGEBLATT. See *Rattermann's* "Deutsch-Amerikanisches Biographikon;" *Groen* states it may have been published daily, and that it was particularly abusive in its attacks on Molitor (p. 235—36, 267—69): "During the hectic presidential campaign of 1852 there was founded in the office of the Democratic TAGEBLATT another German-American newspaper for the express purpose of campaigning for Pierce and the entire Democratic slate both national and local. This paper was called DER ALTE HICKORY. The editor was not mentioned by name, but it was suspected that Albers, who had recently retired from his editorial duties on the TAGEBLATT, was the actual editor. Although Albers had retired from the TAGEBLATT for the alleged reason stated in the announcement below, we may assume that his real reason was to edit the apparently quite obnoxious ALTE HICKORY, and also perhaps to make it appear as though the TAGEBLATT & Rödter had nothing to do with its publication. Perhaps it was because Rödter did not want to drag his TAGEBLATT into the mire of personal polemics which threatened to become worse as the election approached, or it may have been for other reasons; at any rate, on Monday, Aug. 30, 1852, there was begun in the office of the DEMOKRATISCHES TAGEBLATT a German-American campaign newspaper entitled DER ALTE HICKORY, which was destined to cause an unprecedented furor among the German-Americans, and their readers. This campaign sheet was published anonymously, although every one knew that Rödter was its publisher and that his former assistant-editor, Dr. Albers, was the editor. In its opening issue the new paper fired a salvo against the VOLKSBLATT thereby showing not only where it stood on the political issue but also arousing Molitor into a burst of anger... DER ALTE HICKORY not only kept up its attacks, it intensified them, resorting to the grossest insult of persons ever seen in any German-American newspaper, including the VOLKSBLATT, which certainly had shown great aptitude along that line. At this same time, Emil Klauprecht was running a series of sketches in his REPU-BLICANER, which were entitled "Kapitain Hirnbrandt's zwölf Hin- und Hergänge," which were definitely aimed squarely at Rödter... At the same time there began in DER ALTE HICKORY a series of similar sketches, entitled "Aus dem Leben des blondgelockten Jünglings Emil Schüttelmiller Wunderhold," aimed without the shadow of a doubt against Klauprecht. As the days went by, the sketches in each of the 2 papers grew more and more disgusting and increasingly more personal, until the climax was reached on Sept. 16, 1852. On this day, a particularly vile sketch of the "Wunderhold" series had appeared and Klauprecht felt that his wife had been portrayed as a prostitute and that his mother-in-law had been similarly slandered. In a fit of extreme anger he called upon 3 friends to accompany him, went to Albers' home, and after a brief argument in which Klauprecht undoubtedly had the better of Albers since he kept a gun pointed at him, shot him in the chest, whereupon he flung the gun in Albers' face and walked out followed by his friends."
OHi: Oct. 30, 31; Sept, 1, 2, 3, 7, 8, 9, 10, 11, 13, 14, 15, 16, 17, 1852.

Amerikanischer Armen- und Krankenfreund : Jahrgang 1—25, no. 11, Jan. 1904—Nov. 1918.

Monatshefte f. innere Mission und Diakonie. Herausgegeben im Auftrage des Verwaltungsrats des Deutschen Diakonissen- und Krankenhauses. Publication of German Evangelical Protestant Church.
OC: 1913—18.

Cincinnati Anzeiger: Nov. 4, 1880—Oct. 21, 1901.

Daily, evening except Sunday. Republican, 1880—86; Independent, 1887—1901. For weekly edition, see WÖCHENTLICHE CINCINNATI ANZEIGER. For Sunday edition, see SONNTAGSBLATT DES CINCINNATI ANZEIGER. Circulation: 1885, 4300; 1890, 7800; 1900, 7000. Edited & published by Raberg & Paetow, 1880—81; by Emil Paetow & Co., 1881—1900; by Anzeiger Publishing Co., 1901. See *Rowell, 1881—85; Ayer, 1881—1901; Mink; Groen.*

GyAIZ: 1. VIII. 1886. 6 Jg. Nr. 272.
IU: May 31, 1895.
OC: 1881—1901.
OHi: Jan. 1, 1901.
WHi: Jahrgang 21, no. 95, 118, 144, 148, Feb. 18, Mar. 3, Apr. 2, 8, 1901.

Wöchentlicher Cincinnati Anzeiger: Nov. 1880—Oct. 1901.

Weekly edition of CINCINNATI ANZEIGER. Circulation: 1885, 3800; 1890, 4500; 1900, 4000. See *Rowell, 1881—85; Ayer, 1881—1901; Groen; Mink.*

OC: 1881—1901.

Cincinnati Arbeiter Abendzeitung: 1850?—1852?

Daily. United with ARBEITER-UNION. Supported Socialist Labor Party. Edited by Dr. Johannes Peyer, & published by the Arbeiterverein. See *Hillquit; Groen.*

Cincinnati Arbeiterblatt: Sept. 1877—1887?

Daily, evening except Sunday. Follows TÄGLICHE ABEND-PRESSE. One-cent daily. Edited & published by Cincinnater Freie Presse Kompagnie. See *Ayer, 1887, Mink; Groen.*

OCHi: Jahrgang 10, no. 199—263, Jan. 1—June 30, 1887; July—Aug. 27, 1887.

Der Arbeiter-Freund: 1849—?

Edited & published by Dr. Ciolini. See *Stierlin,* who also writes editor's name "Cialdini".

Arbeiter-Union: 1849?—1852?

Daily? Title varies: DIE UNION. Formed by union of CINCINNATI ARBEITER ABENDZEITUNG, and DIE UNION. Edited & published by Dr. Wilhelm Peyer. See *Eickhoff; Groen.*

Die Arbeiter von Ohio: 1877?—?

Socialist weekly. Sub-title: Organ und Eigenthum der Arbeiter-Partei von Cincinnati. See *Kamman; Hillquit; Haskell; Groen.*

NN: Feb. 24—Mar. 3, 1877.

Cincinnati Bau-Vereins Anzeiger: Band 1, no. 1—12, Mar. 1, 1878—Feb. 1, 1879?

Monthly. Published in interests of members of the Verein, the editorial work conducted by the President and Secretary; lists building laws of Ohio; reports of the Verein; some stories printed, as Gerstäcker's "Die Regulatoren in Arkansas." Large quarto, no. 1—4, each 4 pages; no. 5—12, each 8 pages. Published by the Cincinnati Bau-Vereins Anzeiger Compagnie.

OCHi: complete set.

Bauvereins Telephon.

Weekly, established 1885 by E. Daniel. See *Joest; Rowell, 1886.*

Bepler's Banknoten-Liste: Jahrgang 1, no. 1, Mar. 1858—?

Monthly. Octavo, ca. 38 pages; illustrated. A German counterfeit detector and bank-note list. Has supplement entitled "Das Gewicht, Mass und Geld der Vereinigten Staaten und Europas, nebst Notizen für den Geschäftsmann und Handwerker" published 1861, 32 pages. Published by Bepler & Co. [Edward Bepler]. See *Cist; Rowe; Groen.*

DLC: Supplement to no. 1.

Der Bibelforscher: 1871?—1940?

Quarterly. Organ of Deutsche Methodistenkirche. Octavo, each issue ca. 24 pages. Circulation: 1893, 44,500; 1912, 42,000; 1939, 4200. Edited by Heinrich Liebhart. See *Douglass.*

Die Biene auf dem Missionsfeld : 1859—1865.

Monthly. Organ of the Westliche Konferenz der Deutschen Baptisten-Gemeinden von Nord-Amerika. Absorbed by DER SENDBOTE. Edited & published by Philipp W. Bickel. See *Groen;* DER SENDBOTE, Aug. 7, 1940.
GyAIZ: April 1861.

Bildersaal : 1878—?

Organ of Deutsche Methodistenkirche. *North* lists this as a quarterly Sunday School work, established 1878; subscription rate $ 4. *Douglass* describes BILDERSAAL as pictorial cards, published in large volume.

Brauer-Zeitung : vol. 1—49, no. 5, Oct. 2, 1886—Mar. 3, 1934.

Weekly, 1886—1919; bi-weekly, 1920—34. Established as a journal wholly in German; some material published in English as early as Mar. 1893, increasing and becoming more extensive, until last issue contains only one page in German; with the issue of Mar. 3, 1934, the publishers state that "The German language will be abolished;" continued as THE BREWERY WORKER, in English. Title changes reflect the emotions of American politics through wars and Prohibition: 1) DIE BRAUER ZEITUNG, Oct. 1886—Oct. 1910; 2) BRAUEREI ARBEITER ZEITUNG, Nov. 1910—Jan. 4, 1918; 3) BREWERY & SOFT DRINK WORKER'S JOURNAL, Jan. 5, 1918—Nov. 1918; 4) BREW-ERY, FLOUR, CEREAL & SOFT DRINK WORKER'S JOURNAL, Dec. 1918—April 1934 (with this change the German subtitle was dropped, although one or two pages of the paper were printed until March 1934, when it became known as 5) THE BREWERY WORKER, March 1934 to present. Sub-title: 1) Fachblatt des National-Verbandes der Brauer der Vereinigten Staaten; 2) Brauerei Arbeiter Ztg., Brewery Worker Journal; 3) Brauerei- und Mineralwasser-Arbeiter-Zeitung; 4) Brauerei- und Sodawasser-Arbeiter-Zeitung. Place of publication varies: NYC, Oct. 2, 1886—June? 1892; St. Louis, July 1892—May 1899; Cincinnati, May 20, 1899—Mar. 3, 1934. Organ of 1) National Union of Brewers of the U.S., 1886; 2) Brewers National Union, 1887; 3) National Union of the United Brewery Workmen of the U.S., 1887—1903; 4) International Union of the United Brewery Workmen of America, 1903—17; 5) International Union of United Brewery and Soft Drink Workers of America, 1917; 6) International Union of United Brewery, Flour, Cereal, and Soft Drink Workers of America, 1918—34. Size varies slighly: small folio, to large quarto; each issue, 4—8 pages. Edited by Louis Berbrand, Oct. 2, 1886—Dec. 1886 by E. Kurzenknabe, 1886—96; by Jacob L. Franz, 1897—1901; by William E. Trautmann, 1902—Apr. 1905; by J. P. Weigel, Apr. 1905—Sept. 1906; by Gustav Mostler, Sept. 1906—Mar.? 1917; by Julius Zorn, 1917?—1927. See *Schlüter; Barnett; Ayer, 1892—1918, 1927—35.*
DLC: 21—29.
ICJ: 1897—1902 [Npps. in Libraries of Chicago 1936].
KHi: Aug. 12, 1905—Dec. 1917.
NN [on Film]: [6—49, Dec. 5, 1891—Dec. 1934; 1949—50].
OCB: complete set.
WHi [on Film]: [8—49].

C.I.S.V. NEWS : 1952.

Organ of Childrens' International Summer Village. In English, French, German.
OC: 1922.

Der Christliche Apologete : Band 1—103, No. 10, Jan. 4, 1839—Oct. 1, 1941?

Weekly, 1839—1934; monthly, 1935—1941? Sub-title: Deutsches Organ der Bischöflich Metho-distenkirche. Absorbed HAUS UND HERD. *Schneider* states that this was the "pioneer German paper in the West to champion the cause of orthodoxy and to take issue with a growing rationalism;" essentially a family paper of high quality; large quarto in size, with slight variations, each issue 4—16 pages; illustrated, including portraits. Fought for Orthodoxy and Prohibition. A strong force in conversion of Germans to Methodism. Controversy of 1840—41 excited attention of entire church world of U.S.A. Learned polemics based on theological scholarship. Leading articles less concerned with doctrine than problems of life. The general suspicion of anything German brought Congress on Oct. 6, 1917 to pass a law requiring all war reports to be filed with Postmaster at Cincinnati in a true English translation. As a result such news was published in English. The editor, Nast, ultimately was forced to resign, a victim of the war. *Douglass* explains use of word "Apologete," as a more pleasing and satisfactory term than "Verteidiger;" he also speaks of the loyalty of the Church people, and gives early circulation figures. Circulation: 1839, 100; 1840, 1000; 1870, 13,500; 1880, 15,000; 1890, 20,028; 1900, 19,000; 1910, 17,500; 1920, 9847; 1935, 4356; 1938, 4143. Subscription held by Harmony Society, 7 years. Edited by Wilhelm Nast, Jan. 4, 1839—May 1892 [with Heinrich Liebhart, 1869—72; with Jacob Krehbiel, 1880?—July 1890; with August Johann Bucher, 1890—92]; by Albert J. Nast, May 1892—Apr. 1918; by the Rev. August Johann Bucher, May 1918—Dec. 1936; by Book Committee [J. A. Diekmann & A. J. Loeppert, 1937—1941?

Assistant editors: Heinrich Liebhart, 1865—72; Hermann A. Grentzenberg, 1872—76; Jacob Krehbiel, 1876—90; Christian Golder, 1890—1908; F. T. Enderis, Aug. 12, 1908—1918?; F. W. Schneider, 1918—22; A. J. Loeppert, 1920—23; Christian Baumann, 1923—33.

Published by L. Swormstedt & J. H. Power, 1839?—June 10, 1852; by L. Swormstedt & A. Poe, June 17, 1852—June 7, 1860; by A. Poe & L. Hitchcock, June 14, 1860—1870?; by Hitchcock & Walden, 1871?—July? 1880; by Walden & Stowe, Aug. 2? 1880—May 1884; by Cranston & Stowe, June 2, 1884—May 1892; by Cranston & Curts, June 2, 1892—1899; by Curts & Jennings, Jan.—May 1900; by Jennings & Pye, June 7, 1900—May 1904; by Jennings & Graham, June 8, 1904—1915?; by Methodist Book Concern, 1916?—1941? See *Ayer; Groen; Schneider; Douglass.*

BM: Bd. 78, no. 49—Bd. 79, no. 15, 1 Nov. 1916—11 April 1917 imperfect.
CoDU: [98—101]—to date.
GyAIZ: 11. II. 1867; 15. VIII. 1870; 8. VII. 1886; 15. VII. 1886; 19. VIII. 1886; 24. III. 1892.
IEG: 3—6 [46—49]—to date.
InGcD: 33?—41, 1871 –79.
InSbND: 33—41.
MAC: [3]—8.
MnHi: July 15—22, 1886.
NcD: [48—67]—[80—85] 96—to date.
NjMD: [1—3, 31—38, 40—101]—to date.
NN: [42—45]—[48—51]—[56]—[64—68]—[70—71].
OCHi: [1] 12—23 [45].
OClWHi: Apr. 30, May 21—28, 1896.
ODW: [52, 78] 80—89, 91—94, 96.
OHi: 80—82.
OO: [57, 65, 76].

Der Christliche Deutsche Republikaner : 1853?—1870?

Weekly. Of special interest to Methodist Churchmen. Edited & published by Wilhelm Nast. See *Groen.*

Christlicher Hausfreund : June 3, 1848—1860?

Bi-weekly. Organ of the Deutsche Vereinigt-Evangelische Synode in Nord-Amerika. Edited & published by the Reverends Dethlefs, Fischer & Schaad. Continued as CHRISTLICHER HAUSFREUND (Chicago, Ill.). See PHILADELPHIA DEMOKRAT, June 21, 1848; DER DEUTSCHE KIRCHENFREUND, July 1848; *Schneider.* MoSCHi: complete?

Der Christliche Jugendfreund : 1872? 1900?

Semi-monthly. Organ of Evangelische Protestantische Kirche von Nord-Amerika. Large quarto, each issue 4 pages; illustrated. See *Groen; Müller; Steiger.* GyAIZ: 21. III. 1886.

Christliche Sittenschule : 1867?

See the Manuscript of Subscriptions of the Harmony Society, which subscribed for two years.

Congress-Halle : Aug. 1, 1851—?

Monthly. Octavo, each issue 64 pages. Edited by Heinrich Rödter, & published by Rödter & Vieth. Listed by Groen; Cist (1875); Rattermann's "Deutsch-Amerikanisches Biographikon" in which Rattermann quotes from the Prospectus: „Der Zweck dieser Publikation ist, den intelligenten deutschen Lesern, so nahe wie möglich eine ähnliche Gelegenheit zu verschaffen, sich über die Vorgänge im Rath der Nation und am Steuerrade des Staates ebenso zu informiren, als es dem englischen lesenden Publikum durch NILES REGISTER und dem CONGRESSIONAL-GLOBE gewährt wird ..."

Cincinnati Courier : Nov. 1, 1869—Mar. 12, 1874.

Daily, except Sunday. Published for the "freisinniger Theil der republikanischen Partei." Title varies: TÄGLICHER CINCINNATI COURIER, Dec. 6, 1869—Mar. 12, 1874. For weekly edition, see WOCHENBLATT DES CINCINNATI COURIER. For Sunday edition, see SONNTAGSBLATT DES CINCINNATI COURIER. „In diese Zeit, ins Jahr 1872, fällt die Reorganisation oder richtiger gesagt, Neugründung des im Jahre 1869 gegründeten CINCINNATIER COURIERS, was für die Leser der FREIEN PRESSE von besonderem Interesse sein sollte, da der COURIER der Vorgänger der FREIEN PRESSE war und die FREIE PRESSE aus dem COURIER hervorging. Wolfgang Schoenle gesellte sich zu Moritz Jacobi als Besitzer und Leiter der neugegründeten Zeitung; Schoenle übernahm die Redaktion. Mit der Neugründung des COURIERS hängt eine Tragikomödie zusammen, an die ich mich noch aus früher Kindheit lebhaft erinnere. Wolfgang Schoenle, der Schwager Hassaureks, ein wackerer, in Tübingen ausgebildeter Schwabe aus der württembergischen Donaugegend und grundehrlicher Charakter hatte sich zu einer Zeit, als Hassaurek sich noch nicht gegen Grant erklärt hatte, mit seinem Schwager wegen Grants entzweit und dabei die Bemerkung fallen lassen: ‚Lieber haue ich mir die rechte Hand ab, als daß ich wieder für Grant eintrete!' Schoenle trat auch dem zufolge wirklich aus der Redaktion des VOLKSBLATTS aus und verband sich, wie oben ausgeführt, mit Jacobi, um den COURIER als Oppositionsblatt gegen das VOLKSBLATT zu reorganisieren. Und zwar sollte die Zeitung naturlich, *gegen Grant,* der, wie man erwartete, die Unterstützung des VOLKSBLATTS erhalten würde, energisch auftreten. Man glaubte nämlich Hassaurek an Grant gebunden: war doch sein Halbbruder, der junge Kriegsheld Leopold Markbreit, von Grant als Gesandter nach Bolivien in Sudamerika geschickt worden. Doch siehe da! Mit einem Male kam Hassaurek offen gegen Grant heraus. Sein Bruder Markbreit wurde zwar von Grant abberufen. Aber das machte keinen Eindruck auf Hassaurek, der sich niemals durch ein politisches Amt einfangen oder fesseln ließ. Nun war aber die Not groß auf der Redaktion des COURIERS. Ein wirkliches Dilemma! Um dem VOLKSBLATT mit seiner Parteinahme für Grant zu opponieren, war der COURIER doch neugegründet worden. Und nun spielte dieser Hassaurek dem hitzköpfigen Schwaben Schoenle (denn er war eben ein echter Schwab) einen solchen bösen Streich! ... Nolens volens mußte Schoenle in den sauren Apfel beißen und die Kampagne im Interesse des Kandidaten der republischen Partei führen. ... Hassaurek blieb aber dem Reformgedanken treu und kämpfte weiter für notwendige Verbesserungen im öffentlichen Dienst" ... (Schönle).

Circulation: 1871, 3500; 1873, 5800; 1874, 5000 (est.). Edited by August Becker [political editor], Charles F. Johnson, Philipp Strobel, Theodor Schmidt & Victor Zeis [managing editor], Nov. 1—5, 1869; edited by August Necker & Victor Zeis, Nov. 6, 1869—1872; by Georg Franz Eichenlaub; by Philipp Rappaport; by Wolfgang Schoenle, 1872—1874?; by C. A. Honthumb. Published by Cincinnati Courier Co. [Moritz Jacobi]. See *Rowell, 1870—74; Groen; Schönle; Mink.*
OC: 1871—74.
OCHi: Jahrgang 1, no. 1—58, Nov. 1—Dec. 31, 1869.

Die Deborah : Jahrgang 1—45, Aug. 24, 1855—1900; neue Folge, Jahrgang 1—2, Jan. 1901— Dec. 1902.

Weekly, then monthly. Jewish paper printed in German, as supplement to AMERICAN ISRAELITE. Sub-title: 1) Ein Beiblatt zum "Israelit" gewidmet den Töchtern Israels, Aug. 24, 1855—June 1880?; 2) Jüdisch-Amerikanische Familienzeitung; 3) Allgemeine Zeitung des amerikanischen Judenthums, July 1869—June 1870; 4) Eine deutsch-amerikanische Monatsschrift zur Förderung jüdischer Interessen in Gemeinde, Schule und Haus, 1901—02. Omitted in numbering: Jahrgang 33—34. Size varies: in early years, quarto; then folio of various dimensions; octavo, 1901—02; various paging, 8—32 pages; title-page and contents, 4 pages. Circulation: 1870, 5200 (est.); 1880, 3000; 1890, 8000; 1900, 9133. Edited by Isaak Mayer Wise, Aug. 24, 1855—1896; other editors: Rabbi Max Lilienthal; Solomon H. Sonnenschein; associate editors, Rabbies Wolf Rothenheim & Isidor Kalisch. Published by Block & Co., 1855—88; by Leo Wise & Co., 1889—1902. See *Rowell, 1869—75; Groen; Postal.*

BM: [15]—[22].
CtY: [20, 40—41; new series v. 1—2].
DLC: 26—32, 35—[45].
GyAIZ: 10. X. 1856; 15. II. 1857; 5. X. 1860; 28. IX. 1866; 2. VII. 1886; 27. VIII. 1886.
ICHi: [Rowell Collection]: Band 27, no. 13, Sept. 29, 1876.
MH: new series, v. 1—2.
NN: [1—2, 12—18, 25—36]—[42—45]—new series, v. 2.
NNJ: [26—27]—28; new series, v. [1—2].
OC: 41; new series, v. 1—2.
OCH: [1]—2, 6—7, 9—18, 20—[23]—34; new series, v. 1—2.

Der Demokrat : May 27, 1834?—?

Whether this paper was ever published has not yet been proved. However, the following information has been given. The WESTLICHE BLÄTTER, May 6, 1906, states: To be published by Heinrich Rödter as a Democratic weekly, published in the interest of the Jackson Party, with sub-title: Ein deutsches Volksblatt für Politik, Gesetzgebung, Litteratur, Handel und Ackerbau. The "Prospektus" evidently appeared, stating that the first number would appear May 27, 1834. Rattermann in his "Deutsch-Amerikanisches Biographikon" describes this "Prospektus" which he had before him, dated "Cincinnati, May 1834."

Cincinnati Demokrat : Nov. 18, 1845—Feb. 1846.

Daily? Democratic. Followed by DIE LOCOMOTIVE (Louisville, Ky.). Edited by Dr. Wilhelm Albers, & published by W. Albers & Co. (Heinrich Rödter?). See *Groen; Rattermann,* in his "Die Deutschen Pioniere des Scioto-Thales" states that the first number appeared Nov. 18, 1845, but that it lived only 3 months.

Demokratisches Campagne-Blatt : Sept.—Nov.? 1876.

One issue has been located, bound with CINCINNATI VOLKSFREUND, and probably issued by same publisher. It is a small folio, 4 pages, with no separate date-line.
ICHi [Rowell Collection]: Sept. 29, 1876.

Demokratisches Tageblatt : Oct. 1850—1856?

Democratic daily. It is believed, but not proved, that a weekly edition was also published. Follows DIE OHIO STAATSZEITUNG. Edited by Heinrich Rödter, Oct. 1850—Oct. 1851; by Heinrich Rödter & Wilhelm Albers, Oct. 25, 1051 June 7, 1852; by Heinrich Rödter, June 1852—1855; other editors: Georg LaBarre, Oscar Thielemann, and Vieth. Published by Heinrich Rödter & Co., 1850—55; edited & published by Hiller & Becht, 1855—56. In 1852 Dr. Albers got into a violent argument with the editor of the DEUTSCHE REPUBLIKANER, a Whig organ. See *Groen; Körner; Mink.*

DLC: Jahrgang 2, no. 94—308, Jan. 20—Sept. 30, 1851; Jahrgang 3, no. 1—387, Oct. 1, 1851 Dec. 31, 1852. [Several issues wanting].
MWA: Jahrgang 3, no. 296, Sept. 14, 1852.
OCIWHi: Jahrgang 2, no. 182, May 3, 1851; Jahrgang 3, no. 78—387, Jan. 1—Dec. 31, 1852.

Demokratisches Wochenblatt : May 1850—

Democratic weekly. Sub-title: Ein Organ für Politik, Neuigkeiten, Litteratur, Kunst, Handel und Gewerbe. Edited by Heinrich Rödter, & published by H. Rödter & Co. See *ULN.*
DLC: Jahrgang 2, no. 1, May 1, 1851.

Der Deutsch-Amerikaner : 1839—1840?

Democratic weekly. Edited by Georg Walker, & published by August Renz. See *Groen; Klauprecht; Bosse,* who gives Dayton, Ohio as place.

Deutsch-Amerikanische Illustrirte Zeitung : Jahrgang 1, no. 1—10, Oct. 8—Dec. 11, 1886?

IU: vol. 1, no. 1—10, Oct. 8—Dec. 11, 1886 [Lacks pp. 37—38].
OC: vol. 1, no. 2—9, Oct.—Dec. 1886.

Deutsch-Amerikanische Krieger-Zeitung : 1884—1890?
GyAIZ: 18, I. 1888. 4 Jg. Nr. 2.

Deutsch-Amerikanische Lehrer-Zeitung :
Monthly supplement to FAMILIEN-JOURNAL ZUR UNTERHALTUNG UND BELEHRUNG. See *Groen*, as
current in 1892.
GyBIbA: I: 1. 3. 4.   GyMBS: Bd. I. 1887.

Deutsch-Amerikanischer Familien-Kalender : 1880?—?
Octavo; illustrated. Published by M. &. R. Burgheim. See AMERICAN CATALOG, 1876—84.
NN: 1886.

Deutsch-Amerikanisches Magazin : Jahrgang 1, no. 1—4, Oct. 1886—July 1887.
Quarterly. Sub-title: Vierteljahrsschrift für Gedichte, Literatur, Wissenschaft, Kunst, Schule
und Volksleben der Deutschen in Amerika, unter Mitwirkung deutsch-amerikanischer Geschichts-
und Literaturfreunde. Follows DER DEUTSCHE PIONIER. Quarto, each issue 60—160 pages; illu-
strated, including portraits & facsimiles; title-page and contents, 8 pages. Edited & published by
Heinrich Arminius Rattermann; Druck & Spedition, S. Rosenthal & Co.
DLC: complete.   MdBJ: complete.
GyAIZ: Oct. 1886. 1 Jg. Nr. 1.   MWKJA: complete.
GyBIbA: complete.   PHuJ: complete.

Der Deutsche Beobachter.
Weekly.
KHi: June 20, 1888—Jan. 1889.

Der Deutsche Franklin : Jan.? 1835—1837?
Weekly. Established as Whig paper; in 1836 became Democratic; supported Van Buren and
Johnson. Sub-title: Ein demokratisch-republikanisches Volksblatt zur Unterhaltung und Belehrung für Bauern und Handwerker. Follows DER WELTBÜRGER. Edited & published by Benjamin Boffinger. *Ruemelin* gives this interesting account: „DER WELTBUERGER ging bald in die
Haende des Herrn B. Boffinger ueber, der das Blatt in den DEUTSCHEN FRANKLIN umtaufte.
Boffinger hatte schon in Columbus ein deutsches demokratisches Blatt herausgegeben und kam
nach Cincinnati, weil es dort nicht mehr recht gehen wollte. Er fuehrt den DEUTSCHEN FRANKLIN
nach Pennsylvanisch-deutscher Partei-Schablone, ohne eigentlichen inneren Werth. Das Blatt
genuegte den Demokraten nicht, und vielfach wurde Herr Boffinger angegangen, sich einen
guten Redacteur zu sichern und entschieden fuer Van Buren Partei zu nehmen, dieser hatte 1835
im Herbst die Nomination der demokratischen National-Convention erhalten. Boffinger ver-
sprach dies und gab uns zu verstehen, dass er bald Herrn Roedter als Redacteur anstellen werde.
Im Fruehjahr 1836 kam uns nun, gegen alle Vermuthung, die Nachricht zu Ohren, dass Herr
Boffinger mit den Whigs einen Handel abgeschlossen habe, wonach der DEUTSCHE FRANKLIN
um den Preis von 600.00 umsatteln und die Flagge des Gen. Harrison, des sogenannten Volks-
Candidaten aufhissen sollten." See *Groen; Ligowsky*.
DLC: Jahrgang 1, no. 23, May 30, 1835.

Der Deutsche im Westen : 1840—1841?
Whig weekly. Follows DER WESTLICHE MERKUR. Followed by OHIO VOLKSFREUND. Edited &
published by Christian Burghalter & Höfle [Hefley]. Edited also by Rudolph von Maltiz? See
Groen; Körner.

Der Deutsche Patriot : Sept. 14—Nov. 1832?
Whig weekly; a campaign sheet which supported Henry Clay. Published by L. Collignon und
Comp. [Ludwig Collignon], with the support of Heinrich Brachmann, Albert Lange & Karl
von Bonge. Rattermann states that it was probably edited by Christian Burghalter. Heinrich
Rödter was typesetter, according to *Groen*. *Rattermann* states p. 302. „Von der ältesten bisher
aufgefundenen deutschen Zeitung Cincinnatis DER DEUTSCHE PATRIOT, befindet sich eine Nr.
in meinem Besitz, No. 5, vom 12. Oktober 1832. Ich fand dieselbe in Mt. Sterling, Ky. Das Blatt

(12×18 Zoll groß, vierseitig) war eine Wochenzeitung und wurde von Ludwig Collignon in No. 16 Main-strasse gedruckt, drei Seiten deutsch mit deutschen Typen, die vierte aber englisch. Klauprecht, der kein Exemplar des Blattes gesehen hat und seinen Namen nicht einmal kannte, meint, der ehemalige Charlottenburger Jurist, Albert Lange, der später Staats-Auditor von Indiana wurde, sei der Redakteur gewesen; ich vermute jedoch, dass es Christian Burghalter war. Derselbe war Privatsekretär des Fürsten Blücher gewesen, kam 1816 nach Cincinnati, trat 1820 zu den Zitterquäkern über, die in Lebanon, Ohio, ihre Gemeinde hatten, wo ihn auch der Herzog Bernhard von S.-Weimar (1825) besuchte, und kehrte ein Jahr später nach Cincinnati zurück. Der Stil des Blattes ist ganz in Burghalters Schreibweise gehalten, von dem ich auch ein Buch in meinem Besitz habe: ,Geist der Sprache' (1840 gedruckt) ... DER PATRIOT war eine politische Wochenschrift, vertrat die Kandidatur des Whig Kandidaten Henry Clay gegenüber der Wiederwahl Jacksons in der damaligen Präsidentenwahl. Die Artikel des Blattes sind schneidig und scharf geschrieben und boten fast nur politische Polemiken. Lokalneuigkeiten und sonstige Nachrichten waren nur spärlich vertreten. Ich vermute deshalb, daß es eine sogenannte Kampagnezeitung war, die nach der Wahl wieder einschlief. See Groen; Rattermann's "Deutsch-Amerikanischer Journalismus."

P: Oct. 12, 1832.

Der Deutsche Pionier : Jahrgang 1—18, no. 4, Mar. 1869—1887.

Monthly, Mar. 1869—Mar. 1885; quarterly [Jahrgang 17—18], 1885—87. Sub-title: Eine Monatsschrift für Erinnerungen aus dem Deutschen Pionier-Leben in den Vereinigten Staaten, Mar. 1869—Feb. 1876; 2) Erinnerungen aus dem Pionier-Leben der Deutschen in Amerika, Apr. 1876—1887. An indispensable source for the history of Germans in the U.S.A. Objective and constructive. Followed by JAHRESBERICHT DES PIONIER-VEREINS. Supplements issued with numbers for May 1869, May 1870, and June 1871. Octavo, each issue 32—96 pages; illustrated, including plates, portraits, maps. facsimiles. Circulation: 1871, 2000; 1872, 3000; 1873, 1000; 1876, 1879; 1877, 2000. Edited by a Committee of the Verein, Mar. 1869—Feb. 1870; by G. Brühl, Mar. 1870—Feb. 1871; by E. H. Makk, Mar. 1871—Feb. 1872; by Karl Rümelin, Mar. 1872—Apr. 1873; by Karl Knortz, May 1873—Feb. 1874; by Heinrich Arminius Rattermann, Mar. 1874—Mar. 1885; by Hermann Hensel, 1885—87. Published by Der Deutsche Pionier-Verein, Mar. 1869—1887. Printer & business-manager: S. Rosenthal, Mar. 1869—Feb. 1870. See Rowell, 1870—85; Ayer, 1880—88; Groen.

The following libraries have complete sets: CSmH; DLC; IC; ICJ; IU; In; LU; MB; NIC; NN; OC; OCA; OCHi; PPL; TxU; WHi.

CSt: 1—16.	MnHi: 1—4, 7—16, 18.	OClWHi: 1—4, 6—18.
CtY: 1—16.	MnU: 1—6, 8, 10—16.	OCX: 1—8.
ICN: 1—2, 10—11, 13—14.	MoS: 1—4, 7—16.	OOxM: 11—14.
ICU: 1—[17]—18.	MWA: 1—16.	OU: 1—4, 6—10, 14 [15—16]
InSmA: 1—4, 10—16.	NDu: 1—16.	PLaF: 1—16.
MH: 1—[15]—18.	NBuG: 1—4, 9—16.	PPAP: [8—10, 12].
MdU: 1—15.	NjR: [10].	PPHi: 1—17.
MiD-B: 1—2, 10—16.	OCl: 1.	PPU: 1—17.

Der Deutsche Republikaner : Sept. 28, 1842—Mar. 23, 1861?

Daily, evening except Sunday. Established as a Whig paper; became labor paper in Dec. 1858. Sub-title. 1) Ein Tageblatt für Politik, Gewerbe, und Wissenschaft, Jan. 1, 1853—Dec. 1857; 2) Organ der Arbeiter, Dec. 6, 1858—1861. Title varies: CINCINNATI REPUBLIKANER, Jan. 1858—1861? For weekly edition, see DER DEUTSCHE REPUBLIKANER: WOCHENBLATT. Large quarto, each issue 4 pages, but enlarged 1858. Edited by J. H. Schroeder, Sept. 28, 1842—1843; by Dr. C. F. Schmidt, 1843—44; by Wilhelm J. L. Kiderlen, 1844—Aug. 12, 1848; by Heinrich Geider, 1848—49; by Emil Klauprecht, 1849—51; by Ludwig Ferdinand Fenner von Fenneberg, 1851?—May 1852; by Emil Klauprecht, May 15, 1852—1856? (Klauprecht made it a militant, lively newspaper and expanded its influence. He also improved its literary offerings and in general contributed to the elevation of German journalism. He left to become U.S. Consul in Stuttgart) by August Becker, 1856?—Jan. 1858; by August Willich [with Hiller & Becht], Dec. 1858—? Other editors: Jucksch & Rohrbach, associate editors, 1846?; Johann Rittig; Carl Friedrich Guysi. Published by J. H. Schroeder, 1842—44; by Dr. C. F. Schmidt, 1844—49?; by F. C. Schmidt & Co., Feb. 12,

1853?—1855?; by Carl Hiller & Eduard Becht, Jan.?—Nov. 1858; by Socialer Arbeiter-Verein,
Dec. 1, 1858—1861. See *Mink; Groen.*
    CSmH: April 17, 1845.
    DLC: Oct. 1850—July 1851; 1852—54; Apr. 23, 28, 30, 1855; 1858.
    GyAIZ: 2. VIII. 1851; 10. XI. 1859.
    IU: [Nov. 30, 1858—Mar. 23, 1861].
    MWA: Sept. 4, Nov. 20, 1852.
    OCHi: Jahrgang 1, no. 5, Oct. 3, 1842—Aug. 1843.
    OClWHi: Dec. 3, 1850—Apr. 29, 1854.
    OCoC: March 1844—Sept. 18, 1847.
    OHi: Dec. 3, 1852.

Der Deutsche Republikaner : Wochenblatt : Oct. 13, 1842—Mar. 1861?

Weekly edition of DER DEUTSCHE REPUBLICANER. Subscription held by Harmony Society,
1848—49. See *Groen.*
    CSmH: Apr. 17, 1845.
    IU: [Mar. 1860—Mar. 1861].
    MWA: Jahrgang 10, no. 50, Sept. 4, 1852; Jahrgang 11, no. 9, Nov. 20, 1852.
    OCHi: Jahrgang 1, no. 45, Aug. 17, 1843.

Deutscher Advokat : 1890?—?

Weekly. See *Groen,* as current in 1890.

Deutscher Kalender : 1866?—1926?

Annual. Sub-title: Verhandlungen und Berichte der ... jährlichen Sitzung der Südlichen Deutschen Konferenz der Bischöflichen Methodistenkirche. Octavo, with varying paging, 100—208
pages; illustrated, including portraits, tables, etc. Published by the Methodist Book Concern,
and by its predecessors. See *Douglass.*
    PPG: 1869, 1876, 1877, 1866.
    TxU: 1911—1926.

Deutsch-Ungarischer Bote : 1905?—1918?

Weekly, 1905—09; semi-weekly, 1910—13; weekly, 1914—18. Circulation: 1909, 5500; 1910,
7000; 1915, 9400; 1918, 630. Edited & published by Alexander von Dessewffy, 1905—13; published by Deutsch-Ungarischer Bote Co., 1914—18. See *Ayer, 1908—18; Groen.*
    GyStalog: Stg 3, 1914/18.
    IU: Jan.—May 23, 1918.

Englisches Cincinnatier Volksblatt :
    GyStalog: Stg 3, 1914/19.

Der Erfinder und Fabrikant : 1871?—1872?

Monthly: Sub-title: Ein monatliches Journal, den Wissenschaften, Künsten, Erfindungen, und
Fabrikanten gewidmet. Large quarto, each issue 16 pages. Circulation: 1871, 1500 (est.). Edited
by G. von Chateaubriand, & published by T. von Kannel & Co. See *Rowell, 1871—72; Groen;*
DER DEUTSCHE PIONIER, Feb. 1871.

Der Erzähler am Ohio : no. 1—52, 1849—1850.

Weekly. Sub-title: 1) Ein Volksblatt zur Unterhaltung und Belehrung für Stadt und Land;
2) Eine Sammlung der unterhaltendsten Erzählungen, Geschichten, Anekdoten, Witze, &c. Octavo,
each issue 16 pages, paged continuously. Edited & published by Friedrich Stahl & Eduard Bühler.
    IU: complete set.
    NN: no. 1—12, 1849, p. 1—192; no. 13—52, 1850, p. 193—828. (Lacks: p. 829 plus, & no.
      22—29, 52).
    OCHi: no. 1—52.

Evangelisches Gemeindeblatt : 1892—1900?

Weekly, then semi-monthly. Organ of Evangelische Protestantische Kirche von Nord-Amerika.
See *Groen.*

Der Evangelische Kirchenbote : 1846?—1847?

Weekly. Organ of Evangelische Protestantische Kirche von Nord-Amerika. Edited & published by the Rev. Martin Schaad. See *Groen; DER DEUTSCHE PIONIER,* June 1884; *Rattermann (12)* p. *424:* Got into argument with Cincinnati preachers and did not survive.

Familien-Bibliothek : 1850—1855?

Monthly, "Unterhaltungsblatt." Edited & published by Heinrich Rödter. See *Groen; Cist, 1851.*

Familien-Journal zur Unterhaltung und Belehrung : no. 1—52, May 21, 1892—May 13, 1893?

Weekly. Sub-title: Officielles Organ des Nationalen Deutsch-Amerikanischen Lehrer-Bundes. Has monthly "Beilage" entitled: DEUTSCH-AMERIKANISCHE LEHRER-ZEITUNG. Large quarto, each issue 12—16 pages. Edited by Rudolf Burgheim, & published by Burgheim Publishing Co. See *Ayer, 1893—94; Groen.*

DLC: Jahrgang 1892, no. 1—52, May 21, 1892—May 13, 1893 (Lacks: no. 34—35, Jan. 7, 14).

Fest-Zeitung ... des Nord-Amerikanischen Sängerbund : no. 1—33? 1849—1911?

Annual. Title varies: FEST-BULLETIN.

Place of publication varies with city in which the "Fest" was held. See below.

1. Cincinnati: 1849.	16. Chicago: 1868.	27. Cleveland: 1893: Pub. by
2. Louisville: 1850.	17. Cincinnati: 1870.	M. Weinberger & Charles
3. Cincinnati: 1851.	18. St. Louis: 1872.	Haaka.
4. Columbus:	19. Cleveland: 1874.	28. Pittsburgh: 1896, Ed. by
5. Dayton, Ohio:	20. Louisville: 1877.	C. Saam.
6. Canton, Ohio:	21. Cincinnati: 1879.	29. Cincinnati: 1899.
7. Cleveland:	22. Chicago: 1881.	30. Buffalo: 1901.
8. Cincinnati:	23. Buffalo: 1883.	31. St. Louis: 1903.
9. Detroit: 1857.	24. Milwaukee: 1886.	32. Indianapolis: June 17—20,
10. Pittsburgh;	25. St. Louis: 1888.	1908.
11. Cleveland: 1859.	26. New Orleans: 1890:	33. Milwaukee: 1911.
12. Buffalo: 1860.	no. 1—12, May 5,	
13. Columbus: 1865.	1889—Feb. 2, 1890,	
14. Louisville: 1866.	ea. 8 p. Ed.: R. Dietzius.	
15. Indianapolis:		

IU: 15. Gesangfest, 1867.

MWKJA: 26, 27, 28, 1890, 1893, 1896.

Fliegende Blätter : Jahrgang 1, no. 1—52, Aug. 17, 1846—Oct. 2, 1847.

Weekly. Contains short stories and sketches, articles on political, social and literary questions, poetry, altogether a paper of quality, probably soared publication because of lack of financial support and absence of advertising. Large quarto, each issue 12—16 pages; with each issue 4 lithographs. Edited & published by Emil Klauprecht. Printed in "Office of Klauprecht und Munzel's Lithographie." Appears on subscription list of Harmony Society, for 1847. See *Körner; Mink; Groen.*

DLC: Jahrgang 1, no. 18—44, 46, 48—49, 51—52.

ICHi: [1].

NHi: no. 1—52.

OClWHi: [1].

OCHi: complete set.

OHi: no. 18—51.

Fliegende Blätter : 1883?—1900?

Roman Catholic monthly. See *Groen.*

Der Fortschritt : Dec. 1871—1875?

Weekly. Liberal Republican in direction, but independent. Very good style. Carefully chosen reading material. Edited & published by Philipp Rappaport. See *Groen;* in DER DEUTSCHE PIONIER, Nov. 1871.

Cincinnatier Freie Presse : Jg. 1—86, No. 51, Aug. 25, 1874—Dec. 26, 1954 +.

Daily, morning except Sunday, Aug. 25, 1874—Feb. 28, 1920; daily, evening except Sunday, Mar. 1, 1920—Sept. 27? 1941; weekly, Sept. 28, 1941—1954. Republican, 1874—1920; Independent, 1921—54. Title varies slightly: Tᴀ̈ɢʟɪᴄʜᴇ Cɪɴᴄɪɴɴᴀᴛɪᴇʀ Fʀᴇɪᴇ Pʀᴇssᴇ. For weekly edition, see Cɪɴᴄɪɴɴᴀᴛɪᴇʀ Wᴏ̈ᴄʜᴇɴᴛʟɪᴄʜᴇ Fʀᴇɪᴇ Pʀᴇssᴇ. For evening edition, see Tᴀ̈ɢʟɪᴄʜᴇ Aʙᴇɴᴅ-Pʀᴇssᴇ. For Sunday edition, see Sᴏɴɴᴛᴀɢsʙʟᴀᴛᴛ ᴅᴇʀ Cɪɴᴄɪɴɴᴀᴛɪᴇʀ Fʀᴇɪᴇ Pʀᴇssᴇ. Circulation: 1880, 4500; 1890, 12,500; 1900, 11,765; 1905, 12,210; 1910, 11,985; 1915, 18,000; 1920, 23,164; 1925, 22,342; 1930, 12,318; 1940, 14,849; 1950, 8735. Edited by Kaspar Alexander Honthumb, 1874—82; by Moritz Jacobi, 1882—Dec. 1882; by Wolfgang Schönle, 1883; by E. H. Austerlitz, 1883—1903?; by Max Burgheim, 1904—18; by Friedrich Wilhelm Elven [pseud: Der Cincinnarr], Dec. 1919—Jan.? 1941. Other editors: George F. Moser; Fritz M. Witte, Sept. 1, 1928—1941?; Emil Beinecke, 1889?—1929?. Published by Alexander Torges & Co., 1874—76; by Alexander Torges, 1872—1882; by Cincinnatier Freie Presse Kompagnie [Mrs. Torges & E. H. Austerlitz, 1882—85], 1883—Jan. 1941. Edited & published by Max M. Haw, Jan. 1941—1946; by Frederick N. Dittrich, 1947—54. The Vᴏʟᴋsʙʟᴀᴛᴛ and Fʀᴇɪᴇ Pʀᴇssᴇ from the start were political antagonists. Dɪᴇ Fʀᴇɪᴇ Pʀᴇssᴇ was usually Republican. Tʜᴇ Fʀᴇɪᴇ Pʀᴇssᴇ in 1919 absorbed the Vᴏʟᴋsʙʟᴀᴛᴛ. In 1929 the staff of this famous paper was introduced to its readers in the Cɪɴᴄɪɴɴᴀᴛɪ Sᴘɪʀɪᴛ: „Es ist bemerkenswert, daß der Redaktionsstab unserer Zeitung im Gegensatz hierzu ausschliesslich aus wirklichen Berufsjournalisten besteht. Dr. George F. Moser war vor Jahren bereits bei der Fʀᴇɪᴇɴ Pʀᴇssᴇ, ging dann nach Louisville als Telegraphenredakteur und Leitartikler an den L. Aɴ-ᴢᴇɪɢᴇʀ, von wo er im Jahre 1924 zurückkehrte. Dr. Fritz M. Witte kam am 1. Sept. 1928 nach Cincinnati, um den durch den Tod des ehemaligen Lokalredakteurs Richard Greninger freigewordenen Platz zu übernehmen. Er ist Journalist bei Vererbung und Neigung, schnitt bereits sein Universitätsstudium auf diesen Beruf zu, verbrachte seine Lehrzeit bei der Uʟʟsᴛᴇɪɴ Pʀᴇssᴇ in Berlin, und ging für diesen Verlag als Korrespondent für 4 Jahre nach China. Auch in Amerika ist er seiner Liebe zur Journalistik nicht untreu geworden. Die Nachrichten aus dem Staate Ohio werden von Herrn Emil Beinecke bearbeitet, welcher im Betriebe der Fʀᴇɪᴇɴ Pʀᴇssᴇ gross geworden ist. (Und er zählt heute schon mehr Jahre als die Zeitung.) Ja, über 40 Jahre gehört Beinecke zu uns, er hat die Glanztage und die schweren Kriegszeiten mitgemacht und nimmt in der Geschichte unseres Blattes einen Ehrenplatz ein." Jubiläums-Ausgabe: Oct. 29, 1929. 13 sections. Jubiläums-Ausgabe: Nov. 5, 1944 [75th Anniversary]. See *Rowell, 1875—85; Ayer, 1880—1954; Groen; Mink.*

GyStalog: 1 X, 1920/28; Stg 1, 1923/26; 19, 1926/30ff; Stg 1, 1928/30ff; Stg 1, 1922, IV—XII; 19, 25. X—XII. 1925; Stg 1, II. VI—XII. 1927; B 203, n.z.A.

IU: Jan. 18; 1906; Feb. 16, 1907.

OC: 1874—1918 daily; 1925—1940 daily; 1940—1948 weekly (Sunday); 1948—1951 weekly (Sunday); 1951—present weekly (Sunday).

OCHi: [1876—1924]; July 7, 1929—to date.

OHi: [Aug. 24, 1918—Nov. 5, 1920].

Cincinnatier Wöchentliche Freie Presse : Oct. 4, 1876—1906?

Weekly edition of Cɪɴᴄɪɴɴᴀᴛɪᴇʀ Fʀᴇɪᴇ Pʀᴇssᴇ. Title varies slightly. Circulation: 1880, 4000; 1890, 9800; 1895, 12,250; 1900, 11,875; 1905, 8215. See *Rowell, 1877—85; Ayer, 1880—1906; Groen.*

GyAIZ: 4. 14. 15. VII. 1886; 26. III. 1890.

GySIA: 1922—29, 1931—37 (all incomplete except 1929), 1939.

OCHi: Jahrgang 1, no. 1—52, Oct. 4, 1876—Sept. 26, 1877.

Freiheitsbanner :

Weekly. Supported Socialist Labor Party. See *Hillquit.*

Der Freiheitsfreund : 1841?—1860?

See *Körner.*

Der Freisinnige : Oct.? 1841—1845?

Daily, Oct. 19, 1841—Feb. 1844?; weekly, Mar. 1844—1845?. Radical, abolitionist in character. Motto: „Vorwärts! Stillstand ist Rückgang, darum Vorwärts! Wir gehen für die Constitution, für Wahrheit und Recht." Supported Dallas & Polk. Edited & published by C. F. B. Scho und Co.

Groen tells us that "Scho," as he signed his name, was Josef Schoberlechner, a radical Demokrat, who, thus early, advocated abolition of slavery. As far as can be determined, his career was as follows: Landed in New Orleans in early 1830's; married a French girl there; then to Nashville for several years, where they managed an "Ellenwaarenhandlung und Putzmacherei;" because of his abolitionist views, he was forced to sell and leave Nashville; then to Cincinnati where he established DER FREISINNIGE; then to St. Louis, where he seems to have re-established his paper, Nov. 24, 1846; finally, to California, where he died. See *Mink; Groen.*

OCHi: Jahrgang 3, no. 162 [also as: Jahrgang 1, neue Nummer 23], July 18, 1844 [weekly]: States that weekly was established Mar. 1, 1844.

OClWHi: July 18, 1844.

Für Kleine Leute : 1879—1882?

Semi-monthly. Organ of Deutsche Methodistenkirche. Circulation: 1880, 6000. See *Douglass; North.*

Die Glocke : June? 1856?—1900?

Weekly. Sub-title: Für die Sonntagschul- und Jugendwelt. Organ of Deutsche Methodistenkirche. Large quarto, each issue 4 pages. Edited by F. L. Nagler [in 1895]. Published by L. Swormstedt & A. Poe, 1856—June 7, 1860; by A. Poe & L. Hitchcock, June 14, 1860—1865?; by Hitchcock & Walden, 1866?—July? 1880; by Walden & Stowe, Aug. 2? 1880—May 1884; by Cranston & Stowe, June 2, 1884—May 1892; by Cranston & Curts, June 2, 1892—1899; by Curts & Jennings, Jan. —May 1900; by Jennings & Pye, June 7—?, 1900. See *Groen.*

KHi: Band 41, no. 15, Oct. 11, 1896.

Handwerker- und Arbeiter-Union : 1851?—?

Edited & published by John Orff. See DER HOCHWÄCHTER, Oct. 22, 1851.

Haus und Herd : Band 1—46, Jan. 1873—1918.

Monthly. Sub-title: 1) Ein Familien-Magazin für Jung und Alt; 2) Eine Monatsschrift für die Familie und Sonntagschule; 3) Ein illustriertes Familienblatt; 4) Eine illustrierte Monatsschrift für die Familie. Organ of Deutsche Methodistenkirche. Dated also at New York, Chicago & St. Louis. Merged with DER CHRISTLICHE APOLOGETE. Octavo, each issue 56—64 pages; title-page & contents, 4—8 pages; earlier volumes have "Jahrgang" on title-page, but "Band" at mast-head. Richly illustrated, including portraits [volume for 1877 has as many as 12 steel-engravings & 210 woodcuts]; an excellent paper for family reading, rather than a religious periodical. Subscription held by Harmony Society. Circulation: 1875, 5000; 1885, 8050; 1893, 9150; 1900, 8500; 1912, 9090; 1915, 8500. Edited by the Rev. Heinrich Liebhart, Jan. 1873—1895; by Dr. F. Nagler 1896—1900; by Friedrich Munz, 1900—12; by August Johann Bucher, 1912—18; assistant editors: H. A. Schröter; H. W. Liebhart, Friedrich Munz;; Otto Gilbert; J. J. Hoffmann, 1900—01; Friedrich Cramer, 1901—04; Albert Cramer, 1904—09; Carl Fritz, 1909—18. Published by Hitchcock & Walden, Jan. 1873?—July? 1880; by Walden & Stowe, Aug. 2? 1880—May 1884; by Cranston & Stowe, June 2, 1884—May 1892; by Cranston & Curts, June 2, 1892—1899; by Curts & Jennings, Jan. ?—May 1900; by Jennings & Pye, June 7, 1900—May 1904; by Jennings & Graham, June 8, 1904—1915?; by Methodist Book Concern, 1916?—1918. See *Rowell, 1873—85; Ayer, 1880—1910; Groen; Douglass.*

DLC: 1, 30.
GEU: 11.
GyAIZ: Jan., April, May, 1875; Oct. 1886; Oct. 1890; May and Sept. 1891; Jubiläumsnummer: Nov. 1892.
IEG: 3—46.
IEN: 1, 3—5, 8—12, 14—24.
IU: 2—[6]—[9]—[14]—[17].
MnU: 2—5.
MoS: 1, 16—17.
NjMD: [2—5, 8, 12—13, 25—43].
NjR: 4—8.

NN: Fragments.
OC: 1—9, 11—39.
OCl: 1—22.
ODW: 27, 33—35.
OHi: [28].
OO: [18].

Hausblätter : 1855—1867?

Edited by F. W. Hackländer. Literary periodical.
OC: 1855—67.

Heiden Frauenfreund : 1886?—1926?

Missionary paper. Organ of Deutsche Methodistenkirche. See *Douglass*.

Helvetia : Feb. 25, 1857—Feb. 24, 1859.

Weekly. Published in interests of Swiss-Americans. Sub-title: Organ für Fortschritt, Freiheit und Vaterland. Continued as HELVETIA (Tell City, Ind.). Edited by J. H. Walser, & published by Walser & Schellenbaum. See *Schem; Groen; Barba,* "The General Swiss Colonization Society;" *Bocksthaler.*

Cincinnatier Herold : 1895—1897?

Weekly. See *Groen.*

Der Cincinnati Hinkende Bote : 1836?—1927?

Title varies: DER HINKENDE BOTE IN AMERIKA. Published by Benzinger Gebrüder. Also published in other American cities. See ALLGEMEINE ZEITUNG (New York), Mar. 26, 1836; DER DEUTSCHE PIONIER, Dec. 1878; DER DEUTSCHE PIONIER, 1887; GROSS-DAYTONER ZEITUNG, Nov. 23, 1927.
OC: 1847, 1850, 1855.   PPG: 1882.
OCHi: 1856.

Die Hochwacht : 1857?

Weekly. Editors; August Becker; Otto von Reventlow; Wilhelm Rothacker. Groen suggests that this may be merely an alternate title of DER HOCHWÄCHTER after the latter had been sold by Hassaurek.

Der Hochwächter : July 3, 1845—May? 1849.

Weekly. Place of publication varies: Cincinnati, 1846; Louisville, Ky., 1847; Cincinnati, 1848—1849. Edited & published by Johann Georg Walker. See *Groen; Kamman,* who states that the paper disseminated liberal ideas in politics and religion.
IU: 1845—July 17, 1846.

Der Hochwächter : Jahrgang 1—9, Sept. 27, 1850—1859?

Weekly. Sub-title: 1) Ein Organ für religiöse Aufklärung und sociale Reform, June 30, 1852—June 28, 1853; 2) Ein Organ des Gesammt-Fortschritts, July 6, 1853—1855? Organ of the Frei-männer-Verein. Motto: „Wenn Aristokraten und Pfaffen sich vereinigen, ein Volk zu unter-jochen, so machen sie es erst dumm und lauterhaft, denn der Freie und Denkende und Tugend-hafte ist nicht zu unterjochen." Seume. Also as "Ganze Nummer 1—?" Small folio, each issue 4 pages. Edited by Friedrich Hassaurek, Sept. 27, 1850—Jan. 12, 1853; by Friedrich August Hobelmann; by August Becker.
Published by Wilhelm Wachsmuth, Sept. 27, 1850—Jan. 7, 1852; by Friedrich Hassaurek, Jan. 15, 1852—? A militant newspaper. Anti-Roman Catholic and generally anti-clergy as bloodsuckers who produce nothing. Also fought a vigorous battle against the immigration agents in American harbor cities who lived most shamefully off of the ignorance of new arrivals. It opposed all blind adherence to any political party. Hassaurek was an old revolutionist and an agnostic; an excellent orator and fluent in English and German; also successful financially; bitter enemy of Heinzen, his radical and rival colleague in Cincinnati. See *Wittke (5) p. 121; Groen; Klauprecht; Schlicher; Kamman; Mink; ULS.*
GyAIZ: 26. XI. 1856; 19. VIII. 1857.

IU: v. 1—5, no. 1—50, Sept. 27, 1850—Sept. 12, 1855.
MWA: Jahrgang 2, no. 45 (ganze Nummer 97), Aug. 11, 1852.
NN: [8—9].
OCHi: Jahrgang 2, no. 2—52, Oct. 15, 1851—Sept. 29, 1852; Jahrgang 3, no. 1—26, Oct. 6, 1852—Mar. 30, 1853; Jahrgang 5, no. 2, Oct. 11, 1854; Jahrgang 6, no. 16, Jan. 16, 1856.

Cincinnati Industrie Zeitung : 1872.

Issued weekly in preparation for and during Industrie-Ausstellung, which ended Oct. 5, 1872.
OC: complete.

Der Israelitische Volksfreund : vol. 1, no. 1—8, Dec. 1858—July 1859?

Monthly Jewish paper, printed in German. Sub-title: Eine Monatsschrift. Edited & published by G. M. Coen. See *Postal; Friedenberg.*
NNJ: no. 1—8.

Jahresbericht des Vorstandes des Deutschen Pionier-Vereins von Cincinnati : no. 1—63, 1868/69—1930/31?

Annual report. Title varies: 1) BERICHT DER MONATLICHEN VERSAMMLUNG DES DEUTSCHEN PIONIER-VEREINS VON CINCINNATI, 1869/70—1884/85; 2) JAHRESBERICHT DES VORSTANDES DES DEUTSCHEN PIONIER-VEREINS VON CINCINNATI, no. 20, 1887/88; 3) JAHRESBERICHT DES VER-WALTUNGSJAHRES DES DEUTSCHEN PIONIER-VEREINS VON CINCINNATI, no. 21, July, 1888—June 30, 1889; 4) VORSTANDS-BERICHT DES VERWALTUNGSJAHRES DES DEUTSCHEN PIONIER-VEREINS VON CINCINNATI, no. 22—63, 1889/90—1930/31. Number 1–19, 1868/69—1885/86 published in DER DEUTSCHE PIONIER. As a separately published report, it follows DER DEUTSCHE PIONIER. Octavo, with varying pages, up to 48 pages; illustrated including portraits; contains biographical sketches.

CtY: 20—56.	NN: 20.
ICJ: 20—41.	OC: 20—to date.
ICU: 20, 26, 28, 30, 32.	OCHi: 21, 25—26, 28—47, 50—56, 58.
In: 32—50.	OCU: 20—22, 24—63.
IU: 20—42.	OU: 20—21, 30—31, 33—34, 40, 46, 51—54.
MiD: 26, 30, 32, 51—56.	WHi: 20—34, 37.
MnU: [25—46] 51—56.	

Jung-Amerika : Band 1—5, no. 8, Dec. 1901—May 1906.

Monthly during school year; number of issues per "Band" varies slightly. Sub-title: Zeitschrift für Schule und Haus. Octavo, each issue 14—16 pages; title-page and contents, 4 pages; illustrated. Also as "ganze Nummer 1—45," Edited by H. H. Fick, & published by Gus. Mueller. See *Ayer, 1903—07; Stepler.*

IU: [1—5].	NN: complete set.
MoSC: 1906—07.	OCU: complete set.

Kalender für Lustige Leute : 1877?—1890?

See DER DEUTSCHE PIONIER, 1887.

Katholisches Schulblatt : Jahrgang 1—2, Mar. 1, 1864—Feb. 1, 1866.

Roman Catholic monthly. Sub-title: Monatsschrift für Volkserziehung und Völkerunterricht. Unter Mitwirkung von geistlichen und weltlichen Schulmännern. Octavo, each issue 32 pages; title-page and contents, 4 pages.
Edited by G. Miettinger, Mar. 1—Aug. 1864; by H. Johanning, Oct. 1, 1864—Aug. 1865. Published by Jos. A. Hemann, Mar. 1, 1864—Jan. 1866; by Gebrüder Benzinger, Feb. 1, 1866. See *Middleton; Groen;*
OCU: complete set.

Katholische Volkszeitung : 1883?—1892?

Roman Catholic weekly. See *Groen.*

Der Kicker :

See *Groen*, no further information.

Cincinnati Kikeriki : 1872—1884?

Humorous weekly. Sub-title: Wochenblatt für Humor und Satyre. Title varies: DER KIKERIKI. Folio, each issue 4 pages. Circulation: 1877, 4000 (est.); 1880, 3500. Edited & published by Carl Friedrich Lang, 1872—83. See *Rowell, 1876—82; Ayer, 1880—82; Groen.*

Kirchenzeitung : 1899?—1904?

Weekly. Sub-title: Organ der Unabhängigen Evangelischen Protestantischen Gemeinde von Nord-Amerika. Large quarto, each issue 8 pages. Circulation: 1900, 5000. Edited by the Rev. Henry Höfner & Associates, & published by C. G. Wagner, 1899—1904. See *Ayer, 1900—04; Groen.*

Cincinnati Kladderadatsch : 1874?

Humorous weekly. Large quarto, each issue 8 pages. Edited & published by C. H. Austerlitz. See *Rowell, 1874; Groen;* DER DEUTSCHE PIONIER, June 1874.

GyAIZ: 26. X. 1890.

Die Kleine Glocke : July 1897—1918?

Sunday School monthly. Organ of Deutsche Methodistenkirche. 1918 war casualty. Circulation: 1912, 6300. See *Groen; Douglass.*

Kleine Lehrbilder :

Organ of Deutsche Methodistenkirche. Doubtful that this is a "serial." See *Douglass.*

Die Königin des Westens : June? 1849—1850.

Roman Catholic weekly. Merged with CINCINNATI VOLKSFREUND. Edited & published by Hermann Lehmann. See *Groen.*

Die Kratzbürste :

"Witzblatt." Edited & published by C. A. Honthumb. See *Groen,* as current in 1870.

Landlord's Bulletin : 1880?—1881?

Semi-monthly. Published in English and German. Small folio, each 4 pages. Published by Block & Co. See *Rowell, 1881; Groen.*

Die Laterne :

"Witzblatt." See *Schem.*

Der Licht-Freund : Jahrgang 1—3, Aug.? 1840—July? 1843.

Semi-monthly. Sub-title: Organ des Freisinnigen Deutschthums. Circulation: 1840, 500. Edited & published by Eduard Mühl & Karl Strehly, who continued their paper at Hermann, Mo. Published in the Office of the VOLKSBLATT. Very informative for intellectual life of established German Americans. Approved Universalism, attacked American hypocrisy. Ardently for German language in Cincinnati public schools. See *Groen; Körner, Kamman; Falbisaner; Schnake; Bek; Gilmore; Schneider; Organ.*
OCHi: complete file.

Literarischer Anzeiger : no. 1—43, 1893—Feb. 1904?

See *ULS.*
KASB: [2—43].

Der Locofoco : May—June? 1845.

Semi-weekly. Edited & published by Johann Georg Walker & Wilhelm Albers. *Rattermann* (37) explains: „Die bekannte Uneinigkeit der Deutschen liess jedoch bald ein Konkurrenzblatt als wünschenswerth erscheinen, und so kehrte Walker schon im Mai des darauf folgenden Jahres [1845?] von Indianapolis zurück, um auf's Neue eine politische Zeitung herauszugeben, DER

LOCOFOCO, von welcher auch ein paar Nummern erschienen. Den Herausgebern der beiden anderen politischen Blätter [Molitor & Schmidt] kam das natürlich nicht sehr gelegen, und sie bemühten sich nun, unterstützt von einigen anderen einflußreichen Männern, Walker dahin zu bewegen, das begonnene halbwöchentlich erscheinende Blatt wieder fallen zu lassen und statt dessen ein antireligiöses Wochenblatt herauszugeben, das auch in dem von Walker seit dem 3. Juli 1845 bis zu seinem Tode [1849] publizierten HOCHWÄCHTER zu Stande kam."

Ludvigh's Vereinigten Staaten Anzeiger.

See FACKEL, vol. 17.

Lyra : Jahrgang 1, no. 1, July 20, 1897—?

Monthly. Sub-title: Zeitschrift für Musik und Gesang. Officielles Organ des Nord-Amerikanischen Sänger-Bundes. Large quarto, 8 pages. Published by Jacob Willig.
MWKJA: no. 1.

Magazin für Nord-Amerika : Band 1, Apr. 1, 1851—?

Agricultural semi-monthly. Octavo, each issue 16 pages. Edited & published by Dr. Magnus Gross. See *Stuntz; Cist; Groen.*

Die Menschenrechte : 1853—?

Weekly. Edited & published by Wilhelm Rothacker & Johann Rittig. See BELLEVILLER POST UND ZEITUNG, Jan. 11, 1899; *Groen; Kamman.*

Mephistopheles : 1856—?

Humorous paper. Edited & published by Victor Wilhelm Fröhlich & ? Steffens. See *Groen; Pletz.*

Cincinnati Tägliche Morgen-Post : 1877—1878?

Daily, morning except Sunday, edition of TÄGLICHE ABENDPOST. Title varies slightly. Circulation: 1878, 2500 (est.). See *Rowell, 1878; Groen; Mink.*
OC: Mar.—Oct. 13, 1878.

Ohio Volkszeitung : 1876?—1878?

Socialist daily, which supported Socialist Labor Party. Edited & published by Heinrich von Ende. See *Groen; Kamman; Hillquit.*

Neue Glocke : 1882—1887?

Bimonthly organ of Deutsche Methodistenkirche. See *Joest; Douglass.*

Ohio Adler und Volksbühne : 1843—?

See *Joest.*
GyAIZ: 24. IV. 1843.

Die Ohio Chronik : 1826.

Weekly. *Groen* has made a careful study of the sources for material on this first newspaper of Cincinnati, and reports that it was listed in an early history of the city, in "Cincinnati in 1826" by B. Drake & E. D. Mansfield (Cincinnati, 1827), concludes that the paper was short-lived, but that it did exist.

Die Ohio Staatszeitung : 1849—1850.

Daily. Followed by DEMOKRATISCHES TAGEBLATT. Published by J. M. Bürsner, & edited by Friedrich Hassaurek, 1849; edited & published by Heinrich Rödter, Sept. 1850. See *Groen; Körner.*

Ohio Volksfreund : Apr. 1841—Jan. 1842?

Semi-weekly, Apr. 7—July 10, 1841; weekly, July—17—Dec. 25, 1841. Follows DER DEUTSCHE IM WESTEN. Small folio, each issue 4 pages. Edited & published by Rudolph von Maltitz, who, it was reported, was suddenly forced to leave town. See *Groen; Körner; Cist.*
CtY: Dec. 25, 1841.
OCHi: Jahrgang 1, no. 5, Apr. 21, 1841.

Ohio Volkszeitung : 1876—1878?

Socialist daily, which supported Socialist Labor Party. Edited & published by Heinrich von Ende. See *Groen; Kamman; Hillquit;* DER DEUTSCHER PIONIER, Nov. 1879.

Ordenswarte :

Organ der Unabhängigen Orden der Rothmänner.

Periodische Blätter : 1883—1884?

Roman Catholic monthly. See *Groen.*

Cincinnati Tägliche Morgen-Post : 1877—1878.

OC: March.—Oct. 13, 1878.

Cincinnati Wöchentliche Post : 1877?—1880?

Weekly edition of TÄGLICHE ABENDPOST. Circulation: 1880, 6700. See *Rowell, 1877—80; Ayer, 1880.*

Die Propaganda : (1866—?)

Gegründet von Samuel Ludvigh im Monat August 1866, werden folgende Werke in 5 Serien herausgegeben: 1) Frisch und Frei; 2) Der gesunde Menschenverstand; 3) Alt und Neu; 4) Reden und Vorlesungen im Gebiet der Religion, Philosophie und Geschichte; 5) Der Priesterspiegel; 6) Der *Wahre* Glaube, gegründet auf Vernunft. Published by subscription to stocks bought by those interested. Appearance irregular. See second last page of FACKEL, 1866 volume; it lists 126 men all over U.S. who have signed for stocks to support this anti-clerical series.

Der Protestant : no. 1—37?, Nov. 9, 1837?—Sept. 1838?

Weekly. Place of publication given variously: Miamisburg, Ohio [Rümelin, in DER DEUTSCHE PIONIER, June 1872; Rattermann in his „Deutsche Bilder aus der Geschichte der Stadt Cincinnati"]; Germantown, Ohio [Rattermann, „Deutsch-Amerikanisches Biographikon"; Rattermann, „Deutsch-Amerikanischer Journalismus"]; Canal-Dover, Ohio [Rattermann, „Deutsch-Amerikanischer Journalismus"]; Cincinnati [Groen; Stierlin; Eickhoff; Rümelin; Rattermann, „Deutsch-Amerikanischer Journalismus"; DER DEUTSCHE PIONIER, June 1872]. Edited by Johann Georg Walker, & published by ? Espich.

Protestantischer Haus-Freund : 1885?—1899?

Evangelical monthly. Circulation: 1890, 3500; 1895, 5900; 1899, 5000. Edited & published by the Rev. Edward Voss, 1885—89; edited by the Rev. Henry Haefner, 1890—99; published by the Rev. Edward Voss, 1890—92; by the Rev. J. A. Voss, 1893—98; by C. G. Wagner, 1899. See *Ayer, 1888—99; Groen.*

GyAIZ: 17. VI. 1886.

Protestantische Zeitblätter : Jahrgang 1—?, Apr. 8, 1849—1879.

Weekly. Sub-title: 1) Eine Wochenschrift zur Belehrung und Erbauung denkender Christen, Apr. 8, 1849?—1856?; 2) Eine Wochenschrift zur Belehrung und Erbauung sowie für die Ereignisse im kirchlichen und staatlichen Leben, 1856—79? Organ of Vereinigte Lutherische und Reformirte Gemeinden. Organ of Protestantischer Bund der freien christlichen Gemeinden Nord-Amerikas. Circulation: 1875, 912; 1879, 800. Edited & published by Friedrich Bötticher, 1849; edited by August Kröll, Heinrich W. Suhr & Johann Grassow, 1849?—56?; by August Kröll, Mar. 12, 1857—1858?; by August Kröll & Gustav Wilhelm Eisenlohr, 1858?; by Gustav Wilhelm Eisenlohr, 1858?—1879. Published by Deutscher Allgemein-Protestantischer Wittwen-Verein, Jan. 26, 1854—1875?; by Fr. W. Stahl; by David Abbihl, 1875—76; by George Beinert, 1877—79. See *Rowell, 1874—80; Ayer, 1880; Körner; Groen; Rattermann (12).*

GyAIZ: 4. XI. 1869. 21 Jg. Nr. 29.

OCHi: Jahrgang 5, no. 1—52, Apr. 14, 1853—Apr. 6, 1854; Jahrgang 8, no. 1—52, Apr. 10, 1856—Apr. 2, 1857; Jahrgang 10, no. 1—52, Apr. 8, 1858—Mar. 31, 1859.

Reck und Barren : vol. 1, no. 1, Apr. 1889—?

Weekly. Sub-title: Officielles Organ des Ohio Turnbezirks. Propaganda-Schrift und Officielles Organ des Ohio Turnbezirks. Large quarto, 28 pages. Edited by the Redaktions-Committee des Ohio Turnbezirks [in February, 1891: Joel H. Steinberg, Joseph Dauben, Robt. C. Georgi, Ernst A. Weier, F. A. Wayant]. Published by Ernst A. Weier & Co. See *Groen.*
OCHi: Vol. II, No. 47, Feb. 21, 1891.

Republikanisches Volksblatt : 1869?—?

See *Groen; Schem 3:261.*

The Sabbath Visitor : vol. 1—21, 1874—1895?

Weekly. Jewish paper, which Postal states, was at first published partly in German. Title varies: HEBREW SABBATH SCHOOL VISITOR, 1874—80. Edited & published by Rabbi Dr. Max Lilienthal, 1874—95; other editors: Kaufmann Kohler, Isadore Wise, David Phillipson; C. E. Bloch. See *ULS.*
MB: vol. 1, no. 1.
NN: vol. 3, no. 1—51, Jan. 14—Dec. 29, 1876: In English only.
NNJ: 1—3.
OCH: 1—[9], 16, [18, 20—21].

Der Samariter : 1895—1900.

Monthly. See *Groen.*

St. Francisci Glöcklein : 1883—1900.

Roman Catholic monthly. See *Groen.*

St. Franziskus Bote : Jahrgang 1—25, 1892—1917?

Monthly. Sub-title: 1) Monatsschrift für katholische Christen und Organ des III. Ordens in Amerika; 2) Organ des III. Ordens, sowie der frommen Vereine des heiligen Antonius und gewidmet der Verehrung des heiligsten Herzens Mariens. Octavo; each issue ca. 36 pages; illustrated; title-page and contents, 4 pages. Published by Franziskaner-Vätern, Cincinnati. See *Groen.*
DCU: 1—25.   MiDDS: 1—25.
IU: 1—[4—7, 9, 11—18, 20—23].   MoSC: 1—12, 15—21.

Der Cincinnati Schalk : 1882?—1884?

Humorous weekly. Folio, each issue 8 pages. See *Ayer, 1883; Groen.*

Schul- und Jugend-Zeitung : 1855?—?

Edited & published by Carl Beyschlag.

Der Sendbote : 1873.

A monthly published in 1873 by P. Franziskaner. See *Joest.*

Der Sodalist : Vol. 1—54, no. 5, Dec. 1884—June 1938?

Roman Catholic monthly, published in English and German, the German text seems to begin in vol. 50, and to cease in vol. 51, no. 9, Aug. 1935. Published by Sodalities of St. Francis Church. Quarto, each issue 8 pages. See *Middleton; Enzlberger.*
DHN: [51—54].   KASB: [52—53].
DLC: 46—54.

Cincinnatier Sonntagsblatt : 1886?—1887?

Roman Catholic weekly. Circulation: 1887, 6700. Edited & published by Alvis F. Juettner. See *Ayer, 1886—87.*
GyAIZ: 11. VII. 1886.

Sonntagsblatt der Cincinnatier Freien Presse : Aug. 30, 1874—1941?

Sunday edition of CINCINNATIER FREIE PRESSE. Title varies slightly. For special edition, see UMSCHAU. Circulation: 1880, 8000; 1890, 15,000; 1900, 24,600; 1910, 37,808; 1917, 50,310; 1921, 22,281; 1930, 18,720; 1940, 14,849.

GyAIZ: 6. XII. 1891; 8. V. 1892; 24. II., 3. III., 10. III., 1. XII., 1929; 8. II. 1931; 31. V. 1936; 18. X. 1936; 14. XI. 1937.

ICHi [Rowell Collection]: Jahrgang 2, no. 51, Aug. 13, 1876; Jahrgang 3, no. 10, Oct. 29, 1876.

MWKJA: Jahrgang 70, no. 9, Oct. 23, 1938.

OCHi: Jahrgang 1, no. 1—52, Aug. 30, 1874—Aug. 22, 1875; Jahrgang 2—4; Jahrgang 52, no. 1—11, Aug. 22—Oct. 31, 1920.

Sonntagsblatt der Cincinnati Zeitung : 1887?—1901.

Sunday edition of CINCINNATI ZEITUNG. Circulation: 1890, 8000; 1900, 7500. See *Ayer, 1887—1901*.

Sonntagsblatt des Cincinnati Anzeiger : Nov. 1880—Oct. 1901.

Sunday edition of CINCINNATI ANZEIGER. Circulation: 1885, 4700; 1890, 6500; 1900, 6000. See *Rowell, 1881—85; Ayer, 1881—1901; Groen.*

WHi: Jahrgang 21, no. 24, Dec. 16, 1900.

Sonntagsblatt des Cincinnati Courier : Nov. 1869—Mar.? 1874.

Sunday edition of CINCINNATI COURIER. Circulation: 1873, 6000. See *Rowell, 1871—74.*

OCHi: Jahrgang 1, no. 32—53, Dec. 5—26, 1869: [Numbered with daily edition, and bound with it].

Sonntagsblatt des Cincinnati Volksfreund :

Established 1869 as Sunday paper by H. Haache. See *Joest.*

Sonntagsblatt für Schule und Haus : 1899—1900.

Weekly. See *Groen.*

Der Sonntagsmorgen : June 16, 1867—June 11, 1908.

Sunday edition of CINCINNATI VOLKSFREUND. Title varies: SONNTAGSBLATT DES CINCINNATI VOLKSFREUND [in 1876]. Circulation: 1870, 3500 (est.); 1880, 7500; 1890, 7500; 1900, 12,000; 1905, 12,000. See *Rowell, 1869—85; Ayer, 1880—1908; Groen.*

DLC: Jahrgang 6—7, June 8, 1873—May 30, 1875.

GyAIZ: 13. VII., 14. XII., 1890; 22. XI. 1891.

ICHi [Rowell Collection]: Jahrgang 9, no. 17, Sept. 24, 1876.

IU: July 14, 1867; June 27, 1869; Jan. 30, Apr. 17, May 29, 1870.

MWKJA: July 16, 1882 (important article on Harmony Society).

WHi: June 16, 1867—1868; June 12, 1870—June 4, 1871; June 1875—Apr. 1906.

Die Sonntagspost : 1873—?

Monthly. Edited by the Rev. F. J. Werner. See *Groen.*

Cincinnati Sonntagspost : 1877?—1880?

Sunday edition of TÄGLICHE ABENDPOST. Title varies: SONNTAGS-CHRONIK. Circulation: 1880, 7000. See *Rowell, 1880; Ayer, 1880.*

OC: March 11—Dec. 2, 1877: SONNTAGS-CHRONIK, SONNTAGS-AUSGABE DER CINCINNATI ABENDPOST; Dec. 9, 1877—Feb. 24, 1878: TÄGLICHE MORGENPOST (SONNTAGS-AUSGABE).

Sonntagschul-Glocke : Band 1—?, Oct. 1856—1915?

Monthly, 1856—61; semi-monthly, 1862—1915?. Organ of Deutsche Methodistenkirche. Large quarto, each issue 4 pages. Circulation: 1875, 25,000 (est.); 1893, 29,948; 1912, 15,000. Edited by Wilhelm Nast, 1856—May 1892; by the Rev. Heinrich Liebhart, 1871—95. Published by Swormstedt & Poe, 1856—June 7, 1860; by Poe & Hitchcock, June 14, 1860—1870?; by Hitchcock & Walden, 1871?—July ? 1880; by Walden & Stowe, Aug. 2?, 1880—May 1884; by Cranston &

Stowe, June 2, 1884—May 1892; by Cranston & Curts, June 2, 1892—1899; by Curts & Jennings, Jan. ?—May 1900; by Jennings & Pye, June 7, 1900—May 1904; by Jennings & Graham, June 8, 1904—1915?. See *Rowell, 1870—77; Ayer, Douglas.*
   GyAIZ: 1. VIII. 1886.
   IRAu: Band 3, no. 9, 12, June, Sept. 1859.
   MWA [Rowell Periodical Collection]: Band 20, no. 14, Apr. 15, 1876.

Cincinnati South-West : 1877?—1900?

Weekly journal, published in English and German, in interests of liquor trade. Dated also at Louisville, Ky. Circulation: 1890, 5500 [for both Cincinnati & Louisville editions]; 1895, 6200. Title varies?: WEEKLY ARENA, 1895.
Edited by J. B. Chadwick, 1887—1888; by George W. Wood, 1889—1890; by Thorp Burton, 1890—91; by H. van Nes & C. Hartmann, 1892—1893; by H. van Nes, 1893—95.
Published by South-West Publishing Co., 1887—95.
See *Ayer, 1887—95; Groen; Mink.*
   OCHi: Aug. 1891—[1892—May 5, Sept., Oct. 6, 1893; Oct. 5—12, 1894; Sept. 31, 1895].
   OFH: Apr. 13, 1889.

The Cincinnati Sun : vol. 1, no. 1—52?, Dec. 16, 1869—Dec. 1870?

Weekly. Published in English and German. Contains 4 pages, of which pages 2—3 in German, with sub-title: Gewidmet Kaufleuten, Fabrikanten, Handwerkern, und dem Publikum im Allgemeinen. Title of German section: DIE "CINCINNATI SUN". Circulation: 1870, 6365 (est.).
Edited & published by P. Satmar & Co. See *Rowell, 1870; Groen.*
   DLC: vol. 1, no. 2—10, 12—27, 29—38, Dec. 23, 1869—Sept. 30, 1870.

Cincinnati Tageblatt : July 22, 1895—Oct. 17, 1896.

Labor daily. Sub-title: Den Interessen des Lohn-Arbeitenden Volkes gewidmet. Official Organ of Deutscher Gewerkschaftsrath. Published by Cincinnati Co-operative Labor Press Association. See *Groen; Mink.*
   OC: complete set.

Die Tribüne : 1888?—?

Weekly. *Tobias* lists, with circulation of 300.

Turn-Zeitung : no. 1—10, Jan.—Oct. 1851.

Monthly. Sub-title: Herausgegeben von der Turngemeinde zu Cincinnati. Edited by Heinrich Esmann [with Wilhelm Rothacker & Gustav Tafel, no. 2—10?]. Octavo, each issue 8—10 pages. See *Groen; Metzner.*
   NN: no. 1—10.

Turner-Leben : vol. 1, no. 1—12, Nov. 1914—Oct. 1915?

Monthly. Published in English and German. Sub-title: North Cincinnati Turner Life. Large quarto, each issue 12 pages; illustrated, including portraits. Published by Board of Directors of the Nord Cincinnati Turnverein.
   OCHi: complete set.

Die Umschau :

Weekly. Sub-title: Wochenschrift für Politik und verwandte Gebiete. Teilausgabe der Sonntagsausgabe der Cincinnatier Freien Presse. May be part of Sunday edition, gratis, and not a separate title; bears no numbering. Large quarto, each issue 8 pages. See *D-A. Typ. Jb. 1931—32.*
   GyAIZ: 8. III. 1936; 18. X. 1936; 14. XI. 1937.
   GyLDB: 1925—27; 1929—39.
   MWKJA: Oct. 23, 1938.
   OCHi: Oct. 27, 1929.

Der Unabhängige : Nov. 7, 1850—1853?

Weekly. FRANK LESLIE'S ILLUSTRIRTE ZEITUNG, Dec. 7, 1877, refers to issue of Nov. 2, 1852 as "Nr. 1," which may be first number of new "Jahrgang;" it is further stated that it went over to the Arbeiter-Verein von Cincinnati in 1853. Edited by Karl von Schmidt-Bürgeler, & published by Johann Rittig & Wilhelm Rorhacker. See *Groen*.

Die Unabhängige Presse : 1840—?

Tri-weekly. Circulation: 1841, 250. Edited & published by Benjamin Boffinger. See *Groen*.

Die Union :

Daily. Edited by ? Dowiat, & published by Adolf Frey. See *Groen; Mink*.
OClWHi: July 16, Aug. 3, 9, 13, 1866.

Cincinnati Union :

Weekly edition of DIE UNION. See *Mink*.
OClWHi: July 11, 1866.

Die Union : 1879?—1880?

Weekly. Dated also at St. Louis, and at Pittsburgh. Edited & published by Eduard Bosse. See *Groen; Rowell, 1881; Ayer, 1881*. Rattermann, in DER DEUTSCHE PIONIER, May 1884, refers to the paper as a "frei-protestantische Zeitschrift."

Unionist : 1883?—1885?

Weekly organ of trade unions, published in English and German. Edited & published by Penter & Conolly. See *Rowell, 1884—85*.

Unsere Alte Heimath : 1877?—1878?

Weekly. Dated also at New York, and at Fort Wayne, Ind. Edited & published by Wertheimer & Co. See *Rowell, 1878, Groen; Kappel*, who gives facsimile.

Unsere Zeit : Jahrgang 1—3, Dec. 1864?—1867?

Weekly. Sub-title: Organ des Nord-Amerikanischen Turner-Bundes. Small folio, each issue 8 pages. Edited & published by Adolph Frey. See *Groen; ULS*.
NN: Jahrgang 3, no. 33, July 12, 1867.

Der Vereinsbote : Jahrgang 1—3, Nov. 1874—Dec. 1877?

Roman Catholic monthly. Sub-title: Eine Monatsschrift im Interesse des deutschen römisch-katholischen Central-Vereins von Nord-Amerika. Issue for Aug. 1876 never published. Octavo, each issue 32 pages; title-page and contents, 4 pages. Edited & published by the Rev. Anton Schwenniger, im Verlage Fr. Pustet. See *Groen; Middleton; ULS*.
KASB: [1].
NN: complete set.

Tägliches Cincinnatier Volksblatt : Jahrgang 1—83, May 7, 1836—Dec. 5, 1919.

Weekly, May 7, 1836—Nov. [6th to 8th, not precisely known], 1838; daily, morning except Sunday, Nov. 1838—Dec. 5, 1919. The 75th anniversary edition gives a full history of this important newspaper, so rich in local history. Klauprecht, a former editor and Rümelin also have published full accounts. Democratic, 1836—1871?; Republican, 1871?—1875; Independent, 1876—85; Independent Republican, 1886—1919. Title varies slightly: DAS VOLKSBLATT, May 7, 1836—Nov. 1839; VOLKSBLATT, Nov. 1839—?; other slight variations when published daily. For weekly edition, see WÖCHENTLICHES CINCINNATIER VOLKSBLATT. For Sunday edition, see WESTLICHE BLÄTTER.
Circulation: no. 1, May 7, 1836, 300 copies printed & sold; 1840, 1000; 1870, 8500 (est.); 1880, 13,200; 1890, 11,950; 1900, 12,500; 1905, 13,000; 1910, 17,600; 1911, 23,250. Edited by Johann Georg Walker, 1837—1838; by Stephan Molitor, 1838—42; by Eduard Mühl, 1842; by Heinrich Rödter, Apr. 1842—Mar. 21, 1843; by Friedrich Fieser, Apr.—Aug. 2, 1843; by Johann Georg Ritz, Aug. 1843—Feb. 1844; by Viktor Wilhelm Fröhlich, 1844—June 6, 1847; by Richard von

Meysenbug, May 1847—Sept. 1850; by Karl Resch [Roesch], Sept. 5, 1850—May 19, 1851; by Dr. Carl Friedrich Heunisch, Oct. 2, 1851—July 29, 1852; by Karl Resch [Roesch], May 31, 1853—Mar. 1854; by Emil Klauprecht, 1856 [or, 1854?]—1864; by August Becker, 1864; by Moritz Jacobi, 1864—65; by Friedrich Hassaurek, 1865—85 [in Europe, 1875—Summer 1877]; by Leopold Markbreit, 1885—1909; by Wolfgang Schönle, 1876—77; by Henry Danziger, 1909—19. Other editors: August Ligowsky; Wilhelm Kauffmann [in 1892]; Charles F. Johnson; Otto Rothmann; Emil Paetow. Associate editors: Carl Albrecht, 1885—87; Karl Rümelin; Georg Walker; Karl von Schmidt-Bürgeler [1865—?]. City editor: Gustav Tafel. Published by Volksblatt Aktien-Gesellschaft, May 7, 1836—1837; by Heinrich Rödter, 1837—40; by Stephan Molitor, 1840—June 1863; by Gustav Hof & Moritz Jacobi, 1863—65; by Gustav Hof & Friedrich Hassaurek, 1865—Mar. 1875; by Cincinnati Volksblatt Co., Mar. 1875—1919 [President: Fr. Hassaurek, 1875—85; Leopold Markbreit, 1885—1909; Charles Krippendorf, 1909—19]. Jubiläums-Ausgabe, Sept. 3, 1911. See Rowell, 1869—85; Ayer, 1880—1920; Rümelin; Groen; Pletz.

DLC: Jahrgang 2, no. 51, Mar. 4, 1840; Jahrgang 3, no. 233, Oct. 1, 1841; Jahrgang 8, no. 13—304, Jan. 16—Dec. 26, 1846; July 27, 1847—1854; Jan. 5—Nov. 1858; Mar. 6, 1866—Oct. 1869; Apr. 1882—Oct. 1886; Sept. 17, 1888—Aug. 1889; Jan.—May 1890; 1898—to date?

GyAIZ: 13. XI. 1862; 5. IX. 1871. 36 Jg. Nr. 20. 7. VIII. 1872; 6. VII. 1886.

GyMBS: 1914—15 inc.

GyStalog: 12, 1914/15.

ICHi [Rowell Collection]: Jhg. 39, no. 195, Oct. 14, 1876.

IU: May 8, 1885; Mar. 11, 25, May 27, 1894; Nov. 30, 1905; Jan. 18, Dec. 3, 1906; Mar. 3, 1907; Sept. 16, 30, 1910; Nov. 30, Dec. 7, 1911; Jan. 10, Mar. 5, July 16, 1913; Dec. 2, 1915; Feb. 22—June 29, 1918.

MnHi: Mar. 7, 1836.

MWA: Oct. 19, 1837; Sept. 9, 1852; Oct. 11 (extra) 1854. Jahrgang 22, no. 77, Mar. 30, 1860; Jahrgang 39, no. 151, Aug. 24, 1876.

OC: July 12, 1872—1918. [Not available, June 1954].

OCHi: Jahrgang 1, no. 1, May 7, 1836 [2 copies]; Jahrgang 1, no. 10, July 9, 1836; Feb. 15, Mar. 26—28, 30—Apr. 1, Aug. 22, 1839; [Jan. 4, 1843—July 20, 1846]; [April 8, 1847— Sept. 2, 1852]. Jan. 30, 1879; [Nov. 1901—1917]; Dec. 5, 1919.

OClWHi: Oct. 15, 1850—Jan. 14, May 18—Dec. 1852; Aug. 13, 1853. March 3, 24, 1864; Aug. 31, Sept. 28, Nov. 22, 1865.

OHi: [Dec. 1918—1919]; Jan. 1, 1901.

TxU: Jan. 26, 1854—Dec. 20, 1855.

WHi: Sept. 2—Dec. 1889; June 2, 1890—Mar. 1891.

Wöchentliches Cincinnatier Volksblatt : Nov. 1839—Dec. 1919.

Weekly edition of TÄGLICHES CINCINNATIER VOLKSBLATT. Circulation: 1841, 1400; 1870, 7000 (est.); 1880, 12,500; 1890, 12,150; 1900, 13,500; 1910, 18,200. See Rowell, 1869—85; Ayer, 1880—1920; Groen.

ICHi [Rowell Collection]: Jahrgang 41, no. 11 [ganze Nummer 2104], Sept. 5, 1876.

MWA: Jahrgang 2, no. 24 [ganze Nummer 76], Oct. 19, 1837; Jahrgang 19, no. 18 [ganze Nummer 853], Sept. 9, 1852; Oct. 11, 1854 [Extra no.].

OCHi: Mar. 16, 1843; [Apr. 8, 1847—Sept. 2, 1852].

OClWHi: Jahrgang 28, no. 45, 48 [ganze Nummer 1151, 1454]. Mar. 3, 24, 1864; Jahrgang 30, no. 19, 23, 31, Aug. 31, Sept. 28, Nov. 22, 1865.

Volksbote : 1827?—?

Groen gives an interesting account of this title, which he discovered in an unpublished chronological list of Cincinnati newspapers, 1793—1843, compiled by Charles F. Theis, 1832[?]. He noted several inaccuracies in the list and would doubt the existence of the paper. The list is to be found in the Historical & Philosophical Society Library of Cincinnati.

Der Volksbote : 1851?—1854?

Roman Catholic weekly. Edited & published by Joseph Fredewest & Anton Donnersberger. See Groen; DER DEUTSCHE PIONIER, Dec. 1875.

Cincinnati Volksbote : 1879?—?

Religious monthly. See *Groen; North*.

Die Volks-Bühne : June? 1841—1845?

Irregular: weekly, semi-weekly, tri-weekly. Supported Van Buren. Place of publication varies; Louisville, Ky., 1841—42. [Was it ever published in Indianapolis?]. Edited & published by Johann Georg Walker [with August Renz, 1842—45], 1841—45; Friedrich Fieser was associate editor. This paper first gained fame in Louisville and moved to Cincinnati later. The NEW YORKER STAATS-ZEITUNG once had it in mind when saying: „Im Westen wird ein Blatt mit Präriedreck statt mit Druckerschwarz gedruckt." Walker, the editor, rarely published his paper on the day announced. He took it easy, did not work for money but fame. If letters were missing he would use others in inverted form and let his readers practice spelling. Since fame did not pay his Louisville bills he packed his press and opened up in Cincinnati. He died in Cincinnati May 9, 1849, during the great cholera epidemic, forsaken and in poverty. See *Körner; Klauprecht; Groen; Mink.*

GyAIZ: 24. V. 1843. 3. Jg., no. 102.
OCHi: Jahrgang 3, no. 107, June 28, 1843.

Cincinnati Volksfreund : Oct. 12, 1850—June 11, 1908.

Democratic daily, morning except Sunday. Issue for Oct. 12, 1850 is "Probenummer." Title varies slightly. Absorbed DIE KÖNIGIN DES WESTENS. For weekly edition, see CINCINNATI WÖCHENTLICHER VOLKSFREUND. For tri-weekly edition, see CINCINNATI DREIMALWÖCHENTLICHER VOLKSFREUND. For Sunday edition, see SONNTAGSMORGEN. For supplement, see DEMOKRATISCHES CAMPAGNE-BLATT. Circulation: 1870, 5500 (est.); 1880, 6000; 1890, 6000; 1900, 9000; 1905, 10,000. Edited & published by Joseph Anton Hemann, Oct. 12, 1850—July 1863 [with M. Werner, Oct. 12—Nov. 1850; by Johann B. Jeup & Co., July 1863—1869; by Volksfreund Publishing Co., 1870—71; by Limberg & Thilly, 1872; by Limberg & Heinrich Haacke, 1873—79; by Heinrich Haacke, 1880—1908. Other editors: Emil Rothe, Aug. 1869—1872; Dr. Karl Lauenstein, 1863?—Apr. 1866; Heinrich von Martels, 1850—1859?; 1860—1868?; Karl von Schmidt-Bürgeler, 186?—1879? Local editor: Wilhelm Merk, 1880?—1886.

Groen comments, pp. 223—227: "For several years after its founding the CINCINNATI VOLKSFREUND was a dull newspaper, when compared with its contemporaries. It was strictly neutral, although the cause of the Democratic party was favored somewhat, and took no firm stand upon most issues ... Although the VOLKSFREUND was a neutral paper, there were issues against which it took a stand, a very gentlemanly stand, and these were the Know-Nothing agitation, the temperance movement, and rabid abolitionism ... From the moment the VOLKSFREUND openly committed itself to the Democratic party, new life seemed to flow through its columns. Its former lethargy and retiring middle-of-the-road policy discarded, it boldly entered the political arena with a surge of color and brilliance which must have surprised its competing German-American papers. See *Rowell, 1869—85; Ayer, 1880—1908; Groen; Mink.*

DLC: Probe-Nummer, Oct. 12, 1850; Jahrgang 1, no. 2—312, Oct. 15, 1850—Oct. 11, 1851; Jahrgang 2, no. 7—312, Oct. 16, 1851—Oct. 9, 1852; Jahrgang 1—313, Oct. 17, 1852—Oct. 11, 1853; Jahrgang 4, no. 2—69, Oct. 14—Dec. 31, 1853; 1854—Oct. 11, 1863; Oct. 13, 1864—June 1893.
GyAIZ: 21. III. 1861; 18. II. 1870; 15. II. 1883; 21. VIII. 1889; 24. VI. 1983; 27. III. 1895.
ICHi [Rowell Collection]: Jahrgang 26, no. 303, Sept. 29, 1876.
IU: June 4, 1861; Feb. 16, 1881; Mar. 5, 1906.
MWA: Jahrgang 3, no. 68, Dec. 29, 1852.
NcD: Oct. 12—17, 19—31, 1871; Nov. ,Dec. 1—28, 1871.
OC: July 1872—1908. [Not available June 1954.]
OCHi: Jahrgang 19, no. 212—311, June 15—Oct. 9, 1869; Jahrgang 20, no. 1—69, Oct. 12—Dec. 31, 1869.
OClWHi: Jan.—Oct. 10, 1854; Oct. 14—Dec. 1856; Jan. 4, Aug. 16, 1857; Oct. 12, 1858; Jan. 9, 1859; Oct. 12, 1861 [Oct. 13—Dec. 1865]—Feb. 14, Mar. 25, 1866.
WHi: Feb. 16—Oct. 11, 1866; Aug. 7, 1869—Apr. 15, 1908.

Cincinnati Dreimalwöchentlicher Volksfreund:

Tri-weekly edition of CINCINNATI VOLKSFREUND.
Advertised in daily edition, Jahrgang 33, Oct. 1882/Oct. 1883.

Cincinnati Wöchentlicher Volksfreund: Mar. 3, 1853—1908?

Weekly edition of CINCINNATI VOLKSFREUND. Circulation: 1870, 16,000; 1880, 16,000; 1890, 12,000; 1900, 12,000; 1905, 15,000. See *Rowell, 1869—85; Ayer, 1880—1908; Groen; Mink.*
DLC: Jahrgang 1—3, Mar. 3, 1853—Feb. 21, 1856; Jahrgang 5—7, Feb. 26, 1857—Feb. 16, 1860; Jahrgang 10, no. 1—52, Feb. 19, 1862—Feb. 11, 1863.
ICHi [Rowell Collection]: Jahrgang 24, no. 35, Sept. 27, 1876.
MWA: Jahrgang 14, no. 6, Mar. 21, 1866.
OCHi: Jan. 3, 1855; Jan. 10, 24—Feb. 7, 21, Mar. 13—27, Apr. 10—24, July 24—31, Oct. 2, 16, 1856.
OHi: Jan. 1, 1901.
WHi: Feb. 18, 1863—Feb. 18, 1865; Feb. 12, 1868—Feb. 13, 1869; Feb. 13, 1872—Jan. 1873; Feb. 1876—Dec. 25, 1907.

Cincinnati Volkskalender: 1865?—1908?

Edited by von Martels, & published by Limberg & Haacke. See DER DEUTSCHE PIONIER, Nov. 1874, as "Prämie" to subscribers of the VOLKSFREUND.

Wahrheits-Freund: Jahrgang 1—70?, July 20, 1837—1908?

Roman Catholic weekly [daily, 1847, as DER TÄGLICHE WAHRHEITSFREUND]. Prospectus: June 20, 1837. Sub-title: Ein Wochenblatt für katholisches Leben, Wirken und Wissen. Quarto [as daily, small folio], each issue 8 pages.
Circulation: 1870, 13,000 (est.); 1880, 12,000; 1890, 13,000; 1900, 13,500; 1904, 12,210.
Edited by Johann Martin Henni, 1837—43; by Johann Jakob Maximilian Oertel, 1843—46; by Anton Böckling, 1846—50; by J. N. Probst, 1850—1851; by Peter Kröger, Jan. 1851—Dec. 1854; by Anton Böckling, Dec. 1854—Mar. 1857; by Franz Xavier Brandecker, Mar. 1857—Sept. 1862; by Board of Editors [Miettenger, Fasse & Riedel], Sept. 1862—1865? Other editors: Franz Furger [one month]; Anton Schwenniger, 1870?—71; by Hermann Baumstark, 1873—78; J. N. Blum; Joseph Bürgler; Alvis Jeuttner; A. W. Riedel; Joseph Fredewest; Benno Ritter, 1877?—1908?
Published by St. Aloysius Waisen-Verein von Cincinnati, 1837—43?; by Hermann Lehmann, 1843?—Aug. 31, 1850; by Joseph A. Hemann, Sept. 1850—1865?; by Benziger Bros. [Gebrüder Benziger], 1865?—1908.
See *Rowell, 1869—85; Ayer, 1880—1907; Enzlberger.*
DCU: On Film: July 20, 1837—1907.
GyAIZ: 20I X. 1842; 19. VIII. 1852; 11. XI. 1863; 7. VII. 1886; 8. II. 1899; 22. II. 1899.
IU: 1—6, 8, 11, 18—24.
MdEmM: 1—3.
MnColSJ: 2—[34]
MnU: 1, 5—6.
MoSC: 5—[6] 13, 22—28, 31, 48—55, 57—59, 61—67.
MWA: Jahrgang 16, no. 15 [ganze Nummer 795], Dec. 9, 1852.
NYJ: 32—55, 57—70.
WHi: 15, 16.

Wegweiser zur Heiligung: Jan. 7, 1885—1910.

Organ of Deutsche Methodistenkirche. Octavo, each issue 24 pages. Edited & published by Hermann A. Grentzenberg. See *Rowell, 1885; Douglass,* who describes it as the voice of the wing of German Methodism which leaned to "holiness," and translates title as "Guide to Holiness."

Der Weltbürger: Oct. 7, 1834—1835.

Whig weekly. Rattermann, in his "Deutsch-Amerikanischer Journalismus," states that 14 numbers were published. Followed by DER DEUTSCHE FRANKLIN. Edited & published by Karl Eduard [?] Hartmann. Subscription held by Harmony Society. See *Groen; Pletz; Klauprecht; Ligowsky; Eickhoff.*

Westliche Blätter : Jahrgang 1, no. 1—52, Oct. 19, 1851—Oct. 10, 1852.

Weekly. Sub-title: Ein Organ für schöne Literatur, Kunst und Wissenschaft. Large quarto, each issue 8 pages; paged continuously. Edited by Emil Klauprecht & Fenner von Fenneberg. Published by Schmidt, Storch und Co. See *Groen;* advertised in DER DEUTSCHE REPUBLIKANER, Feb. 13, 1853. DLC: complete set. MoS: complete set.

Westliche Blätter : Jahrgang 1—54, no. 39, Nov. 5, 1865—June 29, 1919.

Sunday edition of TÄGLICHES CINCINNATIER VOLKSBLATT. Sub-title: (Sonntagsblatt des Cincinnati Volksblatt.) Sind eine der Unterhaltungs-Lektüre gewidmete Zeitschrift — Romane und Erzählungen, Novelletten, Gedichte, Räthsel, Anekdoten, geschichtliche Aufsätze, Reiseschilderungen, Mode-Artikel, sowie Aufsätze populärer Naturwissenschaften, Literatur, und humoristischen Inhalts. Contains also some telegraphic news. Circulation: 1875, 400 (est.); 1880, 21,000; 1890, 23,000; 1900, 23,400; 1905, 26,000; 1910, 32,100; 1911, 42,750. Jubiläums-Ausgabe: Jahrgang 41, no. 32 [ganze Nummer 2114], May 6, 1906. 32 pages.
See *Rowell, 1872—85; Ayer, 1880—1920, Groen; Mink.*
GyAIZ: 10. VIII. 1873; 28. III. 1886; 11. VII. 1886.
ICHi [Rowell Collection]: Jahrgang 11, no. 48 [ganze Nummer 569], Sept. 24, 1876.
IU: Apr. 22, 1866; Jan. 12, Mar. 15—22, June 28—July 12, 26, Aug. 16, 1868; Apr. 11—18, June 20, Aug. 1, Sept. 5—19, Oct. 10—31, Nov. 14—21, 1869; Jan. 16—23, May 29— June 5, July 3—17, 1870; Mar. 4, 1906; Feb. 10—17, Mar. 22, 1907; June 11—18, July 9, Nov. 26, 1911.
OC: 1865—Feb. 1868; July 14, 1872—1918.
OCHi: June 7, 1900—June 29, 1919.
OHi: Jan. 6, 1901.
WHi: Sept.—Dec. 1889; June 1890—Mar. 1891.

Westlicher Merkur : Nov. 1836—?

Whig weekly. Edited by Christian Burghalter. *Klauprecht* comments: „Im Deer Greek Thale auf Martin Baum's Lande wohnte auch damals als Anachoret, Christian Burkhalter, früher Sekretär des Fürsten ‚Vorwärts' Blücher und später als Zitterquäker und Herausgeber des Westlichen Merkur bekannt. Ganz in religiöse Erbauung versunken, schrieb er Predigten und Gesänge für die Gemeinde." He wrote an excellent style but was too far removed from denominational consistency to please his critics who claimed he was not a "Merkur" but a modern Odysseus because he had been everything except angry. Published by Burghalter & Höfle. See *Groen; Klauprecht; Trepte;* advertised in only issue of tri-weekly seen, $ 2.50.

Westlicher Merkur : vol. 1, no. 1—4?, Feb.—Mar. 1840?

Whig tri-weekly. Probably printed weekly edition also. In only issue seen, dated Mar. 7, 1840, the tri-weekly is advertised at $ 4.00, and weekly at $ 2.50. Sub-title: Gegründet von dem „Deutschen Harrison Club". Small folio, each issue 4 pages, of which pages 1—2 were printed in German., pages 3—4 in English. Followed by DER OHIO VOLKSFREUND. Edited & published by Benjamin Bofinger (sic.) See *Groen.*
DLC: vol. 1, no. 4, Mar. 7, 1840.

Westliche Staatszeitung : 1836?—?

Locofoco organ, published weekly. Edited & published by Benjamin Bofinger. See *Groen; Rattermann.*

Die Windmühle : Apr. 1867?—1870?

Humorous weekly, published Sunday. Sub-title: Die Wind-Mühle ist ein illustrirtes-satyrisches, humoristisch-lyrisches, kritisch-raisonnirendes, ästhetisch-annoncirendes Wochenblatt wo die Woch' sechs Tage hat! Motto: 1) Difficile est satyram non scribere; 2) Wer sich dadurch beleidigt fühlt, Auf seine eigene Dummheit zielt. Delightful humorous paper. Large quarto, each issue 4 pages. Edited & published by Eduard Luther.
NSyG: Jahrgang 4, no. 2, [neue Folge, no. 2], Apr. 24, 1870.

Wochenblatt des Cincinnati Courier : Nov.? 1869—Mar. 1874.

Weekly edition of CINCINNATI COURIER. Circulation: 1873, 6400. See *Rowell, 1870—74.*

Cincinnati Zeitung : 1886—Oct. 20? 1901.

Union labor daily, evening except Sunday. For Sunday edition, see SONNTAGSBLATT DER CIN-CINNATI ZEITUNG. Circulation: 1890, 7500; 1900, 6000. Edited by Ernest A. Weier, 1886—87; by F. Detmers, 1888—89; published by Zeitung Publishing Co., 1886—89; edited & published by Jacob Willig, 1890—95; published by Cincinnati Zeitung Publishing Co., 1896—1901. See *Ayer, 1887—1901; Gruen; Mink.*

  ICHi: June 2, 1897—Oct. 20, 1901.
  ICJ: June 2, 1897—Oct. 1901.
  NN: May 27, June 6, 10, Sept. 1—4, 24, Oct. 2, 12, Dec. 11, 1888; Jan. 17, Dec. 18, 1889;
  Feb. 6—7, 1891; Feb. 19, 1892; Jan. 21, June 7, 12, 1895.
  OC: July 1887—Jan., July—Oct. 1901.
  OHi: Jan. 1, 1901.
  WHi: Apr. 15, 1900.

Die Zukunft : 1864?—1876?

Weekly. Continued as DIE ZUKUNFT (Indianapolis, Ind.). Edited & published by Adolf Frey. See *Groen.*

Part Seven

Imprint Sources

Regarding German imprints, see Franziska C. Ott, Cincinnati German **Imprints: A Checklist.** (New York: Peter Lang, 1993).

Afterword

Cincinnati is a city with a German heritage reaching back to the very beginnings of the city in the 18th century. Today, almost every other person in the area has some German ancestry, which is not all that surprizing in consideration of the fact that Ohioans of German descent number 40% of the state's population. The population of German heritage in the Cincinnati area is, therefore, somewhat larger.

Today, as yesterday, and in the future, such a major dimension is bound to play an important role in the social, cultural, and political life of the area. Clearly, to understand the history and development of the Greater Cincinnati area, it is necessary to take the German heritage into consideration.